An Introduction to
Critical Reading

SIXTH EDITION

LEAH McCRANEY

University of Alabama at Birmingham

THOMSON
WADSWORTH

Australia · Brazil · Canada · Mexico · Singapore · Spain · United Kingdom · United States

An Introduction to Critical Reading, **Sixth Edition**
Leah McCraney

Publisher: *Michael Rosenberg*
Acquisitions Editor: *Stephen Dalphin*
Development Editor: *Cathy Richard Dodson*
Editorial Assistant: *Cheryl Forman*
Technology Project Manager: *Joe Gallagher*
Managing Marketing Manager: *Mandee Eckersley*
Senior Marketing Assistant: *Dawn Giovanniello*
Associate Marketing Communications Manager:
    Patrick Rooney
Associate Content Project Manager:
    Sarah Sherman

Senior Art Director: *Bruce Bond*
Print Buyer: *Betsy Donaghey*
Senior Permissions Editor: *Isabel Alves*
Photo Manager: *Sheri Blaney*
Text/Photo Researcher: *Sue Howard*
Production Service/Compositor: *International
    Typesetting and Composition*
Cover Designer: *Gina Petti*
Cover Printer: *Phoenix Color*
Printer: *Edwards Brothers*

Cover art: *Summer Garden,* 1989 by Larusdottir, Karolina (b. 1944) Private Collection © Noel Oddy Fine Art, Bridgeman Art Library.

Library of Congress Control Number: 2006901300

ISBN 1-4130-1621-9

Thomson Higher Education
25 Thomson Place
Boston, MA 02210-1202
USA

For more information about our products, contact us at:
Thomson Learning Academic Resource Center
1-800-423-0563
For permission to use material from this text or product, submit a request online at
http://www.thomsonrights.com
Any additional questions about permissions can be submitted by e-mail to
thomsonrights@thomson.com

Credits appear on pages 369–371, which constitute a continuation of the copyright page.

In Memory of
Randy Marsh

Deep in December, it's nice to remember,
Without a hurt the heart is hollow.
Deep in December, it's nice to remember,
The fire of September that made us mellow.
Deep in December, our hearts should remember
And follow.

—The Fantasticks

Preface
To the Student

The readings in this book were selected for a number of reasons. First, they are all excellent pieces of writing. Second, they comprise a representative sample of four common types of writing: poetry, fiction, essays, and textbook chapters. Third, they are thought-provoking.

This third reason is of utmost importance to the purposes of this book. Meaningful learning occurs when one is actively involved in the learning process, when one finds something in the process that is of personal importance. The majority of readings in this book offer ideas that are likely to be important to most readers. Literature in particular offers a field of universal ideas—after all, the essence of literature is life—and this is one reason such a wide variety of literature has been included here.

Reading allows one the opportunity to examine one's own principles and the principles of others. The Socratic position is that the unexamined life is not worth living. This position suggests that one must value one's own thinking and judgment, and is grounded in the belief that examining—questioning—is the foundation for being free.

Preface

To the Instructor

An Introduction to Critical Reading is an anthology of poems, short stories, essays, and college textbook chapters. The instructor's manual that accompanies the anthology presents an approach to developmental reading that departs from the traditional, skills-based approach. The manual suggests ways of using the pieces in the anthology to improve reading skills and critical thinking. The anthology is different from other developmental reading texts in its rationale and in its content.

The pieces in the anthology were selected, not on the basis of a "readability formula," but because they are representative of the materials college students are required to read and because they encourage critical thinking. The selections for each genre present a range of difficulties, permitting instructors to choose texts appropriate to the abilities of their specific classes. Texts containing extensive literary allusions or problems of style, such as stream of consciousness, are not included. Such pieces require more time than the primary purposes of a reading course allow.

The selections were also made with critical thinking and critical reading in mind. A detailed discussion of critical thinking, a term that has a variety of meanings, is included in the introductory essay of the instructor's manual. Suffice it to say that the heart of critical thinking is an active, personal involvement stemming from a desire "to know." Students who become actively involved in a text will eventually come to terms with it. This does not mean students will understand all of the information contained in a piece or make every possible inference. But most college students, regardless of their developmental status, can discern the essential message of a piece if they want "to know." The pieces in the anthology revolve around issues that are of interest to most readers: family, relationships, society, and so forth. The selections also reflect the cultural diversity of college readers. Roughly half of the selections are by women and nonwhite writers.

To eliminate some problems of comprehension and to provide the best possible opportunity for active involvement, the anthology provides the following aids:

1. Definitions of difficult words that are not defined in context.
2. Explanatory notes on allusions to literature, history, art, and so on.
3. A glossary that includes definitions and examples of common literary and rhetorical devices.

The anthology does not include questions on the content of the pieces. The instructor's manual discusses the importance of encouraging student questions and student-generated criteria. Questions that come from editors invite a mechanical investigation of what the editors think to be important. Such an investigation limits the possibilities of a piece of writing and limits student thinking to those points addressed by the questions. There is a need, of course, for some teacher questions and teacher-generated criteria. The instructor's manual provides such criteria, not only for evaluating the content of a piece, but also for developing critical thinking. The suggestions in the manual are not meant to limit the teacher's approach, but to suggest typical questions that can accomplish specific goals.

The apparatus is in the instructor's manual. None is included in the anthology for the following reasons:

1. Students tend either to ignore explanatory material or to embrace it so completely that they do not go beyond it and think independently.
2. Students become better readers by reading—not by being told how to read.
3. Textbook generalizations about how an adult *should* read, how *good* readers read, and what a reader *ought* to glean from a piece of writing exclude consideration of the great variety of effective reading styles and of the possible differences in readers' interpretations.
4. An instructor's ideas about the reading process or about a "good" college reader are far more suitable for that teacher's actual audience than a textbook apparatus written for an implied audience.

The instructor's manual contains the following:

1. An introductory essay, providing teachers with the rationale for the anthology, explaining the nature of critical thinking, and providing general guidelines for helping students develop critical thinking.
2. Articles for the instructor on attention deficit hyperactivity disorder and dyslexia.
3. A discussion of each selection in the anthology, explicating content and pointing out issues that teachers may want to explore in class discussions.
4. Specific suggestions for each piece contained in the anthology. These suggestions are intended to involve students in the content of the piece and to encourage the development of critical thinking. Cross-genre studies are suggested frequently to assist those instructors who prefer such studies to the genre-by-genre approach.
5. An essay suggesting a variety of ways in which students might approach textbook reading.
6. The test banks from the textbook chapters' instructor's manuals.
7. Sample outlines of selected textbook chapters.
8. Articles, tables, and charts that can be photocopied and used in conjunction with readings in the anthology.

The method recommended in the instructor's manual is practical. It not only results in measurable improvement, but it also encourages positive treatment of students. The philosophy of the approach presented in this textbook corresponds to the motto of the Scripps Howard newspapers: "Give light and the people will find their own way." The light students need is the practice of critical thinking—a tool they will need regardless of the direction they take.

Acknowledgments

Stephen Dalphin and Cathy Richard Dobson have been remarkable. I thank them for their enthusiasm and direction as well as their patience and flexibility.

I would also like to express my sincere appreciation to the many teachers who have contacted me to ask questions, offer suggestions, and discuss their experiences using this book. This communication has been affirming, exciting, and thought-provoking.

For more types of assistance and kindness than I could possibly name, I thank the following: Bert Andrews, Tom Ashe, Craig Beard, Tia Black, Susan Blair, Henny Bordwin, Malka Bordwin, Milton Bordwin, LaQuita Boswell, Judy Boyer, Joy Brantley, Flowers Braswell, Tom Brown, Sid Burgess, Jason Burnett, Monica Cantwell, John Coley, Stella Cocoris, Kendall Cooper, Tynes Cowan, Robby Cox, Keith Cullen, Randa Graves, Tim Douglas, Betty Duff, Barbara Enlow, Matt Fifolt, Grace Finkel, Paula Fulton, Delores Gallo, Al Gardener, Virginia Gauld, Travis Gordon, Lee Griner, John Haggerty, Lois Harris, Richard Harrison, Barbara Hill, Cindy Holmes, Helen Jackson, Jane Johnson, Jill Johnson, Diana Kato, Tracey Kell, Marilyn Kurata, Susan Labischin, Karin LaGroue, Cindy LeFoy, Pat Lisella, Marcy Ludorf, Anna Lynch, Tracy Lyons, Lisa Madison, Gaines Marsh, Haden Marsh, Randy Marsh, Stephen Marsi, Dot McCraney, Britt McCraney, Nathan McCraney, Niki McCraney, Randy McCraney, Amy McGaughey, Sue McKinnon, Susan Mitchell, Stephen Morris, Mark Myers, Rose Norman, Colm O'Dunlaing, Iris O'Dunlaing, Mary Osthoff, Jane Patton, Bob Penny, Terry Proctor, Candace Ridington, Beebe Roberts, Dave Roberts, John Schnorrenberg, Connie Stavros, Melissa Tate, Judy Traylor, Reuben Triplett, Carol Wada, John Walker, Caroline West, Patty Wheeler-Andrews, Gayle Whidby, Barbara Williams, Debbie Williams, Natasha Womack, and Jason Womack.

Thanks as well to following reviewers: Peggy Johnson, *Saint Mary's University,* Winona, MN; Jared Riddle, *Ivy Tech Community College* of Indiana, East Chicago, IN; Mirian Kopelman, *San Joaquin Valley College,* Bakersfield, CA; Suzanne Hess, *Florida Community College* at Jacksonville, Jacksonville, FL; Janet Cutshan, *Sussex County Community College*; Patricia DeLessio, *Dutchess Community College*; Mary Diedrich, *North Hennepin Community College*; Bryon Ennis, *Jackson Community College*; Kathryn Holmes, *Holyoke Community College*; Bernard LaChance, *Cerro Coso Community College*; Stephan Lucas, *Phoenix College*; Joyce Savage, *North Hennepin Community College*; Mary Soltzer, *Lorain County Community College*; and Cynthia Tober, *Schenectady County Community College.*

Finally, I thank my students, who challenge me, inspire me, and always remind me that true learning involves reaching beyond one's grasp.

Leah McCraney

Contents

Poetry   1

Fiction   *41*

Essays   *211*

Textbook Chapters   *309*

1

Poetry

Lot's Wife

Kristine Batey

While Lot, the conscience of a nation,
struggles with the Lord,
she struggles with the housework.
The City of Sin is where
5   she raises the children.

Ba'al or Adonai—
Whoever is God—
the bread must still be made
and the doorsills swept.

10   The Lord may kill the children tomorrow,
but today they must be bathed and fed.

Well and good to condemn your neighbor's religion;
but weren't they there
when the baby was born,
15   and when the well collapsed?

While her husband communes with God,
she tucks the children into bed.
In the morning when he tells her of the judgment,
she puts down the lamp she is cleaning
20   and calmly begins to pack.

In between bundling up the children
and deciding what will go,
she runs for a moment
to say goodbye to the herd,
25   gently patting each soft head
with tears in her eyes for the animals that will not understand.

She smiles blindly to the woman
who held her hand at childbed.

It is easy for eyes that have always turned to heaven
30   not to look back;
those that have been—by necessity—drawn to earth
cannot forget that life is lived from day to day.
Good, to a God, and good in human terms
are two different things?

35   On the breast of the hill, she chooses to be human,
and turns, in farewell—
and never regrets
the sacrifice.

NOTES

Ba'al or Adonai (l. 6): *Ba'al* is the name for the Canaanite god of Lot's time; *Adonai* (Lord) is one of the terms the Hebrews used when speaking of their god.
communes (l. 16): communicates
at childbed (l. 28): at childbirth

Genesis 19:12–26

The two angels said to Lot, "Have you anyone else here, sons-in-law, sons or daughters, or any who belong to you in the city? Get them out of this place, because we are going to destroy it. The outcry against it has been so great that the Lord has sent us to destroy it." So Lot went out and spoke to his intended sons-in-law. He said, "Be quick and leave this place; the Lord is going to destroy the city." But they did not take him seriously.

As soon as it was dawn, the angels urged Lot to go, saying, "Be quick, take your wife and your two daughters who are here, or you will be swept away when the city is punished." When he lingered, they took him by the hand, with his wife and his daughters, and, because the Lord had spared him, led him on until he was outside the city. When they had brought them out, they said, "Flee for your lives; do not look back and do not stop anywhere in the Plain. Flee to the hills or you will be swept away." Lot replied, "No, sirs. You have shown your servant favour and you have added to your unfailing care for me by saving my life, but I cannot escape to the hills; I shall be overtaken by the disaster, and die. Look, here is a town, only a small place, near enough for me to reach quickly. Let me escape to it—it is very small—and save my life." He said to him, "I grant your request: I will not overthrow this town you speak of. But flee there quickly, because I can do nothing until you are there." That is why the place is called Zoar. The sun had risen over the land as Lot entered Zoar; and then the Lord rained down fire and brimstone from the skies on Sodom and Gomorrah. He overthrew those cities and destroyed all the Plain, with everyone living there and everything growing in the ground. But Lot's wife, behind him, looked back, and she turned into a pillar of salt.

NOTES

two angels (par. 1): messengers sent by God
Zoar (par. 2): The word "Zoar" means "small."

Richard Cory

E. A. Robinson

Whenever Richard Cory went down town,
We people on the pavement looked at him;
He was a gentleman from sole to crown,
Clean favored, and imperially slim.

5   And he was always quietly arrayed,
And he was always human when he talked;

But still he fluttered pulses when he said,
"Good-morning," and he glittered when he walked.

And he was rich—yes, richer than a king—
10   And admirably schooled in every grace:
In fine, we thought that he was everything
To make us wish that we were in his place.

So on we worked, and waited for the light,
And went without the meat, and cursed the bread;
15   And Richard Cory, one calm summer night,
Went home and put a bullet through his head.

NOTES

imperially (l. 4): royally
arrayed (l. 5): finely dressed
in fine (l. 11): in short or in summary

Warren Pryor

Alden Nowlan

When every pencil meant a sacrifice
his parents boarded him at school in town,
slaving to free him from the stony fields,
the meagre acreage that bore them down.

5   They blushed with pride when, at his graduation,
they watched him picking up the slender scroll,
his passport from the years of brutal toil
and lonely patience in a barren hole.

When he went in the Bank their cups ran over.
10   They marvelled how he wore a milk-white shirt
work days and jeans on Sundays, He was saved
from their thistle-strewn farm and its red dirt.

And he said nothing. Hard and serious
like a young bear inside his teller's cage,
15   his axe-hewn hands upon the paper bills
aching with empty strength and throttled rage.

NOTES

barren (l. 8): infertile
thistle (l. 12): prickly weed
axe-hewn (l. 15): shaped as if with an axe
throttled (l. 16): suppressed, stifled

The Road Not Taken

Robert Frost

Two roads diverged in a yellow wood,
And sorry I could not travel both
And be one traveler, long I stood
And looked down one as far as I could
5   To where it bent in the undergrowth;

Then took the other, as just as fair,
And having perhaps the better claim,
Because it was grassy and wanted wear;
Though as for that, the passing there
10   Had worn them really about the same,

And both that morning equally lay
In leaves no step had trodden black.
Oh, I kept the first for another day!
Yet knowing how way leads on to way,
15   I doubted if I should ever come back.

I shall be telling this with a sigh
Somewhere ages and ages hence:
Two roads diverged in a wood, and I—
I took the one less traveled by,
20   And that has made all the difference.

NOTES

two roads diverged (l. 1): The road became two roads that went in different directions.
undergrowth (l. 5): plants or bushes growing beneath trees
wanted wear (l. 8): lacked or needed wear
trodden (l. 12): crushed
hence (l. 17): from this time

I, Too

Langston Hughes

I, too, sing America.

I am the darker brother.
They send me to eat in the kitchen
When company comes,
5   But I laugh,
And eat well,
And grow strong.

Tomorrow,
I'll sit at the table
10   When company comes.

Nobody'll dare
Say to me,
"Eat in the kitchen,"
Then.

15 Besides,
They'll see how beautiful I am
And be ashamed—

I, too, am America.

Harlem

Langston Hughes

What happens to a dream deferred?

Does it dry up
like a raisin in the sun?
Or fester like a sore—
5 And then run?
Does it stink like rotten meat?
Or crust and sugar over—
like a syrupy sweet?

Maybe it just sags
10 like a heavy load.

Or does it explode?

NOTES

Harlem (title): an area of New York City, predominantly African-American

deferred (l. 1): postponed or put off

fester (l. 4) and *run* (l. 5): "Fester" refers to the swelling of inflamed tissue; when the tissue opens, pus is released or "runs."

crust and sugar over . . . (l. 7–8): After a period of time, a sugary crust will form on some syrupy sweets (such as jelly and honey).

Mother to Son

Langston Hughes

Well, son, I'll tell you:
Life for me ain't been no crystal stair.
It's had tacks in it,
And splinters,
5 And boards torn up,
And places with no carpet on the floor—
Bare.
But all the time

I'se been a-climbin' on,
10   And reachin' landin's
And turnin' corners,
And sometimes goin' in the dark
Where there ain't been no light.
So, boy, don't you turn back.
15   Don't you set down on the steps
'Cause you finds it kinder hard.
Don't you fall now—
For I'se still goin', honey,
I'se still climbin',
20   And life for me ain't been no crystal stair.

Those Winter Sundays

Robert Hayden

Sundays too my father got up early
and put his clothes on in the blueblack cold,
then with cracked hands that ached
from labor in the weekday weather made
5   banked fires blaze. No one ever thanked him.

I'd wake and hear the cold splintering, breaking.
When the rooms were warm, he'd call,
and slowly I would rise and dress,
fearing the chronic angers of that house,

10   Speaking indifferently to him,
who had driven out the cold
and polished my good shoes as well.
What did I know, what did I know
of love's austere and lonely offices?

NOTES

banked fires (l. 5): fires that have been smothered with ashes so that the coals will remain hot and can be used later to start another fire
chronic (l. 9): frequently occurring
austere (l. 14): marked by self-denial or self-discipline

Austere

Roland Flint

"What did I know, what did I know . . . ?"

How she left kettles of water
On the kitchen stove for baths
Each Saturday night till hotter
Than needed (add cold), to wash,

5   In the corrugated tub,
     The week's field dirt away,
     Blown even into the crib
     From a North Dakota sky.

     How all of us take turns,
10   The young mother renewing
     Clean heat for each till it runs
     Out, as she's finishing hers.

     I offer you her kettles, stove,
     The kerosene-lamp light,
15   Her palm her soap her olive,
     The tub, its velvety silt.

NOTE

corrugated (l. 5): Corrugated materials (tin, iron, paper, etc.) are shaped in alternating ridges and grooves in order to give them more strength.

A Red Palm

Gary Soto

You're in this dream of cotton plants.
You raise a hoe, swing, and the first weeds
Fall with a sigh. You take another step,
Chop, and the sigh comes again,
5   Until you yourself are breathing that way
With each step, a sigh that will follow you into town.

That's hours later. The sun is a red blister
Coming up in your palm. Your back is strong,
Young, not yet the broken chair
10   In an abandoned school of dry spiders.
Dust settles on your forehead, dirt
Smiles under each fingernail.
You chop, step, and by the end of the first row,
You can buy one splendid fish for wife
15   And three sons. Another row, another fish,
Until you have enough and move on to milk,
Bread, meat. Ten hours and the cupboards creak.
You can rest in the back yard under a tree.
Your hands twitch on your lap,
20   Not unlike the fish on a pier or the bottom
Of a boat. You drink iced tea. The minutes jerk
Like flies.

     It's dusk, now night,
And the lights in your home are on.
25   That costs money, yellow light

In the kitchen. That's thirty steps,
You say to your hands,
Now shaped into binoculars.
You could raise them to your eyes:
30   You were a fool in school, now look at you.
You're a giant among cotton plants,
The lung-shaped leaves that run breathing for miles.

Now you see your oldest boy, also running.
Papa, he says, it's time to come in.
35   You pull him into your lap
And ask, What's forty times nine?
He knows as well as you, and you smile.
The wind makes peace with the trees,
The stars strike themselves in the dark.
40   You get up and walk with the sigh of cotton plants.
You go to sleep with a red sun on your palm,
The sore light you see when you first stir in bed.

Daystar

Rita Dove

She wanted a little room for thinking:
but she saw diapers steaming on the line,
a doll slumped behind the door.

So she lugged a chair behind the garage
5   to sit out the children's naps.
Sometimes there were things to watch—
the pinched armor of a vanished cricket,
a floating maple leaf. Other days
she stared until she was assured
10   when she closed her eyes
she'd see only her own vivid blood.

She had an hour, at best, before Liza appeared
pouting from the top of the stairs.
And just *what* was mother doing
15   out back with the field mice? Why,

building a palace. Later
that night when Thomas rolled over and
lurched into her, she would open her eyes
and think of the place that was hers
20   for an hour—where
she was nothing,
pure nothing, in the middle of the day.

Once a Lady Told Me

Nikki Giovanni

like my mother and her grandmother before
i paddle around the house
in soft-soled shoes
chasing ghosts from corners
5   with incense
they are such a disturbance my ghosts
they break my bric-a-brac and make
me forget to turn my heating stove

the children say you must come to live
10   with us all my life i told them i've lived
with you now i shall live with myself

the grandchildren say it's disgraceful
you in this dark house with the curtains
pulled snuff dripping from your chin
15   would they be happier if i smoked cigarettes
i was very exquisite once very small and well courted
some would say a beauty when my hair was plaited
and i was bustled up

my children wanted my life
20   and now they want my death

but i shall pad around my house
in my purple soft-soled shoes
i'm very happy now
it's not so very neat, you know, but it's my
25   life

My Father's Song

Simon Oriz

Wanting to say things,
I miss my father tonight.
His voice, the slight catch,
the depth from his thin chest,
5   the tremble of emotion
in something he has just said
to his son, his song:

We planted corn one Spring at Acu—
we planted several times
10   but this one particular time

I remember the soft damp sand
in my hand.

My father had stopped at one point
to show me an overturned furrow;
15   the plowshare had unearthed
the burrow nest of a mouse
in the soft moist sand.

Very gently, he scooped tiny pink animals
into the palm of his hand
20   and told me to touch them.
We took them to the edge
of the field and put them in the shade
of a sand moist clod.

I remember the very softness
25   of cool and warm sand and tiny alive mice
and my father saying things.

NOTES

Acu (l. 8): The native village of the Acoma people in New Mexico
furrow (l. 14): shallow trench
plowshare (l. 15): plow

Elegy for My Father, Who Is Not Dead

Andrew Hudgins

One day I'll lift the telephone
and be told my father's dead. He's ready.
In the sureness of his faith, he talks
about the world beyond this world
5   as though his reservations have
been made. I think he wants to go,
a little bit-a new desire
to travel building up, an itch
to see fresh worlds. Or older ones.
10   He thinks that when I follow him
he'll wrap me in his arms and laugh,
the way he did when I arrived
on earth. I do not think he's right.
He's ready. I am not. I can't
15   just say good-bye as cheerfully
as if he were embarking on a trip
to make my later trip go well.
I see myself on deck, convinced

> his ship's gone down, while he's convinced
20 I'll see him standing on the dock
> and waving, shouting, Welcome back.

A Martian Sends a Postcard Home

Craig Raine

Caxtons are mechanical birds with many wings
and some are treasured for their markings—

they cause the eyes to melt
or the body to shriek without pain.

5   I have never seen one fly, but
sometimes they perch on the hand.

Mist is when the sky is tired of flight
and rests its soft machine on ground:

then the world is dim and bookish
10   like engravings under tissue paper.

Rain is when the earth is television.
It has the property of making colours darker.

Model T is a room with the lock inside—
a key is turned to free the world

15   for movement, so quick there is a film
to watch for anything missed.

But time is tied to the wrist
or kept in a box, ticking with impatience.

In homes, a haunted apparatus sleeps,
20   that snores when you pick it up.

If the ghost cries, they carry it
to their lips and soothe it to sleep

with sounds. And yet they wake it up
deliberately, by tickling with a finger.

25   Only the young are allowed to suffer
openly. Adults go to a punishment room

with water but nothing to eat.
They lock the door and suffer the noises

alone. No one is exempt
30   and everyone's pain has a different smell.

At night when all the colours die,
they hide in pairs

and read about themselves—
in colour, with their eyelids shut.

NOTES

Caxtons (l. 1): Literally, a caxton is any book published by William Caxton (1422–1491), the English printer who published the first book in English (*The Recuyell of the Historyes of Troye*, 1475).
Model T (l. 13): an automobile built by Ford Motor company from 1908–1927.
apparatus (l. 19): device, instrument

Bedtime Story

George Macbeth

Long long ago when the world was a wild place
Planted with bushes and peopled by apes, our
Mission Brigade was at work in the jungle.
Hard by the Congo

5   Once, when a foraging detail was active
Scouting for green-fly, it came on a grey man, the
Last living man, in the branch of a baobab
Stalking a monkey

Earlier men had disposed of, for pleasure,
10   Creatures whose names we scarcely remember—
Zebra, Rhinoceros, elephants, wart-hog,
Lion, rats, deer. But

After the wars had extinguished the cities
Only the wild ones were left, half-naked
15   Near the Equator: and here was the last one,
Starved for a monkey.

By then the Mission Brigade had encountered
Hundreds of such men: and their procedure.
History tells us, was only to feed them:
20   Find them and feed them;

Those were the orders. And this was the last one.
Nobody knew that he was, but he was. Mud
Caked on his flat grey flanks. He was crouched, half—
Armed with a shaved spear

25   Glinting between broad leaves. When their jaws cut
Swathes through the bark and he saw fine teeth shine,
Round eyes roll round and forked arms waver
Huge as the rough trunks

Over his head, he was frightened. Our workers
30   Marched through the Congo before he was born, but
This was the first time perhaps that he's seen one.
Starting in hot still

Silence, he crouched there: then jumped. With a long swing
Down from his branch, he had angled his spear too
35   Quickly, before they could hold him, and hurled it
Hard at the soldier

Leading the detail. How could he know the Queen's
Orders were only to help him? The soldier
Winced when the tipped spear pricked him. Unsheathing his
40   Sting was a reflex.

Later the Queen was informed. There were no more
Men. An impetuous soldier had killed off,
Purely by chance, the penultimate primate.
When she was certain

45   Squadrons of workers were fanned through the Congo
Detailed to bring back the man's picked bones to be
Sealed in the archives in amber. I'm quite sure
Nobody found them

After the most industrious search, though.
50   Where had the bones gone? Over the earth, dear,
Ground by the teeth of the termites, blown by the
Wind, like the dodo's.

NOTES

foraging (l. 5): searching (for food)

detail (l. 5): a group of soldiers assigned a specific task

swathes (l. 27): paths

unsheathing (l. 40): pulling out

impetuous (l. 43): rash; impulsive

penultimate (l. 44): next to the last

dodo (l. 53): The dodo bird was larger than a turkey and incapable of flying. It has been extinct since the late 17th century.

Counting the Mad

Donald Justice

This one was put in a jacket,
This one was sent home,
This one was given bread and meat
But would eat none,

5   And this one cried No No No No
All day long.

> This one looked at the window
> As though it were a wall,
> This one saw things that were not there,
>
> 10   And this one cried No No No No
> All day long.
> This one thought himself a bird,
> This one a dog,
>
> And this one thought himself a man,
> 15   An ordinary man,
> And cried and cried No No No No
> All day long.

NOTES
Mad (title): insane
jacket (l. 1): straightjacket

Much Madness Is Divinest Sense

Emily Dickinson

> Much Madness is divinest Sense—
> To a discerning Eye—
> Much Sense—the starkest Madness—
> 'Tis the Majority
> 5   In this, as All, prevail—
> Assent—and you are sane—
> Demur—you're straight away dangerous—
> And handled with a Chain—

NOTES
Madness (title): insanity
discerning (l. 2): perceptive
prevail (l. 5): triumph
Assent (l. 6): agree
Demur (l. 7): object

Four Poems from *Spoon River Anthology*

Edgar Lee Masters

MINERVA JONES

> I am Minerva, the village poetess,
> Hooted at, jeered at by the Yahoos of the street
> For my heavy body, cock-eye, and rolling walk,
> And all the more when "Butch" Weldy

5   Captured me after a brutal hunt.
     He left me to my fate with Doctor Meyers;
     And I sank into death, growing numb from the feet up,
     Like one stepping deeper and deeper into a stream of ice.
     Will some one go to the village newspaper,
10   And gather into a book the verses I wrote?—
     I thirsted so for love!
     I hungered so for life!

NOTES

Spoon River Anthology: A collection of poems about the citizens of Spoon River, a community invented by the poet; each poem is an epitaph, an inscription on the tomb in memory of the person buried there.
Yahoos (l. 2): coarse, rude persons

"INDIGNATION" JONES

     You would not believe, would you,
     That I came from good Welsh stock?
     That I was purer blooded than the white trash here?
     And of more direct lineage than the New Englanders
5   And Virginians of Spoon River?
     You would not believe that I had been to school
     And read some books.
     You saw me only as a run-down man,
     With matted hair and beard
10   And ragged clothes.
     Sometimes a man's life turns into a cancer
     From being bruised and continually bruised,
     And swells into a purplish mass,
     Like growths on stalks of corn.
15   Here was I, a carpenter, mired in a bog of life
     Into which I walked, thinking it was a meadow,
     With a slattern for a wife, and poor Minerva, my daughter,
     Whom you tormented and drove to death.
     So I crept, crept, like a snail through the days
20   Of my life.
     No more you hear my footsteps in the morning,
     Resounding on the hollow sidewalk,
     Going to the grocery store for a little corn meal
     And a nickel's worth of bacon.

NOTES

Welsh (l. 2): descended from a native of Wales, an area in southwest Great Britain
trash (l. 3): worthless people
lineage (l. 4): line of descent from ancestors
mired (l. 15): stuck
bog (l. 15): literally, a swamp-like area
slattern (l. 17): an untidy or immoral woman

DOCTOR MEYERS

No other man, unless it was Doc Hill,
Did more for people in this town than I.
And all the weak, the halt, the improvident
And those who could not pay flocked to me.
5   I was good-hearted, easy Doctor Meyers.
I was healthy, happy, in comfortable fortune,
Blest with a congenial mate, my children raised,
All wedded, doing well in the world.
And then one night, Minerva, the poetess,
10   Came to me in her trouble, crying.
I tried to help her out—she died—
They indicted me, the newspapers disgraced me,
My wife perished of a broken heart.
And pneumonia finished me.

NOTES

halt (l. 3): crippled
improvident (l. 3): those who do not prepare for the future
congenial (l. 7): pleasant and harmonious
indicted (l. 12): to be charged with a crime by a jury

MRS. MEYERS

He protested all his life long
The newspapers lied about him villainously;
That he was not at fault for Minerva's fall,
But only tried to help her.
5   Poor soul so sunk in sin he could not see
That even trying to help her, as he called it,
He had broken the law human and divine.
Passers by, an ancient admonition to you:
If your ways would be ways of pleasantness,
10   And all your pathways peace,
Love God and keep his commandments.

NOTES

villainously (l. 2): viciously
divine (l. 7): relating to God
admonition (l. 8): warning

Digging

Seamus Heaney

Between my finger and my thumb
The squat pen rests; snug as a gun.

Under my window, a clean rasping sound
When the spade sinks into gravelly ground:
5   My father, digging. I look down

Till his straining rump among the flowerbeds
Bends low, comes up twenty years away
Stooping in rhythm through potato drills
Where he was digging.

10   The coarse boot nestled on the lug, the shaft
Against the inside knee was levered firmly.
He rooted out tall tops, buried the bright edge deep
To scatter new potatoes that we picked
Loving their cool hardness in our hands.

15   By God, the old man could handle a spade.
Just like his old man.

My grandfather cut more turf in a day
Than any other man on Toner's bog.
Once I carried him milk in a bottle
20   Corked sloppily with paper. He straightened up
To drink it, then fell to right away
Nicking and slicing neatly, heaving sods
Over his shoulder, going down and down
For the good turf. Digging.

25   The cold smell of potato mould, the squelch and slap
Of soggy peat, the curt cuts of an edge
Through living roots awaken in my head.
But I've no spade to follow men like them.

Between my finger and my thumb
30   The squat pen rests.
I'll dig with it.

NOTES

spade (l. 4): shovel

potato drills (l. 8): rows of potato plants

turf (l. 17): peat

bog (l. 18): peat bog

fell to (l. 21): began energetically

sods (l. 22): pieces of peat

curt (l. 26): short; abrupt

Barbie Doll

Marge Piercy

This girlchild was born as usual
and presented dolls that did pee-pee
and miniature GE stoves and irons
and wee lipsticks the color of cherry candy.
5   Then in the magic of puberty, a classmate said:
You have a great big nose and fat legs.

She was healthy, tested intelligent,
possessed strong arms and back,
abundant sexual drive and manual dexterity.
10   She went to and fro apologizing.
Everyone saw a fat nose on thick legs.

She was advised to play coy,
exhorted to come on hearty,
exercise, diet, smile and wheedle.
15   Her good nature wore out
like a fan belt.
So she cut off her nose and legs
and offered them up.

In the casket displayed on satin she lay
20   with the undertaker's cosmetics painted on,
a turned-up putty nose,
dressed in a pink and white nightie.
Doesn't she look pretty? everyone said.
Consummation at last.
25   To every woman a happy ending.

NOTES

dexterity (l. 9): skillfulness
coy (l. 12): pretended shyness or "cuteness"
exhorted (l. 13): strongly urged or advised
wheedle (l. 14): to influence by flattery
consummation (l. 24): completion or fulfillment of a goal

Mr. Z

M. Carl Holman

Taught early that his mother's skin was the sign of error,
He dressed and spoke the perfect part of honor;
Won scholarships, attended the best schools,
Disclaimed kinship with jazz and spirituals;
5   Chose prudent, raceless views for each situation,
Or when he could not cleanly skirt dissension,

Faced up to the dilemma, firmly seized
Whatever ground was Anglo-Saxonized.
In diet, too, his practice was exemplary:
10   Of pork in its profane forms he was wary;
Expert in vintage wines, sauces, and salads,
His palate shrank from cornbread, yams and collards.

He was as careful whom he chose to kiss:
His bride had somewhere lost her Jewishness,
15   But kept her blue eyes; an Episcopalian
Prelate proclaimed them matched chameleon.
Choosing the right addresses, here, abroad,
They shunned those places where they might be barred;
Even less anxious to be asked to dine
20   Where hosts catered to kosher accent or exotic skin.
And so he climbed, unclogged by ethnic weights,
An airborne plant, flourishing without roots.
Not one false note was struck—until he died:
His subtly grieving widow could have flayed
25   The obit writers, ringing crude changes on a clumsy phrase:
"One of the most distinguished members of his race."

NOTES

disclaimed (l. 4): refused to claim

prudent (l. 5): wise, reasonable

skirt dissension (l. 6): avoid disagreement

dilemma (l. 7): a complex problem

Anglo-Saxonized (l. 8): dominated by Anglo-Saxon thinking, that is, "white" thinking

exemplary (l. 9): worth imitating

profane (l. 10): crude, coarse

wary (l. 10): cautious

vintage (l. 11): fine

palate (l. 12): taste buds

shrank from (l. 12): rejected

Prelate (l. 16): a high-ranking church official, such as a bishop

chameleon (l. 16): literally, a lizard with the ability to change its color

shunned (l. 18): avoided

barred (l. 18): not allowed to enter

catered to (l. 20): provided what was needed or desired

kosher (l. 20): literally, approved by Jewish law

exotic (l. 20): strange, different

unclogged (l. 21): freed from a difficulty

ethnic (l. 21): relating to a group of people that have certain characteristics in common, such as race, language, religion, and so on

subtly (l. 24): quietly, unobviously

flayed (l. 24): literally, to strip off the skin (as by lashing with a whip)

obit (l. 25): short for obituary, a notice of a person's death, usually with a short account of the person's life

ringing . . . changes (l. 25): running through the possible variations

distinguished (l. 26): outstanding

The Vacuum

Howard Nemerov

The house is so quiet now
The vacuum cleaner sulks in the corner closet,
Its bag limp as a stopped lung, its mouth
Grinning into the floor, maybe at my
5   Slovenly life, my dog-dead youth.

I've lived this way long enough,
But when my old woman died her soul
Went into that vacuum cleaner, and I can't bear
To see the bag swell like a belly, eating the dust
10   And the woolen mice, and begin to howl

Because there is old filth everywhere
She used to crawl, in the corner and under the stair.
I know now how life is cheap as dirt,
And still the hungry, angry heart
15   Hangs on and howls, biting at air.

NOTES
sulks (l. 2): pouts
slovenly (l. 5): disorderly

Weakness

Alden Nowlan

Old mare whose eyes
are like cracked marbles
drools blood in her mash,
shivers in her jute blanket.

5   My father hates weakness worse than hail;
in the morning
    without haste
he will shoot her in the ear, once,
shovel her under in the north pasture.

10   Tonight
    leaving the stables,
he stands his lantern on an overturned water pail,
turns,
    cursing her for a bad bargain
15   and spreads his coat
carefully over her sick shoulders.

NOTES
mash (l. 3): feed
jute (l. 4): a type of fiber

Power

Adrienne Rich

Living   in the earth-deposits   of our history

Today a backhoe divulged   out of a crumbling flank of earth
one bottle   amber   perfect   a hundred-year-old
cure for fever   or melancholy   a tonic
5   for living on this earth   in the winters of this climate

Today I was reading about Marie Curie:
she must have known she suffered   from radiation sickness
her body bombarded for years   by the element
she had purified
10   It seems she denied to the end
the source of the cataracts on her eyes
the cracked and suppurating skin   of her finger-ends
till she could no longer hold   a test-tube or a pencil

She died   a famous woman   denying
15   her wounds
denying
her wounds   came   from the same source as her power

NOTES

divulged (l. 2): revealed

flank (l. 2): side

amber (l. 3): brownish-yellow

melancholy (l. 4): sadness

Marie Curie (l. 6): Marie Curie (1867–1934) and her husband, Pierre Curie (1859–1906), searched for the source of radioactivity in pitchblende (a mineral) and discovered two radioactive elements, radium and polonium. In 1903, the Curies were awarded the Nobel Prize for Physics for their discovery. Marie Curie was also awarded the 1911 Nobel Prize for Chemistry for her study of radium. She continued working with radium until her death in 1934 from leukemia, a disease she is believed to have contracted as a result of extensive exposure to high levels of radiation.

cataracts (l. 11): Cloudy spots on the lens of the eye. Today, the types of cataracts that would once have led to blindness can be surgically removed.

suppurating (l. 12): pus filled

The Chimney Sweeper
from *Songs of Innocence*

William Blake

When my mother died I was very young,
And my father sold me while yet my tongue
Could scarcely cry "'weep! 'weep! 'weep! 'weep!"
So your chimneys I sweep & in soot I sleep.

5   There's little Tom Dacre, who cried when his head,
That curl'd like a lamb's back, was shav'd, so I said,
"Hush, Tom! never mind it, for when your head's bare,
You know that the soot cannot spoil your white hair."

And so he was quiet, & that very night,
10   As Tom was a-sleeping he had such a sight!
That thousands of sweepers, Dick, Joe, Ned, & Jack,
Were all of them lock'd up in coffins of black;

And by came an Angel who had a bright key,
And he open'd the coffins & set them all free;
15   Then down a green plain, leaping, laughing they run,
And wash in a river and shine in the Sun.

Then naked & white, all their bags left behind,
They rise upon clouds, and sport in the wind.
And the Angel told Tom, if he'd be a good boy,
20   He'd have God for his father & never want joy.

And so Tom awoke; and we rose in the dark
And got with our bags & our brushes to work.
Tho' the morning was cold, Tom was happy & warm;
So if all do their duty, they need not fear harm.

NOTE

'weep (l. 3): Sweep. Chimney sweepers would advertise their service by walking the streets and calling out
"Sweep!" This child is so young that he cannot clearly pronounce the word.

The Chimney Sweeper
from Songs of Experience

William Blake

A little black thing among the snow
Crying "'weep, 'weep," in notes of woe!
"Where are thy father & mother? say?"
"They are both gone up to the church to pray."
5   "Because I was happy upon the heath,

And smil'd among the winter's snow;
They clothed me in the clothes of death,
And taught me to sing the notes of woe."
"And because I am happy, & dance & sing,
10 They think they have done me no injury,
And are gone to praise God & his Priest & King,
Who make up a heaven of our misery."

NOTES
'weep (l. 2): See note to preceding poem.
heath (l. 5): an area of land covered with small bushes

Dulce et Decorum Est

Wilfred Owen

Bent double, like old beggars under sacks,
Knock-kneed, coughing like hags, we cursed through sludge,
Till on the haunting flares we turned our backs,
And towards our distant rest began to trudge.
5   Men marched asleep. Many had lost their boots,
But limped on, blood-shod. All went lame, all blind;
Drunk with fatigue; deaf even to the hoots
Of Five-Nines dropping softly behind.

Gas! GAS! Quick, boys!—An ecstasy of fumbling,
10 Fitting the clumsy helmets just in time,
But someone still was yelling out and stumbling
And flound'ring like a man in fire or lime . . .
Dim through the misty panes and thick green light,
As under a green sea, I saw him drowning.

15 In all my dreams before my helpless sight
He plunges at me, guttering, choking, drowning.

If in some smothering dreams, you too could pace
Behind the wagon that we flung him in,
And watch the white eyes writhing in his face,
20 His hanging face, like a devil's sick of sin,
If you could hear, at every jolt, the blood
Come gargling from the froth-corrupted lungs,
Obscene as cancer, bitter as the cud
Of vile, incurable sores on innocent tongues—
25 My friend, you would not tell with such high zest
To children ardent for some desperate glory,
The old lie: *Dulce et decorum est
Pro patria mori.*

NOTES

Dulce et Decorum Est (title): A quotation from Horace (Roman poet). The entire statement is given in the last two lines and means "It is sweet and fitting to die for one's country." The action referred to in the poem occurs in World War I, in which Wilfred Owen died a week before the fighting ended.

flares (l. 3): devices containing an explosive material that lights the sky

blood-shod (l. 6): "Shod" literally means wearing shoes.

Five-Nines (l. 8): exploding shells of poisonous gas

ecstasy (l. 9): furious activity

flound'ring (l. 12): floundering; struggling

lime (l. 12): an acid-like chemical

guttering (l. 16): harsh sounds made deep in the throat

writhing (l. 19): twisting in pain

froth-corrupted (l. 22): filled with foam

cud (l. 23): literally, something that is chewed; a wad

vile (l. 24): repulsive

zest (l. 25): great enthusiasm

ardent (l. 26): full of desire

Mending Wall

Robert Frost

Something there is that doesn't love a wall,
That sends the frozen-ground-swell under it,
And spills the upper boulders in the sun;
And makes gaps even two can pass abreast.
5   The work of hunters is another thing:
I have come after them and made repair
Where they have left not one stone on a stone,
But they would have the rabbit out of hiding,
To please the yelping dogs. The gaps I mean,
10   No one has seen them made or heard them made,
But at spring mending-time we find them there.
I let my neighbor know beyond the hill;
And on a day we meet to walk the line
And set the wall between us once again.
15   We keep the wall between us as we go.
To each the boulders that have fallen to each.
And some are loaves and some so nearly balls
We have to use a spell to make them balance:
"Stay where you are until our backs are turned!"
20   We wear our fingers rough with handling them.
Oh, just another kind of outdoor game,
One on a side. It comes to little more:
There where it is we do not need the wall:
He is all pine and I am apple orchard.
25   My apple trees will never get across
And eat the cones under his pines, I tell him.

Stone Wall, Concord, Massachusetts

—Leah McCraney

He only says, "Good fences make good neighbors."
Spring is the mischief in me, and I wonder
If I could put a notion in his head:
30 "*Why* do they make good neighbors? Isn't it
Where there are cows? But here there are no cows.
Before I built a wall I'd ask to know
What I was walling in or walling out,
And to whom I was like to give offense.
35 Something there is that doesn't love a wall,
That wants it down." I could say "Elves" to him,
But it's not elves exactly, and I'd rather
He said it for himself. I see him there
Bringing a stone grasped firmly by the top
40 In each hand, like an old-stone savage armed.
He moves in darkness as it seems to me,
Not of woods only and the shade of trees.
He will not go behind his father's saying,
And he likes having thought of it so well
45 He says again, "Good fences make good neighbors."

NOTES

frozen-ground-swell (l. 2): When the earth freezes, it expands or "swells."
boulders (l. 3): large stones
abreast (l. 4): side by side
yelping (l. 9): barking
spell (l. 18): a magic phrase
Spring is the mischief in me (l. 28): Spring makes me mischievous.
old-stone savage (l. 40): suggesting the image of a stone-age man or "cave man"
go behind (l. 43): dispute, abandon

Lost Sister

Cathy Song

I

In China,
even the peasants
named their first daughters
Jade—
5 the stone that in the far fields
could moisten the dry season,
could make men move mountains
for the healing green of the inner hills
glistening like slices of winter melon.
10 And the daughters were grateful:
They never left home.

To move freely was a luxury
stolen from them at birth.
Instead, they gathered patience,
15   learning to walk in shoes
the size of teacups,
without breaking—
the arc of their movements
as dormant as the rooted willow,
20   as redundant as the farmyard hens.
But they traveled far
in surviving,
learning to stretch the family rice,
to quiet the demons,
25   the noisy stomachs.

II

There is a sister
across the ocean,
who relinquished her name,
diluting jade green
30   with the blue of the Pacific.
Rising with a tide of locusts,
she swarmed with others
to inundate another shore.
In America,
35   there are many roads
and women can stride along with men.
But in another wilderness,
the possibilities,
the loneliness,
40   can strangulate like jungle vines.
The meager provisions and sentiments
of once belonging—
fermented roots, Mah-Jong tiles and firecrackers—set but
a flimsy household
45   in a forest of nightless cities.
A giant snake rattles above,
spewing black clouds into your kitchen.
Dough-faced landlords
slip in and out of your keyholes,
50   making claims you don't understand,
tapping into your communication systems
of laundry lines and restaurant chains.
You find you need China:
your one fragile identification,
55   a jade link
handcuffed to your wrist.

You remember your mother
who walked for centuries,
footless—
60   and like her,
you have left no footprints,
but only because
there is an ocean in between,
the unremitting space of your rebellion.

NOTES

To move freely was . . . stolen from them at birth (l. 13–14): A reference to the Imperial Chinese custom of foot binding. The object of foot binding was to reshape a girl's feet so that her arch was extraordinarily high and her feet would grow to be no longer than 10 cm (3.9 inches). To achieve this shape, a young girl's feet were wrapped with all of her toes (except the first one) pulled under her foot to the sole, a process that necessarily broke the bones in the toes and the foot. The process was repeated numerous times over the next 3–4 years, and the wrappings were regularly tightened.

dormant (l. 19): limited

redundant (l. 20): unchanging

relinquished (l. 28): gave up

diluting (l. 29): weakening

inundate (l. 33): flood

stride (l. 36): walk with long steps

meager (l. 41): barely adequate

Mah-Jong (l. 43): a Chinese game resembling dominoes

unremitting (l. 64): ceaseless, constant

Persimmons

Li-Young Lee

In sixth grade Mrs. Walker
slapped the back of my head
and made me stand in the corner
for not knowing the difference
5   between *persimmon* and *precision*.
How to choose
persimmons. This is precision.
Ripe ones are soft and brown-spotted.
Sniff the bottoms. The sweet one
10   will be fragrant. How to eat:
put the knife away, lay down newspaper.
Peel the skin tenderly, not to tear the meat.
Chew the skin, suck it,
and swallow. Now, eat
15   the meat of the fruit,
so sweet,
all of it, to the heart.

Donna undresses, her stomach is white.
In the yard, dewy and shivering
20   with crickets, we lie naked,
face-up, face-down.
I teach her Chinese.
Crickets: *chiu chiu.* Dew: I've forgotten.
Naked: I've forgotten.
25   *Ni, wo:* you and me.
I part her legs,
remember to tell her
she is beautiful as the moon.

Other words
30   that got me into trouble were
fight and *fright, wren* and *yarn.*
Fight was what I did when I was frightened,
fright was what I felt when I was fighting.
Wrens are small, plain birds,
35   yarn is what one knits with.
Wrens are soft as yarn.
My mother made birds out of yarn.
I loved to watch her tie the stuff;
a bird, a rabbit, a wee man.

40   Mrs. Walker brought a persimmon to class
and cut it up
so everyone could taste
a *Chinese apple.* Knowing
it wasn't ripe or sweet, I didn't eat
45   but watched the other faces.

My mother said every persimmon has a sun
inside, something golden, glowing,
warm as my face.

Once, in the cellar, I found two wrapped in newspaper,
50   forgotten and not yet ripe.
I took them and set both on my bedroom windowsill,
where each morning a cardinal
sang, *The sun, the sun.*

Finally understanding
55   he was going blind,
my father sat up all one night
waiting for a song, a ghost.
I gave him the persimmons,
swelled, heavy as sadness,
60   and sweet as love.

This year, in the muddy lighting
of my parents' cellar, I rummage, looking

for something I lost.
My father sits on the tired, wooden stairs,
65   black cane between his knees,
hand over hand, gripping the handle.

He's so happy that I've come home.
I ask how his eyes are, a stupid question.
All gone, he answers.

70   Under some blankets, I find a box.
Inside the box I find three scrolls.
I sit beside him and untie
three paintings by my father:
Hibiscus leaf and a white flower.
75   Two cats preening.
Two persimmons, so full they want to drop from the cloth.

He raises both hands to touch the cloth,
asks, *Which is this?*

This is persimmons, Father.

80   *Oh, the feel of the wolftail on the silk,*
the strength, the tense
precision in the wrist.
I painted them hundreds of times
eyes closed. These I painted blind.
85   *Some things never leave a person:*
scent of the hair of one you love,
the texture of persimmons,
in your palm, the ripe weight.

NOTES

Persimmons (title): A persimmon is a tomato-sized fruit that is sour and bitter when unripe, but sweet and luscious when ripe.

a **Chinese apple** (l. 43): In the United States, a pomegranate (a fruit that is roughly the size of an orange but looks like a reddish berry) is commonly referred to as a Chinese apple.

wolftail (l. 80): a type of paintbrush that uses wolf-hair as bristles, traditionally used by Asian artists

silk (l. 80): the material of the canvas, traditionally used in certain types of Asian art

Parsley

Rita Dove

1. The Cane Fields

There is a parrot imitating spring
in the palace, its feathers parsley green.
Out of the swamp the cane appears

to haunt us, and we cut it down. El General
5   searches for a word; he is all the world
there is. Like a parrot imitating spring,

we lie down screaming as rain punches through
and we come up green. We cannot speak an R—
out of the swamp, the cane appears

10   and then the mountain we call in whispers *Katalina*.
The children gnaw their teeth to arrowheads.
There is a parrot imitating spring.

El General has found his word: *perejil*.
Who says it, lives. He laughs, teeth shining
15   out of the swamp. The cane appears

in our dreams, lashed by wind and streaming.
And we lie down. For every drop of blood
there is a parrot imitating spring.
Out of the swamp the cane appears.

2. The Palace

20   The word the general's chosen is parsley.
It is fall, when thoughts turn
to love and death; the general thinks
of his mother, how she died in the fall
and he planted her walking cane at the grave
25   and it flowered, each spring stolidly forming
four-star blossoms. The general

pulls on his boots, he stomps to
her room in the palace, the one without
curtains, the one with a parrot
30   in a brass ring. As he paces he wonders
Who can I kill today. And for a moment
the little knot of screams
is still. The parrot, who has traveled

all the way from Australia in an ivory
35   cage, is, coy as a widow, practising

spring. Ever since the morning
his mother collapsed in the kitchen
while baking skull-shaped candies
for the Day of the Dead, the general

40   has hated sweets. He orders pastries
brought up for the bird; they arrive

dusted with sugar on a bed of lace.
The knot in his throat starts to twitch;
he sees his boots the first day in battle

45   splashed with mud and urine
as a soldier falls at his feet amazed—
how stupid he looked!—at the sound
of artillery. *I never thought it would sing*
the soldier said, and died. Now

50   the general sees the fields of sugar
cane, lashed by rain and streaming.
He sees his mother's smile, the teeth
gnawed to arrowheads. He hears
the Haitians sing without R's

55   as they swing the great machetes:
Katalina, they sing, *Katalina*,

mi madle, mi amol en muelte. God knows
his mother was no stupid woman; she
could roll an R like a queen. Even

60   a parrot can roll an R! In the bare room
the bright feathers arch in a parody
of greenery, as the last pale crumbs
disappear under the blackened tongue. Someone

calls out his name in a voice

65   so like his mother's, a startled tear
splashes the tip of his right boot.
My mother, my love in death.
The general remembers the tiny green sprigs
men of his village wore in their capes

70   to honor the birth of a son. He will
order many, this time, to be killed

for a single, beautiful word.

NOTES

"On October 2, 1937, Rafael Trujillo (1891–1961), dictator of the Dominican Republic, ordered 20,000 blacks killed because they could not pronounce the letter 'r' in *perejil*, the Spanish word for parsley." (Dove's note)

El General (l. 4): Trujillo was called *El Jefe* ("The Chief")

Katalina (l. 10): The Haitian pronunciation of *Katarina*. The "r" in the Haitians' native French-based Creole language is not trilled as it is in Spanish (the native language of Dominicans).

The children gnaw their teeth to arrowheads (l. 11): Gnawing on sugarcane can grind teeth into sharp points.

perejil (l. 13) the Spanish word for parsley

coy (l. 35): flirtatiously shy
Baking skull-shaped candies . . . for the Day of the Dead (l. 38–39): The Day of the Dead is a Latin American holiday designed to honor dead relatives as well as the continuity of life. It is traditional to bake dough into skull-shaped cookies called *pan de muerto* or "bread of the dead."
mi madle, mi amol en muelte (l. 57): the Haitian pronunciation of *mi madre, mi amore en muerte*, Spanish for ***My mother, my love in death*** (l. 67)
arch (l. 61): curve
parody (l. 61): poor imitation

The Unknown Citizen

W. H. Auden

(To JS/07/M/378 This Marble Monument Is Erected by the State)

He was found by the Bureau of Statistics to be
One against whom there was no official complaint,
And all the reports on his conduct agree
That, in the modern sense of an old-fashioned word, he was a saint,
5   For in everything he did he served the Greater Community.
Except for the War till the day he retired
He worked in a factory and never got fired,
But satisfied his employers, Fudge Motors Inc.
Yet he wasn't a scab or odd in his views,
10   For his union reports that he paid his dues,
(Our report on his Union shows it was sound)
And our Social Psychology workers found
That he was popular with his mates and liked a drink.
The Press are convinced that he bought a paper every day
15   And that his reactions to advertisements were normal in every way.
Policies taken out in his name prove that he was fully insured,
And his Health-card shows he was once in hospital but left it cured.
Both Producers Research and High-Grade Living declare
He was fully sensible to the advantages of the Installment Plan
20   And had everything necessary to the Modern Man,
A phonograph, a radio, a car and a frigidaire.
Our researchers into Public Opinion are content
That he held the proper opinions for the time of year;
When there was peace, he was for peace; when there was war, he went.
25   He was married and added five children to the population,
Which our Eugenist says was the right number for a parent of his generation.
And our teachers report that he never interfered with their education.
Was he free? Was he happy? The question is absurd:
Had anything been wrong, we should certainly have heard.

NOTES

scab (l. 9): a worker who will not join a labor union or who takes a striker's job
Installment Plan (l. 19): a plan in which goods are paid for over a period of time
frigidaire (l. 21): a refrigerator
Eugenist: (l. 26): an expert on the production of healthy offspring
absurd (l. 28): ridiculous

Curiosity

Alastair Reid

may have killed the cat; more likely
the cat was just unlucky, or else curious
to see what death was like, having no cause
to go on licking paws, or fathering

5   litter on litter of kittens, predictably.
Nevertheless, to be curious
is dangerous enough. To distrust
what is always said, what seems,
to ask odd questions, interfere in dreams,

10   leave home, smell rats, have hunches
do not endear cats to those doggy circles
where well-smelt baskets, suitable wives, good lunches
are the order of things, and where prevails
much wagging of incurious heads and tails.

15   Face it. Curiosity
will not cause us to die—
only lack of it will.
Never to want to see
the other side of the hill

20   or that improbable country
where living is an idyll
(although a probable hell)
would kill us all.
Only the curious

25   have, if they live, a tale
worth telling at all.

Dogs say cats love too much, are irresponsible,
are changeable, marry too many wives,
desert their children, chill all dinner tables

30   with tales of their nine lives.
Well, they are lucky. Let them be
nine-lived and contradictory,
curious enough to change, prepared to pay
the cat price, which is to die

35   and die again and again,
each time with no less pain.
A cat minority of one
is all that can be counted on
to tell the truth. And what cats have to tell

40   on each return from hell
is this: that dying is what the living do,
that dying is what the loving do,

and that dead dogs are those who do not know
that dying is what, to live, each has to do.

NOTE

idyll (l. 21): a simple, peaceful, or carefree existence

What Would Freud Say?

Bob Hicok

Wasn't on purpose that I drilled
through my finger or the nurse
laughed. She apologized
three times and gave me a shot
5   of something that was a lusher
apology. The person
who drove me home
said my smile was a smeared
totem that followed
10   his body that night as it arced
over a cliff in a dream.
He's always flying
in his dreams and lands
on cruise ships or hovers
15   over Atlanta with an erection.
He put me to bed and the drugs
wore off and I woke
to cannibals at my extremities.
I woke with a sense
20   of what nails in the palms
might do to a spirit
temporarily confined to flesh.
That too was an accident
if you believe Judas
25   merely wanted to be loved.
To be loved by God,
Urban the 8th
had heads cut off
that were inadequately
30   bowed by dogma. To be loved
by Blondie, Dagwood
gets nothing right
except the hallucinogenic
architecture of sandwiches.
35   He would have drilled
through a finger too
while making a case for books

on home repair and health.
Drilling through my finger's
40   not the dumbest thing
I've done. Second place
was approaching
a frozen gas-cap with lighter
in hand while thinking
45   *heat melts ice* and not
explosion kills asshole. First
place was passing
through a bedroom door
and removing silk that did not
50   belong to my wife.
Making a bookcase is not
the extent of my apology.
I've also been beaten up
in a bar for saying huevos
55   rancheros in a way
insulting to the patrons'
ethnicity. I've also lost
my job because lying
face down on the couch
60   didn't jibe with my employer's
definition of home
office. I wanted her to come
through the door on Sunday
and see the bookcase
65   she'd asked me to build
for a year and be impressed
that it didn't lean
or wobble even though
I've only leaned and often
70   wobbled. Now it's half
done but certainly
a better gift with its map
of my unfaithful blood.

NOTES

lusher (l. 5): more delicious

totem (l. 9): literally, an object, plant, or animal that serves as a symbol of a family or clan.

arced (l. 10): moved in an arc (the outer circumference of a circle)

extremities (l. 18): fingers and toes

Judas (l. 24): the apostle who betrayed Jesus (Matthew 26:14–15, 26:47–50, 27:1–5; Mark 14:10–11, 14:43–45; Luke 22:1–6, 22:47–49; John 131–3, 13:21–30, 18:1–8; Acts 1:18–20)

Urban the 8th (l. 27): The Pope (1623–1644) who persecuted Galileo Galilei (1564–1642) for supporting Copernicus's theory that all planets revolved around the sun, thus challenging the Catholic Church's teaching that the sun and other planets revolved around the earth.

dogma (l. 30): a church's formal religious principles

Blondie, Dagwood (l. 31): characters from a popular comic strip that focuses on a suburban family headed by the bumbling Dagwood and his beautiful wife Blondie

huevos rancheros (l. 54–55): a Mexican dish comprised of eggs, onion, tomatoes, garlic, chili peppers, and cheese, served on tortillas. The speaker likely misspoke and asked for *huevos de rancheros*—"rancher's testicles"—instead of *huevos rancheros*.

jibe (l. 60): agree with

The Naked and the Nude

Robert Graves

For me, the naked and the nude
(By lexicographers construed
As synonyms that should express
The same deficiency of dress
5   Or shelter) stand as wide apart
As love from lies, or truth from art.

Lovers without reproach will gaze
On bodies naked and ablaze;
The Hippocratic eye will see
10   In nakedness, anatomy;
And naked shines the Goddess when
She mounts her lion among men.

The nude are bold, the nude are sly
To hold each treasonable eye.
15   While draping by a showman's trick
Their dishabille in rhetoric
They grin a mock-religious grin
Of scorn at those of naked skin.

The naked, therefore, who compete
20   Against the nude may know defeat;
Yet when they both together tread
The briary pastures of the dead,
By Gorgons with long whips pursued,
How naked go the sometimes nude!

NOTES

lexicographers (l. 2): dictionary writers

construed (l. 2): interpreted

deficiency (l. 4): lack

Hippocratic eye (l. 9): Scientific eye. The ancient Greek physician Hippocrates is generally considered to be the founder of medical science.

treasonable (l. 14): faithless

dishabille (l. 16): partial or complete lack of clothing

rhetoric (l. 16): literally, clever words

mock (l. 17): fake

tread (l. 21): walk

briary pastures of the dead (l. 22): land of the dead

Gorgons (l. 23): In Greek mythology, three monstrous sisters who had snakes for hair; large, wide eyes; red, lolling tongues; and long, protruding teeth. The Gorgons were so ugly that any man who saw them turned to stone.

2

Fiction

Birthday Party

Katharine Brush

1   They were a couple in their late thirties, and they looked unmistakably married. They sat on the banquette opposite us in a little narrow restaurant, having dinner. The man had a round, self-satisfied face, with glasses on it; the woman was fadingly pretty, in a big hat. There was nothing conspicuous about them, nothing particularly noticeable, until the end of their meal, when it suddenly became obvious that this was an Occasion—in fact, the husband's birthday, and the wife had planned a little surprise for him.

2   It arrived, in the form of a small but glossy birthday cake, with one pink candle burning in the center. The headwaiter brought it in and placed it before the husband, and meanwhile the violin-and-piano orchestra played "Happy Birthday to You," and the wife beamed with shy pride over her little surprise, and such few people as there were in the restaurant tried to help out with a pattering of applause. It became clear at once that help was needed, because the husband was not pleased. Instead he was hotly embarrassed, and indignant at his wife for embarrassing him.

3   You looked at him and saw this and you thought, "Oh, now don't *be* like that!" But he was like that, and as soon as the little cake had been deposited on the table, and the orchestra had finished the birthday piece, and the general attention had shifted from the man and woman, I saw him say something to her under his breath—some punishing thing, quick and curt and unkind. I couldn't bear to look at the woman then, so I stared at my plate and waited for quite a long time. Not long enough, though. She was still crying when I finally glanced over there again. Crying quietly and heartbrokenly and hopelessly, all to herself, under the gay big brim of her best hat.

NOTES

banquette (par. 1): an upholstered bench along a wall
indignant (par. 2): angry

The Lottery

Shirley Jackson

1   The morning of June 27th was clear and sunny, with the fresh warmth of a full-summer day; the flowers were blossoming profusely and the grass was richly green. The people of the village began to gather in the square, between the post office and the bank, around ten o'clock; in some towns there were so many people that the lottery took two days and had to be started on June 26th, but in this village, where there were only about three hundred people, the whole lottery took less than two hours, so it could begin at ten o'clock in the morning and still be through in time to allow the villagers to get home for noon dinner.

NOTE

profusely (par. 1): in great quantity

---

2   The children assembled first, of course. School was recently over for the summer, and the feeling of liberty sat uneasily on most of them; they tended to gather together quietly for a while before they broke into boisterous play, and their talk was still of the classroom and the teacher, of books and reprimands. Bobby Martin had already stuffed his pockets full of stones, and the other boys soon followed his example, selecting the smoothest and roundest stones; Bobby and Harry Jones and Dickie Delacroix—the villagers pronounced this name "Dellacroy"—eventually made a great pile of stones in one corner of the square and guarded it against the raids of the other boys. The girls stood aside, talking among themselves, looking over their shoulders at the boys, and the very small children rolled in the dust or clung to the hands of their older brothers or sisters.

3   Soon the men began to gather, surveying their own children, speaking of planting and rain, tractors, and taxes. They stood together, away from the pile of stones in the corner, and their jokes were quiet and they smiled rather than laughed. The women, wearing faded house dresses and sweaters, came shortly after their menfolk. They greeted one another and exchanged bits of gossip as they went to join their husbands. Soon the women, standing by their husbands, began to call to their children, and the children came reluctantly, having to be called four or five times. Bobby Martin ducked under his mother's grasping hand and ran, laughing, back to the pile of stones. His father spoke up sharply, and Bobby came quickly and took his place between his father and his oldest brother.

4   The lottery was conducted—as were the square dances, the teenage club, the Halloween program—by Mr. Summers, who had time and energy to devote to civic activities. He was a round-faced, jovial man and he ran the coal business, and people were sorry for him, because he had no children and his wife was a scold. When he arrived in the square, carrying the black wooden box, there was a murmur of conversation among the villagers, and he waved and called, "Little late today, folks." The postmaster, Mr. Graves, followed him, carrying a three-legged stool, and the stool was put in the center of the square and Mr. Summers set the black box down on it. The villagers kept their distance, leaving a space between themselves and the stool, and when Mr. Summers said, "Some of you fellows want to give me a hand?" there was a hesitation before two men, Mr. Martin and his oldest son, Baxter, came forward to hold the box steady on the stool while Mr. Summers stirred up the papers inside it.

5   The original paraphernalia for the lottery had been lost long ago, and the black box now resting on the stool had been put into use even before Old Man Warner, the oldest man in town, was born. Mr. Summers spoke frequently to the villagers about making a new box, but no one liked to upset even as much tradition as was represented by the black box. There was a story that the present box had been made with some of the box that had preceded it, the one that had been constructed when the first people settled down to make a village

NOTES

boisterous (par. 2): noisy, rough

reprimands (par. 2): scoldings, criticisms

jovial (par. 4): jolly

paraphernalia (par. 5): the articles or equipment used in some activity

here. Every year, after the lottery, Mr. Summers began talking again about a new box, but every year the subject was allowed to fade off without anything's being done. The black box grew shabbier each year; by now it was no longer completely black but splintered badly along one side to show the original wood color, and in some places faded or stained.

6   Mr. Martin and his oldest son, Baxter, held the black box securely on the stool until Mr. Summers had stirred the papers thoroughly with his hand. Because so much of the ritual had been forgotten or discarded, Mr. Summers had been successful in having slips of paper substituted for the chips of wood that had been used for generations. Chips of wood, Mr. Summers had argued, had been all very well when the village was tiny, but now that the population was more than three hundred and likely to keep on growing, it was necessary to use something that would fit more easily into the black box. The night before the lottery, Mr. Summers and Mr. Graves made up the slips of paper and put them in the box, and it was taken to the safe of Mr. Summers' coal company and locked up until Mr. Summers was ready to take it to the square next morning. The rest of the year, the box was put away, sometimes one place, sometimes another; it had spent one year in Mr. Graves's barn and another year underfoot in the post office, and sometimes it was set on a shelf in the Martin grocery and left there.

7   There was a great deal of fussing to be done before Mr. Summers declared the lottery open. There were the lists to make up—of heads of families, heads of households in each family, members of each household in each family. There was the proper swearing-in of Mr. Summers by the postmaster, as the official of the lottery; at one time, some people remembered, there had been a recital of some sort, performed by the official of the lottery, a perfunctory, tuneless chant that had been rattled off duly each year; some people believed that the official of the lottery used to stand just so when he said or sang it, others believed that he was supposed to walk among the people, but years and years ago this part of the ritual had been allowed to lapse. There had been, also, a ritual salute, which the official of the lottery had had to use in addressing each person who came up to draw from the box, but this also had changed with time, until now it was felt necessary only for the official to speak to each person approaching. Mr. Summers was very good at all this; in his clean white shirt and blue jeans, with one hand resting carelessly on the black box. He seemed very proper and important as he talked interminably to Mr. Graves and the Martins.

8   Just as Mr. Summers finally left off talking and turned to the assembled villagers, Mrs. Hutchinson came hurriedly along the path to the square, her sweater thrown over her shoulders, and slid into place in the back of the crowd. "Clean forgot what day it was," she said to Mrs. Delacroix, who stood next to her, and they both laughed softly. "Thought my old man was out back stacking wood," Mrs. Hutchinson went on, "and then I looked out the window and the kids were gone, and then I remembered it was the twenty-seventh and came a-running." She dried her hands on her apron, and Mrs. Delacroix said, "You're in time, though. They're still talking away up there."

NOTES

perfunctory (par. 7): done automatically or with little personal interest
interminably (par. 7): endlessly

9   Mrs. Hutchinson craned her neck to see through the crowd and found her husband and children standing near the front. She tapped Mrs. Delacroix on the arm as a farewell and began to make her way through the crowd. The people separated good-humoredly to let her through; two or three people said, in voices just loud enough to be heard across the crowd, "Here comes your Missus, Hutchinson," and "Bill, she made it after all." Mrs. Hutchinson reached her husband, and Mr. Summers, who had been waiting, said cheerfully, "Thought we were going to have to get on without you, Tessie." Mrs. Hutchinson said, grinning, "Wouldn't have me leave m'dishes in the sink, now, would you, Joe?" and soft laughter ran through the crowd as the people stirred back into position after Mrs. Hutchinson's arrival. "Well, now," Mr. Summers said soberly, "guess we better get started, get this over with, so's we can go back to work. Anybody ain't here?"

10   "Dunbar," several people said. "Dunbar, Dunbar."

11   Mr. Summers consulted his list. "Clyde Dunbar," he said. "That's right. He's broke his leg, hasn't he? Who's drawing for him?"

12   "Me, I guess," a woman said, and Mr. Summers turned to look at her. "Wife draws for her husband," Mr. Summers said. "Don't you have a grown boy to do it for you, Janey?" Although Mr. Summers and everyone else in the village knew the answer perfectly well, it was the business of the official of the lottery to ask such questions formally. Mr. Summers waited with an expression of polite interest while Mrs. Dunbar answered.

13   "Horace's not but sixteen yet," Mrs. Dunbar said regretfully. "Guess I gotta fill in for the old man this year."

14   "Right," Mr. Summers said. He made a note on the list he was holding. Then he asked, "Watson boy drawing this year?"

15   A tall boy in the crowd raised his hand. "Here," he said. "I'm drawing for m'mother and me." He blinked his eyes nervously and ducked his head as several voices in the crowd said things like "Good fellow, Jack," and "Glad to see your mother's got a man to do it."

16   "Well," Mr. Summers said, "guess that's everyone. Old Man Warner make it?"

17   "Here," a voice said, and Mr. Summers nodded.

18   A sudden hush fell on the crowd as Mr. Summers cleared his throat and looked at the list. "All ready?" he said. "Now, I'll read the names—heads of families first—and the men come up and take a paper out of the box. Keep the paper folded in your hand without looking at it until everyone has had a turn. Everything clear?"

19   The people had done it so many times that they only half listened to the directions; most of them were quiet, wetting their lips, not looking around. Then Mr. Summers raised one hand high and said, "Adams." A man disengaged himself from the crowd and came forward. "Hi, Steve," Mr. Summers said, and Mr. Adams said, "Hi, Joe." They grinned at one another humorlessly and nervously. Then Mr. Adams reached into the black box and took out a folded paper. He held it firmly by one corner as he turned and went hastily back to his place in the crowd, where he stood a little apart from his family, not looking down at his hand.

20   "Allen," Mr. Summers said. "Anderson. . . . Bentham."

21   "Seems like there's no time at all between lotteries any more," Mrs. Delacroix said to Mrs. Graves in the back row. "Seems like we got through with the last one only last week."

22   "Time sure goes fast," Mrs. Graves said.

23   "Clark. . . . Delacroix."

24   "There goes my old man," Mrs. Delacroix said. She held her breath while her husband went forward.

25   "Dunbar," Mr. Summers said, and Mrs. Dunbar went steadily to the box while one of the women said, "Go on, Janey," and another said, "There she goes."

26   "We're next," Mrs. Graves said. She watched while Mr. Graves came around from the side of the box, greeted Mr. Summers gravely, and selected a slip of paper from the box. By now, all through the crowd there were men holding the small folded papers in their large hands, turning them over and over nervously. Mrs. Dunbar and her two sons stood together, Mrs. Dunbar holding the slip of paper.

27   "Harburt. . . . Hutchinson."

28   "Get up there, Bill," Mrs. Hutchinson said, and the people near her laughed.

29   "Jones."

30   "They do say," Mr. Adams said to Old Man Warner, who stood next to him, "that over in the north village they're talking of giving up the lottery."

31   Old Man Warner snorted. "Pack of crazy fools," he said. "Listening to the young folks, nothing's good enough for them. Next thing you know, they'll be wanting to go back to living in caves, nobody work any more, live *that* way for a while. Used to be a saying about 'Lottery in June, corn be heavy soon.' First thing you know, we'd all be eating stewed chickweed and acorns. There's *always* been a lottery," he added petulantly. "Bad enough to see young Joe Summers up there joking with everybody."

32   "Some places have already quit lotteries," Mrs. Adams said.

33   "Nothing but trouble in *that*," Old Man Warner said stoutly. "Pack of young fools."

34   "Martin." And Bobby Martin watched his father go forward. "Overdyke. . . . Percy."

35   "I wish they'd hurry," Mrs. Dunbar said to her older son. "I wish they'd hurry."

36   "They're almost through," her son said.

37   "You get ready to run tell Dad," Mrs. Dunbar said.

38   Mr. Summers called his own name and then stepped forward precisely and selected a slip from the box. Then he called, "Warner."

39   "Seventy-seventh year I been in the lottery," Old Man Warner said as he went through the crowd. "Seventy-seventh time."

40   "Watson." The tall boy came awkwardly through the crowd. Someone said, "Don't be nervous, Jack," and Mr. Summers said, "Take your time, son."

41   "Zanini."

NOTE

petulantly (par. 31): with irritation

42   After that, there was a long pause, a breathless pause, until Mr. Summers, holding his slip of paper in the air, said, "All right, fellows." For a minute, no one moved, and then all the slips of paper were opened. Suddenly, all the women began to speak at once, saying, "Who is it?," "Who's got it?," "Is it the Dunbars?," "Is it the Watsons?" Then the voices began to say, "It's Hutchinson. It's Bill," "Bill Hutchinson's got it."

43   "Go tell your father," Mrs. Dunbar said to her older son.

44   People began to look around to see the Hutchinsons. Bill Hutchinson was standing quiet, staring down at the paper in his hand. Suddenly, Tessie Hutchinson shouted to Mr. Summers, "You didn't give him time enough to take any paper he wanted. I saw you. It wasn't fair."

45   "Be a good sport, Tessie," Mrs. Delacroix called, and Mrs. Graves said, "All of us took the same chance."

46   "Shut up, Tessie," Bill Hutchinson said.

47   "Well, everyone," Mr. Summers said, "that was done pretty fast, and now we've got to be hurrying a little more to get done in time." He consulted his next list. "Bill," he said, "you draw for the Hutchinson family. You got any other households in the Hutchinsons?"

48   "There's Don and Eva," Mrs. Hutchinson yelled. "Make *them* take their chance!"

49   "Daughters draw with their husbands' families, Tessie," Mr. Summers said gently. "You know that as well as anyone else."

50   "It wasn't *fair*," Tessie said.

51   "I guess not, Joe," Bill Hutchinson said regretfully. "My daughter draws with her husband's family, that's only fair. And I've got no other family except the kids."

52   "Then, as far as drawing for families is concerned, it's you," Mr. Summers said in explanation, "and as far as drawing for households is concerned, that's you, too. Right?"

53   "Right," Bill Hutchinson said.

54   "How many kids, Bill?" Mr. Summers asked formally.

55   "Three," Bill Hutchinson said. "There's Bill, Jr., and Nancy, and little Dave. And Tessie and me."

56   "All right, then," Mr. Summers said. "Harry, you got their tickets back?"

57   Mr. Graves nodded and held up the slips of paper. "Put them in the box, then," Mr. Summers directed. "Take Bill's and put it in."

58   "I think we ought to start over," Mrs. Hutchinson said, as quietly as she could. "I tell you it wasn't *fair*. You didn't give him time enough to choose. *Every*body saw that."

59   Mr. Graves had selected the five slips and put them in the box, and he dropped all the papers but those onto the ground, where the breeze caught them and lifted them off.

60   "Listen, everybody," Mrs. Hutchinson was saying to the people around her.

61   "Ready, Bill?" Mr. Summers asked, and Bill Hutchinson, with one quick glance around at his wife and children, nodded.

62   "Remember," Mr. Summers said, "take the slips and keep them folded until each person has taken one. Harry, you help little Dave." Mr. Graves took the hand of the little boy, who came willingly with him up to the box. "Take a paper out of the box, Davy," Mr. Summers said. Davy put his hand into the box and laughed. "Take

just *one* paper," Mr. Summers said. "Harry, you hold it for him." Mr. Graves took the child's hand and removed the folded paper from the tight fist and held it while little Dave stood next to him and looked up at him wonderingly.

63   "Nancy next," Mr. Summers said. Nancy was twelve, and her school friends breathed heavily as she went forward, switching her skirt, and took a slip daintily from the box. "Bill, Jr.," Mr. Summers said, and Billy, his face red and his feet overlarge, nearly knocked the box over as he got a paper out. "Tessie," Mr. Summers said. She hesitated for a minute, looking around defiantly, and then set her lips and went up to the box. She snatched a paper out and held it behind her.

64   "Bill," Mr. Summers said, and Bill Hutchinson reached into the box and felt around, bringing his hand out at last with the slip of paper in it.

65   The crowd was quiet. A girl whispered, "I hope it's not Nancy," and the sound of the whisper reached the edges of the crowd.

66   "It's not the way it used to be," Old Man Warner said clearly. "People ain't the way they used to be."

67   "All right," Mr. Summers said. "Open the papers. Harry, you open little Davy's."

68   Mr. Graves opened the slip of paper and there was a general sigh through the crowd as he held it up and everyone could see that it was blank. Nancy and Bill, Jr., opened theirs at the same time, and both beamed and laughed, turning around to the crowd and holding their slips of paper above their heads.

69   "Tessie," Mr. Summers said. There was a pause, and then Mr. Summers looked at Bill Hutchinson, and Bill unfolded his paper and showed it. It was blank.

70   "It's Tessie," Mr. Summers said, and his voice was hushed. "Show us her paper, Bill."

71   Bill Hutchinson went over to his wife and forced the slip of paper out of her hand. It had a black spot on it, the black spot Mr. Summers had made the night before with the heavy pencil in the coal-company office. Bill Hutchinson held it up, and there was a stir in the crowd.

72   "All right, folks," Mr. Summers said. "Let's finish quickly."

73   Although the villagers had forgotten the ritual and lost the original black box, they still remembered to use stones. The pile of stones the boys had made earlier was ready; there were stones on the ground with the blowing scraps of paper that had come out of the box. Mrs. Delacroix selected a stone so large she had to pick it up with both hands and turned to Mrs. Dunbar. "Come on," she said. "Hurry up."

74   Mrs. Dunbar had small stones in both hands, and she said, gasping for breath, "I can't run at all. You'll have to go ahead and I'll catch up with you."

75   The children had stones already, and someone gave little Davy Hutchinson a few pebbles.

76   Tessie Hutchinson was in the center of a cleared space by now, and she held her hands out desperately as the villagers moved in on her. "It isn't fair," she said. A stone hit her on the side of the head.

NOTE

defiantly (par. 63): with challenge or resistance

77   Old Man Warner was saying, "Come on, come on, everyone." Steve Adams was in the front of the crowd of villagers, with Mrs. Graves beside him.

78   "It isn't fair, it isn't right," Mrs. Hutchinson screamed, and then they were upon her.

Hills Like White Elephants

Ernest Hemingway

1   The hills across the valley of the Ebro were long and white. On this side there was no shade and no trees and the station was between two lines of rails in the sun. Close against the side of the station there was the warm shadow of the building and a curtain, made of strings of bamboo beads, hung across the open door into the bar, to keep out flies. The American and the girl with him sat at a table in the shade, outside the building. It was very hot and the express from Barcelona would come in forty minutes. It stopped at this junction for two minutes and went to Madrid.

2   "What should we drink?" the girl asked. She had taken off her hat and put it on the table.

3   "It's pretty hot," the man said.

4   "Let's drink beer."

5   "*Dos cervezas,*" the man said into the curtain.

6   "Big ones?" a woman asked from the doorway.

7   "Yes. Two big ones."

8   The woman brought two glasses of beer and two felt pads. She put the felt pads and the beer glass on the table and looked at the man and the girl. The girl was looking off at the line of hills. They were white in the sun and the country was brown and dry.

9   "They look like white elephants," she said.

10   "I've never seen one," the man drank his beer.

11   "No, you wouldn't have."

12   "I might have," the man said. "Just because you say I wouldn't have doesn't prove anything."

13   The girl looked at the bead curtain. "They've painted something on it," she said. "What does it say?"

14   "*Anis del Toro.* It's a drink."

15   "Could we try it?"

16   The man called "Listen" through the curtain. The woman came out from the bar.

17   "Four *reales.*"

18   "We want two *Anis del Toro.*"

NOTES

Ebro (par. 1): river in northeastern Spain

Barcelona (par. 1): city in northeastern Spain on the Mediterranean

Madrid (par. 1): the capital of Spain, located in center of the country

reales (par. 17): Spanish coin

19   "With water?"

20   "Do you want it with water?"

21   "I don't know," the girl said. "Is it good with water?"

22   "It's all right."

23   "You want them with water?" asked the woman.

24   "Yes, with water."

25   "It tastes like liquorice," the girl said and put the glass down.

26   "That's the way with everything."

27   "Yes," said the girl. "Everything tastes of liquorice. Especially all the things you've waited so long for, like absinthe."

28   "Oh, cut it out."

29   "You started it," the girl said. "I was being amused. I was having a fine time."

30   "Well, let's try and have a fine time."

31   "All right. I was trying. I said the mountains looked like white elephants. Wasn't that bright?"

32   "That was bright."

33   "I wanted to try this new drink. That's all we do, isn't it—look at things and try new drinks?"

34   "I guess so."

35   The girl looked across at the hills.

36   "They're lovely hills," she said. "They don't really look like white elephants. I just meant the coloring of their skin through the trees."

37   "Should we have another drink?"

38   "All right."

39   The warm wind blew the bead curtain against the table.

40   "The beer's nice and cool," the man said.

41   "It's lovely," the girl said.

42   "It's really an awfully simple operation, Jig," the man said. "It's not really an operation at all."

43   The girl looked at the ground the table legs rested on.

44   "I know you wouldn't mind it, Jig. It's really not anything. It's just to let the air in."

45   The girl did not say anything.

46   "I'll go with you and I'll stay with you all the time. They just let the air in and then it's all perfectly natural."

47   "Then what will we do afterwards?"

48   "We'll be fine afterwards. Just like we were before."

49   "What makes you think so?"

50   "That's the only thing that bothers us. It's the only thing that's made us unhappy."

51   The girl looked at the bead curtain, put her hand out and took hold of two of the strings of beads.

52   "And you think then we'll be all right and be happy."

NOTE

absinthe (par. 27): a liqueur

53   "I know we will. You don't have to be afraid. I've known lots of people that have done it."

54   "So have I," said the girl. "And afterwards they were all so happy."

55   "Well," the man said, "if you don't want to you don't have to. I wouldn't have you do it if you didn't want to. But I know it's perfectly simple."

56   "And you really want to?"

57   "I think it's the best thing to do. But I don't want you to do it if you don't really want to."

58   "And if I do it you'll be happy and things will be like they were and you'll love me?"

59   "I love you now. You know I love you."

60   "I know. But if I do it, then it will be nice again if I say things are like white elephants, and you'll like it?"

61   "I'll love it. I love it now but I just can't think about it. You know how I get when I worry."

62   "If I do it you won't ever worry?"

63   "I won't worry about that because it's perfectly simple."

64   "Then I'll do it. Because I don't care about me."

65   "What do you mean?"

66   "I don't care about me."

67   "Well, I care about you."

68   "Oh, yes. But I don't care about me. And I'll do it and then everything will be fine."

69   "I don't want you to do it if you feel that way."

70   The girl stood up and walked to the end of the station. Across, on the other side, were fields of grain and trees along the banks of the Ebro. Far away, beyond the river, were mountains. The shadow of a cloud moved across the field of grain and she saw the river through the trees.

71   "And we could have all this," she said. "And we could have everything and every day we make it more impossible."

72   "What did you say?"

73   "I said we could have everything."

74   "We can have everything."

75   "No, we can't."

76   "We can have the whole world."

77   "No, we can't."

78   "We can go everywhere."

79   "No, we can't. It isn't ours any more."

80   "It's ours."

81   "No, it isn't. And once they take it away, you never get it back."

82   "But they haven't taken it away."

83   "We'll wait and see."

84   "Come on back in the shade," he said. "You mustn't feel that way."

85   "I don't feel any way," the girl said. "I just know things."

86   "I don't want you to do anything that you don't want to do—"

87   "Nor that isn't good for me," she said. "I know. Could we have another beer?"

88   "All right. But you've got to realize—"

89   "I realize," the girl said. "Can't we maybe stop talking?"

90   They sat down at the table and the girl looked across at the hills on the dry side of the valley and the man looked at her and at the table.

91   "You've got to realize," he said, "that I don't want you to do it if you don't want to. I'm perfectly willing to go through with it if it means anything to you."

92   "Doesn't it mean anything to you? We could get along."

93   "Of course it does. But I don't want anybody but you. I don't want anyone else. And I know it's perfectly simple."

94   "Yes, you know it's perfectly simple."

95   "It's all right for you to say that, but I do know it."

96   "Would you do something for me now?"

97   "I'd do anything for you."

98   "Would you please please please please please please please stop talking?"

99   He did not say anything but looked at the bags against the wall of the station. There were labels on them from all the hotels where they had spent nights.

100   "But I don't want you to," he said, "I don't care anything about it."

101   "I'll scream," the girl said.

102   The woman came out through the curtains with two glasses of beer and put them down on the damp felt pads. "The train comes in five minutes," she said.

103   "What did she say?" asked the girl.

104   "That the train is coming in five minutes."

105   The girl smiled brightly at the woman, to thank her.

106   "I'd better take the bags over to the other side of the station," the man said. She smiled at him.

107   "All right. Then come back and we'll finish the beer."

108   He picked up the two heavy bags and carried them around the station to the other tracks. He looked up the tracks but could not see the train. Coming back, he walked through the barroom, where people waiting for the train were drinking. He drank an *Anis* at the bar and looked at the people. They were all waiting reasonably for the train. He went out through the bead curtain. She was sitting at the table and smiled at him.

109   "Do you feel better?" he asked.

110   "I feel fine," she said. "There's nothing wrong with me. I feel fine."

Harrison Bergeron

Kurt Vonnegut, Jr.

1   The Year was 2081, and everybody was finally equal. They weren't only equal before God and the law. They were equal every which way. Nobody was smarter than anybody else. Nobody was better looking than anybody else. Nobody was stronger or quicker than anybody else. All this equality was due to the 211th, 212th, and 213th Amendments to the Constitution, and to the unceasing vigilance of agents of the United States Handicapper General.

NOTE

vigilance (par. 1): watchfulness

2   Some things about living still weren't quite right, though. April for instance, still drove people crazy by not being springtime. And it was in that clammy month that the H-G men took George and Hazel Bergeron's fourteen-year-old son, Harrison, away.

3   It was tragic, all right, but George and Hazel couldn't think about it very hard. Hazel had a perfectly average intelligence, which meant she couldn't think about anything except in short bursts. And George, while his intelligence was way above normal, had a little mental handicap radio in his ear. He was required by law to wear it at all times. It was tuned to a government transmitter. Every twenty seconds or so, the transmitter would send out some sharp noise to keep people like George from taking unfair advantage of their brains.

4   George and Hazel were watching television. There were tears on Hazel's cheeks, but she'd forgotten for the moment what they were about.

5   On the television screen were ballerinas.

6   A buzzer sounded in George's head. His thoughts fled in panic, like bandits from a burglar alarm.

7   "That was a real pretty dance, that dance they just did," said Hazel.

8   "Huh," said George.

9   "That dance—it was nice," said Hazel.

10   "Yup," said George. He tried to think a little about the ballerinas. They weren't really very good—no better than anybody else would have been, anyway. They were burdened with sash weights and bags of birdshot, and their faces were masked, so that no one, seeing a free and graceful gesture or a pretty face, would feel like something the cat drug in. George was toying with the vague notion that maybe dancers shouldn't be handicapped. But he didn't get very far with it before another noise in his ear radio scattered his thoughts.

11   George winced. So did two out of the eight ballerinas.

12   Hazel saw him wince. Having no mental handicap herself, she had to ask George what the latest sound had been.

13   "Sounded like somebody hitting a milk bottle with a ball peen hammer," said George.

14   "I'd think it would be real interesting, hearing all the different sounds," said Hazel a little envious. "All the things they think up."

15   "Um," said George.

16   "Only, if I was Handicapper General, you know what I would do?" said Hazel. Hazel, as a matter of fact, bore a strong resemblance to the Handicapper General, a woman named Diana Moon Glampers. "If I was Diana Moon Glampers," said Hazel, "I'd have chimes on Sunday—just chimes. Kind of in honor of religion."

17   "I could think, if it was just chimes," said George.

18   "Well—maybe make 'em real loud," said Hazel. "I think I'd make a good Handicapper General."

19   "Good as anybody else," said George.

20   "Who knows better then I do what normal is?" said Hazel.

21   "Right," said George. He began to think glimmeringly about his abnormal son who was now in jail, about Harrison, but a twenty-one-gun salute in his head stopped that.

22   "Boy!" said Hazel, "that was a doozy, wasn't it?"

23   It was such a doozy that George was white and trembling, and tears stood on the rims of his red eyes. Two of the eight ballerinas had collapsed to the studio floor, were holding their temples.

24   "All of a sudden you look so tired," said Hazel. "Why don't you stretch out on the sofa, so's you can rest your handicap bag on the pillows, honeybunch." She was referring to the forty-seven pounds of birdshot in a canvas bag, which was padlocked around George's neck. "Go on and rest the bag for a little while," she said. "I don't care if you're not equal to me for a while."

25   George weighed the bag with his hands. "I don't mind it," he said. "I don't notice it any more. It's just a part of me."

26   "You been so tired lately—kind of wore out," said Hazel. "If there was just some way we could make a little hole in the bottom of the bag, and just take out a few of them lead balls. Just a few."

27   "Two years in prison and two thousand dollars fine for every ball I took out," said George. "I don't call that a bargain."

28   "If you could just take a few out when you came home from work," said Hazel. "I mean—you don't compete with anybody around here. You just set around."

29   "If I tried to get away with it," said George, "then other people'd get away with it—and pretty soon we'd be right back to the dark ages again, with everybody competing against everybody else. You wouldn't like that, would you?"

30   "I'd hate it," said Hazel.

31   "There you are," said George. "The minute people start cheating on laws, what do you think happens to society?"

32   If Hazel hadn't been able to come up with an answer to this question, George couldn't have supplied one. A siren was going off in his head.

33   "Reckon it'd fall all apart," said Hazel.

34   "What would?" said George blankly.

35   "Society," said Hazel uncertainly. "Wasn't that what you just said?"

36   "Who knows?" said George.

37   The television program was suddenly interrupted for a news bulletin. It wasn't clear at first as to what the bulletin was about, since the announcer, like all announcers, had a serious speech impediment. For about half a minute, and in a state of high excitement, the announcer tried to say, "Ladies and Gentlemen."

38   He finally gave up, handed the bulletin to a ballerina to read.

39   "That's all right—" Hazel said of the announcer, "he tried. That's the big thing. He tried to do the best he could with what God gave him. He should get a nice raise for trying so hard."

40   "Ladies and Gentlemen," said the ballerina, reading the bulletin. She must have been extraordinarily beautiful, because the mask she wore was hideous. And it was easy to see that she was the strongest and most graceful of all the dancers, for her handicap bags were as big as those worn by two-hundred pound men.

41   And she had to apologize at once for her voice, which was a very unfair voice for a woman to use. Her voice was a warm, luminous, timeless melody.

NOTE

luminous (par. 41): clear; easily understood

"Excuse me—" she said, and she began again, making her voice absolutely uncompetitive.

42   "Harrison Bergeron, age fourteen," she said in a grackle squawk, "has just escaped from jail, where he was held on suspicion of plotting to overthrow the government. He is a genius and an athlete, is under-handicapped, and should be regarded as extremely dangerous."

43   A police photograph of Harrison Bergeron was flashed on the screen— upside down, then sideways, upside down again, then right side up. The picture showed the full length of Harrison against a background calibrated in feet and inches. He was exactly seven feet tall.

44   The rest of Harrison's appearance was Halloween and hardware. Nobody had ever borne heavier handicaps. He had outgrown hindrances faster than the H-G men could think them up. Instead of a little ear radio for a mental handicap, he wore a tremendous pair of earphones, and spectacles with thick wavy lenses. The spectacles were intended to make him not only half blind, but to give him whanging headaches besides.

45   Scrap metal was hung all over him. Ordinarily, there was a certain symmetry, a military neatness to the handicaps issued to strong people, but Harrison looked like a walking junkyard. In the race of life, Harrison carried three hundred pounds.

46   And to offset his good looks, the H-G men required that he wear at all times a red rubber ball for a nose, keep his eyebrows shaved off, and cover his even white teeth with black caps at snaggle-tooth random.

47   "If you see this boy," said the ballerina, "do not—I repeat, do not—try to reason with him."

48   There was the shriek of a door being torn from its hinges.

49   Screams and barking cries of consternation came from the television set. The photograph of Harrison Bergeron on the screen jumped again and again, as though dancing to the tune of an earthquake.

50   George Bergeron correctly identified the earthquake, and well he might have—for many was the time his own home had danced to the same crashing tune. "My God—" said George, "that must be Harrison!"

51   The realization was blasted from his mind instantly by the sound of an automobile collision in his head.

52   When George could open his eyes again, the photograph of Harrison was gone. A living, breathing Harrison filled the screen.

53   Clanking, clownish, and huge, Harrison stood in the center of the studio. The knob of the uprooted studio door was still in his hand. Ballerinas, technicians, musicians, and announcers cowered on their knees before him, expecting to die.

54   "I am the Emperor!" cried Harrison. "Do you hear? I am the Emperor! Everybody must do what I say at once!" He stamped his foot and the studio shook.

NOTES

calibrated (par. 43): marked
consternation (par. 49): fear
cowered (par. 53): crouched

55   "Even as I stand here" he bellowed, "crippled, hobbled, sickened—I am a greater ruler than any man who ever lived! Now watch me become what I can become!"

56   Harrison tore the straps of his handicap harness like wet tissue paper, tore straps guaranteed to support five thousand pounds.

57   Harrison's scrap-iron handicaps crashed to the floor.

58   Harrison thrust his thumbs under the bar of the padlock that secured his head harness. The bar snapped like celery. Harrison smashed his headphones and spectacles against the wall.

59   He flung away his rubber-ball nose, revealed a man that would have awed Thor, the god of thunder.

60   "I shall now select my Empress!" he said, looking down on the cowering people. "Let the first woman who dares rise to her feet claim her mate and her throne!"

61   A moment passed, and then a ballerina arose, swaying like a willow.

62   Harrison plucked the mental handicap from her ear, snapped off her physical handicaps with marvelous delicacy. Last of all he removed her mask.

63   She was blindingly beautiful.

64   "Now—" said Harrison, taking her hand, "shall we show the people the meaning of the word dance? Music!" he commanded.

65   The musicians scrambled back into their chairs, and Harrison stripped them of their handicaps, too. "Play your best," he told them, "and I'll make you barons and dukes and earls."

66   The music began. It was normal at first—cheap, silly, false. But Harrison snatched two musicians from their chairs, waved them like batons as he sang the music as he wanted it played. He slammed them back into their chairs.

67   The music began again and was much improved.

68   Harrison and his Empress merely listened to the music for a while— listened gravely, as though synchronizing their heartbeats with it.

69   They shifted their weights to their toes.

70   Harrison placed his big hands on the girl's tiny waist, letting her sense the weightlessness that would soon be hers.

71   And then, in an explosion of joy and grace, into the air they sprang!

72   Not only were the laws of the land abandoned, but the law of gravity and the laws of motion as well.

73   They reeled, whirled, swiveled, flounced, capered, gamboled, and spun.

74   They leaped like deer on the moon.

75   The studio ceiling was thirty feet high, but each leap brought the dancers nearer to it.

76   It became their obvious intention to kiss the ceiling. They kissed it.

77   And then, neutralizing gravity with love and pure will, they remained suspended in air inches below the ceiling, and they kissed each other for a long, long time.

78   It was then that Diana Moon Glampers, the Handicapper General, came into the studio with a double-barreled ten-gauge shotgun. She fired twice, and the Emperor and the Empress were dead before they hit the floor.

79   Diana Moon Glampers loaded the gun again. She aimed it at the musicians and told them they had ten seconds to get their handicaps back on.

80   It was then that the Bergerons' television tube burned out.

81   Hazel turned to comment about the blackout to George. But George had gone out into the kitchen for a can of beer.

82   George came back in with the beer, paused while a handicap signal shook him up. And then he sat down again. "You been crying" he said to Hazel.

83   "Yup," she said.

84   "What about?" he said.

85   "I forget," she said. "Something real sad on television."

86   "What was it?" he said.

87   "It's all kind of mixed up in my mind," said Hazel.

88   "Forget sad things," said George.

89   "I always do," said Hazel.

90   "That's my girl," said George. He winced. There was the sound of a riveting gun in his head.

91   "Gee—I could tell that one was a doozy," said Hazel.

92   "You can say that again," said George.

93   "Gee—" said Hazel, "I could tell that one was a doozy."

Crusader Rabbit

Jess Mowry

1   "You could be my dad."

2   Jeremy stood, waist-deep in the dumpster, his arms slimed to the elbows from burrowing, and dropped three beer cans to the buckled asphalt.

3   Raglan lined them up, pop-tops down, and crushed them to crinkled discs under his tattered Nike, then added them to the half-full gunnysack. Finally he straightened, and studied the boy in the dumpster. It wasn't the first time. "I guess I could be."

4   Jeremy made no move to climb out, even though the stink seemed to surround him like a bronze-green cloud, wavering upward like the heat-ghosts off the other dumpster lids along the narrow alley. The boy wore only ragged jeans, the big Airwalks on his sockless feet buried somewhere below. His wiry, dusk-colored body glistened with sweat.

5   Not for the first time Raglan thought that Jeremy was a beautiful kid; thirteen, muscles standing out under tight skin, big hands and feet like puppy paws, and hair like an ebony dandelion puff. A ring glistened gold and fierce in his left ear, and a faded red bandanna, sodden with sweat, hung loosely around his neck. His eyes were bright obsidian but closed now, the bruise-like marks beneath them were fading and his teeth flashed strong and white as he panted. Raglan could have been a larger copy of the boy but looking it only in size, and without the earring. There was an old knife slash on his chest; a deep one with a high ridge of scar.

NOTES

sodden (par. 5): soaked

obsidian (par. 5): shiny black

6   The Oakland morning fog had burned off hours before, leaving the alley to bake in tar-and-rot smell, yet Raglan neither panted nor sweated. There were three more dumpsters to check, and the recycle place across town would be closing soon, but Raglan asked, "Want a smoke?"

7   Jeremy watched through lowered lashes as Raglan's eyes changed, not so much softening as going light-years away somewhere. Jeremy hesitated, his long fingers clenching and unclenching on the dumpster's rusty rim. "Yeah. . . . No . . . I think it's time."

8   Jeremy's movements were stiff and awkward as he tried to climb out. Garbage sucked wetly at his feet. Raglan took the boy, slippery as a seal, under the arms and lifted him over the edge. Together, they walked back to the truck.

9   It was a '55 GMC one-ton, as rusted and battered as the dumpsters. There were splintery plywood sideboards on the bed. The cab was crammed with things, as self-contained as a Land Rover on safari. Even after almost two months it still surprised Jeremy sometimes what Raglan could pull from beneath the seat or out of the piled mess on the floor . . . toilet paper, comic books, or a .45 automatic.

10   Raglan emptied the gunnysack into an almost full garbage can in the back of the truck, then leaned against the sideboard and started to roll a cigarette from Bugler tobacco while Jeremy opened the driver's door and slipped a scarred old Big Bird Band-Aid from under the floormat. The boy's hands shook slightly. He tried not to hurry as he spread out his things on the seat: a little rock bottle, but with grayish-brown powder in the bottom instead of crack crystals; a puff of cotton, stub of a candle, needle, and flame-tarnished spoon. On the cab floor by the shift lever was a gallon plastic jug from Pay-Less Drugs that at one time had held "fresh spring water from clear mountain streams." Raglan filled it from gas station hoses, and the water always tasted like rubber. Jeremy got it out, too.

11   Raglan finished rolling his cigarette, fired it with a Bic, handed the lighter to Jeremy, then started making another as he smoked. His eyes were still far away.

12   Jeremy looked up while he worked. "Yo, I know your other name. I seen it on your driver license. Why you call yourself Raglan?"

13   Smoke drifted from Raglan's nostrils. He came close to smiling. "My dad always called me that. Sposed to be from an old-time cartoon. On TV. When he was only a little kid. *Crusader Rabbit.* I never seen it. The rabbit's homeboy was a tiger. Raglan T. Tiger. Maybe they was something like the Ninja Turtles . . . had adventures and stuff like that. It was a long time ago."

14   "Oh." Jeremy sat on the door sill. He wrapped a strip of innertube around his arm. It was hard to get it right one-handed. He looked up again. "Um . . . ?"

15   "Yeah." Raglan knelt and pulled the strip tighter. His eyes were distant once more, neither watching nor looking away as he put the needle in. "You got good veins. Your muscles make 'em stand out."

16   Jeremy's eyes shifted from the needle, lowering, and his chest hardened a little. "I do got some muscles, huh?"

17   "Yeah. You ain't a bad-lookin kid. Little more exercise . . . "

18   Jeremy chewed his lip. "I used to miss 'em. . . . My veins, I mean. A long time ago. An, sometimes I poked right through."

19 "Yeah. I done that too. A long time ago."

20 The boy's slender body tensed for a moment, then relaxed with a sigh, his face almost peaceful and his eyes closed. But a few seconds later they opened again and searched out Raglan's. "It only makes me normal now."

21 Raglan nodded. "Yeah. On two a day that's all, folks." He handed Jeremy the other cigarette and fired the lighter.

22 The boy pulled in smoke, holding it a long time, then puffing out perfect rings and watching them float in the hot, lifeless air. "Next week it only gonna be one." He held Raglan's eyes. "It gonna hurt some more, huh?"

23 "Yeah."

24 "Um, when you stop wantin it?"

25 Raglan stood, snagging the water jug and taking a few swallows. Traffic rumbled past the alley mouth. Exhaust fumes drifted in from the street. Flies buzzed in clouds over the dumpsters, and a rat scuttled past in no particular hurry. "When you decide there's somethin else you want more."

26 Jeremy began putting his things away. The little bottle was empty. It would take most of today's cans to score another for tomorrow. "Yo. You gots to be my dad, Raglan. Why else you give a shit?"

27 "You figure it out, you let me know."

28 Raglan could have added that when he'd first found Jeremy laying behind a dumpster, the boy hadn't even been breathing. A minute more and it would have been *that's all, folks*. Why? Who in hell knew. Never ask questions if you don't want the answers.

29 Raglan dropped his cigarette on the pavement, slipped the sack off the sideboard, and started toward the other dumpsters. There really wasn't much reason to check them: this was the worst part of West Oaktown, and what poor people threw away was pitiful . . . everything already scraped bony and bare rusted or rotted or beaten beyond redemption, and nothing left of any value at all. Jeremy followed, his moves flowing smooth like a kid's once again.

30 A few paces in front of the boy, Raglan flipped back a lid so it clanged against the sooty brick wall. Flies scattered in swarms. For a second or two he just stood and looked at what lay on top of the trash. He'd seen this before, too many times, just as he'd seen the other Jeremys. But somehow this was even harder to get used to. His hand clamped on Jeremy's shoulder, holding the boy back. But Jeremy saw the baby anyhow.

31 " . . . Oh . . ." Jeremy pressed suddenly close to Raglan, and Raglan's arm went around him.

32 "I . . . heard 'bout them," whispered Jeremy, as if scared he might wake something sleeping. "But . . . I never seen one for real."

33 Raglan's gaze was distant once more, seeing but not seeing the little honey-brown body, the tiny and perfect fingers and toes.

34 Jeremy swallowed. Then his lean chest expanded to pull in air. "What should we do?"

35 Raglan's eyes had turned hard. He was thinking of smirking white cops and their stupid questions . . . or smirking black cops, what in hell was the

NOTE

smirking (par. 35): insincerely smiling

difference? He could make a quick call from a pay phone: there was one at the recycle place. Time was running short. The recycle center closed soon. The truck's tank was still almost full, but there was food to buy after Jeremy's need, and the cans were the only money.

36　　Still, he asked, "What do you want to do?"

37　　The boy looked back at the baby. Automatically he waved flies away. "What do they . . . do with 'em?" He turned to Raglan. "Is there some little coffin . . . An flowers?"

38　　Raglan took his hand off the boy. "They burn 'em."

39　　"*No!*"

40　　"The ones they find. Other times they just get hauled to the dump, an the bulldozers bury 'em. You been to the dump with me."

41　　Almost, the boy clamped his hands to his ears, but then his fists clenched. "NO! Shut the fuck up, goddamn you."

42　　The boy's chest heaved, muscles standing out stark. Raglan stayed quiet a moment. Finally he gripped Jeremy's shoulder once more. Why? Who in hell knew. "Okay."

43　　Raglan walked to the truck while Jeremy watched from the dumpster, still waving away flies. Raglan stopped around back. There was a ragged canvas tarp folded behind the cab. On rainy nights he spread it over the sideboards to make a shelter. A piece of that would do. Who in hell cared? Salty sweat burned Raglan's eyes, and he blinked in the sunlight stabbing down between the buildings. The canvas was oily, and stank. Going around to the cab, he pulled one of his T-shirts from behind the seat.

44　　The old GMC was a city truck . . . an inner city truck . . . that measured its moves in blocks, not miles. It burned oil, the radiator leaked, and its tires were worn almost bald. There were two bullet holes in the right front fender. But it managed to maintain a grudging 55, rattling first across the Bay Bridge into San Francisco, and then over the Golden Gate, headed north. Tourists were taking pictures, but not of the truck. It had a radio/tape-deck, but Jeremy didn't turn on KMEL or play the old Kriss-Kross cassette he'd found in a dumpster and patiently rewound with a pencil. He just stayed silent, rolling cigarettes for Raglan and himself, and looking sometimes through the grimy back window at the little bundle in the bed. Even when they turned off 101 near Novato onto a narrow two-lane leading west, Jeremy only stared through the windshield, his own eyes a lot like Raglan's now, even though an open countryside of gentle green hills spread out around them.

45　　It was early evening with the sunlight slanting gold when Raglan slowed the truck and scanned the roadside ahead. The air was fresh and clean, scented with things that lived and grew, and tasting of the ocean somewhere close at hand. There was a dirt road that Raglan almost missed, hardly much more than twin tracks with a strip of yellow dandelions between. It led away toward more low hills, through fields of tall grass and wild mustard flowers. Raglan turned the truck off the pavement, and they rolled slowly to the hills in third gear. Jeremy began to watch the flowered fields passing by, then looked at Raglan.

46　　"Yo. You been here before?"

47　　"A long time ago."

48   "I never knew there was places like this . . . pretty, an 'out no other people an cars. Not for real."

49   The road entered a cleft between hills, and a little stream ran down to meet it, sparkling over smooth rocks. For a while the road followed the splashing water, then turned and began to wind upward. The truck took the grade, growling in second. The road seemed to fade as it climbed, then finally just ended at the top of a hill. Raglan switched off the engine. A hundred feet ahead a cliff dropped sheer to the sea. Big waves boomed and echoed on rocks somewhere below. Silver streamers of spray drifted up.

50   Jeremy seemed to forget why they'd come. He jumped from the truck and ran to the cliff, stopping as close to the edge as he could, as any boy might. Then he just stood, gazing out over the water.

51   Raglan leaned on the fender and watched.

52   Jeremy spread his arms wide for a moment, his head thrown back. Raglan watched until the boy seemed to discover that if he took off his shoes the grass would feel good underfoot. Then Raglan went to the rear of the truck. There was an old square-nosed cement shovel and an Army trenching tool.

53   Jeremy joined him, his half-naked body gleaming with sea-spray. He was solemn, though his eyes had a sparkle. Raglan said nothing, just taking the shovel in one hand and the little bundle in the crook of his arm. Jeremy followed with the trenching tool.

54   The ground rose again nearby to a point that looked out on the ocean. Raglan and Jeremy climbed to the top. Raglan cut the sweet-smelling sod into blocks with his shovel, and Jeremy set them aside. Earth-scent filled the air. Then they both dug. The sun was almost gone when they finished. Though the evening was growing cooler, Jeremy was sheened once more. But he picked some of the wild mustard and dandelion flowers and laid them on the little mound. Far out on the water the sun grew huge and ruddy as it sank. Raglan built a fire near the truck, and Jeremy unrolled their blankets. He was surprised again when Raglan conjured two dusty cans of Campbell's soup and a pint of Jack Daniel's from somewhere in the cab. A little later, when it was dark and the ocean boomed softly below, and the food was warm inside them, they sat side-by-side near the fire, smoking and sipping the whiskey.

55   "Is this campin out?" asked Jeremy.

56   Raglan looked around. "I guess it is."

57   Jeremy passed the bottle back to Raglan, then glanced at the truck: it seemed small by itself on a hilltop. "Um, we don't got enough gas to get back, huh?"

58   Raglan gazed into the flames. "Maybe there's someplace around here that buys cans. We'll check it out in the mornin."

59   Jeremy stared into the fire for a time. "It gonna hurt a lot, huh?"

NOTES

cleft (par. 49): gap
sheer (par. 49): straight down
sod (par. 54): ground
sheened (par. 54): covered with sweat
ruddy (par. 54): reddish

60   "Yeah. But, I be here with you."

61   "I still glad we come, Raglan."

62   Jeremy moved close to Raglan, shivering. "So, you never seen that Crusader Rabbit? Don't know what he looked like?"

63   "I think he carried a sword . . . an fought dragons."

64   Jeremy smiled. "My dad would say somethin like that."

The Gilded Six-Bits

Zora Neale Hurston

1   It was a Negro yard around a Negro house in a Negro settlement that looked to the payroll of the G and G Fertilizer works for its support.

2   But there was something happy about the place. The front yard was parted in the middle by a sidewalk from gate to doorstep, a sidewalk edged on either side by quart bottles driven neck down to the ground on a slant. A mess of homey flowers planted without a plan but blooming cheerily from their helter-skelter places. The fence and house were whitewashed. The porch and steps scrubbed white.

3   The front door stood open to the sunshine so that the floor of the front room could finish drying after its weekly scouring. It was Saturday. Everything clean from the front gate to the privy house. Yard raked so that the strokes of the rake would make a pattern. Fresh newspaper cut in fancy-edge on the kitchen shelves.

4   Missie May was bathing herself in the galvanized washtub in the bedroom. Her dark-brown skin glistened under the soapsuds that skittered down from her wash rag. Her stiff young breasts thrust forward aggressively like broad-based cones with the tips lacquered in black.

5   She heard men's voices in the distance and glanced at the dollar clock on the dresser.

6   "Humph! Ah'm way behind time t'day! Joe gointer be heah 'fore Ah git mah clothes on if Ah don't make haste."

7   She grabbed the clean meal sack at hand and dried herself hurriedly and began to dress. But before she could tie her slippers, there came the ring of singing metal on wood. Nine times.

NOTES

In this story, the dialogue is written in dialect. This mean that words are spelled the way they would be pronounced by the characters. For example, "I" would be pronounced "Ah," so it is spelled "Ah"; the "r" in "here" would not be pronounced, so it is spelled "heah"; and the "th" in "the" and "that" would be pronounced as a "d," so "the" is spelled "de" and "that" is spelled "dat."

Gilded (title): gold plated, covered with a thin layer of gold

Bits (title): an American slang term for the amount of 12$\frac{1}{2}$ cents, used only with even numbers (2 bits, 25 cents; 4 bits, 50 cents; 6 bits, 75 cents; etc.)

helter-skelter (par. 2): random

privy house (par. 3): outdoor toilet

lacquered (par. 4): varnished

singing (par. 7): ringing

8   Missie May grinned with delight. She had not seen the big tall man come stealing in the gate and creep up the walk grinning happily at the joyful mischief he was about to commit. But she knew that it was her husband throwing silver dollars in the door for her to pick up and pile beside her plate at dinner. It was this way every Saturday afternoon. The nine dollars hurled into the open door, he scurried to a hiding place behind the cape jasmine bush and waited.

9   Missie May promptly appeared at the door in mock alarm.

10   "Who dat chunkin' money in mah do'way?" she demanded. No answer from the yard. She leaped off the porch and began to search the shrubbery. She peeped under the porch and hung over the gate to look up and down the road. While she did this, the man behind the jasmine darted to the chinaberry tree. She spied him and gave chase.

11   "Nobody ain't gointer be chunkin' money at me and Ah not do'em nothin'," she shouted in mock anger. He ran around the house with Missie May at his heels. She overtook him at the kitchen door. He ran inside but could not close it after him before she crowded in and locked with him in a rough and tumble. For several minutes the two were a furious mass of male and female energy. Shouting, laughing, twisting, turning, and Joe trying, but not too hard, to get away.

12   "Missie May, take yo' hand out mah pocket!" Joe shouted out between laughs.

13   "Ah ain't, Joe, not lessen you gwine gimme whateve' it is good you got in yo' pocket. Turn it go Joe, do Ah'll tear yo' clothes."

14   "Go on tear 'em. You de one dat pushes de needles round heah. Move yo' hand Missie May."

15   "Lemme git dat paper sack out yo' pocket. Ah bet its candy kisses."

16   "Tain't. Move yo' hand. Woman ain't got no business in a man's clothes nohow. Go 'way."

17   Missie May gouged way down and gave an upward jerk and triumphed.

18   "Unhhunh! Ah got it. It 'tis so candy kisses. Ah knowed you had somethin' for me in yo' clothes. Now Ah got to see whut's in every pocket you got."

19   Joe smiled indulgently and let his wife go through all of his pockets and take out the things that he had hidden there for her to find. She bore off the chewing gum, the cake of sweet soap, the pocket handkerchief as if she had wrested them from him, as if they had not been bought for the sake of this friendly battle.

20   "Whew! dat play-fight done got me all warmed up," Joe exclaimed. "Got me some water in de kittle?"

21   "Yo' water is on de fire and yo' clean things is cross de bed. Hurry up and wash yo'self and git changed so we kin eat. Ah'm hongry." As Missie said this, she bore the steaming kettle into the bedroom.

NOTES

in mock alarm (par. 9): pretending to be concerned

gouged (par. 17): dug

wrested (par. 19): forced

22   "You ain't hongry, sugar," Joe contradicted her. "Youse jes's little empty. Ah'm de one whut's hongry. Ah could eat up camp meetin', back off 'ssociation, and drink Jurdan dry. Have it on de table when Ah git out de tub."

23   "Don't you mess wid mah business, man. You git in yo' clothes. Ah'm a real wife, not no dress and breath. Ah might not look lak one, but if you burn me, you won't git a thing but wife ashes."

24   Joe splashed in the bedroom and Missie May fanned around in the kitchen. A fresh red and white checked cloth on the table. Big pitcher of buttermilk beaded with pale drops of butter from the churn. Hot fried mullet, crackling bread, ham hocks atop a mound of string beans and new potatoes, and perched on the window-sill a pone of spicy potato pudding.

25   Very little talk during the meal but that little consisted of banter that pretended to deny affection but in reality flaunted it. Like when Missie May reached for a second helping of the tater pone. Joe snatched it out of her reach. After Missie May had made two of three unsuccessful grabs at the pan, she begged, "Aw, Joe gimme some mo' dat tater pone."

26   "Nope, sweetenin' is for us men-folks. Y'all pritty li'l frail eels don't need nothin' lak dis. You too sweet already."

27   "Please, Joe."

28   "Naw, naw. Ah don't want you to git no sweeter than whut you is already. We goin' down de road al li'l piece t'night so you go put on yo' Sunday-go-to-meetin' things."

29   Missie May looked at her husband to see if he was playing some prank. "Sho 'nuff, Joe?"

30   "Yeah. We goin' to de ice cream parlor."

31   "Where de ice cream parlor at, Joe?"

32   "A new man done come heah from Chicago and he done got a place and took and opened it up for a ice cream parlor, and bein' as it's real swell, Ah wants you to be one de first ladies to walk in dere and have some set down."

33   "Do Jesus, Ah ain't knowed nothin' 'bout it. Who de man done it?"

34   "Mister Otis D. Slemmons, of spots and places—Memphis, Chicago, Jacksonville, Philadelphia, and so on."

35   "Dat heavy-set man wid his mouth full of gold teethes?"

36   "Yeah. Where did you see 'im at?"

37   "Ah went down to de sto' tuh git a box of lye and Ah seen 'im standin' on de corner talkin' to some of de mens, and Ah come on back and went to scrubbin' de floor, and he passed and tipped his hat whilst Ah was scourin' de steps. Ah thought never Ah seen *him* befo'."

38   Joe smiled pleasantly. "Yeah, he's up to date. He got de finest clothes Ah ever seen on a colored man's back."

NOTES

camp meetin' (par. 22): an outdoor religious gathering, usually lasting several days

pone (par. 24): oval-shaped cornbread

banter (par. 25): teasing comments

Sunday-go-to-meetin' (par. 28): church

lye (par. 37): an acid-like substance used in making soap

39   "Aw, he don't look no better in his clothes than you do in yourn. He got a puzzlegut on 'im and he so chuckle-headed, he got a pone behind his neck."

40   Joe looked down at his own abdomen and said wistfully, "Wisht Ah had a build on me lak he got. He ain't puzzlegutted, honey. He jes' got a corperation. Dat make 'm look lak a rich white man. All rich mens is got some belly on 'em."

41   "Ah seen de pitchers of Henry Ford and he's a spare-built man and Rockefeller look lak he ain't got but one gut. But Ford and Rockefeller and dis Slemmons and all de rest kin be as many-gutted as dey please, ah'm satisfied wid you jes' lak you is, baby. God took pattern after a pine tree and built you noble. Youse a pretty still man, and if Ah knowed any way to make you mo' pretty still Ah'd take and do it."

42   Joe reached over gently and toyed with Missie May's ear. "You jes' say dat cause you love me, but Ah know Ah can't hold no light to Otis D. Slemmons. Ah ain't never been nowhere and Ah ain't got nothin' but you."

43   "How you know dat, Joe."

44   "He tole us hisself."

45   "Dat don't make it so. His mouf is cut cross-ways, ain't it? Well, he kin lie jes' lak anybody els."

46   "Good Lawd, Missie! You womens sho' is hard to sense into things. He's got a five-dollar gold piece for a stick-pin and he got a ten-dollar gold piece on his watch chain and his mouf is jes' crammed full of gold teethes. Sho' wisht it wuz mine. And whut make it so cool, he got money 'cumulated. And womens give it all to 'im."

47   "Ah don't see whut de womens see on 'im. Ah wouldn't give 'im a wind if de sherff wuz after 'im."

48   "Well, he tole us how de white womens in Chicago give 'im all dat gold money. So he don't 'low nobody to touch it at all. Not even put dey finger on it. Dey tole 'im not to. You kin make 'miration at it, but don't tetch it."

49   "Whyn't he stay up dere where dey so crazy 'bout im?"

50   "Ah reckon dey done made 'im vast-rich and he wants to travel some. He say dey wouldn't leave 'im hit a lick of work. He got mo' lady people crazy 'bout him than he kin shake a stick at."

51   "Joe, Ah hates to see you so dumb. Dat stray nigger jes' tell y'all anything and y'all b'lieve it."

52   "Go 'head on now, honey and put on yo' clothes. He talkin' 'bout his pritty womens—Ah want 'im to see *mine.*"

53   Missie May went off to dress and Joe spent the time trying to make his stomach punch out like Slemmons' middle. He tried the rolling swagger of the stranger, but found that his tall bone-and-muscle stride fitted ill with it. He just had time to drop back into his seat before Missie May came in dressed to go.

54   On the way home that night Joe was exultant. "Didn't Ah say ole Otis was swell? Can't he talk Chicago talk? Wuzn't dat funny whut he said when great big fat ole Ida Armstrong come in? He asted me, 'Who is dat broad wid de

NOTES

His mouf is cut cross-ways (par. 45): his mouth goes from side to side

exultant (par. 54): joyous

forty shake?' Dat's a new word. Us always thought forty was a set of figgers but he showed us where it means a whole heap of things. Sometimes he don't say forty, he jes' say thirty-eight and two and dat mean de same thing. Know whut he tole me when Ah was payin' for our ice cream? He say, 'Ah have to hand it to you, Joe. Dat wife of yours is jes' thirty-eight and two. Yessuh, she's forty!' Ain't he killin'?"

55   "He'll do in case of a rush. But he sho' is got uh heap uh gold on 'im. Dat's de first time Ah ever seed gold money. It lookted good on him sho' nuff, but it'd look a whole heap better on you."

56   "Who, me? Missie May was youse crazy! Where would a po' man lak me git gold money from?"

57   Missie May was silent for a minute, then she said, "Us might find some goin' long de road some time. Us could."

58   "Who would be losin' gold money 'round heah? We ain't even seen none dese white folks wearin' no gold money on dey watch chain. You must be figgeren' Mister Packard or Mister Cadillac goin' pass through heah . . . "

59   "You don't know whut been lost 'round heah. Maybe somebody way back in memorial times lost they gold money and went on off and it ain't never been found. And then if we wuz to find it, you could wear some 'thout havin' no gang of womens lak dat Slemmons say he got."

60   Joe laughed and hugged her. "Don't be so wishful 'bout me. Ah'm satisfied de way Ah is. So long as Ah be yo' husband, ah don't keer 'bout nothin' else. Ah'd ruther all de other womens in de world to be dead than for you to have de toothache. Less we go to bed and git our night rest."

61   It was Saturday night once more before Joe could parade his wife in Slemmons' ice cream parlor again. He worked the night shift and Saturday was his only night off. Every other evening around six o'clock he left home, and dying dawn saw him hustling home around the lake where the challenging sun flung a flaming sword from east to west across the trembling water.

62   That was the best part of life—going home to Missie May. Their whitewashed house, the mock battle on Saturday, the dinner and ice cream parlor afterwards, church on Sunday nights when Missie outdressed any woman in town—all, everything was right.

63   One night around eleven the acid ran out at the G and G. The foreman knocked off the crew and let the steam die down. As Joe rounded the lake on his way home, a lean moon rode the lake in a silver boat. If anybody had asked Joe about the moon on the lake, he would have said he hadn't paid it any attention. But he saw it with his feelings. It made him yearn painfully for Missie. Creation obsessed him. He thought about children. They had been married for more than a year now. They had money put away. They ought to be making little feet for shoes. A little boy child would be about right.

64   He saw a dim light in the bedroom and decided to come in through the kitchen door. He could wash the fertilizer dust off himself before presenting himself to Missie May. It would be nice for her not to know that he was there until he slipped into his place in bed and hugged her back. She always liked that.

65   He eased the kitchen door open slowly and silently, but when he went to set his dinner bucket on the table he bumped it into a pile of dishes, and

something crashed to the floor. He heared his wife gasp in fright and hurried to reassure her.

66   "Iss me, honey. Don't get skeered."

67   There was a quick, large movement in the bedroom. A rustle, a thud, and a stealthy silence. The light went out.

68   What? Robbers? Murderers? Some varmint attacking his helpless wife, perhaps. He struck a match, threw himself on guard and stepped over the doorsill into the bedroom.

69   The great belt on the wheel of Time slipped and eternity stood still. By the match light he could see the man's legs fighting with his breeches in his frantic desire to get them on. He had both chance and time to kill the intruder in his helpless condition—half-in and half-out of his pants—but he was too weak to take action. The shapeless enemies of humanity that live in the hours of Time had waylaid Joe. He was assaulted in his weakness. Like Samson awakening after his haircut. So he just opened his mouth and laughed.

70   The match went out and he struck another and lit the lamp. A howling wind raced across his heart, but underneath its fury he heard his wife sobbing and Slemmons pleading for his life. Offering to buy it with all that he had. "Please, suh, don't kill me. Sixty-two dollars at de sto' gold money."

71   Joe just stood. Slemmons looked at the window, but it was screened. Joe stood out like a rough-backed mountain between him and the door. Barring him from escape, from sunrise, from life.

72   He considered a surprise attack upon the big clown that stood there laughing like a chessy cat. But before his fist could travel an inch, Joe's own rushed out to crush him like a battering ram. Then Joe stood over him.

73   "Git into yo' damn rags, Slemmons, and dat quick."

74   Slemmons scrambled to his feet and into his vest and coat. As he grabbed his hat, Joe's fury overrode his intentions and he grabbed at Slemmons with his left hand and struck at him with his right. The right landed. The left grazed the front of his vest. Slemmons was knocked a somersault into the kitchen and fled through the open door. Joe found himself alone with Missie May, with the golden watch charm clutched in his left fist. A short bit of broken chain dangled between his fingers.

75   Missie May was sobbing. Wails of weeping without words. Joe stood, and after awhile she found out that he had something in his hand. And then he stood and felt without thinking and without seeing with his natural eyes. Missie May kept on crying and Joe kept on feeling so much and not knowing what to do with all his feelings, he put Slemmons' watch charm in his pants pocket and took a good laugh and went to bed.

76   "Missie May, whut you crying for?"

77   "Cause Ah love you so hard and Ah know you don't love *me* no mo'."

78   Joe sank his face into the pillow for a spell then he said huskily, "You don't know de feelings of dat yet, Missie May."

NOTES

waylaid (par. 69): ambushed

a chessy cat (par. 72): a Cheshire cat: a cat that grins broadly and continuously, popularized by Lewis Carroll in *Alice's Adventures in Wonderland*

79   "Oh Joe, honey, he said he wuz gointer gimme dat gold money and he jes' kept on after me—"

80   Joe was very still and silent for a long time. Then he said, "Well, don't cry no mo', Missie May. Ah got yo' gold piece for you."

81   The hours went past on their rusty ankles. Joe still and quiet on one bedrail and Missie May wrung dry of sobs on the other. Finally the sun's tide crept upon the shore of night and drowned all its hours. Missie May with her face stiff and streaked towards the window saw the dawn come into her yard. It was day. Nothing more. Joe wouldn't be coming home as usual. No need to fling open the front door and sweep off the porch, making it nice for Joe. Never no more breakfast to cook; no more washing and starching of Joe's jumper-jackets and pants. No more nothing. So why get up?

82   With this strange man in her bed, she felt embarrassed to get up and dress. She decided to wait till he had dressed and gone. Then she would get up, dress quickly and be gone forever beyond reach of Joe's looks and laughs. But he never moved. Red light turned to yellow, then white.

83   From beyond the no-man's land between them came a voice. A strange voice that yesterday had been Joe's.

84   "Missie May, ain't you gonna fix me no breakfus'?"

85   She sprang out of bed. "Yeah, Joe. Ah didn't reckon you wuz hongry."

86   No need to die today. Joe needed her for a few more minutes anyhow.

87   Soon there was a roaring fire in the cook stove. Water bucket full and two chickens killed. Joe loved fried chicken and rice. She didn't deserve a thing and good Joe was letting her cook him some breakfast. She rushed hot biscuits to the table as Joe took his seat.

88   He ate with his eyes on his plate. No laughter, no banter.

89   "Missie May, you ain't eatin' yo' breakfus'."

90   "Ah don't choose none, Ah thank yuh."

91   His coffee cup was empty. She sprang to refill it. When she turned from the stove and bent to set the cup beside Joe's plate, she saw the yellow coin on the table between them.

92   She slumped into her seat and wept into her arms.

93   Presently Joe said calmly, "Missie May, you cry too much. Don't look back lak Lot's wife and turn to salt."

94   The sun, the hero of every day, the impersonal old man that beams as brightly on death as on birth, came up every morning and raced across the blue dome and dipped into the sea of fire every evening. Water ran down hill and birds nested.

95   Missie knew why she didn't leave Joe. She couldn't. She loved him too much. But she couldn't understand why Joe didn't leave her. He was polite, even kind at times, but aloof.

NOTES

lak Lot's wife and turn to salt (par. 93): According to the Bible, Lot was told by God's angels to flee with his family to the hills in order to escape the destruction of Sodom and Gomorrah and not to look back. Lot's wife looked back and was turned into a pillar of salt (Genesis 19:12–26).

aloof (par. 95): distant

96   There were no more Saturday romps. No ringing silver dollars to stack beside her plate. No pockets to rifle. In fact the yellow coin in his trousers was like a monster hiding in the cave of his pockets to destroy her.

97   She often wondered if he still had it, but nothing could have induced her to ask nor yet to explore his pockets to see for herself. Its shadow was in the house whether or no.

98   One night Joe came home around midnight and complained of pains in the back. He asked Missie to rub him down with liniment. It had been three months since Missie had touched his body and it all seemed strange. But she rubbed him. Grateful for the chance. Before morning, youth triumphed and Missie exulted. But the next day, as she joyfully made up their bed, beneath her pillow she found the piece of money with the bit of chain attached.

99   Alone to herself, she looked at the thing with loathing, but look she must. She took it into the hands with trembling and saw first thing that it was no gold piece. It was a gilded half-dollar. Then she knew why Slemmons had forbidden anyone to touch his gold. He trusted village eyes at a distance not to recognize his stick-pin as a gilded quarter, and his watch charm as a four-bit piece.

100   She was glad at first that Joe had left it there. Perhaps he was through with her punishment. They were man and wife again. Then another thought came clawing at her. He had come home to buy from her as if she were any woman in the long house. Fifty cents for her love. As if to say that he could pay as well as Slemmons. She slid the coin into his Sunday pants pocket and dressed herself and left his house.

101   Halfway between her house and the quarters she met her husband's mother, and after a short talk she turned and went back home. If she had not the substance of marriage, she had the outside show. Joe must leave *her*. She let him see she didn't want his old gold four-bits too.

102   She saw no more of the coin for some time though she knew that Joe could not help finding it in his pocket. But his health kept poor, and he came home at least every ten days to be rubbed.

103   The sun swept around the horizon, trailing its robes of weeks and days. One morning as Joe came in from work, he found Missie May chopping wood. Without a word he took the ax and chopped a huge pile before he stopped.

104   "You ain't got no business choppin' wood, and you know it."

105   "How come? Ah been choppin' it for de last longest."

106   "Ah ain't blind. You makin' feet for shoes."

107   "Won't you be glad to have a li'l baby chile, Joe?"

108   "You know dat 'thout astin' me."

109   "Iss gointer be a boy chile and de very spit of you."

110   "You reckon, Missie May?"

111   "Who else could it look lak?"

112   Joe said nothing, but he thrust his hand deep into his pocket and fingered something there.

NOTE

de very spit of you (par. 109): the very spitting image of you: look just like you

113   It was almost six months later Missie May took to bed and Joe went and got his mother to come wait on the house.

114   Missie May delivered a fine boy. Her travail was over when Joe came in from work one morning. His mother and the old women were drinking great bowls of coffee around the fire in the kitchen.

115   The minute Joe came into the room his mother called him aside.

116   "How did Missie May make out?" he asked quickly.

117   "Who, dat gal? She strong as a ox. She gointer have plenty mo'. We done fixed her wid de sugar and lard to sweeten her for de nex' one."

118   Joe stood silent awhile.

119   "You ain't ast 'bout de baby, Joe. You oughter be mighty proud cause he sho' is de spittin' image of yuh, son. Dat's yourn all right, if you never git another on, dat un is yourn. And you know Ah'm mighty proud too, son, cause Ah never thought well of you marryin' Missie May cause her make used tuh fan her foot 'round right smart and Ah been mighty skeered dat Missie May wuz gointer git misput on her road."

120   Joe said nothing. He fooled around the house till late in the day then just before he went to work, he went and stood at the foot of the bed and asked his wife how she felt. He did this every day during the week.

121   On Saturday he went to Orlando to make his market. It had been a long time since he had done that.

122   Meat and lard, meal and flour, soap and starch. Cans of corn and tomatoes. All the staples. He fooled around town for a while and bought bananas and apples. Way after while he went around to the candy store.

123   "Hellow, Joe," the clerk greeted him. "Ain't seen you in a long time."

124   "Nope, Ah ain't been heah. Been 'round spots and places."

125   "Want some of them molasses kisses you always buy?"

126   "Yessuh." He threw the gilded half-dollar on the counter. "Will dat spend?"

127   "Whut is it, Joe? Well, I'll be doggone! A gold-plated four-bit piece. Where'd you git it, Joe?"

128   "Offen a stray nigger dat come through Eatonville. He had it on his watch chain for a charm—goin' 'round making out iss gold money. Ha ha! He had a quarter on his tie pin and it wuz all golded up too. Tryin' to fool people. Makin' out he is rich and everything. Ha! Ha! Tryin' to tole off folkses wives from home."

129   "How did you git it, Joe? Did he fool you, too?"

130   "Who, me? Naw suh! he ain't fooled me none. Know whut Ah done? He come 'round me wid his smart talk. Ah hauled off and knocked 'im down and took his old four-bits 'way from 'im. Gointer buy my wife some good ole 'lasses kisses wid it. Gimme fifty cents worth of dem candy kisses."

131   "Fifty cents buys a mighty lot of candy kisses, Joe. Why don't you split it up and take some chocolate bars, too. They eat good, too."

132   "Yessuh, dey do, but Ah wants all dat in kisses. Ah got a li'l boy chile home now. Tain't a week old yet, but he kin suck a sugar tit and maybe eat one them kisses hisself."

NOTE

travail (par. 114): labor (of childbirth)

133   Joe got his candy and left the store. The clerk turned to the next customer. "Wisht I could be like these darkies. Laughin' all the time. Nothin' worries 'em."

134   Back in Eatonville, Joe reached his own front door. There was the ring of singing metal on wood. Fifteen times. Missie May couldn't run to the door, but she crept there as quickly as she could.

135   "Joe Banks, Ah hear you chunkin' money in mah do'way. You wait till Ah got mah strength back and Ah'm gointer fix you for dat."

A Very Old Man with Enormous Wings

Gabriel Garcia Marquez

(Trans. Gregory Rabassa)

1   On the third day of rain they had killed so many crabs inside the house that Pelayo had to cross his drenched courtyard and throw them into the sea, because the newborn child had a temperature all night and they thought it was due to the stench. The world had been sad since Tuesday. Sea and sky were a single ash-gray thing and the sands of the beach, which on March nights glimmered like powdered light, had become a stew of mud and rotten shellfish. The light was so weak at noon that when Pelayo was coming back to the house after throwing away the crabs, it was hard for him to see what it was that was moving and groaning in the rear of the courtyard. He had to go very close to see that it was an old man, a very old man, lying face down in the mud, who, in spite of his tremendous efforts, couldn't get up, impeded by his enormous wings.

2   Frightened by that nightmare, Pelayo ran to get Elisenda, his wife, who was putting compresses on the sick child, and he took her to the rear of the courtyard. They both looked at the fallen body with mute stupor. He was dressed like a ragpicker. There were only a few faded hairs left on his bald skull and very few teeth in his mouth, and his pitiful condition of a drenched great-grandfather had taken away any sense of grandeur he might have had. His huge buzzard wings, dirty and half-plucked, were forever entangled in the mud. They looked at him so long and so closely that Pelayo and Elisenda very soon overcame their surprise and in the end found him familiar. Then they dared speak to him, and he answered in an incomprehensible dialect with a strong sailor's voice. That was how they skipped over the inconvenience of the wings and quite intelligently concluded that he was a lonely castaway from some foreign ship wrecked by the storm. And yet, they called in a neighbor woman who knew everything about life and death to see him, and all she needed was one look to show them their mistake.

NOTES

stench (par. 1): disgusting odor

impeded (par. 1): hindered, prevented

mute stupor (par. 2): speechless daze

a ragpicker (par. 2): a person who makes a living by collecting and selling rags and other discarded items

dialect (par. 2): accent

3   "He's an angel," she told them. "He must have been coming for the child, but the poor fellow is so old that the rain knocked him down."

4   On the following day everyone knew that a flesh-and-blood angel was held captive in Pelayo's house. Against the judgment of the wise neighbor woman, for whom angels in those times were the fugitive survivors of a celestial conspiracy, they did not have the heart to club him to death. Pelayo watched over him all afternoon from the kitchen, armed with his bailiff's club, and before going to bed he dragged him out of the mud and locked him up with the hens in the wire chicken coop. In the middle of the night, when the rain stopped, Pelayo and Elisenda were still killing crabs. A short time afterward the child woke up without a fever and with a desire to eat. Then they felt magnanimous and decided to put the angel on a raft with fresh water and provisions for three days and leave him to his fate on the high seas. But when they went out into the courtyard with the first light of dawn, they found the whole neighborhood in front of the chicken coop having fun with the angel, without the slightest reverence, tossing him things to eat through the openings in the wire as if he weren't a supernatural creature but a circus animal.

5   Father Gonzaga arrived before seven o'clock, alarmed at the strange news. By that time onlookers less frivolous than those at dawn had already arrived and they were making all kinds of conjectures concerning the captive's future. The simplest among them thought that he should be named mayor of the world. Others of sterner mind felt that he should be promoted to the rank of five-star general in order to win all wars. Some visionaries hoped that he could be put to stud in order to implant on earth a race of winged wise men who could take charge of the universe. But Father Gonzaga, before becoming a priest, had been a robust woodcutter. Standing by the wire, he reviewed his catechism in an instant and asked them to open the door so that he could take a close look at that pitiful man who looked more like a huge decrepit hen among the fascinated chickens. He was lying in a corner drying his open wings in the sunlight among the fruit peels and breakfast leftovers that the early risers had thrown him. Alien to the impertinences of the world, he only lifted his antiquarian eyes and murmured something in his dialect when Father Gonzaga went into the chicken coop and said good morning to him in Latin. The parish

NOTES

survivors of a celestial conspiracy (par. 4): in other words, angels who had joined Lucifer in his rebellion against God and been cast out of Heaven

bailiff's club (par. 4): nightstick or police officer's club

magnanimous (par. 4): generous

conjectures (par. 5): guesses

catechism (par. 5): a summary of religious beliefs and principles

decrepit (par. 5): broken down, worn out

impertinences (par. 5): rudenesses

antiquarian (par. 5): aged

parasites (par. 5): lice

terrestrial (par. 5): earthly

ingenuous (par. 5): simple, childlike

unwary (par. 5): naïve, unsuspecting

Supreme Pontiff (par. 5): Pope (head of the Catholic Church)

priest had his first suspicion of an impostor when he saw that he did not understand the language of God or know how to greet His ministers. Then he noticed that seen close up he was much too human; he had an unbearable smell of the outdoors, the back side of his wings was strewn with parasites and his main feathers had been mistreated by terrestrial winds, and nothing about him measured up to the proud dignity of angels. Then he came out of the chicken coop and in a brief sermon warned the curious against the risks of being ingenuous. He reminded them that the devil had the bad habit of making use of carnival tricks in order to confuse the unwary. He argued that if wings were not the essential element in determining the difference between a hawk and an airplane, they were even less so in the recognition of angels. Nevertheless, he promised to write a letter to his bishop so that the latter would write to his primate so that the latter would write to the Supreme Pontiff in order to get the final verdict from the highest courts.

6   His prudence fell on sterile hearts. The news of the captive angel spread with such rapidity that after a few hours the courtyard had the bustle of a marketplace and they had to call in troops with fixed bayonets to disperse the mob that was about to knock the house down. Elisenda, her spine all twisted from sweeping up so much marketplace trash, then got the idea of fencing in the yard and charging five cents admission to see the angel.

7   The curious came from far away. A traveling carnival arrived with a flying acrobat who buzzed over the crowd several times, but no one paid any attention to him because his wings were not those of an angel but, rather, those of a sidereal bat. The most unfortunate invalids on earth came in search of health: a poor woman who since childhood had been counting her heartbeats and had run out of numbers; a Portuguese man who couldn't sleep because the noise of the stars disturbed him; a sleepwalker who got up at night to undo the things he had done while awake; and many others with less serious ailments. In the midst of that shipwreck disorder that made the earth tremble, Pelayo and Elisenda were happy with fatigue, for in less than a week they had crammed their rooms with money and the line of pilgrims waiting their turn to enter still reached beyond the horizon.

8   The angel was the only one who took no part in his own act. He spent his time trying to get comfortable in his borrowed nest, befuddled by the hellish heat of the oil lamps and sacramental candles that had been placed along the

NOTES

prudence (par. 6): common sense

sterile (par. 6): infertile; unimaginative

sacramental candles (par. 8): candles intended for use in specific Catholic rituals

papal lunches (par. 8): lunches fit for the Pope

penitents (par. 8): Christians expressing regret for their sins

stellar parasites (par. 8): parasites from the stars

proliferated (par. 8): multiplied

hermetic (par. 8): solitary

lunar (par. 8): moon

gale (par. 8): strong wind

cataclysm (par. 8): violent storm

in repose (par. 8): at rest

wire. At first they tried to make him eat some mothballs, which, according to the wisdom of the wise neighbor woman, were the food prescribed for angels. But he turned them down, just as he turned down the papal lunches that the penitents brought him, and they never found out whether it was because he was an angel or because he was an old man that in the end he ate nothing but eggplant mush. His only supernatural virtue seemed to be patience. Especially during the first days, when the hens pecked at him, searching for the stellar parasites that proliferated in his wings, and the cripples pulled out feathers to touch their defective parts with, and even the most merciful threw stones at him, trying to get him to rise so they could see him standing. The only time they succeeded in arousing him was when they burned his side with an iron for branding steers, for he had been motionless for so many hours that they thought he was dead. He awoke with a start, ranting in his hermetic language and with tears in his eyes, and he flapped his wings a couple of times, which brought on a whirlwind of chicken dung and lunar dust and a gale of panic that did not seem to be of this world. Although many thought that his reaction had been one not of rage but of pain, from then on they were careful not to annoy him, because the majority understood that his passivity was not that of a hero taking his ease but that of a cataclysm in repose.

9   Father Gonzaga held back the crowd's frivolity with formulas of maidservant inspiration while awaiting the arrival of a final judgment on the nature of the captive. But the mail from Rome showed no sense of urgency. They spent their time finding out if the prisoner had a navel, if his dialect had any connection with Aramaic, how many times he could fit on the head of a pin, or whether he wasn't just a Norwegian with wings. Those meager letters might have come and gone until the end of time if a providential event had not put an end to the priest's tribulations.

10   It so happened that during those days, among so many other carnival attractions, there arrived in town the traveling show of the woman who had been changed into a spider for having disobeyed her parents. The admission to see her was not only less than the admission to see the angel, but people were permitted to ask her all manner of questions about her absurd state and to examine her up and down so that no one would ever doubt the truth of her horror. She was a frightful tarantula the size of a ram and with the head of a sad maiden. What was most heart-rending, however, was not her outlandish shape but the sincere affliction with which she recounted the details of her misfortune. While still practically a child she had sneaked out of her parents' house to go to a dance, and while she was coming back through the woods after having danced all night without permission, a fearful thunderclap rent the sky in two and through the crack came the lightning bolt of brimstone that changed her into a spider. Her only nourishment came from the meatballs

NOTES

frivolity (par. 9): playfulness
providential (par. 9): fortunate; heaven-sent
rent (par. 10): tore
haughty (par. 10): arrogant
deigned (par. 10): consented

that charitable souls chose to toss into her mouth. A spectacle like that, full of so much human truth and with such a fearful lesson, was bound to defeat without even trying that of a haughty angel who scarcely deigned to look at mortals. Besides, the few miracles attributed to the angel showed a certain mental disorder, like the blind man who didn't recover his sight but grew three new teeth, or the paralytic who didn't get to walk but almost won the lottery, and the leper whose sores sprouted sunflowers. Those consolation miracles, which were more like mocking fun, had already ruined the angel's reputation when the woman who had been changed into a spider finally crushed him completely. That was how Father Gonzaga was cured forever of his insomnia and Pelayo's courtyard went back to being as empty as during the time it had rained for three days and crabs walked through the bedrooms.

11   The owners of the house had no reason to lament. With the money they saved they built a two-story mansion with balconies and gardens and high netting so that crabs wouldn't get in during the winter, and with iron bars on the windows so that angels wouldn't get in. Pelayo also set up a rabbit warren close to town and gave up his job as bailiff for good, and Elisenda bought some satin pumps with high heels and many dresses of iridescent silk, the kind worn on Sunday by the most desirable women in those times. The chicken coop was the only thing that didn't receive any attention. If they washed it down with creolin and burned tears of myrrh inside it every so often, it was not in homage to the angel but to drive away the dungheap stench that still hung everywhere like a ghost and was turning the new house into an old one. At first, when the child learned to walk, they were careful that he not get too close to the chicken coop. But then they began to lose their fears and got used to the smell, and before the child got his second teeth he'd gone inside the chicken coop to play, where the wires were falling apart. The angel was no less standoffish with him than with other mortals, but he tolerated the most ingenious infamies with the patience of a dog who had no illusions. They both came down with chicken pox at the same time. The doctor who took care of the child couldn't resist the temptation to listen to the angel's heart, and he found so much whistling in the heart and so many sounds in his kidneys that it seemed impossible for him to be alive. What surprised him most, however, was the logic of his wings. They seemed so natural on that completely human organism that he couldn't understand why other men didn't have them too.

12   When the child began school it had been some time since the sun and rain had caused the collapse of the chicken coop. The angel went dragging himself about here and there like a stray dying man. They would drive him out of the bedroom with a broom and a moment later find him in the kitchen.

NOTES

lament (par. 11): mourn

iridescent (par. 11): colorful

creolin (par. 11): a compound used to disinfect and deodorize animal enclosures

tears of myrrh (par. 11): sap of a myrrh tree

ingenious (par. 11): inventive

infamies (par. 11): shameful, abusive acts

cannulae (par. 12): literally, small flexible tubes that are inserted into the body to withdraw or administer fluids

delirious (par. 12): hallucinating

He seemed to be in so many places at the same time that they grew to think that he'd been duplicated, that he was reproducing himself all through the house, and the exasperated and unhinged Elisenda shouted that it was awful living in that hell full of angels. He could scarcely eat and his antiquarian eyes had also become so foggy that he went about bumping into posts. All he had left were the bare cannulae of his last feathers. Pelayo threw a blanket over him and extended him the charity of letting him sleep in the shed, and only then did they notice that he had a temperature at night, and was delirious with the tongue twisters of an old Norwegian. That was one of the few times they became alarmed, for they thought he was going to die and not even the wise neighbor woman had been able to tell them what to do with dead angels.

13   And yet he not only survived his worst winter, but seemed improved with the first sunny days. He remained motionless for several days in the farthest corner of the courtyard, where no one would see him, and at the beginning of December some large, stiff feathers began to grow on his wings, the feathers of a scarecrow, which looked more like another misfortune of decrepitude. But he must have known the reason for those changes, for he was quite careful that no one should notice them, that no one should hear the sea chanteys that he sometimes sang under the stars. One morning Elisenda was cutting some bunches of onions for lunch when a wind that seemed to come from the high seas blew into the kitchen. Then she went to the window and caught the angel in his first attempts at flight. They were so clumsy that his fingernails opened a furrow in the vegetable patch and he was on the point of knocking the shed down with the ungainly flapping that slipped on the light and couldn't get a grip on the air. But he did manage to gain altitude. Elisenda let out a sigh of relief, for herself and for him, when she saw him pass over the last houses, holding himself up in some way with the risky flapping of a senile vulture. She kept watching him even when she was through cutting the onions and she kept on watching until it was no longer possible for her to see him, because then he was no longer an annoyance in her life but an imaginary dot on the horizon of the sea.

NOTE

chanteys (par. 13): sailors' work songs

The Veldt

Ray Bradbury

I

1   "George, I wish you'd look at the nursery."
2   "What's wrong with it?"
3   "I don't know."
4   "Well, then."
5   "I just want you to look at it, is all, or call a psychologist in to look at it."
6   "What would a psychologist want with a nursery?"

NOTE

Veldt (title): grassland

7   "You know very well what he'd want." His wife paused in the middle of the kitchen and watched the stove busy humming to itself, making supper for four.

8   "It's just that the nursery is different now than it was."

9   "All right, let's have a look."

10   They walked down the hall of their soundproofed, Happylife Home, which had cost them thirty thousand dollars installed, this house which clothed and fed and rocked them to sleep and played and sang and was good to them. Their approach sensitized a switch somewhere and the nursery light flicked on when they came within ten feet of it. Similarly, behind them, in the halls, lights went on and off as they left them behind, with a soft automaticity.

11   "Well," said George Hadley.

12   They stood on the thatched floor of the nursery. It was forty feet across by forty feet long and thirty feet high; it had cost half again as much as the rest of the house. "But nothing's too good for our children," George had said.

13   The nursery was silent. It was empty as a jungle glade at hot high noon. The walls were blank and two dimensional. Now, as George and Lydia Hadley stood in the center of the room, the walls began to purr and recede into crystalline distance, it seemed, and presently an African veldt appeared, in three dimensions; on all sides, in colors reproduced to the final pebble and bit of straw. The ceiling above them became a deep sky with a hot yellow sun.

14   George Hadley felt the perspiration start on his brow.

15   "Let's get out of the sun," he said. "This is a little too real. But I don't see anything wrong."

16   "Wait a moment, you'll see," said his wife.

17   Now the hidden odorophonics were beginning to blow a wind of odor at the two people in the middle of the baked veldtland. The hot straw smell of lion grass, the cool green smell of the hidden water hole, the great rusty smell of animals, the smell of dust like a red paprika in the hot air. And now the sounds: the thump of distant antelope feet on grassy sod, the papery rustling of vultures. A shadow passed through the sky. The shadow flickered on George Hadley's upturned, sweating face.

18   "Filthy creatures," he heard his wife say.

19   "The vultures."

20   "You see, there are the lions, far over, that way. Now they're on their way to the water hole. They've just been eating," said Lydia. "I don't know what."

21   "Some animal." George Hadley put his hand up to shield off the burning light from his squinted eyes. "A zebra or a baby giraffe, maybe."

22   "Are you sure?" His wife sounded peculiarly tense.

23   "No, it's a little late to be sure," he said, amused. "Nothing over there I can see but cleaned bone, and the vultures dropping for what's left."

24   "Did you hear that scream?" she asked.

NOTES

thatched (par. 12): straw covered

glade (par. 13): an open space in the middle of a forest

two dimensional (par. 13): having height and width

recede into crystalline distance (par. 13): become transparent

three dimensions (par. 13): having height, width, and depth

25   "No."

26   "About a minute ago?"

27   "Sorry, no."

28   The lions were coming. And again George Hadley was filled with admiration for the mechanical genius who had conceived this room. A miracle of efficiency selling for an absurdly low price. Every home should have one. Oh, occasionally they frightened you with their clinical accuracy, they startled you, gave you a twinge, but most of the time what fun for everyone, not only your own son and daughter, but for yourself when you felt like a quick jaunt to a foreign land, a quick change of scenery. Well, here it was!

29   And here were the lions now, fifteen feet away, so real, so feverishly and startlingly real that you could feel the prickling fur on your hand, and your mouth was stuffed with the dusty upholstery smell of their heated pelts, and the yellow of them was in your eyes like the yellow of an exquisite French tapestry, the yellows of lions and summer grass, and the sound of the matted lion lungs exhaling on the silent noontide, and the smell of meat from the panting, dripping mouths.

30   The lions stood looking at George and Lydia Hadley with terrible green-yellow eyes.

31   "Watch out!" screamed Lydia.

32   The lions came running at them.

33   Lydia bolted and ran. Instinctively, George sprang after her. Outside, in the hall, with the door slammed, he was laughing and she was crying, and they both stood appalled at the other's reaction.

34   "George!"

35   "Lydia! Oh, my dear poor sweet Lydia!"

36   "They almost got us!"

37   "Walls, Lydia, remember; crystal walls, that's all they are. Oh, they look real, I must admit—Africa in your parlor—but it's all dimensional superreactionary, supersensitive color film and mental tape film behind glass screens. It's all odorophonics and sonics, Lydia. Here's my handkerchief."

38   "I'm afraid." She came to him and put her body against him and cried steadily. "Did you see? Did you *feel*? It's too real."

39   "Now, Lydia . . . "

40   "You've got to tell Wendy and Peter not to read any more on Africa."

41   "Of course—of course." He patted her.

42   "Promise?"

43   "Sure."

44   "And lock the nursery for a few days until I get my nerves settled."

45   "You know how difficult Peter is about that. When I punished him a month ago by locking the nursery for even a few hours—the tantrum he threw! And Wendy too. They *live* for the nursery."

NOTES

jaunt (par. 28): pleasure trip

tapestry (par. 29): a heavy cloth woven with designs, frequently used as a wall hanging

bolted (par. 33): jerked, moved suddenly

appalled (par. 33): shocked

46   "It's got to be locked, that's all there is to it."

47   "All right." Reluctantly he locked the huge door. "You've been working too hard. You need a rest."

48   "I don't know—I don't know," she said, blowing her nose, sitting down in a chair that immediately began to rock and comfort her. "Maybe I don't have enough to do. Maybe I have time to think too much. Why don't we shut the whole house off for a few days and take a vacation?"

49   "You mean you want to fry my eggs for me?"

50   "Yes." She nodded.

51   "And darn my socks?"

52   "Yes." A frantic, watery-eyed nodding.

53   "And sweep the house?"

54   "Yes, yes—oh, yes!"

55   "But I thought that's why we bought this house, so we wouldn't have to do anything?"

56   "That's just it. I feel like I don't belong here. The house is wife and mother now and nursemaid. Can I compete with an African veldt? Can I give a bath and scrub the children as efficiently or quickly as the automatic scrub bath can? I cannot. And it isn't just me. It's you. You've been awfully nervous lately."

57   "I suppose I have been smoking too much."

58   "You look as if you didn't know what to do with yourself in this house, either. You smoke a little more every morning and drink a little more every afternoon and need a little more sedative every night. You're beginning to feel unnecessary too."

59   "Am I?" He paused and tried to feel into himself to see what was really there.

60   "Oh, George!" She looked beyond him, at the nursery door: "Those lions can't get out of there, can they?"

61   He looked at the door and saw it tremble as if something had jumped against it from the other side.

62   "Of course not," he said.

63   At dinner they ate alone, for Wendy and Peter were at a special plastic carnival across town and had televised home to say they'd be late, to go ahead eating. So George Hadley, bemused, sat watching the dining-room table produce warm dishes of food from its mechanical interior.

64   "We forgot the ketchup," he said.

65   "Sorry," said a small voice within the table, and ketchup appeared.

66   As for the nursery, thought George Hadley, it won't hurt for the children to be locked out of it awhile. Too much of anything isn't good for anyone. And it was clearly indicated that the children had been spending a little too much time on Africa. That sun. He could feel it on his neck, still, like a hot paw. And the lions. And the smell of blood. Remarkable how the nursery caught the telepathic emanations of the children's minds and created life to fill their every desire.

NOTES

bemused (par. 63): lost in thought

telepathic emanations (par. 66): thoughts

The children thought lions, and there were lions. The children thought zebras, and there were zebras. Sun—sun. Giraffes—giraffes. Death and death.

67   That last. He chewed tastelessly on the meat that the table had cut for him. Death thoughts. They were awfully young, Wendy and Peter, for death thoughts. Or, no, you were never too young, really. Long before you knew what death was you were wishing it on someone else. When you were two years old you were shooting people with cap pistols.

68   But this—the long, hot African veldt—the awful death in the jaws of a lion. And repeated again and again.

69   "Where are you going?"

70   He didn't answer Lydia. Preoccupied, he let the lights glow softly on ahead of him, extinguished behind him as he padded to the nursery door. He listened against it. Far away, a lion roared.

71   He unlocked the door and opened it. Just before he stepped inside, he heard a faraway scream. And then another roar from the lions, which subsided quickly.

72   He stepped into Africa. How many times in the last year had he opened this door and found Wonderland, Alice, the Mock Turtle, or Aladdin and his Magical Lamp, or Jack Pumpkinhead of Oz, or Dr. Doolittle, or the cow jumping over a very real-appearing moon—all the delightful contraptions of a make-believe world. How often had he seen Pegasus flying in the sky ceiling, or seen fountains of red fireworks, or heard angel voices singing. But now, this yellow hot Africa, this bake oven with murder in the heat. Perhaps Lydia was right. Perhaps they needed a little vacation from the fantasy which was growing a bit too real for ten-year-old children. It was all right to exercise one's mind with gymnastic fantasies, but when the lively child mind settled on *one* pattern . . . ? It seemed that, at a distance, for the past month, he had heard lions roaring, and smelled their strong odor seeping as far away as his study door. But, being busy, he had paid it no attention.

73   George Hadley stood on the African grassland alone. The lions looked up from their feeding, watching him. The only flaw to the illusion was the open door through which he could see his wife, far down the dark hall, like a framed picture, eating her dinner abstractedly.

74   "Go away," he said to the lions.

75   They did not go.

76   He knew the principle of the room exactly. You sent out your thoughts. Whatever you thought would appear.

77   "Let's have Aladdin and his lamp," he snapped.

78   The veldtland remained; the lions remained.

79   "Come on, room! I demand Aladdin!" he said.

80   Nothing happened. The lions mumbled in their baked pelts.

NOTES

subsided (par. 71): stopped

Wonderland, Alice . . . moon (par. 72): places and characters from children's stories

contraptions (par. 72): inventions

Pegasus (par. 72): a winged horse in Greek mythology

81   "Aladdin!"

82   He went back to dinner. "The fool room's out of order," he said. "It won't respond."

83   "Or—"

84   "Or what?"

85   "Or it *can't* respond," said Lydia, "because the children have thought about Africa and lions and killing so many days that the room's in a rut."

86   "Could be."

87   "Or Peter's set it to remain that way."

88   "*Set* it?"

89   "He may have got into the machinery and fixed something."

90   "Peter doesn't know machinery."

91   "He's a wise one for ten. That I.Q. of his—"

92   "Nevertheless—"

93   "Hello, Mom. Hello, Dad."

94   The Hadleys turned. Wendy and Peter were coming in the front door, cheeks like peppermint candy, eyes like bright blue agate marbles, a smell of ozone on their jumpers from their trip in the helicopter.

95   "You're just in time for supper," said both parents.

96   "We're full of strawberry ice cream and hot dogs," said the children, holding hands. "But we'll sit and watch."

97   "Yes, come tell us about the nursery," said George Hadley.

98   The brother and sister blinked at him and then at each other. "Nursery?"

99   "All about Africa and everything," said the father with false joviality.

100   "I don't understand," said Peter.

101   "Your mother and I were just traveling through Africa with rod and reel; Tom Swift and his Electric Lion," said George Hadley.

102   "There's no Africa in the nursery," said Peter simply.

103   "Oh, come now, Peter. We know better."

104   "I don't remember any Africa," said Peter to Wendy. "Do you?"

105   "No."

106   "Run see and come tell."

107   She obeyed.

108   "Wendy, come back here!" said George Hadley, but she was gone.

109   The house lights followed her like a flock of fireflies. Too late, he realized he had forgotten to lock the nursery door after his last inspection.

110   "Wendy'll look and come tell us," said Peter.

111   "She doesn't have to tell *me*. I've seen it."

112   "I'm sure you're mistaken, Father."

113   "I'm not, Peter. Come along now."

114   But Wendy was back. "It's not Africa," she said breathlessly.

NOTES

agate (par. 94): quartz

ozone (par. 94): A gaseous substance with a strong, irritating odor; high concentrations of ozone are found in the upper atmosphere.

joviality (par. 99): jolliness

Tom Swift (par. 101): a character in the novels of Victor Appleton (1892–1965)

115   "We'll see about this," said George Hadley, and they all walked down the hall together and opened the nursery door.

116   There was a green, lovely forest, a lovely river, a purple mountain, high voices singing, and Rima, lovely and mysterious, lurking in the trees with colorful flights of butterflies, like animated bouquets, lingering on her long hair. The African veldtland was gone. The lions were gone. Only Rima was here now, singing a song so beautiful that it brought tears to your eyes.

117   George Hadley looked in at the changed scene. "Go to bed," he said to the children.

118   They opened their mouths.

119   "You heard me," he said.

120   They went off to the air closet, where a wind sucked them like brown leaves up the flue to their slumber rooms.

121   George Hadley walked through the singing glade and picked up something that lay in the corner near where the lions had been. He walked slowly back to his wife.

122   "What is that?" she asked.

123   "An old wallet of mine," he said.

124   He showed it to her. The smell of hot grass was on it and the smell of a lion. There were drops of saliva on it, it had been chewed, and there were blood smears on both sides.

125   He closed the nursery door and locked it, tight.

126   In the middle of the night he was still awake and he knew his wife was awake. "Do you think Wendy changed it?" she said at last, in the dark room.

127   "Of course."

128   "Made it from a veldt into a forest and put Rima there instead of lions?"

129   "Yes."

130   "Why?"

131   "I don't know. But it's staying locked until I find out."

132   "How did your wallet get there?"

133   "I don't know anything," he said, "except that I'm beginning to be sorry we bought that room for the children. If children are neurotic at all, a room like that—"

134   "It's supposed to help them work off their neuroses in a healthful way."

135   "I'm starting to wonder." He stared at the ceiling.

136   "We've given the children everything they ever wanted. Is this our reward—secrecy, disobedience?"

137   "Who was it said, 'Children are carpets, they should be stepped on occasionally'? We've never lifted a hand. They're insufferable—let's admit it. They come and go when they like; they treat us as if *we* were offspring. They're spoiled and we're spoiled."

NOTES

Rima (par. 116): a character in the novel *Green Mansions* by William H. Hudson (1841–1922)

lurking (par. 116): hiding

animated (par. 116): moving, living

flue (par. 120): passageway

neurotic (par. 133): mentally unstable

insufferable (par. 137): intolerable

138   "They've been acting funny ever since you forbade them to take the rocket to New York a few months ago."

139   "They're not old enough to do that alone, I explained."

140   "Nevertheless, I've noticed they've been decidedly cool toward us since."

141   "I think I'll have David McClean come tomorrow morning to have a look at Africa."

142   "But it's not Africa now, it's Green Mansions country and Rima."

143   "I have a feeling it'll be Africa again before then."

144   A moment later they heard the screams.

145   Two screams. Two people screaming from downstairs. And then a roar of lions.

146   "Wendy and Peter aren't in their rooms," said his wife.

147   He lay in his bed with his beating heart. "No," he said. "They've broken into the nursery."

148   "Those screams—they sound familiar."

149   "Do they?"

150   "Yes, awfully."

151   And although their beds tried very hard, the two adults couldn't be rocked to sleep for another hour. A smell of cats was in the night air.

152   "Father?" said Peter.

153   "Yes."

154   Peter looked at his shoes. He never looked at his father any more, nor at his mother. "You aren't going to lock up the nursery for good, are you?"

155   "That all depends."

156   "On what?" snapped Peter.

157   "On you and your sister. If you intersperse this Africa with a little variety—oh, Sweden perhaps, or Denmark or China—"

158   "I thought we were free to play as we wished."

159   "You are, within reasonable bounds."

160   "What's wrong with Africa, Father?"

161   "Oh, so now you admit you have been conjuring up Africa, do you?"

162   "I wouldn't want the nursery locked up," said Peter coldly. "Ever."

163   "Matter of fact, we're thinking of turning the whole house off for about a month. Live sort of a carefree one-for-all existence."

164   "That sounds dreadful! Would I have to tie my own shoes instead of letting the shoe tier do it? And brush my own teeth and comb my hair and give myself a bath?"

165   "It would be fun for a change, don't you think?"

166   "No, it would be horrid. I didn't like it when you took out the picture painter last month."

167   "That's because I wanted you to learn to paint all by yourself, son."

168   "I don't want to do anything but look and listen and smell; what else *is* there to do?"

169   "All right, go play in Africa."

NOTE

intersperse (par. 157): mix

170   "Will you shut off the house sometime soon?"

171   "We're considering it."

172   "I don't think you'd better consider it any more, Father."

173   "I won't have any threats from my son!"

174   "Very well." And Peter strolled off to the nursery.

175   "Am I on time?" said David McClean.

176   "Breakfast?" asked George Hadley.

177   "Thanks, had some. What's the trouble?"

178   "David, you're a psychologist."

179   "I should hope so."

180   "Well, then, have a look at our nursery. You saw it a year ago when you dropped by; did you notice anything peculiar about it then?"

181   "Can't say I did; the usual violences, a tendency toward a slight paranoia here or there, usual in children because they feel persecuted by parents constantly, but, oh, really nothing."

182   They walked down the hall. "I locked the nursery up," explained the father, "and the children broke back into it during the night. I let them stay so they could form the patterns for you to see."

183   There was a terrible screaming from the nursery.

184   "There it is," said George Hadley. "See what you make of it."

185   They walked in on the children without rapping.

186   The screams had faded. The lions were feeding.

187   "Run outside a moment, children," said George Hadley. "No, don't change the mental combination. Leave the walls as they are. Get!"

188   With the children gone, the two men stood studying the lions clustered at a distance, eating with great relish whatever it was they had caught.

189   "I wish I knew what it was," said George Hadley. "Sometimes I can almost see. Do you think if I brought high-powered binoculars here and—"

190   David McClean laughed dryly. "Hardly." He turned to study all four walls. "How long has this been going on?"

191   "A little over a month."

192   "It certainly doesn't *feel* good."

193   "I want facts, not feelings."

194   "My dear George, a psychologist never saw a fact in his life. He only hears about feelings; vague things. This doesn't feel good, I tell you. Trust my hunches and my instincts. I have a nose for something bad. This is very bad. My advice to you is to have the whole damn room torn down and your children brought to me every day during the next year for treatment."

195   "Is it that bad?"

196   "I'm afraid so. One of the original uses of these nurseries was so that we could study the patterns left on the walls by the child's mind, study at our leisure, and help the child. In this case, however, the room has become a channel toward—destructive thoughts, instead of a release away from them."

NOTES

paranoia (par. 181): unreasonable suspicion or distrust

rapping (par. 185): knocking

197   "Didn't you sense this before?"

198   "I sensed only that you had spoiled your children more than most. And now you're letting them down in some way. What way?"

199   "I wouldn't let them go to New York."

200   "What else?"

201   "I've taken a few machines from the house and threatened them, a month ago, with closing up the nursery unless they did their homework. I did close it for a few days to show I meant business."

202   "Ah, ha!"

203   "Does that mean anything?"

204   "Everything. Where before they had a Santa Claus now they have a Scrooge. Children prefer Santas. You've let this room and this house replace you and your wife in your children's affections. This room is their mother and father, far more important in their lives than their real parents. And now you come along and want to shut it off. No wonder there's hatred here. You can feel it coming out of the sky. Feel that sun. George, you'll have to change your life. Like too many others, you've built it around creature comforts. Why, you'd starve tomorrow if something went wrong in your kitchen. You wouldn't know how to tap an egg. Nevertheless, turn everything off. Start new. It'll take time. But we'll make good children out of bad in a year, wait and see."

205   "But won't the shock be too much for the children, shutting the room up abruptly, for good?"

206   "I don't want them going any deeper into this, that's all."

207   The lions were finished with their red feast.

208   The lions were standing on the edge of the clearing watching the two men.

209   "Now *I'm* feeling persecuted," said McClean. "Let's get out of here. I never have cared for these damned rooms. Make me nervous."

210   "The lions look real, don't they?" said George Hadley. "I don't suppose there's any way—"

211   "What?"

212   "—that they could *become* real?"

213   "Not that I know."

214   "Some flaw in the machinery, a tampering or something?"

215   "No."

216   They went to the door.

217   "I don't imagine the room will like being turned off," said the father.

218   "Nothing ever likes to die—even a room."

219   "I wonder if it hates me for wanting to switch it off?"

220   "Paranoia is thick around here today," said David McClean. "You can follow it like a spoor. Hello." He bent and picked up a bloody scarf. "This yours?"

221   "No." George Hadley's face was rigid. "It belongs to Lydia."

222   They went to the fuse box together and threw the switch that killed the nursery.

223   The two children were in hysterics. They screamed and pranced and threw things. They yelled and sobbed and swore and jumped at the furniture.

NOTE

spoor (par. 220): trail or droppings of a wild animal

224   "You can't do that to the nursery, you can't!"

225   "Now, children."

226   The children flung themselves on to a couch, weeping.

227   "George," said Lydia Hadley, "turn on the nursery, just for a few moments. You can't be so abrupt."

228   "No."

229   "You can't be so cruel."

230   "Lydia, it's off, and it stays off. And the whole damn house dies as of here and now. The more I see of the mess we've put ourselves in, the more it sickens me. We've been contemplating our mechanical, electronic navels for too long. My God, how we need a breath of honest air!"

231   And he marched about the house turning off the voice clocks, the stoves, the heaters, the shoe shiners, the shoe lacers, the body scrubbers and swabbers and massagers, and every other machine he could put his hand to.

232   The house was full of dead bodies, it seemed. It felt like a mechanical cemetery. So silent. None of the humming hidden energy of machines waiting to function at the tap of a button.

233   "Don't let them do it!" wailed Peter at the ceiling, as if he was talking to the house, the nursery. "Don't let Father kill everything." He turned to his father. "Oh, I hate you!"

234   "Insults won't get you anywhere."

235   "I wish you were dead!"

236   "We were, for a long while. Now we're going to really start living. Instead of being handled and massaged, we're going to *live*."

237   Wendy was still crying and Peter joined her again. "Just a moment, just one moment, just another moment of nursery," they wailed.

238   "Oh, George," said the wife, "It can't hurt."

239   "All right—all right, if they'll only just shut up. One minute, mind you, and then off forever."

240   "Daddy, Daddy, Daddy!" sang the children, smiling with wet faces.

241   "And then we're going on a vacation. David McClean is coming back in half an hour to help us move out and get to the airport. I'm going to dress. You turn the nursery on for a minute, Lydia, just a minute, mind you."

242   And the three of them went babbling off while he let himself be vacuumed upstairs through the air flue and set about dressing himself. A minute later Lydia appeared.

243   "I'll be glad when we get away," she sighed.

244   "Did you leave them in the nursery?"

245   "I wanted to dress too. Oh, that horrid Africa. What can they see in it?"

246   "Well, in five minutes we'll be on our way to Iowa. Lord, how did we ever get in this house? What prompted us to buy a nightmare?"

247   "Pride, money, foolishness."

248   "I think we'd better get downstairs before those kids get engrossed with those damned beasts again."

NOTES

wailed (par. 233): cried

engrossed with (par. 248): deeply involved with, totally occupied by

249   Just then they heard the children calling, "Daddy, Mommy, come quick—quick!"

250   They went downstairs in the air flue and ran down the hall. The children were nowhere in sight. "Wendy? Peter!"

251   They ran into the nursery. The veldtland was empty save for the lions waiting, looking at them. "Peter, Wendy?"

252   The door slammed.

253   "Wendy, Peter!"

254   George Hadley and his wife whirled and ran back to the door.

255   "Open the door!" cried George Hadley, trying the knob. "Why, they've locked it from the outside! Peter!" He beat at the door. "Open up!"

256   He heard Peter's voice outside, against the door.

257   "Don't let them switch off the nursery and the house," he was saying.

258   Mr. and Mrs. George Hadley beat at the door. "Now, don't be ridiculous, children. It's time to go. Mr. McClean'll be here in a minute and . . . "

259   And then they heard the sounds.

260   The lions on three sides of them, in the yellow veldt grass, padding through the dry straw, rumbling and roaring in their throats.

261   The lions.

262   Mr. Hadley looked at his wife and they turned and looked back at the beasts edging slowly forward, crouching, tails stiff.

263   Mr. and Mrs. Hadley screamed.

264   And suddenly they realized why those other screams had sounded familiar.

265   "Well, here I am," said David McClean in the nursery doorway. "Oh, hello." He stared at the two children seated in the center of the open glade eating a little picnic lunch. Beyond them was the water hole and the yellow veldtland; above was the hot sun. He began to perspire. "Where are your father and mother?"

266   The children looked up and smiled. "Oh, they'll be here directly."

267   "Good, we must get going." At a distance Mr. McClean saw the lions fighting and clawing and then quieting down to feed in silence under the shady trees.

268   He squinted at the lions with his hand up to his eyes.

269   Now the lions were done feeding. They moved to the water hole to drink.

270   A shadow flickered over Mr. McClean's hot face. Many shadows flickered. The vultures were dropping down the blazing sky.

271   "A cup of tea?" asked Wendy in the silence.

Everyday Use

Alice Walker

for your grandmama

1   I will wait for her in the yard that Maggie and I made so clean and wavy yesterday afternoon. A yard like this is more comfortable than most people know. It is not just a yard. It is like an extended living room. When the hard clay is swept clean as a floor and the fine sand around the edges lined with tiny, irregular grooves, anyone can come and sit and look up into the elm tree and wait for the breezes that never come inside the house.

2   Maggie will be nervous until after her sister goes: she will stand hopelessly in corners, homely and ashamed of the burn scars down her arms and legs, eyeing her sister with a mixture of envy and awe. She thinks her sister has held life always in the palm of one hand, that "no" is a word the world never learned to say to her.

3   You've no doubt seen those TV shows where the child who has "made it" is confronted, as a surprise, by her own mother and father, tottering in weakly from backstage. (A pleasant surprise, of course: What would they do if parent and child came on the show only to curse out and insult each other?) On TV mother and child embrace and smile into each other's faces. Sometimes the mother and father weep, the child wraps them in her arms and leans across the table to tell how she would not have made it without their help. I have seen these programs.

4   Sometimes I dream a dream in which Dee and I are suddenly brought together on a TV program of this sort. Out of a dark and soft-seated limousine I am ushered into a bright room filled with many people. There I meet a smiling, gray, sporty man like Johnny Carson who shakes my hand and tells me what a fine girl I have. Then we are on the stage and Dee is embracing me with tears in her eyes. She pins on my dress a large orchid, even though she has told me once that she thinks orchids are tacky flowers.

5   In real life I am a large, big boned woman with rough, man-working hands. In the winter I wear flannel nightgowns to bed and overalls during the day. I can kill and clean a hog as mercilessly as a man. My fat keeps me hot in zero weather. I can work outside all day, breaking ice to get water for washing; I can eat pork liver cooked over the open fire minutes after it comes steaming from the hog. One winter I knocked a bull calf straight in the brain between the eyes with a sledge hammer and had the meat hung up to chill before nightfall. But of course all this does not show on television. I am the way my daughter would want me to be: a hundred pounds lighter, my skin like an uncooked barley pancake. My hair glistens in the hot bright lights. Johnny Carson has much to do to keep up with my quick and witty tongue.

6   But that is a mistake. I know even before I wake up. Who ever knew a Johnson with a quick tongue? Who can even imagine me looking a strange white man in the eye? It seems to me I have talked to them always with one foot raised in flight, with my head fumed in whichever way is farthest from them. Dee, though. She would always look anyone in the eye. Hesitation was no part of her nature.

7   "How do I look, Mama?" Maggie says, showing just enough of her thin body enveloped in pink skirt and red blouse for me to know she's there, almost hidden by the door.

8   "Come out into the yard," I say.

NOTES

awe (par. 2): a combination of fear and wonder
confronted (par. 3): brought face to face
tottering (par. 3): walking unsteadily
glistens (par. 5): shines

9   Have you ever seen a lame animal, perhaps a dog run over by some careless person rich enough to own a car, sidle up to someone who is ignorant enough to be kind to him? That is the way my Maggie walks. She has been like this, chin on chest, eyes on ground, feet in shuffle, ever since the fire that burned the other house to the ground.

10   Dee is lighter than Maggie, with nicer hair and a fuller figure. She's a woman now, though sometimes I forget. How long ago was it that the other house burned? Ten, twelve years? Sometimes I can still hear the flames and feel Maggie's arms sticking to me, her hair smoking, and her dress falling off her in little black papery flakes. Her eyes seemed stretched open, blazed open by the flames reflected in them. And Dee. I see her standing off under the sweet gum tree she used to dig gum out of; a look of concentration on her face as she watched the last dingy gray board of the house fall in toward the red hot brick chimney. Why don't you do a dance around the ashes? I'd wanted to ask her. She had hated the house that much.

11   I used to think she hated Maggie, too. But that was before we raised money, the church and me, to send her to Augusta to school. She used to read to us without pity; forcing words, lies, other folks' habits, whole lives upon us two, sitting trapped and ignorant underneath her voice. She washed us in a river of make believe, burned us with a lot of knowledge we didn't necessarily need to know. Pressed us to her with the serf' ous way she read, to shove us away at just the moment, like dimwits, we seemed about to understand.

12   Dee wanted nice things. A yellow organdy dress to wear to her graduation from high school; black pumps to match a green suit she'd made from an old suit somebody gave me. She was determined to stare down any disaster in her efforts. Her eyelids would not flicker for minutes at a time. Often I fought off the temptation to shake her. At sixteen she had a style of her own: and knew what style was.

13   I never had an education myself. After second grade the school was closed down. Don't ask my why: in 1927 colored asked fewer questions than they do now. Sometimes Maggie reads to me. She stumbles along good naturedly but can't see well. She knows she is not bright. Like good looks and money, quickness passes her by. She will marry John Thomas (who has mossy teeth in an earnest face) and then I'll be free to sit here and I guess just sing church songs to myself. Although I never was a good singer. Never could carry a tune. I was always better at a man's job. I used to love to milk till I was hooked in the side in '49. Cows are soothing and slow and don't bother you, unless you try to milk them the wrong way.

14   I have deliberately turned my back on the house. It is three rooms, just like the one that burned, except the roof is tin; they don't make shingle roofs any more.

NOTES

sidle up (par. 9): to move sideways toward something
Augusta (par. 11): city in Georgia
organdy (par. 12): a type of fabric
mossy (par. 13): dark and coated
earnest (par. 13): sincere
hooked (par. 13): struck by the horns of a cow
shingle roofs (par. 14): here, roofs with wooden shingles

There are no real windows, just some holes cut in the sides, like the portholes in a ship, but not round and not square, with rawhide holding the shutters up on the outside. This house is in a pasture, too, like the other one. No doubt when Dee sees it she will want to tear it down. She wrote me once that no matter where we "choose" to live, she will manage to come see us. But she will never bring her friends. Maggie and I thought about this and Maggie asked me, "Mama, when did Dee ever *have* any friends?"

15 She had a few. Furtive boys in pink shirts hanging about on washday after school. Nervous girls who never laughed. Impressed with her they worshiped the well-turned phrase, the cute shape, the scalding humor that erupted like bubbles in lye. She read to them.

16 When she was courting Jimmy T she didn't have much time to pay to us, but turned all her faultfinding power on him. He flew to marry a cheap city girl from a family of ignorant flashy people. She hardly had time to recompose herself.

17 When she comes I will meet—but there they are!

18 Maggie attempts to make a dash for the house, in her shuffling way, but I stay her with my hand. "Come back here," I say. And she stops and tries to dig a well in the sand with her toe.

19 It is hard to see them clearly through the strong sun. But even the first glimpse of leg out of the car tells me it is Dee. Her feet were always neat looking, as if God himself had shaped them with a certain style. From the other side of the car comes a short, stocky man. Hair is all over his head a foot long and hanging from his chin like a kinky mule tail. I hear Maggie suck in her breath. "Uhnnnh," is what it sounds like. Like when you see the wriggling end of a snake just in front of your foot on the road. "Uhnnnh."

20 Dee next. A dress down to the ground, in this hot weather. A dress so loud it hurts my eyes. There are yellows and oranges enough to throw back the light of the sun. I feel my whole face warming from the heat waves it throws out. Earrings gold, too, and hanging down to her shoulders. Bracelets dangling and making noises when she moves her arm up to shake the folds of the dress out of her armpits. The dress is loose and flows, and as she walks closer, I like it. I hear Maggie go "Uhnnnh" again. It is her sister's hair. It stands straight up like the wool on a sheep. It is black as night and around the edges are two long pigtails that rope about like small lizards disappearing behind her ears.

21 "Wa su zo Tean o!" she says, coming on in that gliding way the dress makes her move. The short stocky fellow with the hair to his navel is all grinning and he follows up with "Asalamalakim, my mother and sister!" He moves to hug Maggie but she falls back, right up against the back of my chair. I feel her trembling there and when I look up I see the perspiration falling off her chin.

NOTES

furtive (par. 15): sly, sneaky

well-turned phrase (par. 15): clever statement

lye (par. 15): a chemical that bubbles when mixed with a liquid

courting (par 16): dating

recompose (par. 16): to return to a calm state

stay (par. 18): stop

22   "Don't get up," says Dee. Since I am stout it takes something of a push. You can see me trying to move a second or two before I make it. She turns, showing white heels through her sandals, and goes back to the car. Out she peeks next with a Polaroid. She stoops down quickly and lines up picture after picture of me sitting there in front of the house with Maggie cowering behind me. She never takes a shot without making sure the house is included. When a cow comes nibbling around the edge of the yard she snaps it and me and Maggie *and* the house. Then she puts the Polaroid in the back seat of the car, and comes up and kisses me on the forehead.

23   Meanwhile Asalamalakim is going through motions with Maggie's hand. Maggie's hand is as limp as a fish, and probably as cold, despite the sweat, and she keeps trying to pull it back. It looks like Asalamalakim wants to shake hands but wants to do it fancy. Or maybe he don't know how people shake hands. Anyhow, he soon gives up on Maggie.

24   "Well," I say. "Dee."

25   "No, Mama," she says. "Not 'Dee,' Wangero Leewanika Kemanjo!"

26   "What happened to 'Dee'?" I wanted to know.

27   "She's dead," Wangero said. "I couldn't bear it any longer, being named after the people who oppress me."

28   "You know as well as me you was named after your aunt Dicie," I said. Dicie is my sister. She named Dee. We called her "Big Dee" after Dee was born.

29   "But who was *she* named after?" asked Wangero.

30   "I guess after Grandma Dee," I said.

31   "And who was she named after?" asked Wangero.

32   "Her mother," I said, and saw Wangero was getting tired. "That's about as far back as I can trace it," I said. Though, in fact, I probably could have carried it back beyond the Civil War through the branches.

33   "Well," said Asalamalakim, "there you are."

34   "Uhnnnh," I heard Maggie say.

35   "There I was not," I said, "before 'Dicie' cropped up in our family, so why should I try to trace it that far back?"

36   He just stood there grinning, looking down on me like somebody inspecting a Model A car. Every once in a while he and Wangero sent eye signals over my head.

37   "How do you pronounce this name?" I asked.

38   "You don't have to call me by it if you don't want to," said Wangero.

39   "Why shouldn't I?" I asked. "If that's what you want us to call you, we'll call you."

40   "I know it might sound awkward at first," said Wangero.

41   "I'll get used to it," I said. "Ream it out again."

NOTES

stout (par. 22): heavy

cowering (par. 22): shrinking away, as in fear

oppress (par. 27): burden, persecute

branches (par. 32): that is, the branches of a "family tree"

Model A (par. 36): a Ford car produced from 1927 to 1931

ream it out again (par. 41): repeat it

42   Well, soon we got the name out of the way. Asalamalakim had a name twice as long and three times as hard. After I tripped over it two or three times he told me to just call him Hakim a barber. I wanted to ask him was he a barber, but I didn't really think he was, so I didn't ask.

43   "You must belong to those beef cattle peoples down the road," I said. They said "Asalamalakim" when they met you, too, but they didn't shake hands. Always too busy: feeding the cattle, fixing the fences, putting up salt lick shelters, throwing down hay. When the white folks poisoned some of the herd the men stayed up all night with rifles in their hands. I walked a mile and a half just to see the sight.

44   Hakim a barber said, "I accept some of their doctrines, but farming and raising cattle is not my style." (They didn't tell me, and I didn't ask, whether Wangero (Dee) had really gone and married him.)

45   We sat down to eat and right away he said he didn't eat collards and pork was unclean. Wangero, though, went on through the chitlins and corn bread, the greens and everything else. She talked a blue streak over the sweet potatoes. Everything delighted her. Even the fact that we still used the benches her daddy made for the table when we couldn't afford to buy chairs.

46   "Oh, Mama!" she cried. Then turned to Hakim-a-barber. "I never knew how lovely these benches are. You can feel the rump prints," she said, running her hands underneath her and along the bench. Then she gave a sigh and her hand closed over Grandma Dee's butter dish. "That's it!" she said. "I knew there was something I wanted to ask you if I could have." She jumped up from the table and went over in the corner where the churn stood, the milk in it crabber by now. She looked at the churn and looked at it.

47   "This churn top is what I need," she said. "Didn't Uncle Buddy whittle it out of a tree you all used to have?"

48   "Yes," I said.

49   "Un huh," she said happily. "And I want the dasher, too."

50   "Uncle Buddy whittle that, too?" asked the barber.

51   Dee (Wangero) looked up at me.

52   "Aunt Dee's first husband whittled the dash," said Maggie so low you almost couldn't hear her. "His name was Henry, but they called him Stash."

53   "Maggie's brain is like an elephant's," Wangero said, laughing. "I can use the chute top as a centerpiece for the alcove table," she said, sliding a plate over the chute, "and I'll think of something artistic to do with the dasher."

54   When she finished wrapping the dasher the handle stuck out. I took it for a moment in my hands. You didn't even have to look close to see where hands pushing the dasher up and down to make butter had left a kind of sink in the wood. In fact, there were a lot of small sinks; you could see where thumbs and

NOTES

salt-lick (par. 42): a block of salt that cows lick

doctrines (par. 44): principles by which one lives

chitlins (par. 45): hog intestines

churn (par. 46): a container in which milk is placed and allowed to sour and thicken ("clabber," par. 46); a "dasher" (par. 49) is moved up and down in the churn to separate the butter from the milk

alcove (par. 53): an area separated from the main part of the room

fingers had sunk into the wood. It was beautiful light yellow wood, from a tree that grew in the yard where Big Dee and Stash had lived.

55   After dinner Dee (Wangero) went to the trunk at the foot of my bed and started rifling through it. Maggie hung back in the kitchen over the dishpan. Out came Wangero with two quilts. They had been pieced by Grandma Dee and then Big Dee and me had hung them on the quilt frames on the front porch and quilted them. One was in the Lone State pattern. The other was Walk Around the Mountain. In both of them were scraps of dresses Grandma Dee had worn fifty and more years ago. Bits and pieces of Grandpa Jattell's Paisley shirts. And one teeny faded blue piece, about the size of a penny matchbox, that was from Great Grandpa Ezra's uniform that he wore in the Civil War.

56   "Mama," Wangro said sweet as a bird. "Can I have these old quilts?"

57   I heard something fall in the kitchen, and a minute later the kitchen door slammed.

58   "Why don't you take one or two of the others?" I asked. "These old things was just done by me and Big Dee from some tops your grandma pieced before she died."

59   "No," said Wangero. "I don't want those. They are stitched around the borders by machine."

60   "That'll make them last better," I said.

61   "That's not the point," said Wangero. "These are all pieces of dresses Grandma used to wear. She did all this stitching by hand. Imagine!" She held the quilts securely in her arms, stroking them.

62   "Some of the pieces, like those lavender ones, come from old clothes her mother handed down to her," I said, moving up to touch the quilts. Dee (Wangero) moved back just enough so that I couldn't reach the quilts. They already belonged to her.

63   "Imagine!" she breathed again, clutching them closely to her bosom.

64   "The truth is," I said, "I promised to give them quilts to Maggie, for when she marries John Thomas."

65   She gasped like a bee had stung her.

66   "Maggie can't appreciate these quilts!" she said. "She'd probably be backward enough to put them to everyday use."

67   "I reckon she would," I said. "God knows I been saving 'em for long enough with nobody using 'em. I hope she will!" I didn't want to bring up how I had offered Dee (Wangero) a quilt when she went away to college. Then she had told they were old-fashioned, out of style.

68   "But they're *priceless*!" she was saying now, furiously; for she has a temper. "Maggie would put them on the bed and in five years they'd be in rags. Less than that!"

69   "She can always make some more," I said. "Maggie knows how to quilt."

70   Dee (Wangero) looked at me with hatred. "You just will not understand. The point is these quilts, *these* quilts!"

71   "Well," I said, stumped. "What would *you* do with them?"

NOTES

rifling (par. 55): rummaging, plundering
pieced (par. 55): put together
backward (par. 66): ignorant

72   "Hang them," she said. As if that was the only thing you *could* do with quilts.

73   Maggie by now was standing in the door. I could almost hear the sound her feet made as they scraped over each other.

74   "She can have them, Mama," she said, like somebody used to never winning anything, or having anything reserved for her. "I can 'member Grandma Dee without the quilts."

75   I looked at her hard. She had filled her bottom lip with checkerberry snuff and gave her face a kind of dopey, hangdog look. It was Grandma Dee and Big Dee who taught her how to quilt herself. She stood there with her scarred hands hidden in the folds of her skirt. She looked at her sister with something like fear but she wasn't mad at her. This was Maggie's portion. This was the way she knew God to work.

76   When I looked at her like that something hit me in the top of my head and ran down to the soles of my feet. Just like when I'm in church and the spirit of God touches me and I get happy and shout. I did some thing I never done before: hugged Maggie to me, then dragged her on into the room, snatched the quilts out of Miss Wangero's hands and dumped them into Maggie's lap. Maggie just sat there on my bed with her mouth open.

77   "Take one or two of the others," I said to Dee.

78   But she turned without a word and went out to Hakim-a-barber.

79   "You just don't understand," she said, as Maggie and I came out to the car.

80   "What don't I understand?" I wanted to know.

81   "Your heritage," she said, And then she turned to Maggie, kissed her, and said, "You ought to try to make something of yourself, too, Maggie. It's really a new day for us. But from the way you and Mama still live you'd never know it."

82   She put on some sunglasses that hid everything above the tip of her nose and chin.

83   Maggie smiled; maybe at the sunglasses. But a real smile, not scared. After we watched the car dust settle I asked Maggie to bring me a dip of snuff. And then the two of us sat there just enjoying, until it was time to go in the house and go to bed.

NOTES

snuff (par. 75): ground tobacco that is inhaled or placed inside the lip or cheek
hangdog (par. 75): defeated

Gimpel the Fool

Isaac Bashevis Singer

(Trans. Saul Bellow)

1   I am Gimpel the fool. I don't think myself a fool. On the contrary. But that's what folks call me. They gave me the name while I was still in school. I had seven names in all: imbecile, donkey, flax-head, dope, glump, ninny, and fool.

NOTE

rabbi's (par. 1): teacher and leader of a Jewish congregation

The last name stuck. What did my foolishness consist of? I was easy to take in. They said, "Gimpel, you know the rabbi's wife has been brought to childbed?" So I skipped school. Well, it turned out to be a lie. How was I supposed to know? She hadn't had a big belly. But I never looked at her belly. Was that really so foolish? The gang laughed and hee-hawed, stomped and danced, and chanted a good-night prayer. And instead of the raisins they give when a woman's lying-in, they stuffed my hand full of goat turds. I was no weakling. If I slapped someone he'd see all the way to Cracow. But I'm really not a slugger by nature. I think to myself: Let it pass. So they take advantage of me.

2   I was coming home from school and heard a dog barking. I'm not afraid of dogs, but of course I never want to start up with them. One of them may be mad, and if he bites there's not a Tartar in the world who can help you. So I made tracks. Then I looked around and saw the whole market place wild with laughter. It was no dog at all but Wolf-Leib the Thief. How was I supposed to know it was he? It sounded like a howling bitch.

3   When the pranksters and leg-pullers found that I was easy to fool, every one of them tried his luck with me. "Gimpel, the Czar is coming to Frampol; Gimpel, the moon fell down in Turbeen; Gimpel, little Hodel Furpiece found a treasure behind the bathhouse." And I like a golem believed everyone. In the first place, everything is possible, as it is written in the Wisdom of the Fathers, I've forgotten just how. Second, I had to believe when the whole town came down on me! If I ever dared to say, "Ah, you're kidding!" there was trouble. People got angry. "What do you mean! You want to call everyone a liar?" What was I to do? I believed them, and I hope at least that did them some good.

4   I was an orphan. My grandfather who brought me up was already bent toward the grave. So they turned me over to a baker, and what a time they gave me there! Every woman or girl who came to bake a batch of noodles had to fool me at least once. "Gimpel, there's a fair in heaven; Gimpel, the rabbi gave birth to a calf in the seventh month; Gimpel, a cow flew over the roof and laid brass eggs." A student from the yeshiva came once to buy a roll, and he said, "You, Gimpel, while you stand here scraping with your baker's shovel the Messiah has come. The dead have arisen." "What do you mean?" I said.

NOTES

has been brought to childbed (par. 1): is in the process of giving birth

lying-in (par. 1): giving birth

Cracow (par. 1): a city in Poland

mad (par. 2): rabid (i.e., affected by rabies)

Tartar (par. 2): figuratively, a fierce and violent person. Literally, Tartar refers to the peoples of Central Asia who invaded Western Asia and Eastern Europe under the leadership of Genghis Khan (1202–1227).

bitch (par. 2): female dog

Czar (par. 3): king, emperor

golem (par. 3): blockhead

yeshiva (par. 4): Orthodox Jewish schools where young men study Jewish law, usually in preparation for becoming rabbis

Messiah (par. 4): the promised and awaited deliverer of the Jews

blowing the ram's horn (par. 4): According to Zechariah, the Messiah's arrival will be announced by the blowing of the ram's horn (Zech 9:14).

"I heard no one blowing the ram's horn!" He said, "Are you deaf?" And all began to cry, "We heard it, we heard!" Then in came Rietze the Candle-dipper and called out in her hoarse voice, "Gimpel, your father and mother have stood up from the grave. They're looking for you."

5   To tell the truth, I knew very well that nothing of the sort had happened, but all the same, as folks were talking, I threw on my wool vest and went out. Maybe something had happened. What did I stand to lose by looking? Well, what a cat music went up! And then I took a vow to believe nothing more. But that was no go either. They confused me so that I didn't know the big end from the small.

6   I went to the rabbi to get some advice. He said, "It is written, better to be a fool all your days than for one hour to be evil. You are not a fool. They are the fools. For he who causes his neighbor to feel shame loses Paradise himself." Nevertheless the rabbi's daughter took me in. As I left the rabbinical court she said, "Have you kissed the wall yet?" I said, "No; what for?" She answered, "It's the law; you've got to do it after every visit." Well, there didn't seem to be any harm in it. And she burst out laughing. It was a fine trick. She put one over on me, all right.

7   I wanted to go off to another town, but then everyone got busy matchmaking, and they were after me so they nearly tore my coat tails off. They talked at me and talked until I got water on the ear. She was no chaste maiden, but they told me she was virgin pure. She had a limp, and they said it was deliberate, from coyness. She had a bastard, and they told me the child was her little brother. I cried, "You're wasting your time. I'll never marry that whore." But they said indignantly, "What a way to talk! Aren't you ashamed of yourself? We can take you to the rabbi and have you fined for giving her a bad name." I saw then that I wouldn't escape them so easily and I thought: They're set on making me their butt. But when you're married the husband's the master, and if that's all right with her it's agreeable to me too. Besides, you can't pass through life unscathed, nor expect to.

8   I went to her clay house, which was built on the sand, and the whole gang hollering and chorusing, came after me. They acted like bear-baiters. When we came to the well they stopped all the same. They were afraid to start anything with Elka. Her mouth would open as if it were on a hinge, and she had a fierce tongue. I entered the house. Lines were strung from wall to wall and clothes were drying. Barefoot she stood by the tub, doing the wash. She was dressed in a worn hand-me-down gown of plush. She had her hair put up in braids and pinned across her head. It took my breath away, almost, the reek of it all.

9   Evidently she knew who I was. She took a look at me and said, "Look who's here! He's come, the drip. Grab a seat."

NOTES

chaste maiden (par. 7): virgin

bastard (par. 7): illegitimate child

indignantly (par. 7): angrily

unscathed (par. 7): unharmed, without injury

bear-baiters (par. 8): people who participate in bear-baiting, a sport (now illegal in most countries) in which a bear is chained by a hind leg or the neck to a post and dogs are released to attack it

10   I told her all; I denied nothing. "Tell me the truth," I said, "are you really a virgin; and is that mischievous Yechiel actually your little brother? Don't be deceitful with me, for I'm an orphan."

11   "I'm an orphan myself," she answered, "and whoever tries to twist you up, may the end of his nose take a twist. But don't let them think they can take advantage of me. I want a dowry of fifty guilders, and let them take up a collection besides. Otherwise they can kiss my you-know-what." She was very plainspoken. I said, "It's the bride and not the groom who gives a dowry." Then she said, "Don't bargain with me. Either a flat 'yes' or a flat 'no'—Go back where you came from."

12   I thought: No bread will ever be baked from this dough. But ours is not a poor town. They consented to everything and proceeded with the wedding. It so happened that there was a dysentery epidemic at the time. The ceremony was held at the cemetery gates, near the little corpse-washing hut. The fellows got drunk. While the marriage contract was being drawn up I heard the most pious high rabbi ask, "Is the bride a widow or a divorced woman?" And the sexton's wife answered for her, "Both a widow and divorced." It was a black moment for me. But what was I to do, run away from under the marriage canopy?

13   There was singing and dancing. An old granny danced opposite me, hugging a braided white *chalah*. The master of revels made a "God 'a mercy" in memory of the bride's parents. The schoolboys threw burrs, as on Tishe b'Av fast day. There were a lot of gifts after the sermon: a noodle board, a kneading trough, a bucket, brooms, ladles, household articles galore. Then I took a look and saw two strapping young men carrying a crib. "What do we need this for?" I asked. So they said, "Don't rack your brains about it. It's all right, it'll come in handy." I realized I was going to be rooked. Take it another way though, what did I stand to lose? I reflected: I'll see what comes of it. A whole town can't go altogether crazy.

II

14   At night I came where my wife lay, but she wouldn't let me in. "Say, look here, is this what they married us for?" I said. And she said, "My monthly has come." "But yesterday they took you to the ritual bath, and that's afterward,

---

NOTES

deceitful (par. 10): dishonest

dowry (par. 11): money or property given by a bride's family to her husband

guilder (par. 11): the basic monetary unit of the Netherlands

dysentery (par. 12): a disease of the bowels that causes severe pain and diarrhea

epidemic (par. 12): outbreak

pious (par. 12): religious

sexton's wife (par. 12): wife of the sexton, an official of the synagogue (Jewish house of worship)

the marriage canopy (par. 12): During one part of the Jewish wedding ceremony, the groom, the bride, their parents, and the rabbi stand under the *chuppah* or "marriage canopy," symbolic of the home of the new couple. The rabbi offers blessings and prayers of thanks to God.

chalah (par. 13): braided bread traditionally eaten by Jews on the Sabbath and holidays

revels (par. 13): festivities

Tishe b'Av (par. 13): a Jewish holy day observed with fasting

rooked (par. 13): cheated

isn't it supposed to be?" "Today isn't yesterday," said she, "and yesterday's not today. You can beat it if you don't like it." In short, I waited.

15   Not four months later she was in childbed. The townsfolk hid their laughter with their knuckles. But what could I do? She suffered intolerable pains and clawed at the walls. "Gimpel," she cried, "I'm going. Forgive me!" The house filled with women. They were boiling pans of water. The screams rose to the welkin.

16   The thing to do was to go to the House of Prayer to repeat Psalms, and that was what I did.

17   The townsfolk liked that, all right. I stood in a corner saying Psalms and prayers, and they shook their heads at me. "Pray, pray!" they told me. "Prayer never made any woman pregnant." One of the congregation put a straw to my mouth and said, "Hay for the cows." There was something to that too, by God!

18   She gave birth to a boy. Friday at the synagogue the sexton stood up before the Ark, pounded on the reading table, and announced, "The wealthy Reb Gimpel invites the congregation to a feast in honor of the birth of a son." The whole House of Prayer rang with laughter. My face was flaming. But there was nothing I could do. After all, I was the one responsible for the circumcision honors and rituals. Half the town came running. You couldn't wedge another soul in. Women brought peppered chickpeas, and there was a keg of beer from the tavern. I ate and drank as much as anyone, and they all congratulated me. Then there was a circumcision, and I named the boy after my father, may he rest in peace. When all were gone and I was left with my wife alone, she thrust her head through the bed-curtain and called me to her. "Gimpel," said she, "why are you silent? Has your ship gone and sunk?"

19   "What shall I say?" I answered. "A fine thing you've done to me! If my mother had known of it she'd have died a second time."

20   She said, "Are you crazy, or what?"

21   "How can you make such a fool," I said, "of one who should be your lord and master?"

22   "What's the matter with you?" she said. "What have you taken it into your head to imagine?"

23   I saw that I must speak bluntly and openly. "Do you think this is the way to use an orphan?" I said. "You have borne a bastard."

24   She answered, "Drive this foolishness out of your head. The child is yours."

25   "How can he be mine?" I argued. "He was born seventeen weeks after the wedding?"

NOTES

childbed (par. 15): giving birth

welkin (par. 15): heaven

synagogue (par. 18): Jewish house of worship and instruction

Reb (par. 18): used as a title of respect, like "Mister"

the circumcision honors and rituals (par. 18): Circumcision is the surgical removal of part or all of the foreskin of the penis. Jewish law requires that male children be circumcised when they are eight days old (Genesis 17: 10–12; Leviticus 12:3). The ritual circumcision (*Bris* or *Brit Mila*) takes place among family and friends and is a time for celebration.

26   She told me then that he was premature. I said, "Isn't he a little too premature?" She said, she had had a grandmother who carried just as short a time and she resembled this grandmother of hers as one drop of water does another. She swore to it with such oaths that you would have believed a peasant at the fair if he had used them. To tell the plain truth, I didn't believe her; but when I talked it over next day with the schoolmaster he told me that the very same thing had happened to Adam and Eve. Two they went up to bed, and four they descended.

27   "There isn't a woman in the world who is not the granddaughter of Eve," he said.

28   That was how it was; they argued me dumb. But then, who really knows how such things are?

29   I began to forget my sorrow. I loved the child madly, and he loved me too. As soon as he saw me he'd wave his little hands and want me to pick him up, and when he was colicky I was the only one who could pacify him. I bought him a little bone teething ring and a little gilded cap. He was forever catching the evil eye from someone, and then I had to run to get one of those abracadabras for him that would get him out of it. I worked like an ox. You don't know how expenses go up with there's an infant in the house. I don't want to lie about it; I didn't dislike Elka either, for that matter. She swore at me and cursed, and I couldn't get enough of her. What strength she had! One of her looks could rob you of the power of speech. And her orations! Pitch and sulphur, that's what they were full of, and yet somehow also full of charm. I adored her every word. She gave me bloody wounds though.

30   In the evening I brought her a white loaf as well as a dark one, and also poppyseed rolls I baked myself. I thieved because of her and swiped everything I could get my hands on: macaroons, raisins, almonds, cakes. I hope I may be forgiven for stealing from the Saturday pots the women left to warm in the baker's oven. I would take out scraps of meat, a chunk of pudding, a chicken leg or head, a piece of tripe, whatever I could nip quickly. She ate and became fat and handsome.

31   I had to sleep away from home all during the week, at the bakery. On Friday nights when I got home she always made an excuse of some sort. Either she had heartburn, or a stitch in the side, or hiccups, or headaches. You know what women's excuses are. I had a bitter time of it. It was rough. To add to it, this little brother of hers, the bastard, was growing bigger. He'd put lumps on me, and when I wanted to hit back she'd open her mouth and curse so powerfully I saw a green haze floating before my eyes. Ten times a day she threatened to divorce me. Another man in my place would have taken French leave

NOTES

dumb (par. 28): speechless, silent

colicky (par. 29): irritable, crying

abracadabras (par. 29): magical charms that ward off disease or disaster

orations (par. 29): elaborate speeches

Pitch and sulphur (par. 29): nonsense

tripe (par. 30): the stomach lining of animals such as cows, sheep, and oxen, which is used for food

and disappeared. But I'm the type that bears it and says nothing. What's one to do? Shoulders are from God, and burdens too.

32   One night there was a calamity in the bakery; the oven burst, and we almost had a fire. There was nothing to do but go home, so I went home. Let me, I thought, also taste the joy of sleeping in bed in midweek. I didn't want to wake the sleeping mite and tiptoed into the house. Coming in, it seemed to me that I heard not the snoring of one but, as it were, a double snore, one a thin enough snore and the other like the snoring of a slaughtered ox. Oh, I didn't like that! I didn't like it at all. I went up to the bed, and things suddenly turned black. Next to Elka lay a man's form. Another in my place would have made an uproar, and enough noise to rouse the whole town, but the thought occurred to me that I might wake the child. A little thing like that—why frighten a little swallow, I thought. All right then, I went back to the bakery and stretched out on a sack of flour and till morning I never shut an eye. I shivered as if I had had malaria. "Enough of being a donkey," I said to myself. "Gimpel isn't going to be a sucker all his life. There's a limit even to the foolishness of a fool like Gimpel."

33   In the morning I went to the rabbi to get advice, and it made a great commotion in the town. They sent the beadle for Elka right away. She came, carrying the child. And what do you think she did? She denied it, denied everything, bone and stone! "He's out of his head," she said. "I know nothing of dreams or divinations." They yelled at her, warned her, hammered on the table, but she stuck to her guns: it was a false accusation, she said.

34   The butchers and the horse traders took her part. One of the lads from the slaughterhouse came by and said to me, "We've got our eye on you, you're a marked man." Meanwhile the child started to bear down and soiled itself. In the rabbinical court there was an Ark of the Covenant, and they couldn't allow that, so they sent Elka away.

35   I said to the rabbi, "What shall I do?"

36   "You must divorce her at once," said he.

37   "And what if she refuses?" I asked.

38   He said, "You must serve the divorce. That's all you have to do."

39   I said, "Well, all right, Rabbi. Let me think about it."

40   "There's nothing to think about," said he. "You mustn't remain under the same roof with her."

41   "And if I want to see the child?" I asked.

42   "Let her go, the harlot," said he, "and her brood of bastards with her."

43   The verdict he gave was that I mustn't even cross her threshold—never again, as long as I should live.

NOTES

calamity (par. 32): disaster, catastrophe

mite (par. 32): literally, a tiny animal similar to a spider; figuratively, a small child

swallow (par. 32): literally, a type of small bird

beadle (par. 33): an official of the synagogue

divinations (par. 33): fortune-telling

Ark of the Covenant (par. 34): a chest in which the scrolls of the Torah (the first five books of the Old Testament) are kept

threshold (par. 43): path, doorway

44   During the day it didn't bother me so much. I thought: It was bound to happen, the abscess had to burst. But at night when I stretched out upon the sacks I felt it all very bitterly. A longing took me, for her and for the child. I wanted to be angry, but that's my misfortune exactly, I don't have it in me to be really angry. In the first place—this was how my thoughts went—there's bound to be a slip sometimes. You can't live without errors. Probably that lad who was with her led her on and gave her presents and what not, and women are often long on hair and short on sense, and so he got around her. And then since she denies it so, maybe I was only seeing things? Hallucinations do happen. You see a figure or a mannikin or something, but when you come up closer it's nothing, there's not a thing there. And if that's so, I'm doing her an injustice. And when I got so far in my thoughts I started to weep. I sobbed so that I wet the flour where I lay. In the morning I went to the rabbi and told him that I had made a mistake. The rabbi wrote on with his quill, and he said that if that were so he would have to reconsider the whole case. Until he had finished I wasn't to go near my wife, but I might send her bread and money by messenger.

III

45   Nine months passed before all the rabbis could come to an agreement. Letters went back and forth. I hadn't realized that there could be so much erudition about a matter like this.

46   Meanwhile Elka gave birth to still another child, a girl this time. On the Sabbath I went to the synagogue and invoked a blessing on her. They called me up to the Torah, and I named the child for my mother-in-law—may she rest in peace. The louts and loudmouths of the town who came into the bakery gave me a going over. All Frampol refreshed its spirits because of my trouble and grief. However, I resolved that I would always believe what I was told. What's the good of *not* believing? Today it's your wife you don't believe; tomorrow it's God Himself you won't take stock in.

47   By an apprentice who was her neighbor I sent her daily a corn or a wheat loaf, or a piece of pastry, rolls or bagels, or, when I got the chance, a slab of pudding, a slice of honeycake, or wedding strudel—whatever came my way. The apprentice was a good-hearted lad, and more than once he added something on his own. He had formerly annoyed me a lot, plucking my nose and digging me in the ribs, but when he started to be a visitor to my house he became kind and friendly. "Hey, you, Gimpel," he said to me, "you have a very decent little wife and two fine kids. You don't deserve them."

48   "But the things people say about her," I said.

49   "Well, they have long tongues," he said, "and nothing to do with them but babble. Ignore it as you ignore the cold of last winter."

NOTES

abscess (par. 44): literally, a pus-filled sore

erudition (par. 45): scholarship, knowledge

invoked (par. 46): called for earnestly

Torah (par. 46): the first five books of the Old Testament

louts (par. 46): stupid people

50   One day the rabbi sent for me and said, "Are you certain, Gimpel, that you were wrong about your wife?"

51   I said, "I'm certain."

52   "Why, but look here! You yourself saw it."

53   "It must have been a shadow," I said.

54   "The shadow of what?"

55   "Just one of the beams, I think."

56   "You can go home then. You owe thanks to the Yanover rabbi. He found an obscure reference in Maimonides that favored you."

57   I seized the rabbi's hand and kissed it.

58   I wanted to run home immediately. It's no small thing to be separated for so long a time from wife and child. Then I reflected: I'd better go back to work now, and go home in the evening. I said nothing to anyone, although as far as my heart was concerned it was like one of the Holy Days. The women teased and twitted me as they did every day, but my thought was: Go on, with your loose talk. The truth is out, like the oil upon the water. Maimonides says it's right, and therefore it is right!

59   At night, when I had covered the dough to let it rise, I took my share of bread and a little sack of flour and started homeward. The moon was full and the stars were glistening, something to terrify the soul. I hurried onward, and before me darted a long shadow. It was winter, and a fresh snow had fallen. I had a mind to sing, but it was growing late and I didn't want to wake the householders. Then I felt like whistling, but I remembered that you don't whistle at night because it brings the demons out. So I was silent and walked as fast as I could.

60   Dogs in the Christian yards barked at me when I passed, but I thought: Bark your teeth out! What are you but mere dogs? Whereas I am a man, the husband of a fine wife, the father of promising children.

61   As I approached the house my heart started to pound as though it were the heart of a criminal. I felt no fear, but my heart went thump! thump! Well, no drawing back. I quietly lifted the latch and went in. Elka was asleep. I looked at the infant's cradle. The shutter was closed, but the moon forced its way through the cracks. I saw the newborn child's face and loved it as soon as I saw it—immediately—each tiny bone.

62   Then I came nearer to the bed. And what did I see but the apprentice lying there beside Elka. The moon went out all at once. It was utterly black, and I trembled. My teeth chattered. The bread fell from my hands, and my wife waked and said, "Who is that, ah?"

63   I muttered, "It's me."

64   "Gimpel?" she asked. "How come you're here? I thought it was forbidden."

65   "The rabbi said," I answered and shook as with a fever.

66   "Listen to me, Gimpel," she said, "go out to the shed and see if the goat's all right. It seems she's been sick." I have forgotten to say that we had a goat.

NOTES

obscure (par. 56): little known
Maimonides (par. 56): a Jewish theologian (1135–1204)

When I heard she was unwell I went into the yard. The nanny goat was a good little creature. I had a nearly human feeling for her.

67   With hesitant steps I went up to the shed and opened the door. The goat stood there on her four feet. I felt her everywhere, drew her by the horns, examined her udders, and found nothing wrong. She had probably eaten too much bark. "Good night, little goat," I said. "Keep well." And the little beast answered with a "Maa" as though to thank me for the good will.

68   I went back. The apprentice had vanished. "Where," I asked, "is the lad?"

69   "What lad?" my wife answered.

70   "What do you mean?" I said. "The apprentice. You were sleeping with him."

71   "The things I have dreamed this night and the night before," she said, "may they come true and lay you low, body and soul! An evil spirit has taken root in you and dazzles your sight." She screamed out, "You hateful creature! You moon calf! You spook! You uncouth man! Get out, or I'll scream all Frampol out of bed!"

72   Before I could move, her brother sprang out from behind the oven and struck me a blow on the back of the head. I thought he had broken my neck. I felt that something about me was deeply wrong, and I said, "Don't make a scandal. All that's needed now is that people should accuse me of raising spooks and *dybbuks*." For that was what she had meant. "No one will touch bread of my baking."

73   In short, I somehow calmed her.

74   "Well," she said, "that's enough. Lie down, and be shattered by wheels."

75   Next morning I called the apprentice aside. "Listen here. Brother!" I said. And so on and so forth. "What do you say?" He stared at me as though I had dropped from the roof or something.

76   "I swear," he said, "you'd better go to an herb doctor or some healer. I'm afraid you have a screw loose, but I'll hush it up for you." And that's how the thing stood.

77   To make a long story short, I lived twenty years with my wife. She bore me six children, four daughters and two sons. All kinds of things happened, but I neither saw nor heard. I believed, and that's all. The rabbi recently said to me, "Belief in itself is beneficial. It is written that a good man lives by his faith."

78   Suddenly my wife took sick. It began with a trifle, a little growth upon the breast. But she evidently was not destined to live long; she had no years. I spent a fortune on her. I have forgotten to say that by this time I had a bakery of my own and in Frampol was considered to be something of a rich man. Daily the healer came, and every witch doctor in the neighborhood was brought. They decided to use leeches, and after that to try cupping. They even called a doctor from Lublin, but it was too late. Before she died she called me to her bed and said, "Forgive me, Gimpel."

NOTES

udders (par. 67): mammary glands (in which milk is stored)

uncouth (par. 71): vulgar

dybbuks (par. 72): demons

trifle (par. 78): something of little importance

leeches . . . cupping (par. 78): treatments used to remove blood from a patient

79   I said, "What is there to forgive? You have been a good and faithful wife."

80   "Woe, Gimpel!" she said. "It was ugly how I deceived you all these years. I want to go clean to my Maker, and so I have to tell you that the children are not yours."

81   If I had been clouted on the head with a piece of wood it couldn't have bewildered me more.

82   "Whose are they?" I asked.

83   "I don't know," she said. "There were a lot . . . but they're not yours." And as she spoke she tossed her head to the side, her eyes turned glassy, and it was all up with Elka. On her whitened lips there remained a smile.

84   I imagined that, dead as she was, she was saying, "I deceived Gimpel. That was the meaning of my brief life."

IV

85   One night, when the period of mourning was done, as I lay dreaming on the flour sacks, there came the Spirit of Evil himself and said to me, "Gimpel, why do you sleep?"

86   I said, "What should I be doing? Eating *kreplach*?"

87   "The whole world deceives you," he said, "and you ought to deceive the world in your turn."

88   "How can I deceive the world?" I asked him.

89   He answered, "You might accumulate a bucket of urine every day and at night pour it in the dough. Let the sages of Frampol eat filth."

90   "What about the judgment in the world to come?" I said.

91   "There is no world to come," he said. "They've sold you a bill of goods and talked you into believing you carried a cat in your belly. What nonsense!"

92   "Well then," I said, "and is there a God?"

93   He answered, "There is no God either."

94   "What," I said, "*is* there, then?"

95   "A thick mire."

96   He stood before my eyes with a goatish beard and horn, long-toothed, and with a tail. Hearing such words, I wanted to snatch him by the tail, but I tumbled for the flour sacks and nearly broke a rib. Then it happened that I had to answer the call of nature, and, passing, I saw the risen dough, which seemed to say to me, "Do it!" In brief, I let myself be persuaded.

97   At dawn the apprentice came. We kneaded the bread, scattered caraway seeds on it, and set it to bake. Then the apprentice went away, and I was left sitting in the little trench by the oven, on a pile of rags. Well, Gimpel, I thought, you've revenged yourself on them for all the shame they've put on you. Outside the frost glittered, but it was warm beside the oven. The flames heated my face. I bent my head and fell into a doze.

NOTES

clouted (par. 81): hit
bewildered (par. 81): confused
kreplach (par. 86): dumplings
sages (par. 89): wise men
mire (par. 95): swamp

98   I saw in a dream, at once, Elka in her shroud. She called to me, "What have you done, Gimpel?"

99   I said to her, "It's all your fault," and started to cry.

100   "You fool!" she said. "You fool! Because I was false is everything false too? I never deceived anyone but myself. I'm paying for it all, Gimpel. They spare you nothing here."

101   I looked at her face. It was black; I was startled and waked, and remained sitting dumb. I sensed that everything hung in the balance. A false step now and I'd lose Eternal Life. But God gave me His help. I seized the long shovel and took out the loaves, carried them into the yard, and started to dig a hole in the frozen earth.

102   My apprentice came back as I was doing. "What are you doing, boss?" he said, and grew pale as a corpse.

103   "I know what I'm doing," I said, and I buried it all before his very eyes.

104   Then I went home, took my hoard from its hiding place, and divided it among the children. "I saw your mother tonight," I said. "She's turning black, poor thing."

105   They were so astounded they couldn't speak a word.

106   "Be well," I said, "and forget that such a one as Gimpel ever existed." I put on my short coat, a pair of boots, took the bag that held my prayer shawl in one hand, my stock in the other, and kissed the *mezuzah*. When people saw me in the street they were greatly surprised.

107   "Where are you going?" they said.

108   I answered, "Into the world." And so I departed from Frampol.

109   I wandered over the land, and good people did not neglect me. After many years I became old and white; I heard a great deal, many lies and falsehoods, but the longer I lived the more I understood that there were really no lies. Whatever doesn't really happen is dreamed at night. It happens to one if it doesn't happen to another, tomorrow if not today, or a century hence if not next year. What difference can it make? Often I heard tales of which I said, "Now this is a thing that cannot happen." But before a year had elapsed I heard that it actually had come to pass somewhere.

110   Going from place to place, eating at strange tables, it often happens that I spin yarns—improbable things that could never have happened—about devils, magicians, windmills, and the like. The children run after me, calling, "Grandfather, tell us a story." Sometimes they ask for particular stories, and I try to please them. A fat young boy once said to me, "Grandfather, it's the same story you told us before." The little rogue, he was right.

NOTES

shroud (par. 98): burial cloth

hoard (par. 104): stored supply of money and valuables

mezuzah (par. 106): a small piece of parchment inscribed on one side with biblical passages (Deuteronomy 6:4–9 and 11:13–21) and on the other with *Shaddai* (a name for God), enclosed in a case is attached to the door post, in fulfillment of Jewish law (Deuteronomy 6:9 and 11:20). Upon entering and leaving the house, Jews touch the mezuzah with their fingers and then touch their fingers to their lips, repeating the words of Psalms 121:8 ("God will guard your going and coming from now and for all time").

hence (par. 109): from now

111   So it is with dreams too. It is many years since I left Frampol, but as soon as I shut my eyes I am there again. And whom do you think I see? Elka. She is standing by the washtub, as at our first encounter, but her face is shining and her eyes are as radiant as the eyes of a saint, and she speaks outlandish words to me, strange things. When I wake I have forgotten it all. But while the dream lasts I am comforted. She answers all my queries, and what comes out is that all is right. I weep and implore, "Let me be with you." And she consoles me and tells me to be patient. The time is nearer than it is far. Sometimes she strokes and kisses me and weeps upon my face. When I awaken I feel her lips and taste the salt of her tears.

112   No doubt the world is entirely an imaginary world, but it is only once removed from the true world. At the door of the hovel where I lie, there stands the plank on which the dead are taken away. The gravedigger Jew has his spade ready. The grave waits and the worms are hungry; the shrouds are prepared— I carry them in my beggar's sack. Another *shnorrer* is waiting to inherit my bed of straw. When the time comes I will go joyfully. Whatever may be there, it will be real, without complication, without ridicule, without deception. God be praised: there even Gimpel cannot be deceived.

NOTES

radiant (par. 111): bright
queries (par. 111): questions
implore (par. 111): plead
consoles (par. 111): comforts
hovel (par. 112): shack
plank (par. 112): wooden board
shnorrer (par. 112): begger

A Worn Path

Eudora Welty

1   It was December—a bright frozen day in the early morning. Far out in the country there was an old Negro woman with her head tied in a red rag, coming along a path through the pinewoods. Her name was Phoenix Jackson. She was very old and small and she walked slowly in the dark pine shadows, moving a little from side to side in her steps, with the balanced heaviness and lightness of a pendulum in a grandfather clock. She carried a thin, small cane made from an umbrella, and with this she kept tapping the frozen earth in front of her. This made a grave and persistent noise in the still air, that seemed meditative like the chirping of a solitary little bird.

NOTES

Phoenix (par. 1): The phoenix is an Egyptian mythological bird that lived in the desert for 500 years and then flew to Heliopolis to the temple of Re, the god of the sun. In the temple, the phoenix flew into the altar fire, was consumed by it, and arose from the ashes, renewed.
meditative (par. 1): religiously or philosophically thoughtful

---

2   She wore a dark striped dress reaching down to her shoe tops, and an equally long apron of bleached sugar sacks, with a full pocket: all neat and tidy, but every time she took a step she might have fallen over her shoelaces, which dragged from her unlaced shoes. She looked straight ahead. Her eyes were blue with age. Her skin had a pattern all its own of numberless branching wrinkles and as though a whole little tree stood in the middle of her forehead, but a golden color ran underneath, and the two knobs of her cheeks were illuminated by a yellow burning under the dark. Under the red rag her hair came down on her neck in the frailest of ringlets, still black, and with an odor like copper.

3   Now and then there was a quivering in the thicket. Old Phoenix said, "Out of my way, all you foxes, owls, beetles, jack rabbits, coons, and wild animals! . . . Keep out from under these feet, little bobwhites. . . . Keep the big wild hogs out of my path. Don't let none of those come running my direction. I got a long way." Under her small black-freckled hand her cane, limber as a buggy whip, would switch at the brush as if to rouse up any hiding things.

4   On she went. The woods were deep and still. The sun made the pine needles almost too bright to look at, up where the wind rocked. The cones dropped as light as feathers. Down in the hollow was the mourning dove—it was not too late for him.

5   The path ran up a hill. "Seem like there is chains about my feet, time I get this far," she said, in the voice of argument old people keep to use with themselves. "Something always take a hold of me on this hill—pleads I should stay."

6   After she got to the top she turned and gave a full, severe look behind her where she had come. "Up through pines," she said at length. "Now down through oaks."

7   Her eyes opened their widest, and she started down gently. But before she got to the bottom of the hill a bush caught her dress.

8   Her fingers were busy and intent, but her skirts were full and long, so that before she could pull them free in one place they were caught in another. It was not possible to allow the dress to tear. "I in the thorny bush," she said. "Thorns, you doing your appointed work. Never want to let folks pass, no sir. Old eyes thought you was a pretty little *green* bush."

9   Finally, trembling all over, she stood free, and after a moment dared to stoop for her cane.

10   "Sun so high!" she cried, leaning back and looking, while the thick tears went over her eyes. "The time getting all gone here."

11   At the foot of this hill was a place where a log was laid across the creek.

12   "Now comes the trial," said Phoenix.

13   Putting her right foot out, she mounted the log and shut her eyes. Lifting her skirt, leveling her cane fiercely before her, like a festival figure in some parade, she began to march across. Then she opened her eyes and she was safe on the other side.

14   "I wasn't as old as I thought," she said.

NOTE

rouse up (par. 3): startle

15   But she sat down to rest. She spread her skirts on the bank around her and folded her hands over her knees. Up above her was a tree in a pearly cloud of mistletoe. She did not dare to close her eyes, and when a little boy brought her a plate with a slice of marble-cake on it she spoke to him. "That would be acceptable," she said. But when she went to take it there was just her own hand in the air.

16   So she left that tree, and had to go through a barbed-wire fence. There she had to creep and crawl, spreading her knees and stretching her fingers like a baby trying to climb the steps. But she talked loudly to herself: she could not let her dress be torn now, so late in the day, and she could not pay for having her arm or her leg sawed off if she got caught fast where she was.

17   At last she was safe through the fence and risen up out in the clearing. Big dead trees, like black men with one arm, were standing in the purple stalks of the withered cotton field. There sat a buzzard.

18   "Who you watching?"

19   In the furrow she made her way along.

20   "Glad this not the season for bulls," she said, looking sideways, "and the good Lord made his snakes to curl up and sleep in the winter. A pleasure I don't see no two-headed snake coming around that tree, where it come once. It took a while to get by him, back in the summer."

21   She passed through the old cotton and went into a field of dead corn. It whispered and shook and was taller than her head. "Through the maze now," she said, for there was no path.

22   Then there was something tall, black, and skinny there, moving before her.

23   At first she took it for a man. It could have been a man dancing in the field. But she stood still and listened, and it did not make a sound. It was as silent as a ghost.

24   "Ghost," she said sharply, "who be you the ghost of? For I have heard of nary death close by."

25   But there was no answer—only the ragged dancing in the wind.

26   She shut her eyes, reached out her hand, and touched a sleeve. She found a coat and inside that an emptiness, cold as ice.

27   "You scarecrow," she said. Her face lighted. "I ought to be shut up for good," she said with laughter. "My senses is gone. I too old. I the oldest people I ever know. Dance, old scarecrow," she said, "while I dancing with you."

28   She kicked her foot over the furrow, and with mouth drawn down, shook her head once or twice in a little strutting way. Some husks blew down and whirled in streamers about her skirts.

29   Then she went on, parting her way from side to side with the cane, through the whispering field. At last she came to the end, to a wagon track where the silver grass blew between the red ruts. The quail were walking around like pullets, seeming all dainty and unseen.

30   "Walk pretty," she said. "This the easy place. This the easy going."

NOTE

furrow (par. 19): plowed row

31   She followed the track, swaying through the quiet bare fields, through the little strings of trees silver in their dead leaves, past cabins silver from weather, with the doors and windows boarded shut, all like old women under a spell sitting there. "I walking in their sleep," she said, nodding her head vigorously.

32   In a ravine she went where a spring was silent flowing through a hollow log. Old Phoenix bent and drank. "Sweet-gum makes the water sweet," she said, and drank more. "Nobody know who made this well, for it was here when I was born."

33   The track crossed a swampy part where the moss hung as white as lace from every limb. "Sleep on, alligators, and blow your bubbles." Then the track went into the road.

34   Deep, deep the road went down between the high green-colored banks. Overhead the live oaks met, and it was as dark as a cave.

35   A black dog with a lolling tongue came up out of the weeds by the ditch. She was meditating, and not ready, and when he came at her she only hit him a little with her cane. Over she went in the ditch, like a little puff of milkweed.

36   Down there, her senses drifted away. A dream visited her, and she reached her hand up, but nothing reached down and gave her a pull. So she lay there and presently went to talking. "Old woman," she said to herself, "that black dog come up out of the weeds to stall you off, and now there he sitting on his fine tail, smiling at you."

37   A white man finally came along and found her—a hunter, a young man, with his dog on a chain.

38   "Well, Granny!" he laughed. "What are you doing there?"

39   "Lying on my back like a June-bug waiting to be turned over, mister," she said, reaching up her hand.

40   He lifted her up, gave her a swing in the air, and set her down. "Anything broken, Granny?"

41   "No, sir, them old dead weeds is springy enough," said Phoenix, when she had got her breath. "I thank you for your trouble."

42   "Where do you live, Granny?" he asked, while the two dogs were growling at each other.

43   "Away back yonder, sir, behind the ridge. You can't even see it from here."

44   "On your way home?"

45   "No sir, I going to town."

46   "Why, that's too far! That's as far as I walk when I come out myself, and I get something for my trouble." He patted the stuffed bag he carried, and there hung down a little closed claw. It was one of the bobwhites, and its beak hooked bitterly to show it was dead. "Now you go home, Granny!"

47   "I bound to go to town, mister," said Phoenix. "The time come around."

48   He gave another laugh, filling the whole landscape. "I know you old colored people! Wouldn't miss going to town to see Santa Claus!"

NOTES

ravine (par. 32): a deep, narrow valley

a lolling tongue (par. 35): its tongue hanging out

49   But something held old Phoenix very still. The deep lines in her face went into a fierce and different radiation. Without warning, she had seen with her own eyes a flashing nickel fall out of the man's pocket onto the ground.

50   "How old are you, Granny?" he was saying.

51   "There is no telling, mister," she said, "no telling."

52   Then she gave a little cry and clapped her hands and said, "Git on away from here, dog! Look! Look at that dog!" She laughed as if in admiration. "He ain't scared of nobody. He a big black dog." She whispered, "Sic him!"

53   "Watch me get rid of that cur," said the man. "Sic him, Pete! Sic him!"

54   Phoenix heard the dogs fighting, and heard the man running and throwing sticks. She even heard a gunshot. But she was slowly bending forward by that time, further and further forward, the lids stretched down over her eyes, as if she were doing this in her sleep. Her chin was lowered almost to her knees. The yellow palm of her hand came out from the fold of her apron. Her fingers slid down and along the ground under the piece of money with the grace and care they would have in lifting an egg from under a setting hen. Then she slowly straightened up, she stood erect, and the nickel was in her apron pocket. A bird flew by. Her lips moved. "God watching me the whole time. I come to stealing."

55   The man came back, and his own dog panted about them. "Well, I scared him off that time," he said, and then he laughed and lifted his gun and pointed it at Phoenix.

56   She stood straight and faced him.

57   "Doesn't the gun scare you?" he said, still pointing it.

58   "No, sir, I seen plenty go off closer by, in my day, and for less than what I done," she said, holding utterly still.

59   He smiled, and shouldered the gun. "Well, Granny," he said, "you must be a hundred years old, and scared of nothing. I'd give you a dime if I had any money with me. But you take my advice and stay home, and nothing will happen to you."

60   "I bound to go on my way, mister," said Phoenix. She inclined her head in the red rag. Then they went in different directions, but she could hear the gun shooting again and again over the hill.

61   She walked on. The shadows hung from the oak trees to the road like curtains. Then she smelled wood-smoke, and smelled the river, and she saw a steeple and the cabins on their steep steps. Dozens of little black children whirled around her. There ahead was Natchez shining. Bells were ringing. She walked on.

62   In the paved city it was Christmas time. There were red and green electric lights strung and criss-crossed everywhere, and all turned on in the daytime. Old Phoenix would have been lost if she had not distrusted her eyesight and depended on her feet to know where to take her.

NOTES

cur (par. 53): mutt

Natchez (par. 61): a port city in Mississippi, on the banks of the Mississippi River

63   She paused quietly on the sidewalk where people were passing by. A lady came along in the crowd, carrying an armful of red-, green- and silver-wrapped presents; she gave off perfume like the red roses in hot summer, and Phoenix stopped her.

64   "Please, missy, will you lace up my shoe?" She held up her foot.

65   "What do you want, Grandma?"

66   "See my shoe," said Phoenix. "Do all right for out in the country, but wouldn't look right to go in a big building."

67   "Stand still then, Grandma" said the lady. She put her packages down on the sidewalk beside her and laced and tied both shoes tightly.

68   "Can't lace 'em with a cane," said Phoenix. "Thank you, missy. I doesn't mind asking a nice lady to tie up my shoe, when I gets out on the street."

69   Moving slowly and from side to side, she went into the big building, and into a tower of steps, where she walked up and around and around until her feet knew to stop.

70   She entered a door, and there she saw nailed up on the wall the document that had been stamped with the gold seal and framed in the gold frame, which matched the dream that was hung up in her head.

71   "Here I be," she said. There was a fixed and ceremonial stiffness over her body.

72   "A charity case, I suppose," said an attendant who sat at the desk before her.

73   But Phoenix only looked above her head. There was sweat on her face, the wrinkles in her skin shone like a bright net.

74   "Speak up, Grandma," the woman said. "What's your name? We must have your history, you know. Have you been here before? What seems to be the trouble with you?"

75   Old Phoenix only gave a twitch to her face as if a fly were bothering her.

76   "Are you deaf?" cried the attendant.

77   But then the nurse came in.

78   "Oh, that's just old Aunt Phoenix," she said. "She doesn't come for herself—she has a little grandson. She makes these trips just as regular as clockwork. She lives away back off the Old Natchez Trace." She bent down. "Well, Aunt Phoenix, why don't you just take a seat? We won't keep you standing after your long trip." She pointed.

79   The old woman sat down, bolt upright in the chair.

80   "Now, how is the boy?" asked the nurse.

81   Old Phoenix did not speak.

82   "I said, how is the boy?"

83   But Phoenix only waited and stared straight ahead, her face very solemn and withdrawn into rigidity.

84   "Is his throat any better?" asked the nurse. "Aunt Phoenix, don't you hear me? Is your grandson's throat any better since the last time you came for the medicine?"

85   With her hands on her knees, the old woman waited, silent, erect and motionless, just as if she were in armor.

86   "You mustn't take up our time this way, Aunt Phoenix," the nurse said. "Tell us quickly about your grandson, and get it over. He isn't dead, is he?"

87   At last there came a flicker and then a flame of comprehension across her face, and she spoke.

88   "My grandson. It was my memory had left me. There I sat and forgot why I made my long trip."

89   "Forgot?" the nurse frowned. "After you came so far?"

90   Then Phoenix was like an old woman begging a dignified forgiveness for waking up frightened in the night. "I never did go to school, I was too old at the Surrender," she said in a soft voice. "I'm an old woman without an education. It was my memory fail me. My little grandson, he is just the same, and I forgot it in the coming."

91   "Throat never heals, does it?" said the nurse, speaking in a loud, sure voice to old Phoenix. By now she had a card with something written on it, a little list. "Yes. Swallowed lye. When was it?—January—two–three years ago—"

92   Phoenix spoke unasked now. "No, missy, he not dead, he just the same. Every little while his throat begin to close up again, and he not able to swallow. He not get his breath. He not able to help himself. So the time come around, and I go on another trip for the soothing medicine."

93   "All right. The doctor said as long as you came to get it, you could have it," said the nurse. "But it's an obstinate case."

94   "My little grandson, he sit up there in the house all wrapped up, waiting by himself," Phoenix went on. "We is the only two left in the world. He suffer and it don't seem to put him back at all. He got a sweet look. He going to last. He wear a little patch quilt and peep out holding his mouth open like a little bird. I remembers so plain now. I not going to forget him again, no, the whole enduring time. I could tell him from all the others in creation."

95   "All right." The nurse was trying to hush her now. She brought her a bottle of medicine. "Charity," she said, making a check mark in a book.

96   Old Phoenix held the bottle close to her eyes, and then carefully put it into her pocket.

97   "I thank you," she said.

98   "It's Christmas time, Grandma," said the attendant. "Could I give you a few pennies out of my purse?"

99   "Five pennies is a nickel," said Phoenix stiffly.

100   "Here's a nickel," said the attendant.

101   Phoenix rose carefully and held out her hand. She received the nickel and then fished the other nickel out of her pocket and laid it beside the new one. She stared at her palm closely, with her head on one side.

102   Then she gave a tap with her cane on the floor.

103   "This is what come to me to do," she said. "I going to the store and buy my child a little windmill they sells, made out of paper. He going to find it hard to believe there such a thing in the world. I'll march myself back where he waiting, holding it straight up in this hand."

104   She lifted her free hand, gave a little nod, turned around, and walked out of the doctor's office. Then her slow step began on the stairs, going down.

NOTES

the Surrender (par. 90): The April 9, 1865 surrender of the South to the North. The act officially ended the Civil War in the United States.

lye (par. 91): an acid-like substance used in making soap

obstinate (par. 93): stubborn

I Stand Here Ironing

Tillie Olsen

1   "I stand here ironing, and what you asked me moves tormented back and forth with the iron."

2   "I wish you would manage the time to come in and talk with me about your daughter. I'm sure you can help me understand her. She's a youngster who needs help and whom I'm deeply interested in helping."

3   "Who needs help. . . . " Even if I came, what good would it do? You think because I am her mother I have a key, or that in some way you could use me as a key? She has lived for nineteen years. There is all that life that has happened outside of me, beyond me.

4   And when is there time to remember, to sift, to weigh, to estimate, to total? I will start and there will be an interruption and I will have to gather it all together again. Or I will become engulfed with all I did or did not do, with what should have been and what cannot be helped.

5   She was a beautiful baby. The first and only one of our five that was beautiful at birth. You do not guess how new and uneasy her tenancy in her now-loveliness. You did not know her all those years she was thought homely, or see her poring over her baby pictures, making me tell her over and over how beautiful she had been—and would be, I would tell her—and was now, to the seeing eye. But the seeing eyes were few or non-existent. Including mine.

6   I nursed her. They feel that's important nowadays. I nursed all the children, but with her, with all the fierce rigidity of first motherhood, I did like the books then said. Though her cries battered me to trembling and my breasts ached with swollenness, I waited till the clock decreed.

7   Why do I put that first? I do not even know if it matters, or if it explains anything.

8   She was a beautiful baby. She blew shining bubbles of sound. She loved motion, loved light, loved color and music and textures. She would lie on the floor in her blue overalls patting the surface so hard in ecstasy her hands and feet would blur. She was a miracle to me, but when she was eight months old I had to leave her daytimes with the woman downstairs to whom she was no miracle at all, for I worked or looked for work and for Emily's father, who "could no longer endure" (he wrote in his good-bye note) "sharing want with us."

9   I was nineteen. It was the pre-relief, pre-WPA world of the depression. I would start running as soon as I got off the streetcar, running up the stairs, the

NOTES

engulfed (par. 4): overwhelmed

tenancy (par. 5): occupancy

ecstasy (par. 8): great joy

pre-relief (par. 9): before welfare

pre-WPA (par. 9): before Work Projects Administration, a government program that provided jobs during the 1930s

the depression (par. 9): a time of terrible economic conditions, beginning with the great stock market crash in 1929 and lasting until about 1940

place smelling sour, and awake or asleep to startle awake, when she saw me she would break into a clogged weeping that could not be comforted, a weeping I can hear yet.

10 After a while I found a job hashing at night so I could be with her days, and it was better. But it came to where I had to bring her to his family and leave her.

11 It took a long time to raise the money for her fare back. Then she got chicken pox and I had to wait longer. When she finally came, I hardly knew her, walking quick and nervous like her father, looking like her father, thin, and dressed in a shoddy red that yellowed her skin and glared at the pock-marks. All the baby loveliness gone.

12 She was two. Old enough for nursery school they said, and I did not know then what I know now—the fatigue of the long day, and the lacerations of group life in the kinds of nurseries that are only parking places for children.

13 Except that it would have made no difference if I had known. It was the only place there was. It was the only way we could be together, the only way I could hold a job.

14 And even without knowing, I knew. I knew the teacher that was evil because all these years it has curdled into my memory, the little boy hunched in the corner, her rasp, "why aren't you outside, because Alvin hits you? that's no reason, go out, scaredy." I knew Emily hated it even if she did not clutch and implore "don't go Mommy" like the other children, mornings.

15 She always had a reason why we should stay home. Momma, you look sick, Momma. I feel sick. Momma, the teachers aren't there today, they're sick. Momma, we can't go, there was a fire there last night. Momma, it's a holiday today, no school, they told me.

16 But never a direct protest, never rebellion. I think of our others in their three-, four-year-oldness—the explosions, the tempers, the denunciations, the demands—and I feel suddenly ill. I put the iron down. What in me demanded that goodness in her? And what was the cost, the cost to her of such goodness?

17 The old man living in the back once said in his gentle way: "You should smile at Emily more when you look at her." What *was* in my face when I looked at her? I loved her. There were all the acts of love.

18 It was only with others I remembered what he said, and it was the face of joy, and not of care or tightness or worry I turned to them—too late for Emily. She does not smile easily, let alone almost always as her brothers and sisters

NOTES

hashing (par. 10): cooking

shoddy (par. 11): cheap

lacerations (par. 12): literally, wounds

curdled (par. 14): literally, thickened and soured

rasp (par. 14): harsh voice

denunciations (par. 16): accusations

sombre (par. 18): serious

fluid (par. 18): full of expression

pantomimes (par. 18): acting in which the performer communicates by movements rather than by speech

rouses a laughter out of the audience (par. 18): excites from the audience

do. Her face is closed and sombre, but when she wants, how fluid. You must have seen it in her pantomimes, you spoke of her rare gift for comedy on the stage that rouses a laughter out of the audience so dear they applaud and applaud and do not want to let her go.

19   Where does it come from, that comedy? There was none of it in her when she came back to me that second time, after I had had to send her away again. She had a new daddy now to learn to love, and I think perhaps it was a better time.

20   Except when we left her alone nights, telling ourselves she was old enough.

21   "Can't you go some other time, Mommy, like tomorrow?" she would ask. "Will it be just a little while you'll be gone? Do you promise?"

22   The time we came back, the front door open, the clock on the floor in the hall. She rigid awake. "It wasn't just a little while. I didn't cry. Three times I called you, just three times, and then I ran downstairs to open the door so you could come faster. The clock talked loud. I threw it away, it scared me what it talked."

23   She said the clock talked loud again that night I went to the hospital to have Susan. She was delirious with the fever that comes before red measles, but she was fully conscious all the week I was gone and the week after we were home when she could not come near the new baby or me.

24   She did not get well. She stayed skeleton thin, not wanting to eat, and night after night she had nightmares. She would call for me, and I would rouse from exhaustion to sleepily call back: "You're all right, darling, go to sleep, it's just a dream," and if she still called, in a sterner voice, "now go to sleep, Emily, there's nothing to hurt you." Twice, only twice, when I had to get up for Susan anyhow, I went in to sit with her.

25   Now when it is too late (as if she would let me hold and comfort her like I do the others) I get up and go to her at once at her moan or restless stirring. "Are you awake, Emily? Can I get you something?" And the answer is always the same: "No, I'm all right, go back to sleep, Mother."

26   They persuaded me at the clinic to send her away to a convalescent home in the country where "she can have the kind of food and care you can't manage for her, and you'll be free to concentrate on the new baby." They still send children to that place. I see pictures on the society page of sleek young women planning affairs to raise money for it, or dancing at the affairs, or decorating Easter eggs or filling Christmas stockings for the children.

27   They never have a picture of the children so I do not know if the girls still wear those gigantic red bows and the ravaged looks on the every other Sunday when parents can come to visit "unless otherwise notified"—as we were notified the first six weeks.

28   Oh it is a handsome place, green lawns and tall trees and fluted flower beds. High up on the balconies of each cottage the children stand, the girls in

NOTES

delirious (par. 23): mentally confused

rouse (par. 24): wake up

convalescent home (par. 26): an institution where people go to rest and recover from an illness

sleek (par. 26): slender and graceful

ravaged (par. 27): defeated

their red bows and the white dresses, the boys in white suits and giant red ties. The parents stand below shrieking up to be heard and the children shriek down to be heard, and between them the invisible wall "Not to Be Contaminated by Parental Germs or Physical Affection."

29   There was a tiny girl who always stood hand in hand with Emily. Her parents never came. One visit she was gone. "They moved her to Rose Cottage," Emily shouted in explanation. "They don't like you to love anybody here."

30   She wrote once a week, the labored writing of a seven-year-old. "I am fine. How is the baby. If I write my letter nicely I will have a star. Love." There never was a star. We wrote every other day, letters she could never hold or keep but only hear read—once. "We simply do not have room for children to keep any personal possessions," they patiently explained when we pieced one Sunday's shrieking together to plead how much it would mean to Emily, who loved so to keep things, to be allowed to keep her letters and cards.

31   Each visit she looked frailer. "She isn't eating," they told us.

32   (They had runny eggs for breakfast or mush with lumps, Emily said later, I'd hold it in my mouth and not swallow. Nothing ever tasted good, just when they had chicken.)

33   It took us eight months to get her released home, and only the fact that she gained back so little of her seven lost pounds convinced the social worker.

34   I used to try to hold and love her after she came back, but her body would stay stiff, and after a while she'd push away. She ate little. Food sickened her, and I think much of life too. Oh she had physical lightness and brightness, twinkling by on skates, bouncing like a ball up and down over the jump rope, skimming over the hill; but these were momentary.

35   She fretted about her appearance, thin and dark and foreign-looking at a time when every little girl was supposed to look or thought she should look a chubby blonde replica of Shirley Temple. The doorbell sometimes rang for her, but no one seemed to come and play in the house or be a best friend. Maybe because we moved so much.

36   There was a boy she loved painfully through two school semesters. Months later she told me how she had taken pennies from my purse to buy him candy. "Licorice was his favorite and I brought him some every day, but he still liked Jennifer better'n me. Why, Mommy?" The kind of question for which there is no answer.

37   School was a worry to her. She was not glib or quick in a world where glibness and quickness were easily confused with ability to learn. To her overworked and exasperated teachers she was an overconscientious "slow learner" who kept trying to catch up and was absent entirely too often.

NOTES

labored (par. 30): showing much effort

mush (par. 32): boiled cornmeal

fretted (par. 35): worried

replica (par. 35): copy

glib (par. 37): quick with words

exasperated (par. 37): frustrated

overconscientious (par. 37): overly dedicated

38   I let her be absent, though sometimes the illness was imaginary. How different from my now-strictness about attendance with the others. I wasn't working. We had a new baby, I was home anyhow. Sometimes, after Susan grew old enough, I would keep her home from school, too, to have them all together.

39   Mostly Emily had asthma, and her breathing, harsh and labored, would fill the house with a curiously tranquil sound. I would bring the two old dresser mirrors and her boxes of collections to her bed. She would select beads and single earrings, bottle tops and shells, dried flowers and pebbles, old postcards and scraps, all sorts of oddments; then she and Susan would play Kingdom, setting up landscapes and furniture, peopling them with action.

40   Those were the only times of peaceful companionship between her and Susan. I have edged away from it, that poisonous feeling between them, that terrible balancing of hurts and needs I had to do between the two, and did so badly, those earlier years.

41   Oh there are conflicts between the others too, each one human, needing, demanding, hurting, taking—but only between Emily and Susan, no, Emily toward Susan that corroding resentment. It seems so obvious on the surface, yet it is not obvious. Susan, the second child, Susan, golden- and curly-haired and chubby, quick and articulate and assured, everything in appearance and manner Emily was not; Susan, not able to resist Emily's precious things, losing or sometimes clumsily breaking them: Susan telling jokes and riddles to company for applause while Emily sat silent (to say to me later: that was *my* riddle, Mother. I told it to Susan); Susan, who for all the five years' difference in age was just a year behind Emily in developing physically.

42   I am glad for that slow physical development that widened the difference between her and her contemporaries, though she suffered over it. She was too vulnerable for that terrible world of youthful competition, of preening and parading, of constant measuring of yourself against every other, of envy, "If I had that copper hair," "If I had that skin. . . . " She tormented herself enough about not looking like the others, there was enough of the unsureness, the having to be conscious of words before you speak, the constant caring—what are they thinking of me? without having it all magnified by the merciless physical drives.

43   Ronnie is calling. He is wet and I change him. It is rare there is such a cry now. That time of motherhood is almost behind me when the ear is not one's own but must always be racked and listening for the child cry, the child call. We sit for a while and I hold him, looking out over the city spread in charcoal with its soft aisles of light. "*Shoogily*," he breathes and curls closer. I carry him back to bed, asleep. *Shoogily*. A funny word, a family word, inherited from Emily, invented by her to say: *comfort*.

NOTES

tranquil (par. 39): peaceful
corroding (par. 41): destructive
articulate (par. 41): good with words
vulnerable (par. 42): defenseless
preening (par. 42): primping
racked (par. 43): strained

44   In this and other ways she leaves her seal, I say aloud. And startle at my saying it. What do I mean? What did I start to gather together, to try and make coherent? I was at the terrible, growing years. War years. I do not remember them well. I was working, there were four smaller ones now, there was not time for her. She had to help be a mother, and housekeeper, and shopper. She had to set her seal. Mornings of crisis and near hysteria trying to get lunches packed, hair combed, coats and shoes found, everyone to school or Child Care on time, the baby ready for transportation. And always the paper scribbled on by a smaller one, the book looked at by Susan then mislaid, the homework not done. Running out to that huge school where she was one, she was lost, she was a drop; suffering over the unpreparedness, stammering and unsure in her classes.

45   There was so little time left at night after the kids were bedded down. She would struggle over books, always eating (it was those years she developed her enormous appetite that is legendary in our family) and I would be ironing, or preparing food for the next day, or writing V-mail to Bill, or tending the baby. Sometimes, to make me laugh, or out of her despair, she would imitate happenings or types at school.

46   I think I said once: "Why don't you do something like this in the school amateur show?" One morning she phoned me at work, hardly understandable through the weeping: "Mother, I did it. I won, I won; they gave me first prize; they clapped and clapped and wouldn't let me go."

47   Now suddenly she was Somebody, and as imprisoned in her difference as she had been in anonymity.

48   She began to be asked to perform at other high schools, even in colleges, then at city and statewide affairs. The first one we went to, I only recognized her that first moment when thin, shy, she almost drowned herself into the curtains. Then: Was this Emily? The control, the command, the convulsing and deadly clowning, the spell, then the roaring, stamping audience, unwilling to let this rare and precious laughter out of their lives.

49   Afterwards: You ought to do something about her with a gift like that—but without money or knowing how, what does one do? We have left it all to her, and the gift has as often eddied inside, clogged and clotted, as been used and growing.

50   She is coming. She runs up the stairs two at a time with her light graceful step, and I know she is happy tonight. Whatever it was that occasioned your call did not happen today.

51   "Aren't you ever going to finish the ironing, Mother? Whistler painted his mother in a rocker. I'd have to paint mine standing over an ironing board."

NOTES

coherent (par. 44): understandable

hysteria (par. 44): panic

V-mail (par. 45): Victory mail—the name given to mail sent to soldiers during World War II

anonymity (par. 47): state of being unknown

convulsing (par. 48): laughable

occasioned (par. 50): caused

Whistler (par. 51): James Abbot Whistler (1834–1903), American painter

icebox (par. 51): refrigerator

This is one of her communicative nights and she tells me everything and nothing as she fixes herself a plate of food out of the icebox.

52   She is so lovely. Why did you want me to come in at all? Why were you concerned? She will find her way.

53   She starts up the stairs to bed. "Don't get me up with the rest in the morning." "But I thought you were having midterms." "Oh, those," she comes back in, kisses me, and says lightly, "in a couple of years when we'll all be atom-dead they won't matter a bit."

54   She has said it before. She *believes* it. But because I have been dredging the past, and all that compounds a human being is so heavy and meaningful in me, I cannot endure it tonight.

55   I will never total it all. I will never come in to say: She was a child seldom smiled at. Her father left me before she was a year old. I had to work her first six years when there was work, or I sent her home and to his relatives. There were years she had care she hated. She was dark and thin and foreign-looking in a world where the prestige went to blondeness and curly hair and dimples, she was slow where glibness was prized. She was a child of anxious, not proud, love. We were poor and could not afford for her the soil of easy growth. I was a young mother, I was a distracted mother. There were the other children pushing up, demanding. Her younger sister seemed all that she was not. There were years she did not want me to touch her. She kept too much in herself, her life was such she had to keep too much in herself. My wisdom came too late. She has much to her and probably little will come of it. She is a child of her age, of depression, of war, of fear.

56   Let her be. So all that is in her will not bloom—but in how many does it? There is still enough left to live by. Only help her to know—help make it so there is cause for her to know—that she is more than this dress on the ironing board, helpless before the iron.

NOTES

dredging (par. 54): digging up
anxious (par. 55): nervous, worried
distracted (par. 55): distressed

The Fat Girl

Andre Dubus

1   Her name was Louise. Once when she was sixteen a boy kissed her at a barbecue; he was drunk and he jammed his tongue into her mouth and ran his hands up and down her hips. Her father kissed her often. He was thin and kind and she could see in his eyes when he looked at her the lights of love and pity.

2   It started when Louise was nine. You must start watching what you eat, her mother would say. I can see you have my metabolism. Louise also had her

NOTE

metabolism (par. 2): the chemical process through which the body breaks down and uses food

mother's pale blonde hair. Her mother was slim and pretty, carried herself erectly, and ate very little. The two of them would eat bare lunches, while her older brother ate sandwiches and potato chips, and then her mother would sit smoking while Louise eyed the bread box, the pantry, the refrigerator. Wasn't that good, her mother would say. In five years you'll be in high school and if you're fat the boys won't like you; they won't ask you out. Boys were as far away as five years, and she would go to her room and wait for nearly an hour until she knew her mother was no longer thinking of her, then she would creep into the kitchen and, listening to her mother talking on the phone, or her footsteps upstairs, she would open the bread box, the pantry, the jar of peanut butter. She would put the sandwich under her shirt and go outside or to the bathroom to eat it.

3   Her father was a lawyer and made a lot of money and came home looking pale and happy. Martinis put color back in his face, and at dinner he talked to his wife and two children. Oh give her a potato, he would say to Louise's mother. She's a growing girl. Her mother's voice then became tense: If she has a potato she shouldn't have dessert. She should have both, her father would say, and he would reach over and touch Louise's cheek or hand or arm.

4   In high school she had two girl friends and at night and on weekends they rode in a car or went to movies. In movies she was fascinated by fat actresses. She wondered why they were fat. She knew why she was fat: she was fat because she was Louise. Because God had made her that way. Because she wasn't like her friends Joan and Marjorie, who drank milk shakes after school and were all bones and tight skin. But what about those actresses, with their talents, with their broad and profound faces? Did they eat as heedlessly as Bishop Humphries and his wife who sometimes came to dinner and, as Louise's mother said, gorged between amenities? Or did they try to lose weight, did they go about hungry and angry and thinking of food? She thought of them eating lean meats and salads with friends, and then going home and building strange large sandwiches with French bread. But mostly she believed they did not go through these failures; they were fat because they chose to be. And she was certain of something else too: she could see it in their faces: they did not eat secretly. Which she did: her creeping to the kitchen when she was nine became, in high school, a ritual of deceit and pleasure. She was a furtive eater of sweets. Even her two friends did not know her secret.

5   Joan was thin, gangling, and flat-chested; she was attractive enough and all she needed was someone to take a second look at her face, but the school was large and there were pretty girls in every classroom and walking all the corridors, so no one ever needed to take a second look at Joan. Marjorie was

NOTES

heedlessly (par. 4): unconcerned

gorged (par. 4): stuffed themselves

amenities (par. 4): polite conversations

furtive (par. 4): secret

gangling (par. 5): tall and awkward

untrammelled (par. 5): unrestricted

ecstatically (par. 5): overwhelmingly, joyfully

thin too, an intense, heavy-smoking girl with brittle laughter. She was very intelligent, and with boys she was shy because she knew she made them uncomfortable, and because she was smarter than they were and so could not understand or could not believe the levels they lived on. She was to have a nervous breakdown before earning her PhD. in philosophy at the University of California, where she met and married a physicist and discovered within herself an untrammelled passion: she made love with her husband on the couch, the carpet, in the bathtub, and on the washing machine. By that time much had happened to her and she never thought of Louise. Joan would finally stop growing and begin moving with grace and confidence. In college she would have two lovers and then several more during the six years she spent in Boston before marrying a middle-aged editor who had two sons in their early teens, who drank too much, who was tenderly, boyishly grateful for her love, and whose wife had been killed while rock climbing in New Hampshire with her lover. She would not think of Louise either, except in an earlier time, when lovers were still new to her and she was ecstatically surprised each time one of them loved her and, sometimes at night, lying in a man's arms, she would tell how in high school no one dated her, she had been thin and plain (she would still believe that: that she had been plain; it had never been true) and so had been forced into the weekend and nighttime company of a neurotic smart girl and a shy fat girl. She would say this with self-pity exaggerated by Scotch and her need to be more deeply loved by the man who held her.

6   She never eats, Joan and Marjorie said of Louise. They ate lunch with her at school, watched her refusing potatoes, ravioli, fried fish. Sometimes she got through the cafeteria line with only a salad. That is how they would remember her: a girl whose hapless body was destined to be fat. No one saw the sandwiches she made and took to her room when she came home from school. No one saw the store of Milky Ways, Butterfingers, Almond Joys, and Hersheys far back on her closet shelf, behind the stuffed animals of her childhood. She was not a hypocrite. When she was out of the house she truly believed she was dieting; she forgot about the candy, as a man speaking into his office dictaphone may forget the lewd photographs hidden in an old shoe in his closet. At other times, away from home, she thought of the waiting candy with near lust. One night driving home from a movie, Marjorie said: "You're lucky you don't smoke; it's incredible what I go through to hide it from my parents." Louise turned to her a smile which was elusive and mysterious; she yearned to be home in bed, eating chocolate in the dark. She did not need to smoke; she already had a vice that was insular and destructive.

7   She brought it with her to college. She thought she would leave it behind. A move from one place to another, a new room without the haunted closet

NOTES

hapless (par. 6): unfortunate

hypocrite (par. 6): a person who says one thing and does the opposite

lewd (par. 6): obscene

elusive (par. 6): deceptive

insular (par. 6): concealed

elaborate (par. 7): careful

shelf, would do for her what she could not do for herself. She packed her large dresses and went. For two weeks she was busy with registration, with shyness, with classes; then she began to feel at home. Her room was no longer like a motel. Its walls had stopped watching her, she felt they were her friends, and she gave them her secret. Away from her mother, she did not have to be as elaborate; she kept the candy in her drawer now.

8   The school was in Massachusetts, a girls' school. When she chose it, when she and her father and mother talked about it in the evenings, everyone so carefully avoided the word boys that sometimes the conversations seemed to be about nothing but boys. There are no boys there, the neuter words said; you will not have to contend with that. In her father's eyes were pity and encouragement; in her mother's was disappointment, and her voice was crisp. They spoke of courses, of small classes where Louise would get more attention. She imagined herself in those small classes; she saw herself as a teacher would see her, as the other girls would; she would get no attention.

9   The girls at the school were from wealthy families, but most of them wore the uniform of another class: blue jeans and work shirts, and many wore overalls. Louise bought some overalls, washed them until the dark blue faded, and wore them to classes. In the cafeteria she ate as she had in high school, not to lose weight nor even to sustain her lie, but because eating lightly in public had become as habitual as good manners. Everyone had to take gym, and in the locker room with the other girls, and wearing shorts on the volleyball and badminton courts, she hated her body. She liked her body most when she was unaware of it: in bed at night, as sleep gently took her out of her day, out of herself. And she liked parts of her body. She liked her brown eyes and sometimes looked at them in the mirror: they were not shallow eyes, she thought; they were indeed windows of a tender soul, a good heart. She liked her lips and nose, and her chin, finely shaped between her wide and sagging cheeks. Most of all she liked her long pale blonde hair, she liked washing and drying it and lying naked on her bed, smelling of shampoo, and feeling the soft hair at her neck and shoulders and back.

10   Her friend at college was Carrie, who was thin and wore thick glasses and often at night she cried in Louise's room. She did not know why she was crying. She was crying, she said, because she was unhappy. She could say no more. Louise said she was unhappy too, and Carrie moved in with her. One night Carrie talked for hours, sadly and bitterly, about her parents and what they did to each other. When she finished she hugged Louise and they went to bed. Then in the dark Carrie spoke across the room: "Louise? I just wanted to tell you. One night last week I woke up and smelled chocolate. You were eating chocolate, in your bed. I wish you'd eat it in front of me, Louise, whenever you feel like it."

11   Stiffened in her bed, Louise could think of nothing to say. In the silence she was afraid Carrie would think she was asleep and would tell her again in

NOTES

neuter (par. 8): literally, having neither male nor female characteristics
sustain (par. 9): maintain

the morning or tomorrow night. Finally she said Okay. Then after a moment she told Carrie if she ever wanted any she could feel free to help herself; the candy was in the top drawer. Then she said "Thank you."

12   They were roommates for four years and in the summers they exchanged letters. Each fall they greeted with embraces, laughter, tears, and moved into their old room, which had been stripped and cleansed of them for the summer. Neither girl enjoyed summer. Carrie did not like being at home because her parents did not love each other. Louise lived in a small city in Louisiana. She did not like summer because she had lost touch with Joan and Marjorie; they saw each other, but it was not the same. She liked being with her father but with no one else. The flicker of disappointment in her mother's eyes at the airport was a vanguard of the army of relatives and acquaintances who awaited her: they would see her on the streets, in stores, at the country club, in her home, and in theirs; in the first moments of greeting, their eyes would tell her she was still fat Louise, who had been fat as long as they could remember, who had gone to college and returned as fat as ever. Then their eyes dismissed her, and she longed for school and Carrie, and she wrote letters to her friend. But that saddened her too. It wasn't simply that Carrie was her only friend, and when they finished college they might never see each other again. It was that her existence in the world was so divided; it had begun when she was a child creeping to the kitchen; now that division was much sharper, and her friendship with Carrie seemed disproportionate and perilous. The world she was destined to live in had nothing to do with the intimate nights in their room at school.

13   In the summer before their senior year, Carrie fell in love. She wrote to Louise about him, but she did not write much, and this hurt Louise more than if Carrie had shown the joy her writing tried to conceal. That fall they returned to their room; they were still close and warm, Carrie still needed Louise's ears and heart at night as she spoke of her parents and her recurring malaise whose source the two friends never discovered. But on most weekends Carrie left, and caught a bus to Boston where her boyfriend studied music. During the week she often spoke hesitantly of sex; she was not sure if she liked it. But Louise, eating candy and listening, did not know whether Carrie was telling the truth or whether, as in her letters of the past summer, Carrie was keeping from her those delights she may never experience.

14   Then one Sunday night when Carrie had just returned from Boston and was unpacking her overnight bag, she looked at Louise and said: "I was thinking about you. On the bus coming home tonight." Looking at Carrie's concerned, determined face, Louise prepared herself for humiliation. "I was thinking about when we graduate. What you're going to do. What's to become of you. I want you to be loved the way I love you. Louise, if I help you, *really* help you, will you go on a diet?"

NOTES

vanguard (par. 12): literally, the troops at the head of an army
perilous (par. 12): risky
destined (par. 12): certain
intimate (par. 12): very personal
malaise (par. 13): depression

15   Louise entered a period of her life she would remember always, the way some people remember having endured poverty. Her diet did not begin the next day. Carrie told her to eat on Monday as though it were the last day of her life. So for the first time since grammar school Louise went into a school cafeteria and ate everything she wanted. At breakfast and lunch and dinner she glanced around the table to see if the other girls noticed the food on her tray. They did not. She felt there was a lesson in this, but it lay beyond her grasp. That night in their room she ate the four remaining candy bars. During the day Carrie rented a small refrigerator, bought an electric skillet, an electric broiler, and bathroom scales.

16   On Tuesday morning Louise stood on the scales, and Carrie wrote in her notebook: *October 14: 184 lbs.* Then she made Louise a cup of black coffee and scrambled one egg and sat with her while she ate. When Carrie went to the dining room for breakfast, Louise walked about the campus for thirty minutes. That was part of the plan. The campus was pretty, on its lawns grew at least one of every tree native to New England, and in the warm morning sun Louise felt a new hope. At noon they met in their room, and Carrie broiled her a piece of hamburger and served it with lettuce. Then while Carrie ate in the dining room Louise walked again. She was weak with hunger and she felt queasy. During her afternoon classes she was nervous and tense and she chewed her pencil and tapped her heels on the floor and tightened her calves. When she returned to her room late that afternoon, she was so glad to see Carrie that she embraced her; she had felt she could not bear another minute of hunger, but now with Carrie she knew she could make it at least through tonight. Then she would sleep and face tomorrow when it came. Carrie broiled her a steak and served it with lettuce. Louise studied while Carrie ate dinner, then they went for a walk.

17   That was her ritual and her diet for the rest of the year, Carrie alternating fish and chicken breasts with the steaks for dinner, and every day was nearly as bad as the first. In the evenings she was irritable. In all her life she had never been afflicted by ill temper and she looked upon it now as a demon which, along with hunger, was taking possession of her soul. Often she spoke sharply to Carrie. One night during their after-dinner walk Carrie talked sadly of night, of how darkness made her more aware of herself, and at night she did not know why she was in college, why she studied, why she was walking the earth with other people. They were standing on a wooden foot bridge looking down at a dark pond. Carrie kept talking; perhaps soon she would cry. Suddenly Louise said: "I'm sick of lettuce. I never want to see a piece of lettuce for the rest of my life. I hate it. We shouldn't even buy it, it's immoral."

18   Carrie was quiet. Louise glanced at her, and the pain and irritation in Carrie's face soothed her. Then she was ashamed. Before she could say she was sorry, Carrie turned to her and said gently: "I know. I know how terrible it is."

NOTES

queasy (par. 16): nauseated
afflicted (par. 17): troubled

19   Carrie did all the shopping, telling Louise she knew how hard it was to go into a supermarket when you were hungry. And Louise was always hungry. She drank diet soft drinks and started smoking Carrie's cigarettes, learned to enjoy inhaling, thought of cancer and emphysema but they were as far away as those boys her mother had talked about when she was nine. By Thanksgiving she was smoking over a pack a day and her weight in Carrie's notebook was one hundred and sixty-two pounds. Carrie was afraid if Louise went home at Thanksgiving she would lapse from the diet, so Louise spent the vacation with Carrie, in Philadelphia. Carrie wrote her family about the diet, and told Louise that she had. On the phone to Philadelphia, Louise said: "I feel like a bedwetter. When I was a little girl I had a friend who used to come spend the night and Mother would put a rubber sheet on the bed and we all pretended there wasn't a rubber sheet and that she hadn't wet the bed. Even me, and I slept with her." At Thanksgiving dinner she lowered her eyes as Carrie's father put two slices of white meat on her plate and passed it to her over the bowls of steaming food.

20   When she went home at Christmas she weighed a hundred and fifty-five pounds; at the airport her mother marvelled. Her father laughed and hugged her and said: "But now there's less of you to love." He was troubled by her smoking but only mentioned it once; he told her she was beautiful and, as always, his eyes bathed her with love. During the long vacation her mother cooked for her as Carrie had, and Louise returned to school weighing a hundred and forty-six pounds.

21   Flying north on the plane she warmly recalled the surprised and congratulatory eyes of her relatives and acquaintances. She had not seen Joan or Marjorie. She thought of returning home in May, weighing the hundred and fifteen pounds which Carrie had in October set as their goal. Looking toward the stoic days ahead, she felt strong. She thought of those hungry days of fall and early winter (and now: she was hungry now: with almost a frown, almost a brusque shake of the head, she refused peanuts from the stewardess): those first weeks of the diet when she was the pawn of an irascibility which still, conditioned to her ritual as she was, could at any moment take command of her. She thought of the nights of trying to sleep while her stomach growled. She thought of her addiction to cigarettes. She thought of the people at school: not one teacher, not one girl, had spoken to her about her loss of weight, not even about her absence from meals. And without warning her spirit collapsed. She did not feel strong, she did not feel she was committed to and within reach of achieving a valuable goal. She felt that somehow she had lost more than pounds of fat; that some time during her dieting she had lost herself too. She tried to remember what it had felt like to be Louise before she had started living on meat and fish, as an unhappy adult may look sadly in the memory of

NOTES

stoic (par. 21): literally, showing no reaction to pleasure or pain
brusque (par. 21): abrupt, rude
pawn (par. 21): literally, one who is controlled by another
irascibility (par. 21): anger, irritability

childhood for lost virtues and hopes. She looked down at the earth far below, and it seemed to her that her soul, like her body aboard the plane, was in some rootless flight. She neither knew its destination or where it had departed from; it was on some passage she could not even define.

22   During the next few weeks she lost weight more slowly and once for eight days Carrie's daily recording stayed at a hundred and thirty-six. Louise woke in the morning thinking of one hundred and thirty-six and then she stood on the scales and they echoed her. She became obsessed with that number, and there wasn't a day when she didn't say it aloud, and through the days and nights the number stayed in her mind, and if a teacher had spoken those digits in a classroom she would have opened her mouth to speak. What if that's me, she said to Carrie. I mean what if a hundred and thirty-six is my real weight and I just can't lose anymore. Walking hand-in-hand with her despair was a longing for this to be true, and that longing angered her and wearied her, and every day she was gloomy. On the ninth day she weighed a hundred and thirty-five and a half pounds. She was not relieved; she thought bitterly of the months ahead, the shedding of the last twenty and a half pounds.

23   On Easter Sunday, which she spent at Carrie's, she weighed one hundred and twenty pounds, and she ate one slice of glazed pineapple with her ham and lettuce. She did not enjoy it: she felt she was being friendly with a recalcitrant enemy who had once tried to destroy her. Carrie's parents were laudative. She liked them and she wished they would touch sometimes, and look at each other when they spoke. She guessed they would divorce when Carrie left home, and she vowed that her own marriage would be one of affection and tenderness. She could think about that now: marriage. At school she had read in a Boston paper that this summer the cicadas would come out of their seventeen year hibernation on Cape Cod, for a month they would mate and then die, leaving their young to burrow into the ground where they would stay for seventeen years. That's me, she had said to Carrie. Only my hibernation lasted twenty-one years.

24   Often her mother asked in letters and on the phone about the diet, but Louise answered vaguely. When she flew home in late May she weighed a hundred and thirteen pounds, and at the airport her mother cried and hugged her and said again and again: You're so beautiful. Her father blushed and bought her a martini. For days her relatives and acquaintances congratulated her, and the applause in their eyes lasted the entire summer, and she loved their eyes, and swam in the country club pool, the first time she had done this since she was a child.

25   She lived at home and ate the way her mother did and every morning she weighed herself on the scales in her bathroom. Her mother liked to take her shopping and buy her dresses and they put her old ones in the Goodwill box at the shopping center; Louise thought of them existing on the body of a poor

NOTES

recalcitrant (par. 23): difficult to control or overcome

laudative (par. 23): extremely complimentary

cicadas (par. 23): an insect

woman whose cheap meals kept her fat. Louise's mother had a photographer come to the house, and Louise posed on the couch and standing beneath a live oak and sitting in a wicker lawn chair next to an azalea bush. The new clothes and the photographer made her feel she was going to another country or becoming a citizen of a new one. In the fall she took a job of no consequence, to give herself something to do.

26   Also in the fall a young lawyer joined her father's firm, he came one night to dinner, and they started seeing each other. He was the first man outside her family to kiss her since the barbecue when she was sixteen. Louise celebrated Thanksgiving not with rice dressing and candied sweet potatoes and mince meat and pumpkin pies, but by giving Richard her virginity which she realized, at the very last moment of its existence, she had embarked on giving him over thirteen months ago, on that Tuesday in October when Carrie had made her a cup of black coffee and scrambled one egg. She wrote this to Carrie, who replied happily by return mail. She also, through glance and smile and innuendo, tried to tell her mother too. But finally she controlled that impulse, because Richard felt guilty about making love with the daughter of his partner and friend. In the spring they married. The wedding was a large one, in the Episcopal church, and Carrie flew from Boston to be maid of honor. Her parents had recently separated and she was living with the musician and was still victim of her unpredictable malaise. It overcame her on the night before the wedding, so Louise was up with her until past three and woke next morning from a sleep so heavy that she did not want to leave it.

27   Richard was a lean, tall, energetic man with the metabolism of a pencil sharpener. Louise fed him everything he wanted. He liked Italian food and she got recipes from her mother and watched him eating spaghetti with the sauce she had only tasted, and ravioli and lasagna, while she ate antipasto with her chianti. He made a lot of money and borrowed more and they bought a house whose lawn sloped down to the shore of a lake; they had a wharf and a boathouse, and Richard bought a boat and they took friends waterskiing. Richard bought her a car and they spent his vacations in Mexico, Canada, the Bahamas, and in the fifth year of their marriage they went to Europe and, according to their plan, she conceived a child in Paris. On the plane back, as she looked out the window and beyond the sparkling sea and saw her country, she felt that it was waiting for her, as her home by the lake was, and her parents, and her good friends who rode in the boat and waterskied; she thought of the accumulated warmth and pelf of her marriage, and how by slimming her body she had bought into the pleasures of the nation. She felt cunning, and she smiled to herself, and took Richard's hand.

28   But these moments of triumph were sparse. On most days she went about her routine of leisure with a sense of certainty about herself that came merely

NOTES

had embarked on (par. 26): had begun

innuendo (par. 26): suggestion

pelf (par. 27): wealth

sparse (par. 28): few

from not thinking. But there were times, with her friends, or with Richard, or alone in the house, when she was suddenly assaulted by the feeling that she had taken the wrong train and arrived at a place where no one knew her, and where she ought not to be. Often, in bed with Richard, she talked of being fat: "I was the one who started the friendship with Carrie, I chose her, I started the conversations. When I understood that she was my friend I understood something else: I had chosen her for the same reason I'd chosen Joan and Marjorie. They were all thin. I was always thinking about what people saw when they looked at me and I didn't want them to see two fat girls. When I was alone I didn't mind being fat but then I'd have to leave the house again and then I didn't want to look like me. But at home I didn't mind except when I was getting dressed to go out of the house and when Mother looked at me. But I stopped looking at her when she looked at me. And in college I felt good with Carrie; there weren't any boys and I didn't have any other friends and so when I wasn't with Carrie I thought about her and I tried to ignore the other people around me, I tried to make them not exist. A lot of the time I could do that. It was strange, and I felt like a spy."

29   If Richard was bored by her repetition he pretended not to be. But she knew the story meant very little to him. She could have been telling him of a childhood illness, or wearing braces, or a broken heart at sixteen. He could not see her as she was when she was fat. She felt as though she were trying to tell a foreign lover about her life in the United States, and if only she could command the language he would know and love all of her and she would feel complete. Some of the acquaintances of her childhood were her friends now, and even they did not seem to remember her when she was fat.

30   Now her body was growing again, and when she put on a maternity dress for the first time she shivered with fear. Richard did not smoke and he asked her, in a voice just short of demand, to stop during her pregnancy. She did. She ate carrots and celery instead of smoking, and at cocktail parties she tried to eat nothing, but after her first drink she ate nuts and cheese and crackers and dips. Always at these parties Richard had talked with his friends and she had rarely spoken to him until they drove home. But now when he noticed her at the hors d'oeuvres table he crossed the room and, smiling, led her back to his group. His smile and his hand on her arm told her he was doing his clumsy, husbandly best to help her through a time of female mystery.

31   She was gaining weight but she told herself it was only the baby, and would leave with its birth. But at other times she knew quite clearly that she was losing the discipline she had fought so hard to gain during her last year with Carrie. She was hungry now as she had been in college, and she ate between meals and after dinner and tried to eat only carrots and celery, but she grew to hate them, and her desire for sweets was as vicious as it had been long ago. At home she ate bread and jam and when she shopped for groceries she bought a candy bar and ate it driving home and put the wrapper in her purse and then in the garbage can under the sink. Her cheeks had filled out, there was loose flesh under her chin, her arms and legs were plump, and her mother was concerned. So was Richard. One night when she brought pie and milk to the living room where they were watching television, he said: "You already had a piece. At dinner."

32   She did not look at him.

33   "You're gaining weight. It's not all water, either. It's fat. It'll be summertime. You'll want to get into your bathing suit."

34   The pie was cherry. She looked at it as her fork cut through it; she speared the piece and rubbed it in the red juice on the plate before lifting it to her mouth.

35   "You never used to eat pie," he said. "I just think you ought to watch it a bit. It's going to be tough on you this summer."

36   In her seventh month, with a delight reminiscent of climbing the stairs to Richard's apartment before they were married, she returned to her world of secret gratification. She began hiding candy in her underwear drawer. She ate it during the day and at night while Richard slept, and at breakfast she was distracted, waiting for him to leave.

37   She gave birth to a son, brought him home, and nursed both him and her appetites. During this time of celibacy she enjoyed her body through her son's mouth; while he suckled she stroked his small head and back. She was hiding candy but she did not conceal her other indulgences: she was smoking again but still she ate between meals, and at dinner she ate what Richard did, and coldly he watched her, he grew petulant, and when the date marking the end of their celibacy came they let it pass. Often in the afternoons her mother visited and scolded her and Louise sat looking at the baby and said nothing until finally, to end it, she promised to diet. When her mother and father came for dinners, her father kissed her and held the baby and her mother said nothing about Louise's body, and her voice was tense. Returning from work in the evenings Richard looked at a soiled plate and glass on the table beside her chair as if detecting traces of infidelity, and at every dinner they fought.

38   "Look at you," he said. "Lasagna, for God's sake. When are you going to start? It's not simply that you haven't lost any weight. You're gaining. I can see it. I can feel it when you get in bed. Pretty soon you'll weigh more than I do and I'll be sleeping on a trampoline."

39   "You never touch me anymore."

40   "I don't want to touch you. Why should I? Have you *looked* at yourself?"

41   "You're cruel," she said. "I never knew how cruel you were."

42   She ate, watching him. He did not look at her. Glaring at his plate, he worked with fork and knife like a hurried man at a lunch counter.

43   "I bet you didn't either," she said.

44   That night when he was asleep she took a Milky Way to the bathroom. For a while she stood eating in the dark, then she turned on the light. Chewing, she looked at herself in the mirror; she looked at her eyes and hair. Then she stood on the scales and looking at the numbers between her feet, one hundred

NOTES

reminiscent of (par. 36): remindful of and similar to

gratification (par. 36): pleasure

distracted (par. 36): occupied with other thoughts

celibacy (par. 37): refraining from sexual intercourse

petulant (par. 37): irritable

infidelity (par. 37): adultery

and sixty-two, she remembered when she had weighed a hundred and thirty-six pounds for eight days. Her memory of those eight days was fond and amusing, as though she were recalling an Easter egg hunt when she was six. She stepped off the scales and pushed them under the lavatory and did not stand on them again.

45   It was summer and she bought loose dresses and when Richard took friends out on the boat she did not wear a bathing suit or shorts; her friends gave her mischievous glances, and Richard did not look at her. She stopped riding on the boat. She told them she wanted to stay with the baby, and she sat inside holding him until she heard the boat leave the wharf. Then she took him to the front lawn and walked with him in the shade of the trees and talked to him about the blue jays and mockingbirds and cardinals she saw on their branches. Sometimes she stopped and watched the boat out on the lake and the friend skiing behind it.

46   Every day Richard quarreled, and because his rage went no further than her weight and shape, she felt excluded from it, and she remained calm within layers of flesh and spirit, and watched his frustration, his impotence. He truly believed they were arguing about her weight. She knew better: she knew that beneath the argument lay the question of who Richard was. She thought of him smiling at the wheel of his boat, and long ago courting his slender girl, the daughter of his partner and friend. She thought of Carrie telling her of smelling chocolate in the dark and, after that, watching her eat it night after night. She smiled at Richard, teasing his anger.

47   He is angry now. He stands in the center of the living room, raging at her, and he wakes the baby. Beneath Richard's voice she hears the soft crying, feels it in her heart, and quietly she rises from her chair and goes upstairs to the child's room and takes him from the crib. She brings him to the living room and sits holding him in her lap, pressing him gently against the folds of fat at her waist. Now Richard is pleading with her. Louise thinks tenderly of Carrie broiling meat and fish in their room, and walking with her in the evenings. She wonders if Carrie still has the malaise. Perhaps she will come for a visit. In Louise's arms now the boy sleeps.

48   "I'll help you," Richard says. "I'll eat the same things you eat."

49   But his face does not approach the compassion and determination and love she had seen in Carrie's during what she now recognizes as the worst year of her life. She can remember nothing about that year except hunger, and the meals in her room. She is hungry now. When she puts the boy to bed she will get a candy bar from her room. She will eat it here, in front of Richard. This room will be hers soon. She considers the possibilities: all these rooms and the lawn where she can do whatever she wishes. She knows he will leave soon. It has been in his eyes all summer. She stands, using one hand to pull herself out of the chair. She carries the boy to his crib, feels him against her large breasts, feels that his sleeping body touches her soul. With a surge of vindication and

NOTES

impotence (par. 46): powerlessness

vindication (par. 49): a feeling of being right or blameless

relief she holds him. Then she kisses his forehead and places him in the crib. She goes to the bedroom and in the dark takes a bar of candy from her drawer. Slowly she descends the stairs. She knows Richard is waiting but she feels his departure so happily that, when she enters the living room, unwrapping the candy, she is surprised to see him standing there.

Life after High School

Joyce Carol Oates

1   "Sunny? Sun-ny?"

2   On that last night of March, 1959, in soiled sheepskin parka and unbuckled overshoes, but bareheaded in the lightly falling snow, Zachary Graff, eighteen years old, six feet one and a half inches tall, weight 203 pounds, IQ 160, stood beneath Sunny Burhman's second-story bedroom window, calling her name softly, urgently, as if his very life depended on it. It was nearly midnight: Sunny had been in bed for a half hour, and woke from a thin dissolving sleep to hear her name rising mysteriously out of the dark, the voice low, gravelly, repetitive as the surf. "*Sun-ny—?*" She had not spoken with Zachary Graff since the previous week, when she'd told him, quietly, tears shining in her eyes, that she did not love him; she could not accept his engagement ring, still less marry him. This was the first time in the twelve weeks of Zachary's pursuit of her that he'd dared to come to the rear of the Burhmans' house, by day or night—the first time, as Sunny would say afterward, that he'd ever appealed to her in such a way.

3   They would ask, In what way?

4   Sunny would hesitate, and say, So—emotionally. In a way that scared me.

5   So you sent him away?

6   She did. She sent him away.

7   It was much talked of at South Lebanon High School, how, in this winter of their senior year, Zachary Graff, who had never to anyone's recollection asked a girl out before, let alone pursued her so publicly and with such clumsy devotion, seemed to have fallen in love with Sunny Burhman.

8   Of all people—Sunny Burhman.

9   Odd, too, that Zachary should seem to have discovered Sunny only now, though the two had been classmates in the South Lebanon, New York, public schools since first grade.

10   Zachary, whose father was Homer Graff, the town's pre-eminent physician, had since ninth grade cultivated a clipped, mock-gallant manner when speaking

NOTES

parka (par. 2): coat with a hood

pre-eminent (par. 10): most notable

mock-gallant (par. 10): exaggeratedly courteous

Clifton Webb (par. 10): American actor (1893–1966)

impervious to (par. 10): unaffected by

giddy (par. 10): flighty

myopia (par. 10): nearsightedness

with female classmates—his Clifton Webb style. He was unfailingly courteous, but unfailingly cool, measured, formal. He seemed impervious to the giddy rise and ebb of adolescent emotion, moving, clumsy but determined, like a grizzly bear on its hind legs, through the school corridors, rarely glancing to left or right: his gaze, its myopia corrected by lenses encased in chunky black-plastic frames, was firmly fixed on the horizon. Dr. Graff's son was not so much unpopular as feared, and thus disliked.

11   If Zachary's excellent academic record continued uninterrupted through final papers and final exams, and no one suspected that it would not, Zachary would be valedictorian of the class of 1959. Barbara ("Sunny") Burhman, later to distinguish herself at Cornell, would graduate only ninth, in a class of eighty-two.

12   Zachary's attentiveness to Sunny had begun, with no warning, immediately after Christmas recess, when classes resumed in January. Suddenly, a half-dozen times a day, in Sunny's vicinity, looming large, eyeglasses glittering, there Zachary was. His Clifton Webb pose had dissolved; he was shy, stammering, yet forceful, even bold, waiting for the advantageous moment (for Sunny was always surrounded by friends) to push forward and say, "Hi, Sunny!" The greeting, utterly commonplace in content, sounded in Zachary's mouth like a Latin phrase torturously translated.

13   Sunny, so named for her really quite astonishing smile, a dazzling white Sunny-smile that transformed a girl of conventional freckled, snub-nosed prettiness into a true beauty, might have been surprised initially but gave no sign, saying "Hi, Zach!"

14   In those years the corridors of South Lebanon High School were lyric crossfires of *Hi!* and *H'lo!* and *Good to see ya!* uttered hundred of times daily by the golden girls, the popular, confident, good-looking girls—club officers, prom queens, cheerleaders like Sunny Burhman and her friends—tossed out indiscriminately, for that was the style.

15   Most of the students were in fact practicing Christians, of Lutheran, Presbyterian, and Methodist stock. Like Sunny Burhman, who was, or seemed, even at the time of this story, too good to be true. That's to say—*good*.

16   So, though Sunny soon wondered why on earth Zachary Graff was hanging around her, why, again, at her elbow, or lying in wait for her at the foot of a stairway, why, for the *n*th time that week, *him*, she was too *good* to indicate impatience or exasperation—too *good* to tell him, as her friends advised, to get lost.

17   He telephoned her too. Poor Zachary. Stammering over the phone, his voice lowered as if he were in terror of being overheard, "Is S-Sunny there, Mrs. B-Burhman? May I speak with her, please?" And Mrs. Burhman, who knew Dr. Graff and his wife, of course, since everyone in South Lebanon, population 3,800, knew everyone else or knew of them, including frequently their family histories and facts about them of which their children were entirely unaware, hesitated, and said, "Yes, I'll put her on, but I hope you won't talk

NOTES

conventional (par. 13): usual
lyric (par. 14): musical
indiscriminately (par. 14): unselectively
exasperation (par. 16): annoyance

long—Sunny has homework tonight." Or, apologetically but firmly, "No, I'm afraid she isn't here. May I take a message?"

18   "N-no message," Zachary murmured, and hurriedly hung up.

19   Sunny, standing close by, thumbnail in the just perceptible gap between her front teeth, expression crinkled in dismay, whispered, "Oh, Mom. I feel so *bad*. I just feel so—*bad*."

20   Mrs. Burhman said briskly, "You don't have time for all of them, honey."

21   Still, Zachary was not discouraged, and in time their schoolmates began to observe Sunny engaged in conversations with him—the two of them sitting alone in a corner of the cafeteria, or walking together after a meeting of the Debate Club, of which Zachary was president and Sunny a member. They were both on the staff of the South Lebanon High *Beacon* and the 1959 South Lebanon High yearbook and the South Lebanon *Torch* (the literary magazine). They were both members of the National Honor Society and the Quill & Scroll Society. Though Zachary Graff, in his aloofness and impatience with most of his peers, would be remembered as antisocial—a "loner," in fact—his record of activities, printed beneath his photograph in the yearbook, suggested that he had time, or made time, for things that mattered to him.

22   He shunned sports, however. High school sports, at least. His life's game, he informed Sunny Burhman, unaware of the solemn pomposity with which he spoke, would be *golf*. His father had been instructing him informally since his twelfth birthday.

23   Zachary said, "I have no natural talent for it, and I find it profoundly boring, but golf will be my game." And he pushed his chunky black glasses roughly against the bridge of his nose, something he did countless times a day, as if they were in danger of sliding off.

24   Zachary Graff had such a physical presence that few of his contemporaries would have described him as unattractive, still less as homely. His head appeared oversized, even for his massive body; his eyes were deep-set, with a look of watchfulness and secrecy; his skin was tallow-colored and blemished in wavering patches like topographical maps. His big teeth glinted with filaments of silver, and his breath, oddly for one whose father was a doctor, was stale, musty—not that Sunny Burhman ever mentioned this fact to others.

25   Her friends began to ask, a bit jealously, reproachfully, "What do you two talk about so much—you and *him*?" and Sunny replied, taking care not to hint with the slightest movement of her eyebrows, or rolling of her eyes, that, yes, she found the situation peculiar too, "Oh—Zachary and I talk about all kinds of things. *He*

NOTES

dismay (par. 19): distress

aloofness (par. 21): indifference toward

antisocial (par. 21): not sociable

shunned (par. 22): purposely avoided

pomposity (par. 22): self-importance

contemporaries (par. 24): peers

tallow (par. 24): hard animal fat used to make candles and soap

topographical maps (par. 24): maps that show the surface features (such as elevation) of a place or region

filaments (par. 24): threads

reproachfully (par. 25): disapprovingly

talks, mainly. He's brilliant. He's" —pausing, her forehead delicately crinkling in thought, her lovely brown eyes for a moment clouded— "well, *brilliant.*"

26   In fact, at first Zachary spoke, in his intense, obsessive way, of impersonal subjects: the meaning of life, the future of Earth, whether science or art best satisfies the human hunger for self-expression. He said, laughing nervously, fixing Sunny with his bold stare, "Just to pose certain questions is, I guess, to show your hope that they can be answered."

27   Early on, Zachary seemed to have understood that if he expressed doubt about "whether God exists," and so forth, Sunny Burhman would listen seriously, and would talk with him earnestly, with the air of a nurse giving a transfusion to a patient in danger of expiring from loss of blood. She was not a religious fanatic but she *was* a devout Christian; the Burhmans were members of the First Presbyterian Church of South Lebanon, and Sunny was president of her youth group and, among other good deeds, did YWCA volunteer work on Saturday afternoons; she had not the slightest doubt that Jesus Christ—that is to say, His spirit—dwelled in her heart, and that simply by speaking the truth of what she believed, she could convince others.

28   Though one day soon Sunny would examine her beliefs, and question the faith into which she'd been born, she had not yet done so. She was a virgin, and virginal in all, or most, of her thoughts.

29   Sometimes, behind her back, even by friends, Sunny was laughed at, gently— never ridiculed, for no one would ridicule Sunny.

30   When popular Chuck Crueller, a quarterback for the South Lebanon varsity football team, was injured during a game and carried off by ambulance to undergo emergency surgery, Sunny mobilized the other cheerleaders, tears fierce in her eyes: "We can do it for Chuck—we can *pray.*" And so the eight girls in their short-skirted crimson jumpers and starched white cotton blouses had gripped one another's hands tightly, and weeping, on the verge of hysteria, had prayed, prayed, *prayed*—hidden away in the depths of the girls' locker room for hours. Sunny had led the prayers, and Chuck Crueller had recovered.

31   So you wouldn't ridicule Sunny Burhman. Somehow it wouldn't be appropriate.

32   As her classmate Tobias Shanks wrote of her, in his function as literary editor of the 1959 South Lebanon literary yearbook: "*Sunny Burhman!—an all-American girl too good to be true who is nonetheless TRUE!*"

33   If Tobias Shanks's praise obscured a slyly mocking tone, a hint that such goodness was predictable and superficial, perhaps of no genuine merit, the

---

NOTES

giving a transfusion (par. 27): putting blood into the bloodstream

expiring (par. 27): dying

fanatic (par. 27): extremist

devout (par. 27): faithful, sincere

mobilized (par. 30): assembled and motivated

hysteria (par. 30): an uncontrollable outburst of emotion

obscured (par. 33): concealed

slyly mocking (par. 33): secretly scornful

superficial (par. 33): shallow

merit (par. 33): worth

caption, mere print, beneath Sunny's dazzlingly beautiful photograph conveyed nothing but admiration and affection.

34   Surprisingly, for all his pose of skepticism and superiority, Zachary Graff, too, was a Christian. He'd been baptized Lutheran, and never failed to attend Sunday services with his parents at the First Lutheran Church. Amid the congregation of somber, somnambulant worshippers, Zachary Graff's frowning young face, the set of his beefy shoulders, drew the minister's uneasy eye; some parishioners murmured of Dr. Graff's precocious son, in retrospect, that he'd been perhaps too *serious*.

35   Before falling in love with Sunny Burhman, and discussing his religious doubts with her, Zachary had often discussed them with Tobias Shanks, who'd been his friend, you might say his only friend, since seventh grade. (But only sporadically since seventh grade, because the boys, each highly intelligent and inclined to impatience and sarcasm, got on each other's nerves.) Once, Zachary confided in Tobias that he prayed every morning of his life. Immediately upon waking he scrambled out of bed, knelt, hid his face in his hands, and prayed—for his sinful soul, for his sinful thoughts, deeds, desires. He lacerated his soul the way he'd been taught by his mother to tug a fine-toothed steel comb through his coarse, oily hair: never less than once a day.

36   Tobias Shanks, a self-proclaimed agnostic since the age of fourteen, laughed and asked derisively, "Yes, but what do you pray *for*, exactly?" Zachary had thought a bit and said, not ironically, but altogether seriously, "To get through the day. Doesn't everyone?"

37   Zachary's parents urged him to go to Muhlenberg College, which was church-affiliated; Zachary hoped to go elsewhere. He said humbly to Sunny Burhman, "If you go to Cornell, Sunny, I—maybe I'll go there too?"

38   Sunny hesitated and then smiled. "Oh. That would be nice."

39   "You wouldn't mind, Sunny?"

40   "Why would I *mind*, Zachary?" Sunny laughed, to hide her impatience. They were headed for Zachary's car, parked just up the hill from the YM-YWCA building. It was a gusty Saturday afternoon in early March. Leaving the YWCA, Sunny had seen Zachary Graff standing at the curb as if accidentally, his hands in the pockets of his sheepskin parka, his head lowered but his eyes nervously alert.

41   She couldn't avoid him, and so had to allow him to drive her home. She was beginning to feel panic, however, like darting tongues of flame, at the prospect of Zachary Graff always *there*.

NOTES

skepticism (par. 34): doubt

somnambulant (par. 34): sleepwalking

precocious (par. 34): gifted

in retrospect (par. 34): looking back (in time)

sporadically (par. 35): irregularly

lacerated (par. 35): distressed

agnostic (par. 36): one who neither believes nor disbelieves in the existence of God, maintaining that one cannot *know* whether or not God exists

derisively (par. 36): scornfully

prospect (par. 41): possibility

42   Tell the creep to get lost, her friends counseled. Even her nice friends were unsentimental about Zachary Graff.

43   Until sixth grade Sunny had been plain little Barbara Burhman. Then, one day, her teacher had said to all the class, in one of those moments of inspiration that can alter, by whim, the course of an entire life, "Tell you what, boys and girls: let's call Barbara 'Sunny' from now on—that's what she *is*."

44   Ever afterward in South Lebanon she was "Sunny" Burhman. Plain little Barbara had been left behind, seemingly forever.

45   So of course Sunny could not tell Zachary Graff to get lost. Such words were not part of her vocabulary.

46   Zachary owned a plum-colored 1956 Plymouth, which other boys envied—why should Zachary, of all people, have his own car, when so few of them, who loved cars, did? But Zachary was oblivious of their resentment, as, in a way, he seemed oblivious of his own good fortune. He drove the car as if it were an adult duty, with middle-aged fussiness and worry. Yet driving Sunny home he talked—chattered—continuously. He spoke of college and of religious "obligations" and of his parents' expectations, of medical school, the future, life—"beyond South Lebanon."

47   He asked again, in that gravelly, irksomely humble voice, if Sunny would mind if he went to Cornell. And Sunny said, trying to sound reasonable, "Zachary, it's *a free world.*"

48   Zachary said, "Oh, no, it isn't, Sunny. For some of us, it isn't."

49   This enigmatic remark Sunny was determined not to pursue.

50   Braking to a careful stop in front of the Burhman's house, Zachary said, with an almost boyish enthusiasm, "So—Cornell? In the fall? We'll both go to Cornell?"

51   Sunny was out of the car before Zachary could put on the emergency brake and come around, ceremoniously, to open her door. Gaily, recklessly, infinitely relieved to be out of his company, she called back over her shoulder, "Why not?"

52   Sunny's secret vanity must have been what linked them. For several times, gravely, Zachary had said to her, "When I'm with you, Sunny, it's possible for me to believe."

53   He meant, she thought, believe in God. In Jesus. In the life hereafter.

54   The next time Zachary maneuvered Sunny into his car, under the pretext of driving her home, he presented the startled girl with an engagement ring.

55   He'd bought the ring at Stern's Jewelers, South Lebanon's single good jewelry store, with money withdrawn from his savings account. This was his "college fund," or had been—out of the $2,245 saved, only $1,090 remained. How

NOTES

whim (par. 43): a sudden impulse

oblivious (par. 46): unaware

irksomely (par. 47): annoyingly

enigmatic (par. 49): puzzling

vanity (par. 52): pride

under the pretext (par. 54): using the excuse

astonished, upset, furious, his parents would be when they learned, Zachary hadn't allowed himself to contemplate.

56   The Graffs knew nothing about Sunny Burhman. So far as they knew, their son's frequent absences from home were nothing out of the ordinary. He'd always spent time at the public library, where his preferred reading was reference books. Sometimes he'd begin with Volume One of a set and make his way through successive volumes like a horse grazing a field, rarely glancing up, uninterested in his surroundings.

57   "Please—will you accept it?"

58   Sunny was staring incredulously at the diamond ring, which was presented to her not in Zachary's big clumsy fingers, with the dirt-edged nails, but in a plush-lined little box, as if it might be more attractive that way, more like a gift. The ring was 24-carat gold and the diamond was small but distinctive, and coldly glittering. The ring was beautiful, but Sunny did not see it that way.

59   She whispered, "Oh. Zachary. Oh, *no*—there must be some misunderstanding."

60   Zachary seemed prepared for her reaction, because he said, quickly, "Will you just try it on?—see if it fits?"

61   Sunny shook her head. No, she couldn't.

62   "They'll take it back to adjust it, if it's too big," Zachary said. "They promised."

63   "Zachary, no," Sunny said gently. "I'm so sorry." Tears flooded her eyes and spilled over onto her cheeks.

64   Zachary was saying eagerly, his lips flecked with spittle, "I realize you don't l-love me, Sunny, at least not yet, but—you could wear the ring, couldn't you? Just wear it?" He continued to hold the little box out to her, his hand visibly shaking. "On your right hand, if you don't want to wear it on your left? Please?"

65   "Zachary, no. That's impossible."

66   "Just, you know, as a, a gift? Oh, Sunny . . ."

67   They were sitting in the plum-colored Plymouth, parked in an awkwardly public place, on Upchurch Avenue, three blocks from Sunny's house. It was 4:25 P.M., March 26, a Thursday: Zachary had lingered after school in order to drive Sunny home after choir practice. Sunny would afterward recall, with an odd haltingness, as if her memory of the episode were blurred with tears, that Zachary, as usual, had done most of the talking. He had not argued with her, nor exactly begged, but had spoken almost formally, as if setting out the basic points of his debating strategy: if Sunny did not love him, he could love enough for both; and if Sunny did not want to be "officially" engaged, she could wear his ring anyway, couldn't she?

68   It would mean so much to him, Zachary said.

69   Life or death, Zachary said.

70   Sunny closed the lid of the little box and pushed it from her, gently. She was crying, and her smooth pageboy was now disheveled. "Oh, Zachary, I'm *sorry*. I can't."

NOTES

contemplate (par. 55): consider
incredulously (par. 58): disbelieving
pageboy (par. 70): a shoulder-length hair style
disheveled (par. 70): messy

71   Sunny knelt by her bed, hid her face in her hands, and prayed.

72   Please help Zachary not to be in love with me. Please help me not to be cruel. Have mercy on us both, O God.

73   God, help him to realize he doesn't love me, doesn't know *me*.

74   Days passed, and Zachary did not call.

75   Sunny Burhman was not a girl of secrets. She was not a girl of stealth. Still, though she had confided in her mother all her life, she did not tell her mother about Zachary's desperate proposal; perhaps, flattered, she did not see it as desperate. She reasoned that if she told either of her parents, they would telephone Zachary's parents immediately. I can't betray him, she thought.

76   Nor did she tell her closest girl friends, or the boy she was seeing most frequently at the time, knowing that the account would turn comical in the telling, that she and her listeners would collapse into laughter, and this, too, would be a betrayal of Zachary.

77   She happened to see Tobias Shanks one day looking oddly at her. Sunny knew that he was, or had been, a friend of Zachary Graff's; she wondered if Zachary confided in him, yet she made no effort to speak with him. He didn't like her, she sensed.

78   No, Sunny didn't tell anyone about Zachary and the engagement ring. Of all sins, she thought, betrayal is surely the worst.

79   "Sunny? Sun-ny?"

80   She did not believe she had been sleeping, but the low, persistent, gravelly sound of Zachary's voice penetrated her consciousness like a dream voice, felt, not heard.

81   She got out of bed and crouched at her window without turning on the light. She saw, to her horror, Zachary down below, standing in the shrubbery, his large head uplifted, face round like the moon, and shadowed like the moon's face. Blossom-like clumps of snow had fallen on the boy's broad shoulders, in his matted hair. Sighting her, he began to wave excitedly, like an impatient child.

82   "Oh. Zachary. My God."

83   In haste, fumbling, she put on a bulky-knit ski sweater over her flannel nightgown, kicked on bedroom slippers, hurried downstairs. The house was already dark; the Burhmans were in the habit of going to bed early. Sunny's hope was that she could send Zachary away without her parents' knowing he was there. Even in her distress she was not thinking of the trouble Zachary might make for her: she was thinking of the trouble he might make for himself.

84   Yet as soon as she saw him close up, she realized that something was gravely wrong. Here was Zachary Graff—yet not Zachary.

85   He told her he had to talk with her, and he had to talk with her now. His car was parked in the alley, he said.

86   He made a gesture as if to take her hand, but Sunny drew back. He loomed over her, his breath steaming. She could not see his eyes.

NOTES

stealth (par. 75): sneakiness
betray him (par. 75): reveal his secret
loomed (par. 86): towered

87   She said no, she couldn't go with him. She said he must go home, at once, before her parents woke up.

88   He said he couldn't leave without her, he had to talk with her. The raw urgency, the forcefulness in him, Sunny had never seen before, and she was frightened.

89   She said no. He said yes.

90   He reached again for her hand, this time taking hold of her wrist.

91   His fingers were strong.

92   "I told you, I can love enough for both!"

93   Sunny stared up at him, for an instant mute, paralyzed, seeing not Zachary Graff's eyes but the lenses of his glasses, which appeared in the semi-dark, opaque. Large snowflakes were falling languidly through the still night air. Sunny saw Zachary Graff's face, which was pale and clenched as a muscle, and she heard his voice, which was the voice of a stranger, and she felt him tug at her so roughly that her arm was strained in its very socket, and she cried, "No! No! Go away! No!" The spell was broken; the boy gaped at her another moment and then released her, turned, and ran.

94   No more than two or three minutes had passed, yet afterward Sunny would recall the encounter as if it had lasted a very long time, like a scene in a protracted and repetitive nightmare.

95   That was the last time Sunny Burhman saw Zachary Graff alive.

96   Next morning all of South Lebanon talked about the death of Dr. Graff's son, Zachary: he'd committed suicide by parking his car in a garage behind an unoccupied house on Upchurch Avenue, and letting the motor run until the gas tank was empty. Death was diagnosed as the result of carbon monoxide poisoning, the time estimated at approximately 4:30 A.M., April 1, 1959.

97   Was the date deliberate? Zachary had left only a single note behind, printed in firm block letters and taped to the outside of the car windshield:

April Fool's Day 1959

> *To Whom It May (Or May Not) Concern:*
> *I, Zachary A. Graff, being of sound mind & body, do hereby declare that I have taken my own life of my own free will & I hereby declare all others guiltless as they are ignorant of the death of the aforementioned & the life.*

ZACHARY A. GRAFF

98   Police officers, called to the scene at 7:45 A.M., reported finding Zachary lifeless, stripped to his underwear, in the rear seat of the car. The sheepskin parka was oddly draped over the steering wheel, and the interior of the car was littered with numerous items: a Bible, several high school textbooks, a pizza carton and some uneaten crusts of pizza, several empty Pepsi bottles, an empty bag of M&M candies, a pair of unlaced gym shoes (size 11), a ten-foot

NOTES

mute (par. 93): unable to speak

opaque (par. 93): cloudy, not clear

languidly (par. 93): listlessly, lazily

gaped (par. 93): stared in openmouthed amazement

protracted (par. 94): long, drawn-out

length of clothesline (in the glove compartment), and a diamond ring in its plush-lined box from Stern's Jewelers (in a pocket of the parka).

99   Sunny Burhman heard the news of Zachary's suicide before leaving for school that morning, when a friend telephoned. Within earshot of both her astonished parents, Sunny burst into tears and sobbed, "Oh, my God—it's my fault."

100   The consensus in South Lebanon, following the police investigation and much public speculation, proved to be not that it was Sunny Burhman's fault, exactly, not that the girl was to blame, exactly, but that, yes, poor Zachary Graff, the doctor's son, had killed himself in despondency over her, over her refusal of his engagement ring, her rejection of his love.

101   That was the final season of her life as "Sunny" Burhman.

102   She was out of school for a full week following Zachary's death, and when she returned, conspicuously paler, more subdued, in all ways less sunny, she did not speak of the tragedy, even with her closest friends; nor did anyone else bring up the subject. She withdrew her name from balloting for senior-prom queen, she withdrew from her part in the senior play, she dropped out of the school choir, she did not participate in the annual statewide debating competition—in which, in previous years, Zachary Graff had excelled. Following her last class of the day she went home immediately, and rarely saw her friends on weekends. Was she in mourning? Was she ashamed? Like the bearer of a deadly virus, herself unaffected, Sunny knew how, on all sides, her classmates and her teachers were regarding her: she was the girl for whose love a boy had thrown away his life; she was an unwitting agent of death.

103   Her family, of course, told her that she shouldn't blame herself, that Zachary Graff had been mentally unbalanced.

104   Even the Graffs did not blame her—or said they didn't.

105   Sunny said, "Yes. But it's my fault he's dead."

106   The Presbyterian minister, who counseled Sunny and prayed with her, assured her that Jesus surely understood, that she had not sinned—that Zachary Graff had been mentally unbalanced. And Sunny replied matter-of-factly, sadly, as if stating a self-evident truth, "Yes. But it's my fault he's dead."

107   Her older sister, Helen, later that summer, meaning only well, said exasperatedly, "Sunny, when are you going to cheer *up*?" Sunny turned on her with uncharacteristic fury and said, "Don't call me that idiotic name ever again! I want it gone!"

108   When, in the fall, she enrolled at Cornell University, she was "Barbara Burhman."

109   She remained "Barbara" for the rest of her life.

110   Barbara Burhman excelled as an undergraduate, concentrating on academic work almost exclusively; she went on to graduate school at Harvard, in

NOTES

consensus (par. 100): opinion of the majority

despondency (par. 100): despair

conspicuously (par. 102): obviously

unwitting (par. 102): unintentional

prestigious (par. 110): highly regarded

nostalgia (par. 110): longing for the past

American studies; she taught at several prestigious universities, rising rapidly through the administrative ranks before accepting a position, both highly paid and politically visible, with a well-known research foundation in Manhattan. She was the author of numerous books and articles; she was married and the mother of three children; she lectured widely; she was frequently interviewed in the popular press; she lent her name to good causes. She did not think of herself as extraordinary—in the world she now inhabited, she was surrounded by similarly active, energetic, professionally engaged men and women—except in recalling, as she sometimes did, with a mild pang of nostalgia, her old, lost self, sweet "Sunny" Burhman, of South Lebanon, New York.

111   She hadn't been queen of the senior prom. She hadn't even continued to be a Christian.

112   The irony had not escaped Barbara Burhman that in casting away his young life so recklessly, Zachary Graff had freed her for hers.

113   With the passage of time grief had lessened. Perhaps it had disappeared. After twenty, and then twenty-five, and now thirty-one years, it was difficult for Barbara, known in her adult life as an exemplar of practical sense, to feel a kinship with the adolescent girl she'd been, or with that claustrophobic high school world of the late 1950s. She'd never returned for a single high school reunion. If she thought of Zachary Graff—about whom, incidentally, she'd never told her husband of twenty-eight years—it was with the regret with which we think of remote acquaintances, lost to us by accidents of fate. Forever Zachary Graff, the most brilliant member of the class of 1959 of South Lebanon High, would remain a high school boy, trapped in his eighteenth year.

114   Of his classmates, the only other person to have acquired what might be called a national reputation was Tobias Shanks, now known as T. R. Shanks, a playwright and director of experimental drama. Barbara had followed Tobias's career with interest, and had sent him a telegram congratulating him on his most recent play, which went on to win a number of awards, dealing, as it did, with the vicissitudes of gay life in the 1980s. In the winter of 1990 Barbara and Tobias began to encounter each other socially; Tobias was the playwright-in-residence at Bard College, close by Hazelton-on-Hudson, where Barbara lived. At first they were strangely shy of each other, and guarded, as if, even in this neutral setting, their South Lebanon ghost selves exerted a powerful influence. The golden girl and the loner. The splendidly normal, the defiantly "odd." One night Tobias Shanks, shaking Barbara's hand, had smiled wryly and said, "It *is* Sunny, isn't it?" and Barbara, laughing nervously, hoping no one had overheard, said, "No, in fact it isn't. It's Barbara."

115   They looked at each other, mildly dazed. For one saw a small-boned but solidly built man of youthful middle age, sweet-faced, yet with ironic, pouched eyes, thinning gray hair, and a close-trimmed gray beard; the other

NOTES

exemplar (par. 113): ideal example

kinship (par. 113): connection

claustrophobic (par. 113): confining, inhibiting

vicissitudes (par. 114): changing conditions

impeccably (par. 115): perfectly

saw a woman of youthful middle age, striking in appearance, impeccably groomed, with fading hair of no distinctive color, and faint, white, puckering lines at the edges of her eyes. Their ghost selves *were* there—not aged, or not aged merely, but transformed, as the genes of one generation are transformed by the next.

116   Tobias stared at Barbara for a long moment, as if unable to speak. Finally he said, "I have something to tell you, Barbara. When can we meet?"

117   Tobias Shanks handed the much-folded letter across the table to Barbara, and watched as she opened it and read it with an expression of increasing astonishment and wonder.

118   "*He* wrote this? Zachary? To you?"

119   "He did."

120   "And you—? Did you—?"

121   Tobias shook his head.

122   His expression was carefully neutral, but his eyes swam suddenly with tears.

123   "We'd been friends, very close friends, for years. Each other's only friend, most of the time. The way kids that age can be, in certain restricted environments—kids who aren't what's called 'average' or 'normal.' We talked a good deal about religion—Zachary was afraid of hell. We both liked science fiction. We both had very strict parents. I suppose I might have been attracted to Zachary at times—I knew I was attracted to other guys—but of course I never acted on it; I wouldn't have dared. Almost no one dared, in those days." He laughed, with a mild shudder. He passed a hand over his eyes. "I couldn't have *loved* Zachary Graff, as he claimed he loved me, because—I couldn't. But I could have allowed him to know that he wasn't sick, crazy, 'perverted,' as he called himself in that letter." He paused. For a long, painful moment Barbara thought he wasn't going to continue. Then he said, with that same mirthless, shuddering laugh, "I could have made him feel less lonely. But I didn't. I failed him. My only friend."

124   Barbara had taken out a tissue and was dabbing at her eyes.

125   She felt as if she'd been dealt a blow so hard she could not gauge how she'd been hurt—or if she'd been hurt at all.

126   She said, "Then he never really loved a 'Sunny'—she was an illusion."

127   Tobias said thoughtfully, "I don't know. I suppose so. I got a sense, at least as I saw it at the time, that, yes, he'd chosen you, decided on you."

128   "As a symbol."

129   "Not just as a symbol. We all adored you—we were all a little in love with you." Tobias laughed, embarrassed. "Even me."

130   "I wish you had come to me and told me, back then. After—it happened."

131   "I was too frightened. I was terrified of being exposed, and, maybe, doing to myself what he'd done to himself. Suicide is so very attractive to adolescents."

NOTES

mirthless (par. 123): unhappy
gauge (par. 125): judge
illusion (par. 126): fantasy

Tobias paused, and reached over to touch Barbara's hand. His fingertips were cold. "I'm not proud of myself, Barbara, and I've tried to deal with it in my writing, but—that's how I was, back then." Again he paused. He pressed a little harder against Barbara's hand. "Another thing—after Zachary went to you that night, he came to me."

132   "To you?"

133   "To me."

134   "And—?"

135   "And I refused to go with him too. I was furious with him for coming to the house like that, risking my parents' discovering us. I guess I got a little hysterical. And he fled."

136   "He fled."

137   "Then, afterward, I just couldn't bring myself to come forward. Why I saved that letter, I don't know—I'd thrown away some others that were less incriminating. I suppose I figured—no one knew about me, everyone knew about you. 'Sunny' Burhman."

138   They ordered two more drinks—they'd forgotten their surroundings—and they talked.

139   After an hour or so Barbara leaned across the table, as at one of her professional meetings, and asked, in a tone of intellectual curiosity, "What do you think Zachary planned to do with the clothesline?"

Islands on the Moon

Barbara Kingsolver

1   Annemarie's mother, Magda, is one of a kind. She wears sandals and one-hundred-percent cotton dresses and walks like she's crossing plowed ground. She makes necklaces from the lacquered vertebrae of nonendangered species. Her hair is wavy and long and threaded with gray. She's forty-four.

2   Annemarie has always believed that if life had turned out better her mother would have been an artist. As it is, Magda just has to ooze out a little bit of art in everything she does, so that no part of her life is exactly normal. She paints landscapes on her teakettles, for example, and dates younger men. Annemarie's theory is that everyone has some big thing, the rock in their road, that has kept them from greatness or so they would like to think. Magda had Annemarie when she was sixteen and has been standing on tiptoe ever since to see over or around her difficult daughter to whatever is on the other side. Annemarie just assumed that she was the rock in her mother's road. Until now. Now she has no idea.

3   On the morning Magda's big news arrived in the mail, Annemarie handed it over to her son Leon without even reading it, thinking it was just one of her standard cards. "Another magic message from Grandma Magda," she'd said, and Leon had rolled his eyes. He's nine years old, but that's only part of it. Annemarie influences him, telling my-most-embarrassing-moment stories about growing up with a mother like Magda, and Leon buys them wholesale, right along with nine-times-nine and the capital of Wyoming.

4   For example, Magda has always sent out winter solstice cards of her own design, printed on paper she makes by boiling down tree bark and weeds. The neighbors always smell it, and once, when Annemarie was a teenager, they reported Magda as a nuisance.

5   But it's April now so this isn't a solstice card. It's not homemade, either. It came from one of those stores where you can buy a personalized astrology chart for a baby gift. The paper is yellowed and smells of incense. Leon holds it to his nose, then turns it in his hands, not trying to decipher Magda's slanty handwriting but studying the ink drawing that runs around the border. Leon has curly black hair, like Magda's—and like Annemarie's would be, if she didn't continually crop it and bleach it and wax it into spikes. But Leon doesn't care who he looks like. He's entirely unconscious of himself as he sits there, ears sticking out, heels banging the stool at the kitchen counter. One of Annemarie's cats rubs the length of its spine along his green hightop sneaker.

6   "It looks like those paper dolls that come out all together, holding hands," he says. "Only they're fattish, like old ladies. Dancing."

7   "That's about what I'd decided," says Annemarie.

8   Leon hands the card back and heads for fresh air. The bang of the screen door is the closest she gets these days to a good-bye kiss.

9   Where, in a world where kids play with Masters of the Universe, has Leon encountered holding-hands paper dolls? This is what disturbs Annemarie. Her son is normal in every obvious way but has a freakish awareness of old-fashioned things. He collects things: old Coke bottles, license-plate slogans, anything. They'll be driving down Broadway and he'll call out "Illinois Land of Lincoln!" And he saves string. Annemarie found it in a ball, rolled into a sweatsock. It's as if some whole piece of Magda has come through to Leon without even touching her.

10   She reads the card and stares at the design, numb, trying to see what these little fat dancing women have to be happy about. She and her mother haven't spoken for months, although either one can see the other's mobile home when she steps out on the porch to shake the dust mop. Magda says she's willing to wait until Annemarie stops emitting negative energy toward her. In the meantime she sends cards.

11   Annemarie is suddenly stricken, as she often is, with the feeling she's about to be abandoned. Leon will take Magda's side. He'll think this new project of hers is great, and mine's awful. Magda always wins without looking like she was trying.

12   Annemarie stands at the kitchen sink staring out the window at her neighbor's porch, which is twined with queen's wreath and dusty honeysuckle, a stalwart oasis in the desert of the trailer court. A plaster Virgin Mary, painted in blue and rose and the type of cheap, shiny gold that chips easily, presides

NOTES

solstice (par. 4): Either of the two times a year when the sun, at its highest point, is furthest from the equator. In the northern half of the earth, the winter solstice, the shortest day of the year, occurs about December 22; the summer solstice, the longest day of the year, about June 21.

emitting (par. 10): sending out

stalwart (par. 12): hardy

over the barbecue pit, and three lawn chairs with faded webbing are drawn up close around it as if for some secret family ceremony. A wooden sign hanging from the porch awning proclaims that they are "Navarrete's" over there. Their grandson, who lives with them, made the sign in Boy Scouts. Ten years Annemarie has been trying to get out of this trailer court, and the people next door are so content with themselves they hang out a shingle.

13   Before she knows it she's crying, wiping her face with the backs of her dishpan hands. This is completely normal. All morning she sat by herself watching nothing in particular on TV, and cried when Luis and Maria got married on *Sesame Street*. It's the hormones. She hasn't told him yet, but she's going to have another child besides Leon. The big news in Magda's card is that she is going to have another child too, besides Annemarie.

14   When she tries to be reasonable—and she is trying at the moment, sitting in a Denny's with her best friend Kay Kay—Annemarie knows that mid-forties isn't too old to have boyfriends. But Magda doesn't seem mid-forties, she seems like Grandma Moses in moonstone earrings. She's the type who's proud about not having to go to the store for some little thing because she can rummage around in the kitchen drawers until she finds some other thing that will serve just as well. For her fifth birthday Annemarie screamed for a Bubble-Hairdo Barbie just because she knew there wouldn't be one in the kitchen drawer.

15   Annemarie's side of the story is that she had to fight her way out of a family that smelled like an old folks' home. Her father was devoted and funny, chasing her around the house after dinner in white paper-napkin masks with eyeholes, and he could fix anything on wheels, and then without warning he turned into a wheezing old man with taut-skinned hands rattling a bottle of pills. Then he was dead, leaving behind a medicinal pall that hung over Annemarie and followed her to school. They'd saved up just enough to move to Tucson, for his lungs, and the injustice of it stung her. He'd breathed the scorched desert air for a single autumn, and Annemarie had to go on breathing it one summer after another. In New Hampshire she'd had friends, as many as the trees had leaves, but they couldn't get back there now. Magda was vague and useless, no protection from poverty. Only fathers, it seemed, offered that particular safety. Magda reminded her that the Little Women were poor too, and for all practical purposes fatherless, but Annemarie didn't care. The March girls didn't have to live in a trailer court.

16   Eventually Magda went on dates. By that time Annemarie was sneaking Marlboros and fixing her hair and hanging around by the phone, and would have given her eyeteeth for as many offers—but Magda threw them away. Even back then, she didn't get attached to men. She devoted herself instead to saving

NOTES

moonstone (par. 14): a type of stone that has a pearly appearance

rummage (par. 14): search

taut-skinned (par. 15): tight-skinned

pall (par. 15): cloud

Little Women (par. 15): *Little Women*, a novel by American author Louisa May Alcott (1832–1888), revolves around the lives of the adolescent ***March girls*** (par. 15), four sisters named Meg, Jo, Beth, and Amy.

stewardship (par. 16): literally, the management of something entrusted to one's care

every rubber band and piece of string that entered their door. Magda does the things people used to do in other centuries, before it occurred to them to pay someone else to do them. Annemarie's friends think this is wonderful. Magda is so old-fashioned she's come back into style. And she's committed. She intends to leave her life savings, if any, to Save the Planet, and tells Annemarie she should be more concerned about the stewardship of the earth. Kay Kay thinks she ought to be the president. "You want to trade?" she routinely asks. "You want my mother?"

17   "What's wrong with your mother?" Annemarie wants to know.

18   "What's wrong with my mother," Kay Kay answers, shaking her head. Everybody thinks they've got a corner on the market, thinks Annemarie.

19   Kay Kay is five feet two and has green eyes and drives a locomotive for Southern Pacific. She's had the same lover, a rock 'n' roll singer named Connie Skylab, for as long as Annemarie has known her. Kay Kay and Connie take vacations that just amaze Annemarie: they'll go skiing, or hang-gliding, or wind-surfing down in Puerto Penasco. Annemarie often wishes she could do just one brave thing in her lifetime. Like hang-gliding.

20   "Okay, here you go," says Kay Kay. "For my birthday my mother sent me one of those fold-up things you carry in your purse for covering up the toilet seat. 'Honey, you're on the go so much,' she says to me. 'And besides there's AIDS to think about now.' The guys at work think I ought to have it bronzed."

21   "At least she didn't try to *knit* you a toilet-seat cover, like Magda would," says Annemarie. "She bought it at a store, right?"

22   "Number one," Kay Kay says, "I don't carry a purse when I'm driving a train. And number two, I don't know how to tell Ma this, but the bathrooms in those engines don't even *have* a seat."

23   Annemarie and Kay Kay are having lunch. Kay Kay spends her whole life in restaurants when she isn't driving a train. She says if you're going to pull down thirty-eight thousand a year, why cook?

24   "At least you had a normal childhood," Annemarie says, taking a mirror-compact out of her purse, confirming that she looks awful, and snapping it shut. "I was the only teenager in America that couldn't use hairspray because it's death to the ozone layer."

25   "I just don't see what's so terrible about Magda caring what happens to the world," Kay Kay says.

26   "It's morbid. All those war marches she goes on. How can you think all the time about nuclear winter wiping out life as we know it, and still go on making your car payments?"

27   Kay Kay smiles.

NOTES

ozone layer (par. 24): A layer of the earth's upper atmosphere which contains a concentration of ozone, a gaseous substance that absorbs ultraviolet radiation. Certain chemical compounds that have been used in aerosol sprays (such as hairspray) destroy ozone.

morbid (par. 26): depressing

nuclear winter (par. 26): Some scientists believe that the global dust cloud created by a nuclear war would block sunlight, resulting initially in worldwide darkness and cold and ultimately in the destruction of surviving life forms.

28   "She mainly just does it to remind me what a slug I am. I didn't turn out all gung-ho like she wanted me to."

29   "That's not true," Kay Kay says. "You're very responsible, in your way. I think Magda wants a safe world for you and Leon. My mother couldn't care less if the world went to hell in a handbasket, as long as her nail color was co-ordinated with her lipstick."

30   Annemarie can never make people see. She cradles her chin mournfully in her palms. Annemarie has surprisingly fair skin for a black-haired person, which she is in principle.

31   That particular complexion, from Magda's side of the family, has dropped unaltered through the generations like a rock. They are fine-boned, too, with graceful necks and fingers that curve outward slightly at the tips. Annemarie had wished for awful things in her lifetime, even stubby fingers, something to set her apart.

32   "I got my first period," she tells Kay Kay, unable to drop the subject, "at this *die-in* she organized against the Vietnam War. I had horrible cramps and no-body paid any attention; they all thought I was just dying-in."

33   "And you're never going to forgive her," Kay Kay says. "You ought to have a T-shirt made up: 'I hate my mother because I got my first period at a die-in.'"

34   Annemarie attends to her salad, which she has no intention of eating. Two tables away, a woman in a western shirt and heavy turquoise jewelry is watching Annemarie in a maternal way over her husband's shoulder. "She just has to one-up me," says Annemarie. "Her due date is a month before mine."

35   "I can see where you'd be upset," Kay Kay says, "but she didn't know. You didn't even tell me till a month ago. It's not like she grabbed some guy off the street and said, 'Quick, knock me up so I can steal my daughter's thunder.'"

36   Annemarie doesn't like to think about Magda having sex with some guy off the street. "She should have an abortion," she says. "Childbirth is unsafe at her age."

37   "Your mother can't part with the rubber band off the Sunday paper."

38   This is true. Annemarie picks off the alfalfa sprouts, which she didn't ask for in the first place. Magda used to make her wheat-germ sandwiches, know-ing full well she despised sprouts and anything else that was recently a seed. Annemarie is crying now and there's no disguising it. She was still a kid when she had Leon, but this baby she'd intended to do on her own. With a man maybe, but not with her mother prancing around on center stage.

39   "Lots of women have babies in their forties," Kay Kay says. "Look at Goldie Hawn."

40   "Goldie Hawn isn't my mother. *And* she's married."

41   "Is the father that guy I met? Bartholomew?"

NOTES

in principle (par. 30): fundamentally

maternal (par. 34): motherly

steal . . . thunder (par. 35): To "steal someone's thunder" is to take for oneself the attention due another person.

alfalfa sprouts (par. 38): young shoots from an alfalfa seed; alfalfa is a legume (a plant of the pea and bean family)

wheat-germ (par. 38): the vitamin-filled core of the wheat kernel

42   "The father is not in the picture. That's a quote. You know Magda and men; she's not going to let the grass grow under *her* bed."

43   Kay Kay is looking down at her plate, using her knife and fork in a serious way that shows all the tendons in her hands. Kay Kay generally argues with Annemarie only if she's putting herself down. When she starts in on Magda, Kay Kay mostly just listens.

44   "Ever since Daddy died she's never looked back," Annemarie says, blinking. Her contact lenses are foundering, like skaters on a flooded rink.

45   "And you think she ought to look back?"

46   "I don't know. Yeah." She dabs at her eyes, trying not to look at the woman with the turquoise bracelets. "It bothers me. Bartholomew's in love with her. Another guy wants to marry her. All these guys are telling her how beautiful she is. And look at me, it seems like every year I'm crying over another boyfriend gone west, not even counting Leon's dad." She takes a bite of lettuce and chews on empty calories. "I'm still driving the Pontiac I bought ten years ago, but I've gone through six boyfriends and a husband. Twice. I was married to Buddy twice."

47   "Well, look at it this way, at least you've got a good car," says Kay Kay.

48   "Now that this kid's on the way he's talking about going for marriage number three. Him and Leon are in cahoots, I think."

49   "You and Buddy again?"

50   "Buddy's settled down a lot," Annemarie insists. "I think I could get him to stay home more this time." Buddy wears braids like his idol, Willie Nelson, and drives a car with flames painted on the hood. When Annemarie says he has settled down, she means that whereas he used to try to avoid work in his father's lawnmower repair shop, now he owns it.

51   "Maybe it would be good for Leon. A boy needs his dad."

52   "Oh, Leon's a rock, like me," says Annemarie. "It comes from growing up alone. When I try to do any little thing for Leon he acts like I'm the creature from the swamp. I know he'd rather live with Buddy. He'll be out the door for good one of these days."

53   "Well, you never know, it might work out with you and Buddy," Kay Kay says brightly. "Maybe third time's a charm."

54   "Oh, sure. Seems like guys want to roll through my life like the drive-in window. Probably me and Buddy'll end up going for divorce number three." She pulls a paper napkin out of the holder and openly blows her nose.

55   "Why don't you take the afternoon off?" Kay Kay suggests. "Go home and take a nap. I'll call your boss for you, and tell him you've got afternoon sickness or something."

56   Annemarie visibly shrugs off Kay Kay's concern. "Oh, I couldn't, he'd kill me. I'd better get back." Annemarie is assistant manager of a discount delivery service called "Yesterday!" and really holds the place together, though she denies it.

NOTES

foundering (par. 44): falling down

in cahoots (par. 48): secretly plotting together

57   "Well, don't get down in the dumps," says Kay Kay gently. "You've just got the baby blues."

58   "If it's not one kind of blues it's another. I can't help it. Just the sound of the word 'divorced' makes me feel like I'm dragging around a suitcase of dirty handkerchiefs."

59   Kay Kay nods.

60   "The thing that gets me about Magda is, man or no man, it's all the same to her," Annemarie explains, feeling the bitterness of this truth between her teeth like a sour apple. "When it comes to men, she doesn't even carry any luggage."

61   The woman in the turquoise bracelets stops watching Annemarie and gets up to go to the restroom. The husband, whose back is turned, waits for the bill.

62   The telephone wakes Annemarie. It's not late, only a little past seven, the sun is still up, and she's confused. She must have fallen asleep without meaning to. She is cut through with terror while she struggles to place where Leon is and remember whether he's been fed. Since his birth, falling asleep in the daytime has served up to Annemarie this momentary shock of guilt.

63   When she hears the voice on the phone and understands who it is, she stares at the receiver, thinking somehow that it's not her phone. She hasn't heard her mother's voice for such a long time.

64   "All I'm asking is for you to go with me to the clinic," Magda is saying. "You don't have to look at the needle. You don't even have to hold my hand." She waits, but Annemarie is speechless. "You don't even have to talk to me. Just peck on the receiver: once if you'll go, twice if you won't." Magda is trying to sound light-hearted, but Annemarie realizes with a strange satisfaction that she must be very afraid. She's going to have amniocentesis.

65   "Are you all right?" Magda asks. "You sound woozy."

66   "Why wouldn't I be all right," Annemarie snaps. She runs a hand through her hair, which is spiked with perspiration, and regains herself. "Why on earth are you even having it done, the amniowhatsis, if you think it's going to be so awful?"

67   "My doctor won't be my doctor anymore unless I have it. It's kind of a requirement for women my age."

68   A yellow tabby cat walks over Annemarie's leg and jumps off the bed. Annemarie is constantly taking in strays, joking to Kay Kay that if Leon leaves her at least she won't be alone, she'll have the cats. She has eleven or twelve at the moment.

69   "Well, it's probably for the best," Annemarie tells Magda, in the brisk voice she uses to let Magda know she is a citizen of the world, unlike some people. "It will ease your mind, anyway, to know the baby's okay."

70   "Oh, I'm not going to look at the results," Magda explains. "I told Dr. Lavinna I'd have it, and have the results sent over to his office, but I don't want to know. That was our compromise."

NOTE

amniocentesis (par. 64): A procedure in which a long hollow needle is inserted through a woman's abdomen into her uterus in order to obtain a sample of the amniotic fluid surrounding a fetus. The sample is analyzed to detect fetal abnormalities and to discover the sex of the fetus.

71 "Why don't you want to know the results?" asks Annemarie. "You could even know if it was a boy or a girl. You could pick out a name."

72 "As if it's such hard work to pick out an extra name," says Magda, "that I should go have needles poked into me to save myself the trouble?"

73 "I just don't see why you wouldn't want to know."

74 "People spend their whole lives with labels stuck on them, Annemarie. I just think it would be nice for this one to have nine months of being a plain human being."

75 "Mother knows best," sighs Annemarie, and she had the feeling she's always had, that she's sinking in a bog of mud. "You two should just talk," Kay Kay sometimes insists, and Annemarie can't get across that it's like quicksand. It's like reasoning with the sand trap at a golf course. There is no beginning and no end to the conversation she needs to have with Magda, and she'd rather just steer clear.

76 The following day, after work, Kay Kay comes over to help Annemarie get her evaporative cooler going for the summer. It's up on the roof of her mobile home. They have to climb up there with the vacuum cleaner and a long extension cord and clean out a winter's worth of dust and twigs and wayward insect parts. Then they will paint the bottom of the tank with tar, and install new pads, and check the water lines. Afterward, Kay Kay has promised she'll take Annemarie to the Dairy Queen for a milkshake. Kay Kay is looking after her friend in a carefully offhand way that Annemarie hasn't quite noticed.

77 It actually hasn't dawned on Annemarie that she's halfway through a pregnancy. She just doesn't think about what's going on in there, other than having some vague awareness that someone has moved in and is rearranging the furniture of her body. She's been thinking mostly about what pants she can still fit into. It was this way the first time, too. At six months she marched with Buddy down the aisle in an empire gown and seed-pearl tiara and no one suspected a thing, including, in her heart-of-hearts, Annemarie. Seven weeks later Leon sprang out of her body with his mouth open, already yelling, and neither one of them has ever quite gotten over the shock.

78 It's not that she doesn't want this baby, she tells Kay Kay; she didn't at first, but now she's decided. Leon has reached the age where he dodges her kisses like wild pitches over home plate, and she could use someone around to cuddle. "But there are so many things I have to get done, before I can have it," she says.

79 "Like what kind of things?" Kay Kay has a bandanna tied around her head and is slapping the tar around energetically. She's used to dirty work. She says after you've driven a few hundred miles with your head out the window of a locomotive, you don't just take a washcloth to your face, you have to wash your *teeth*.

NOTES

bog (par. 75): literally, a swamp-like area

wayward (par. 76): stubborn, unpredictable

empire gown (par. 77): a high-waisted, full-length dress

tiara (par. 77): a semicircular head ornament worn atop a woman's hair

80   "Oh, I don't know." Annemarie sits back on her heels. The metal roof is too hot to touch, but the view from up there is interesting, almost like it's not where she lives. The mobile homes are arranged like shoeboxes along the main drive, with cars and motorbikes parked beside them, just so many toys in a sandbox. The shadows of things trail away everywhere in the same direction like long oil leaks across the gravel. The trailer court is called "Island Breezes," and like the names of most trailer courts, it's a joke. No swaying palm trees. In fact, there's no official vegetation at all except for cactus plants in straight, symmetrical rows along the drive, like some bizarre desert organized by a child.

81   "Well, deciding what to do about Buddy, for instance," Annemarie says at last, after Kay Kay has clearly forgotten the question. "I need to figure that out first. And also what I'd do with a baby while I'm at work. I couldn't leave it with Magda, they'd all be down at the Air Force Base getting arrested to stop the cruise missiles."

82   Kay Kay doesn't say anything. She wraps the tarred, spiky paintbrush in a plastic bag and begins to pry last year's cooler pads out of the frames. Annemarie is being an absentminded helper, staring into space, sometimes handing Kay Kay a screwdriver when she's asked for the pliers.

83   With a horrible screeching of claws on metal, one of Annemarie's cats, Lone Ranger, has managed to get himself up to the roof in pursuit of a lizard. He's surprised to see the women up there; he freezes and then slinks away along the gutter. Lone Ranger is a problem cat. Annemarie buys him special food, anything to entice him, but he won't come inside and be pampered. He cowers and shrinks from love like a blast from the hose.

84   "How long you think you'll take off work?" Kay Kay asks.

85   "Take off?"

86   "When the baby comes."

87   "Oh, I don't know," Annemarie says, uneasily. She could endanger her job there if she doesn't give them some kind of advance notice. She's well aware, even when Kay Kay refrains from pointing it out, that she's responsible in a hit-or-miss way. Once, toward the end of their first marriage, Buddy totaled his car and she paid to have it repaired so he wouldn't leave her. The next weekend he drove to Reno with a woman who sold newspapers from a traffic island.

88   Annemarie begins to unwrap the new cooler pads, which look like huge, flat sponges and smell like fresh sawdust. According to the label they're made of aspen, which Annemarie thought was a place you go skiing and try to get a glimpse of Jack Nicholson. "You'd think they could make these things out of plastic," she says. "They'd last longer, and it wouldn't smell like a damn camping trip every time you turn on your cooler."

NOTES

vegetation (par. 80): plant life
symmetrical (par. 80): balanced
entice (par. 83): tempt
cowers (par. 83): crouches in fear
aspen (par. 88): a type of tree

89   "They have to absorb water, though," explains Kay Kay. "That's the whole point. When the fan blows through the wet pads it cools down the air."

90   Annemarie is in the mood where she can't get particularly interested in the way things work. She holds two of the pads against herself like a hula skirt. "I could see these as a costume, couldn't you? For Connie?"

91   "That's an idea," Kay Kay says, examining them thoughtfully. "Connie's allergic to grasses, but not wood fibers."

92   Annemarie's bones ache to be known and loved this well. What she wouldn't give for someone to stand on a roof, halfway across the city, and say to some other person, "Annemarie's allergic to grasses, but not wood fibers."

93   "I'll mention it," Kay Kay says. "The band might go for it." Connie Skylab and the Falling Debris are into outlandish looks. Connie performs one number, "My Mother's Teeth," dressed in a black plastic garbage bag and a necklace of sheep's molars. A line Annemarie remembers is: "My mother's teeth grow in my head, I'll eat my children's dreams when she is dead."

94   Connie's mother is, in actual fact, dead. But neither she nor Kay Kay plans to produce any children. Annemarie thinks maybe that's how they can be so happy and bold. Their relationship is a sleek little boat of their own construction, untethered in either direction by the knotted ropes of motherhood, free to sail the open seas. Some people can manage it. Annemarie once met a happily married couple who made jewelry and traveled the nation in a dented microbus, selling their wares on street corners. They had no permanent address whatsoever, no traditions, no family. They told Annemarie they never celebrated holidays.

95   And then on the other hand there are the Navarretes next door with their little nest of lawn chairs. They're happy too. Annemarie feels permanently disqualified from either camp, the old-fashioned family or the new. It's as if she somehow got left behind, missed every boat across the river, and now must watch happiness being acted out on the beach of a distant shore.

96   Two days later, on Saturday, Annemarie pulls on sweat pants and a T-shirt, starts up her Pontiac—scattering cats in every direction—and drives a hundred feet to pick up Magda and take her to the clinic. There just wasn't any reasonable way out.

97   The sun is reflected so brightly off the road it's like driving on a mirage. The ground is as barren as some planet where it rains once per century. It has been an unusually dry spring, though it doesn't much matter here in Island Breezes, where the lawns are made of gravel. Some people, deeply missing the Midwest, have spray-painted their gravel green.

NOTES

outlandish (par. 93): bizarre
untethered (par. 94): not tied
microbus (par. 94): a bus-shaped station wagon
mirage (par. 97): A mirage is an optical effect caused by the bending of light-rays off of differently heated layers of air; it creates the illusion of a pool of water or a mirror in which distant objects are sometimes reflected upside down.
barren (par. 97): empty, infertile

98   Magda's yard is naturally the exception. It's planted with many things, including clumps of aloe vera, which she claims heals burns, and most recently, a little hand-painted sign with a blue dove that explains to all and sundry passersby that you can't hug your kids with nuclear arms. When Annemarie drives up, Magda's standing out on the wooden steps in one of her loose India-print cotton dresses, and looks cool. Annemarie is envious. Magda's ordinary wardrobe will carry her right through the ninth month.

99   Magda's hair brushes her shoulders like a lace curtain as she gets into the car, and she seems flushed and excited, though perhaps it's nerves. She fishes around in her enormous woven bag and pulls out a bottle of green shampoo. "I thought you might like to try this. It has an extract of nettles. I know to you that probably sounds awful, but it's really good; it can repair damaged hair shafts."

100   Annemarie beeps impatiently at some kids playing kickball in the drive near the front entrance. "Magda, can we please not start right in *immediately* on my hair? Can we at least say, 'How do you do' and 'fine thank you' before we start in on my hair?"

101   "Sorry."

102   "Believe it or not, I actually *want* my hair to look like something dead beside the road. It's the style now."

103   Magda looks around behind the seat for the seat belt and buckles it up. She refrains from saying anything about Annemarie's seat belt. They literally don't speak again until they get where they're going.

104   At the clinic they find themselves listening to a lecture on AIDS prevention. Apparently it's a mandatory part of the services here. Before Magda's amniocentesis they need to sit with the other patients and learn about nonoxynol-number-9 spermicide and the proper application of a condom.

105   "You want to leave a little room at the end, like this," says the nurse, who's wearing jeans and red sneakers. She rolls the condom carefully onto a plastic banana. All the other people in the room look fourteen, and there are some giggles. Their mothers probably go around saying that they and their daughters are "close," and have no idea they're here today getting birth control and what not.

106   Finally Magda gets to see the doctor, but it's a more complicated procedure than Annemarie expected: first they have to take a sonogram, to make sure that when they stick in the needle they won't poke the baby.

107   "Even if that did happen," the doctor explains, "the fetus will usually just move out of the way." Annemarie is floored to imagine a five-month-old fetus fending for itself. She tries to think of what's inside her as being an actual baby, or a baby-to-be, but can't. She hasn't even felt it move yet.

NOTES

all and sundry (par. 98): collective and individual

extract (par. 99): a concentrated form of plant juice

nettles (par. 99): a type of plant

nonoxynol-number-9 spermicide (par. 104): a contraceptive substance that kills sperm

sonogram (par. 106): a computerized image of the internal body produced with ultrasound (very high sound frequencies)

108   The doctor rubs Magda's belly with Vaseline and then places against it something that looks like a Ping-Pong paddle wired for sound. She frowns at the TV screen, concentrating, and then points. "Look, there, you can see the head."

109   Magda and Annemarie watch a black-and-white screen where meaningless shadows move around each other like iridescent ink blots. Suddenly they can make out one main shadow, fish-shaped with a big head, like Casper the Friendly Ghost.

110   "The bladder's full," the doctor says. "See that little clear spot? That's a good sign, it means the kidneys are working. Oops, there it went."

111   "There what went?" asks Magda.

112   "The bladder. It voided." She looks closely at the screen, smiling. "You know, I can't promise you but I think what you've got here . . ."

113   "Don't tell me," Magda says. "If you're going to tell me if it's a boy or a girl, I don't want to know."

114   "I do," says Annemarie. "Tell me."

115   "Is that okay with you?" the doctor asks Magda, and Magda shrugs. "Close your eyes, then," she tells Magda. She holds up two glass tubes with rubber stoppers, one pink and the other blue-green. She nods at the pink one.

116   Annemarie smiles. "Okay, all clear," she tells Magda. "My lips are sealed."

117   "That's the face, right there," the doctor says, pointing out the eyes. "It has one fist in its mouth; that's very common at this stage. Can you see it?"

118   They can see it. The other fist, the left one, is raised up alongside its huge head like the Black Panther salute. Magda is transfixed. Annemarie can see the flickering light of the screen reflected in her eyes, and she understands for the first time that what they are looking at here is not a plan or a plot, it has nothing to do with herself. It's Magda's future.

119   Afterward they have to go straight to the park to pick up Leon from softball practice. It's hot, and Annemarie drives distractedly, worrying about Leon because they're late. She talked him into joining the league in the first place; he'd just as soon stay home and collect baseball cards. But now she worries that he'll get hit with a ball, or kidnapped by some pervert that hangs around in the park waiting for the one little boy whose mother's late. She hits the brakes at a crosswalk to let three women pass safely through the traffic, walking with their thin brown arms so close together they could be holding hands. They're apparently three generations of a family: The grandmother is draped elaborately in a sari, the mother is in pink slacks, and the daughter wears a bleached denim miniskirt. But from the back they could be triplets. Three long braids, woven as thin and tight as ropes, bounce placidly against their backs as they walk away from the stopped cars.

NOTES

iridescent (par. 109): bright

Black Panther (par. 118): The Black Panther Party, active from the mid-1960s through the mid-1970s, was a militant group formed to advance the rights of African Americans.

transfixed (par. 118): fascinated

sari (par. 119): a garment worn by Hindu women, consisting of a long piece of cotton or silk that is wrapped around the waist to form a skirt and draped over the head or shoulder

placidly (par. 119): calmly

120   "Was it as bad as you thought it would be?" Annemarie asks Magda. It's awkward to be speaking after all this time, so suddenly, and really for no good reason.

121   "It was worse."

122   "I liked the sonogram," Annemarie says. "I liked seeing it, didn't you?"

123   "Yes, but not that other part. I hate doctors and needles and that whole thing. Doctors treat women like a disease in progress."

124   That's Magda, Annemarie thinks. You never know what's going to come out of her mouth next. Annemarie thinks the doctor was just about as nice as possible. But in fairness to Magda, the needle was unbelievably long. It made her skin draw up into goose pimples just to watch. Magda seems worn out from the experience.

125   Annemarie rolls down the window to signal a left turn at the intersection. Her blinkers don't work, but at least the air conditioning still does. In the summer when her mobile home heats up like a toaster oven, the car is Annemarie's refuge. Sometimes she'll drive across town on invented, insignificant errands, singing along with Annie Lennox on the radio and living for the moment in a small, safe, perfectly cool place.

126   "I'd have this baby at home if I could," says Magda.

127   "Why can't you?"

128   "Too old," she says, complacently. "I talked to the midwife program but they risked me out."

129   The sun seems horribly bright. Annemarie thinks she's read something about pregnancy making your eyes sensitive to light. "Was it an awful shock, when you found out?" she asks Magda.

130   "About the midwives?"

131   "No. About the pregnancy."

132   Magda looks at her as if she's dropped from another planet.

133   "What's the matter?" asks Annemarie.

134   "I've been trying my whole life to have more babies. You knew that, that I'd been trying."

135   "No, I didn't. Just lately?"

136   "No, Annemarie, not just lately, forever. The whole time with your father we kept trying, but the drugs he took for the cancer knocked out his sperms. The doctor told us they were still alive, but were too confused to make a baby."

137   Annemarie tries not to smile. "Too confused?"

138   "That's what he said."

139   "And you've kept on ever since then?" she asks.

140   "I kept hoping, but I'd about given up. I feel like this baby is a gift."

141   Annemarie thinks of one of the customers at Yesterday! who sent relatives a Christmas fruitcake that somehow got lost; it arrived two and a half years later on the twelfth of July. Magda's baby is like the fruitcake, she thinks, and she shakes her head and laughs.

NOTES

refuge (par. 125): retreat

complacently (par. 128): unconcernedly

midwives (par. 130): people trained to assist women in childbirth

142   "What's so funny?"

143   "Nothing. I just can't believe you wanted a bunch of kids. You never said so. I thought even having just me got in your way."

144   "Got in my way?"

145   "Well, yeah. Because you were so young. I thought that's why you weren't mad when Buddy and I had to get married, because you'd done the same thing. I always figured my middle name ought to have been Whoops."

146   Magda looks strangely at Annemarie again. "I had to douche with vinegar to get pregnant with you," she says.

147   They've reach the park, and Leon is waiting with his bat slung over his shoulder like a dangerous character. "The other kids' moms already came ten hours ago," he says when he gets into the car. He doesn't seem at all surprised to see Magda and Annemarie in the same vehicle.

148   "We got held up," Annemarie says. "Sorry, Leon."

149   Leon stares out the window for a good while. "Leon's a stupid name," he says, eventually. This is a complaint of his these days.

150   "There have been a lot of important Leons in history," Annemarie says.

151   "Like who?"

152   She considers this. "Leon Russell," she says. "He's a rock and roll singer."

153   "Leon Trotsky," says Magda.

154   Annemarie heard all about Leon Trotsky in her time, and Rosa Luxemburg, and Mother Jones.

155   "Trotsky was an important socialist who disagreed with Stalin's methodology," Magda explains. "Stalin was the kingpin at the time, so Trotsky had to run for his life to Mexico."

156   "This all happened decades ago, I might add," Annemarie says, glancing at Leon in the rear-view mirror.

157   "He was killed by his trusted secretary," Magda continues. "With an axe in the head."

158   "Magda, please. You think he'll like his name better if he knows many famous Leons have been axed?"

159   "I'm telling him my girlhood memories. I'm trying to be a good grandmother."

160   "Your girlhood memories? What, were you there?"

161   "Of course not, it happened in Mexico, before I was born. But it affected me. I read about it when I was a teenager, and I cried. My father said, 'Oh, I

NOTES

Rosa Luxemburg (par. 154): Rosa Luxemburg (1870–1919) was a German socialist leader and cofounder of the Spartacus League, which became the Communist Party of Germany.

Mother Jones (par. 154): Mary Harris Jones (1830–1930) was an Irish-born American labor leader, union organizer, and opponent of child labor. She helped found the Social Democratic Party and the Industrial Workers of the World.

socialist (par. 155): a supporter of socialism (a social system in which the collective community owns and controls the means of production and distribution of goods)

Stalin's (par. 155): Joseph Stalin (1879–1953) was the dictator of the Union of Soviet Socialist Republics (USSR) and secretary-general of the Communist Party in the USSR from 1922 to 1953.

methodology (par. 155): methods

remember seeing that headline in the paper and thinking, What, Trotsky's dead? Hal Trotsky, first baseman for the Cleveland Indians.'"

162 "Live Free or Die, New Hampshire!" shouts Leon at an approaching car.

163 Magda says, "Annemarie's father came from New Hampshire."

164 Annemarie runs a stop sign.

165 It isn't clear to her what's happened. There is a crunch of metal and glass, and some white thing plowing like a torpedo into the left side of the Pontiac, and they spin around, seeing the same view pass by again and again. Then Annemarie is lying across Magda with her mouth open and her head out the window on the passenger's side. Magda's arms are tight around her chest. The window has vanished, and there is a feeling like sand trickling through Annemarie's hair. After a minute she realizes that a sound is coming out of her mouth. It's a scream. She closes her mouth and it stops.

166 With some effort she unbuckles Magda's seat belt and pulls the door handle and they more or less tumble out together onto the ground. It strikes Annemarie, for no good reason, that Magda isn't a very big person. She's Annemarie's own size, if not smaller. The sun is unbelievably bright.

167 There's no other traffic. A woman gets out of the white car with the New Hampshire plates, brushing her beige skirt in a businesslike way and straightening her hair. Oddly, she has on stockings but no shoes. She looks at the front end of her car, which resembles a metal cauliflower, and then at the two women hugging each other on the ground.

168 "There was a stop sign," she says. Her voice is clear as a song in the strange silence. A series of rapid clicks emanates from the underside of one of the cars, then stops.

169 "I guess I missed it," Annemarie says.

170 "Are you okay?" the woman asks. She looks hard at Annemarie's face. Annemarie puts her hand on her head, and it feels wet.

171 "I'm fine," she and Magda say at the same time.

172 "You're bleeding," the woman says to Annemarie. She looks down at herself, and then carefully unbuttons her white blouse and holds it out to Annemarie. "You'd better let me tie this around your head," she says. "Then I'll go call the police."

173 "All right," says Annemarie. She pries apart Magda's fingers, which seem to be stuck, and they pull each other up. The woman pulls the blouse across Annemarie's bleeding forehead and knots the silk sleeves tightly at the nape of her neck. She does this while standing behind Annemarie in her stocking feet and brassiere, with Magda looking on, and somehow it has the feeling of some ordinary female ritual.

174 "Oh, God," says Annemarie. She looks at the Pontiac and sits back down on the ground. The back doors of the car are standing wide open, and Leon is gone. "My son," she says. The child inside her flips and arches its spine in a graceful, hungry movement, like a dolphin leaping for a fish held out by its tail.

NOTES

emanates (par. 168): comes
nape (par. 173): back (of the neck)

175   "Is that him?" the woman asks, pointing to the far side of the intersection. Leon is there, sitting cross-legged on a mound of dirt. On one side of him there is a jagged pile of broken cement. On the other side is a stack of concrete pipes. Leon looks at his mother and grandmother, and laughs.

176   Annemarie can't stop sobbing in the back of the ambulance. She knows that what she's feeling would sound foolish put into words: that there's no point in living once you understand that at any moment you could die.

177   She and Magda are strapped elaborately onto boards, so they can't turn their heads even to look at each other. Magda says over and over again, "Leon's okay. You're okay. We're all okay." Out the window Annemarie can only see things that are high up: telephone wires, clouds, an airplane full of people who have no idea how near they could be to death. Daily there are reports of mid-air collisions barely averted. When the ambulance turns a corner she can see the permanent landmark of the Catalina Mountains standing over the city. In a saddle between two dark peaks a storm cloud spreads out like a fan, and Annemarie sees how easily it could grow into something else, tragically roiling up into itself, veined with blinding light: a mushroom cloud.

178   "Magda," she says, "me too. I'm having a baby too."

179   At the hospital Magda repeats to everyone, like a broken record, that she and her daughter are both pregnant. She's terrified they'll be given some tranquilizer that will mutate the fetuses. Whenever the nurses approach, she confuses them by talking about Thalidomide babies. "Annemarie is allergic to penicillin," she warns the doctor when they're separated. It's true, Annemarie is, and she always forgets to mark it on her forms.

180   It turns out that she needs no penicillin, just stitches in her scalp. Magda has cuts and serious contusions from where her knees hit the dash. Leon has nothing. Not a bruise.

181   During the lecture the doctor gives them about seat belts, which Annemarie will remember for the rest of her life, he explains that in an average accident the human body becomes as heavy as a piano dropping from a ten-story building. She has bruises on her rib cage from where Magda held on to her, and the doctor can't understand how she kept Annemarie from going out the window. He looks at the two of them, pregnant and dazed, and tells them many times over that they are two very lucky ladies. "Sometimes the strength of motherhood is greater than natural laws," he declares.

182   The only telephone number Annemarie can think to give them is the crew dispatcher for Southern Pacific, which is basically Kay Kay's home number. Luckily she's just brought in the Amtrak and is next door to the depot, at Wendy's, when the call comes. She gets there in minutes, still dressed in her work boots and blackened jeans, with a green bandanna around her neck.

NOTES

averted (par. 177): prevented
roiling (par. 177): churning
mutate (par. 179): deform
Thalidomide (par. 179): a drug that caused severe deformities in babies of women who took it while pregnant; it was taken off of the market
contusions (par. 180): bruises

183　　"They didn't want me to come in here," Kay Kay tells Annemarie in the recovery room. "They said I was too dirty. Can you imagine?"

184　　Annemarie tries to laugh, but tears run from her eyes instead, and she squeezes Kay Kay's hand. She still can't think of anything that seems important enough to say. She feels as if life has just been handed to her in a heavy and formal way, like a microphone on a stage, and the audience is waiting to see what great thing she intends to do with it.

185　　But Kay Kay is her everyday self. "Don't worry about Leon, he's got it all worked out, he's staying with me," she tells Annemarie, not looking at her stitches. "He's going to teach me how to hit a softball."

186　　"He doesn't want to go to Buddy's?" Annemarie asks.

187　　"He didn't say he did."

188　　"Isn't he scared to death?" Annemarie feels so weak and confused she doesn't believe she'll ever stand up again.

189　　Kay Kay smiles. "Leon's a rock," she says, and Annemarie thinks of the pile of dirt he landed on. She believes now that she can remember the sound of him hitting it.

190　　Annemarie and Magda have to stay overnight for observation. They end up in maternity, with their beds pushed close together so they won't disturb the other woman in the room. She's just given birth to twins and is watching *Falcon Crest.*

191　　"I just keep seeing him there on that pile of dirt," whispers Annemarie. "And I think, he could have been dead. There was just that one little safe place for him to land. Why did he land there? And then I think, *we* could have been dead, and he'd be alone. He'd be an orphan. Like that poor little girl that survived that plane wreck."

192　　"That poor kid," Magda agrees. "People are just burying her with teddy bears. How could you live with a thing like that?" Magda seems a little dazed too. They each accepted a pill to calm them down, once the doctor came and personally guaranteed Magda it wouldn't cause fetal deformity.

193　　"I think that woman's blouse was silk. Can you believe it?" Annemarie asks.

194　　"She was kind," says Magda.

195　　"I wonder what became of it? I suppose it's ruined."

196　　"Probably," Magda says. She keeps looking over at Annemarie and smiling. "When are you due?" she asks.

197　　"October twelfth," says Annemarie. "After you."

198　　"Leon came early, remember. And I went way late with you, three weeks I think. Yours could come first."

199　　"Did you know Buddy wants us to get married again?" Annemarie asks after a while. "Leon thinks it's a great idea."

200　　"What do you think? That's the question."

201　　"That's the question," Annemarie agrees.

202　　A nurse comes to take their blood pressure. "How are the mamas tonight?" she asks. Annemarie thinks about how nurses wear that same calm face stewardesses have, never letting on like you're sitting on thirty thousand feet of thin air. Her head has begun to ache in no uncertain terms, and she thinks of poor old Leon Trotsky, axed in the head.

203   "I dread to think of what my hair's going to look like when these bandages come off. Did they have to shave a lot?"

204   "Not too much," the nurse says, concentrating on the blood-pressure dial.

205   "Well, it's just as well my hair was a wreck to begin with."

206   The nurse smiles and rips off the Velcro cuff, and then turns her back on Annemarie, attending to Magda. Another nurse rolls in their dinners and sets up their tray tables. Magda props herself up halfway, grimacing a little, and the nurse helps settle her with pillows under her back. She pokes a straw into a carton of milk, but Annemarie doesn't even take the plastic wrap off her tray.

207   "Ugh," she complains, once the nurses have padded away on their white soles. "This reminds me of the stuff you used to bring me when I was sick."

208   "Milk toast," says Magda.

209   "That's right. Toast soaked in milk. Who could dream up such a disgusting thing?"

210   "I like it," says Magda. "When I'm sick, it's the only thing I can stand. Seems like it always goes down nice."

211   "It went down nice with Blackie," Annemarie says. "Did you know he's the one that always ate it? I told you a million times I hated milk toast."

212   "I never knew what you expected from me, Annemarie. I never could be the mother you wanted."

213   Annemarie turns up one corner of the cellophane and pleats it with her fingers. "I guess I didn't expect anything, and you kept giving it to me anyway. When I was a teenager you were always making me drink barley fiber so I wouldn't have colon cancer when I was fifty. All I wanted was Cokes and Twinkies like the other kids."

214   "I know that," Magda says. "Don't you think I know that? You didn't want anything. A Barbie doll, and new clothes, but nothing in the way of mothering. Reading to you or anything like that. I could march around freeing South Africa or saving Glen Canyon but I couldn't do one thing for my own child."

215   They are both quiet for a minute. On TV, a woman in an airport knits a longer and longer sweater, apparently unable to stop, while her plane is delayed again and again.

216   "I know you didn't want to be taken care of, honey," Magda says. "But I guess I just couldn't help it."

217   Annemarie turns her head to the side, ponderously, as if it has become an enormous egg. She'd forgotten and now remembers how pain seems to increase the size of things. "You know what's crazy?" she asks. "Now I want to be taken care of and nobody will. Men, I mean."

218   "They would if you'd let them. You act like you don't deserve any better."

NOTES

grimacing (par. 206): twisting her face in pain

Glen Canyon (par. 214): Glen Canyon is located in north-central Arizona and southern Utah. In 1960, amid much controversy, construction began on the Glen Canyon Dam, one of a series of dams built along the Colorado River to control it and to provide water and electricity. The dam was completed in 1963, and Glen Canyon is now filled with over 25 million acre-feet of water. Opposition to the dam continues.

ponderously (par. 217): clumsily

219   "That's not true." Annemarie is surprised and a little resentful at Magda's analysis.

220   "It is true. You'll take a silk blouse from a complete stranger, but not the least little thing from anybody that loves you. Not even a bottle of shampoo. If it comes from somebody that cares about you, you act like it's not worth having."

221   "Well, you're a good one to talk."

222   "What do you mean?" Magda pushes the tray table back and turns toward her daughter, carefully, resting her chin on her hand.

223   "What I mean is you beat men off with a stick. Bartholomew thinks you're Miss America and you don't want him around you. You don't even miss Daddy."

224   Magda stares at Annemarie. "You don't know the first thing about it. Where were you when he was dying? Outside playing hopscotch."

225   That is true. That's exactly where Annemarie was.

226   "Do you remember that upholstered armchair we had, Annemarie, with the grandfather clocks on it? He sat in that chair, morning till night, with his lungs filling up. Worrying about us. He'd say, 'You won't forget to lock the doors, will you? Let's write a little note and tape it there by the door.' And I'd do it. And then he'd say, 'You know that the brakes on the car have to be checked every so often. They loosen up. And the oil will need to be changed in February.' He sat there looking out the front window and every hour he'd think of another thing, till his face turned gray with the pain, knowing he'd never think of it all."

227   Annemarie can picture them there in the trailer: two people facing a blank, bright window, waiting for the change that would permanently disconnect them.

228   Magda looks away from Annemarie. "What hurt him wasn't dying. It was not being able to follow you and me through life looking after us. How could I ever give anybody that kind of grief again?"

229   The woman who just had the twins has turned off her program, and Annemarie realizes their voices have gradually risen. She demands in a whisper, "I didn't know it was like that for you when he died. How could I not ever have known that, that it wrecked your life, too?"

230   Magda looks across Annemarie, out the window, and Annemarie tries to follow her line of vision. There is a parking lot outside, and nothing else to see. A sparse forest of metal poles. The unlit streetlamps stare down at the pavement like blind eyes.

231   "I don't know," Magda says. "Seem like just how it is with you and me. We're like islands on the moon."

232   "There's no water on the moon," says Annemarie.

233   "That's what I mean. A person could walk from one to the other if they just decided to do it."

234   It's dark. Annemarie is staring out the window when the lights in the parking lot come on all together with a soft blink. From her bed she can only see

NOTES

sparse (par. 230): thin, skimpy
luminous (par. 234): shining

the tops of the cars glowing quietly in the pink light like some strange crop of luminous mushrooms. Enough time passes, she thinks, and it's tomorrow. Buddy or no Buddy, this baby is going to come. For the first time she lets herself imagine holding a newborn against her stomach, its helplessness and rage pulling on her heart like the greatest tragedy there ever was.

235   There won't be just one baby, either, but two: her own, and her mother's second daughter. Two more kids with dark, curly hair. Annemarie can see them kneeling in the gravel, their heads identically bent forward on pale, slender necks, driving trucks over the moonlike surface of Island Breezes. Getting trikes for their birthdays, skinning their knees, starting school. Once in a while going down with Magda to the Air Force Base, most likely, to fend off nuclear war.

236   Magda is still lying on her side, facing Annemarie, but she has drawn the covers up and her eyes are closed. The top of the sheet is bunched into her two hands like a bride's bouquet. The belly beneath pokes forward, begging as the unborn do for attention, some reassurance from the outside world, the flat of a palm. Because she can't help it, Annemarie reaches across and lays a hand on her little sister.

What You Pawn I Will Redeem

Sherman Alexie

NOON

1   One day you have a home and the next you don't, but I'm not going to tell you my particular reasons for being homeless, because it's my secret story, and Indians have to work hard to keep secrets from hungry white folks.

2   I'm a Spokane Indian boy, an Interior Salish, and my people have lived within a hundred-mile radius of Spokane, Washington, for at least ten thousand years. I grew up in Spokane, moved to Seattle twenty-three years ago for college, flunked out after two semesters, worked various blue- and bluer-collar jobs, married two or three times, fathered two or three kids, and then went crazy. Of course, crazy is not the official definition of my mental problem, but I don't think asocial disorder fits it, either, because that makes me sound like I'm a serial killer or something. I've never hurt another human being, or, at least, not physically. I've broken a few hearts in my time, but we've all done that, so I'm nothing special in that regard. I'm a boring heartbreaker, too. I never dated or married more than one woman at a time. I didn't break hearts into pieces overnight. I broke them slowly and carefully. And I didn't set any land-speed records running out the door. Piece by piece, I disappeared. I've been disappearing ever since.

NOTES

Interior Salish (par. 2): a group of Native Americans inhabiting parts of British Columbia, northern Washington, northern Idaho, and western Montana
asocial (par. 2): unwilling or unable to abide by social rules
serial killer (par. 2): someone who kills four or more people over a period of time, usually using the same method

3   I've been homeless for six years now. If there's such a thing as an effective homeless man, then I suppose I'm effective. Being homeless is probably the only thing I've ever been good at. I know where to get the best free food. I've made friends with restaurant and convenience-store managers who let me use their bathrooms. And I don't mean the public bathrooms, either. I mean the employees' bathrooms, the clean ones hidden behind the kitchen or the pantry or the cooler. I know it sounds strange to be proud of this, but it means a lot to me, being trustworthy enough to piss in somebody else's clean bathroom. Maybe you don't understand the value of a clean bathroom, but I do.

4   Probably none of this interests you. Homeless Indians are everywhere in Seattle. We're common and boring, and you walk right on by us, with maybe a look of anger or disgust or even sadness at the terrible fate of the noble savage. But we have dreams and families. I'm friends with a homeless Plains Indian man whose son is the editor of a big-time newspaper back East. Of course, that's his story, but we Indians are great storytellers and liars and mythmakers, so maybe that Plains Indian hobo is just a plain old everyday Indian. I'm kind of suspicious of him, because he identifies himself only as Plains Indian, a generic term, and not by a specific tribe. When I asked him why he wouldn't tell me exactly what he is, he said, "Do any of us know exactly what we are?" Yeah, great, a philosophizing Indian. "Hey," I said, "you got to have a home to be that homely." He just laughed and flipped me the eagle and walked away.

5   I wander the streets with a regular crew—my teammates, my defenders, my posse. It's Rose of Sharon, Junior, and me. We matter to each other if we don't matter to anybody else. Rose of Sharon is a big woman, about seven feet tall if you're measuring overall effect and about five feet tall if you're only talking about the physical. She's a Yakama Indian of the Wishram variety. Junior is a Colville, but there are about a hundred and ninety-nine tribes that make up the Colville, so he could be anything. He's good-looking, though, like he just stepped out of some "Don't Litter the Earth" public-service advertisement. He's got those great big cheekbones that are like planets, you know, with little moons orbiting them. He gets me jealous, jealous, and jealous. If you put Junior and me next to each other, he's the Before Columbus Arrived Indian and I'm the After Columbus Arrived Indian. I am living proof of the horrible damage that colonialism has done to us Skins. But I'm not going to let you know how scared I sometimes get of history and its ways. I'm a strong man, and I know that silence is the best method of dealing with white folks.

NOTES

Plains Indian (par. 4): a member of any of the Native American peoples inhabiting the Great Plains, or Midwest region, of the United States

generic (par. 4): general

Yakama Indian (par. 5): a Native American nation of south-central Washington

Wishram (par. 5): one of the tribes comprising the Yakama nation

Colville (par. 5): the descendants of eleven bands of Native Americans who were settled on the Colville Reservation in 1872 in north-central Washington

colonialism (par. 5): the practice of controlling another nation, occupying it with settlers, and exploiting its people and resources for profit

Skins (par. 5): short for "redskins," an offensive slang term for Native Americans

6   This whole story really started at lunchtime, when Rose of Sharon, Junior, and I were panning the handle down at Pike Place Market. After about two hours of negotiating, we earned five dollars—good enough for a bottle of fortified courage from the most beautiful 7-Eleven in the world. So we headed over that way, feeling like warrior drunks, and we walked past this pawnshop I'd never noticed before. And that was strange, because we Indians have built-in pawnshop radar. But the strangest thing of all was the old pow-wow dance regalia I saw hanging in the window.

7   "That's my grandmother's regalia," I said to Rose of Sharon and Junior.

8   "How you know for sure?" Junior asked.

9   I didn't know for sure, because I hadn't seen that regalia in person ever. I'd only seen photographs of my grandmother dancing in it. And those were taken before somebody stole it from her, fifty years ago. But it sure looked like my memory of it, and it had all the same color feathers and beads that my family sewed into our pow-wow regalia.

10   "There's only one way to know for sure," I said.

11   So Rose of Sharon, Junior, and I walked into the pawnshop and greeted the old white man working behind the counter.

12   "How can I help you?" he asked.

13   "That's my grandmother's pow-wow regalia in your window," I said. "Somebody stole it from her fifty years ago, and my family has been searching for it ever since."

14   The pawnbroker looked at me like I was a liar. I understood. Pawnshops are filled with liars.

15   "I'm not lying," I said. "Ask my friends here. They'll tell you."

16   "He's the most honest Indian I know," Rose of Sharon said.

17   "All right, honest Indian," the pawnbroker said. "I'll give you the benefit of the doubt. Can you prove it's your grandmother's regalia?"

18   Because they don't want to be perfect, because only God is perfect, Indian people sew flaws into their powwow regalia. My family always sewed one yellow bead somewhere on our regalia. But we always hid it so that you had to search really hard to find it.

19   "If it really is my grandmother's," I said, "there will be one yellow bead hidden somewhere on it."

20   "All right, then," the pawnbroker said. "Let's take a look."

21   He pulled the regalia out of the window, laid it down on the glass counter, and we searched for that yellow bead and found it hidden beneath the armpit.

22   "There it is," the pawnbroker said. He didn't sound surprised. "You were right. This is your grandmother's regalia."

23   "It's been missing for fifty years," Junior said.

24   "Hey, Junior," I said. "It's my family's story. Let me tell it."

25   "All right," he said. "I apologize. You go ahead."

26   "It's been missing for fifty years," I said.

NOTES

fortified (par. 6): strengthened

pow-wow dance regalia (par. 6): A *pow-wow* is a formal meeting of Native American during which they perform ceremonial dances and rituals. *Regalia* refers to the ceremonial costumes worn by participants.

27   "That's his family's sad story," Rose of Sharon said. "Are you going to give it back to him?"

28   "That would be the right thing to do," the pawnbroker said. "But I can't afford to do the right thing. I paid a thousand dollars for this. I can't just give away a thousand dollars."

29   "We could go to the cops and tell them it was stolen," Rose of Sharon said.

30   "Hey," I said to her. "Don't go threatening people."

31   The pawnbroker sighed. He was thinking about the possibilities.

32   "Well, I suppose you could go to the cops," he said. "But I don't think they'd believe a word you said."

33   He sounded sad about that. As if he was sorry for taking advantage of our disadvantages.

34   "What's your name?" the pawnbroker asked me.

35   "Jackson," I said.

36   "Is that first or last?"

37   "Both," I said.

38   "Are you serious?"

39   "Yes, it's true. My mother and father named me Jackson Jackson. My family nickname is Jackson Squared. My family is funny."

40   "All right, Jackson Jackson," the pawnbroker said. "You wouldn't happen to have a thousand dollars, would you?"

41   "We've got five dollars total," I said.

42   "That's too bad," he said, and thought hard about the possibilities. "I'd sell it to you for a thousand dollars if you had it. Heck, to make it fair, I'd sell it to you for nine hundred and ninety-nine dollars. I'd lose a dollar. That would be the moral thing to do in this case. To lose a dollar would be the right thing."

43   "We've got five dollars total," I said again.

44   "That's too bad," he said once more, and thought harder about the possibilities. "How about this? I'll give you twenty-four hours to come up with nine hundred and ninety-nine dollars. You come back here at lunchtime tomorrow with the money and I'll sell it back to you. How does that sound?"

45   "It sounds all right," I said.

46   "All right, then," he said. "We have a deal. And I'll get you started. Here's twenty bucks."

47   He opened up his wallet and pulled out a crisp twenty-dollar bill and gave it to me. And Rose of Sharon, Junior, and I walked out into the daylight to search for nine hundred and seventy-four more dollars.

1 P.M.

48   Rose of Sharon, Junior, and I carried our twenty-dollar bill and our five dollars in loose change over to the 7-Eleven and bought three bottles of imagination. We needed to figure out how to raise all that money in only one day. Thinking hard, we huddled in an alley beneath the Alaska Way Viaduct and finished off those bottles—one, two, and three.

NOTE

Viaduct (par. 48): bridge

2 P.M.

49   Rose of Sharon was gone when I woke up. I heard later that she had hitchhiked back to Toppenish and was living with her sister on the reservation.

50   Junior had passed out beside me and was covered in his own vomit, or maybe somebody else's vomit, and my head hurt from thinking, so I left him alone and walked down to the water. I love the smell of ocean water. Salt always smells like memory.

51   When I got to the wharf, I ran into three Aleut cousins, who sat on a wooden bench and stared out at the bay and cried. Most of the homeless Indians in Seattle come from Alaska. One by one, each of them hopped a big working boat in Anchorage or Barrow or Juneau, fished his way south to Seattle, jumped off the boat with a pocketful of cash to party hard at one of the highly sacred and traditional Indian bars, went broke and broker, and has been trying to find his way back to the boat and the frozen North ever since.

52   These Aleuts smelled like salmon, I thought, and they told me they were going to sit on that wooden bench until their boat came back.

53   "How long has your boat been gone?" I asked.

54   "Eleven years," the elder Aleut said.

55   I cried with them for a while.

56   "Hey," I said. "Do you guys have any money I can borrow?"

57   They didn't.

3 P.M.

58   I walked back to Junior. He was still out cold. I put my face down near his mouth to make sure he was breathing. He was alive, so I dug around in his blue jeans pockets and found half a cigarette. I smoked it all the way down and thought about my grandmother.

59   Her name was Agnes, and she died of breast cancer when I was fourteen. My father always thought Agnes caught her tumors from the uranium mine on the reservation. But my mother said the disease started when Agnes was walking back from a pow-wow one night and got run over by a motorcycle. She broke three ribs, and my mother always said those ribs never healed right, and tumors take over when you don't heal right.

60   Sitting beside Junior, smelling the smoke and the salt and the vomit, I wondered if my grandmother's cancer started when somebody stole her pow-wow regalia. Maybe the cancer started in her broken heart and then leaked out into her breasts. I know it's crazy, but I wondered whether I could bring my grandmother back to life if I bought back her regalia.

61   I needed money, big money, so I left Junior and walked over to the Real Change office.

NOTES

Toppenish (par. 49): a tourist town located on the Yakima Indian Reservation
Aleut (par. 51): Native Americans inhabiting the Aleutian Islands and coastal areas of southwestern Alaska
uranium (par. 59): a radioactive and poisonous element occurring in several minerals and used for nuclear fuel and nuclear weapons

4 P.M.

62   Real Change is a multifaceted organization that publishes a newspaper, supports cultural projects that empower the poor and the homeless, and mobilizes the public around poverty issues. Real Change's mission is to organize, educate, and build alliances to create solutions to homelessness and poverty. It exists to provide a voice for poor people in our community.

63   I memorized Real Change's mission statement because I sometimes sell the newspaper on the streets. But you have to stay sober to sell it, and I'm not always good at staying sober. Anybody can sell the paper. You buy each copy for thirty cents and sell it for a dollar, and you keep the profit.

64   "I need one thousand four hundred and thirty papers," I said to the Big Boss.

65   "That's a strange number," he said. "And that's a lot of papers."

66   "I need them."

67   The Big Boss pulled out his calculator and did the math.

68   "It will cost you four hundred and twenty-nine dollars for that many," he said.

69   "If I had that kind of money, I wouldn't need to sell the papers."

70   "What's going on, Jackson-to-the-Second-Power?" he asked. He is the only person who calls me that. He's a funny and kind man.

71   I told him about my grandmother's pow-wow regalia and how much money I needed in order to buy it back.

72   "We should call the police," he said.

73   "I don't want to do that," I said. "It's a quest now. I need to win it back by myself."

74   "I understand," he said. "And, to be honest, I'd give you the papers to sell if I thought it would work. But the record for the most papers sold in one day by one vender is only three hundred and two."

75   "That would net me about two hundred bucks," I said.

76   The Big Boss used his calculator. "Two hundred and eleven dollars and forty cents," he said.

77   "That's not enough," I said.

78   "And the most money anybody has made in one day is five hundred and twenty-five. And that's because somebody gave Old Blue five hundred-dollar bills for some dang reason. The average daily net is about thirty dollars."

79   "This isn't going to work."

80   "No."

81   "Can you lend me some money?"

82   "I can't do that," he said. "If I lend you money, I have to lend money to everybody."

83   "What can you do?"

84   "I'll give you fifty papers for free. But don't tell anybody I did it."

85   "O.K.," I said.

NOTES

alliances (par. 62): partnerships
quest (par. 73): search

86   He gathered up the newspapers and handed them to me. I held them to my chest. He hugged me. I carried the newspapers back toward the water.

5 P.M.

87   Back on the wharf, I stood near the Bainbridge Island Terminal and tried to sell papers to business commuters boarding the ferry.

88   I sold five in one hour, dumped the other forty-five in a garbage can, and walked into McDonald's, ordered four cheeseburgers for a dollar each, and slowly ate them.

89   After eating, I walked outside and vomited on the sidewalk. I hated to lose my food so soon after eating it. As an alcoholic Indian with a busted stomach, I always hope I can keep enough food in me to stay alive.

6 P.M.

90   With one dollar in my pocket, I walked back to Junior. He was still passed out, and I put my ear to his chest and listened for his heartbeat. He was alive, so I took off his shoes and socks and found one dollar in his left sock and fifty cents in his right sock.

91   With two dollars and fifty cents in my hand, I sat beside Junior and thought about my grandmother and her stories.

92   When I was thirteen, my grandmother told me a story about the Second World War. She was a nurse at a military hospital in Sydney, Australia. For two years, she healed and comforted American and Australian soldiers.

93   One day, she tended to a wounded Maori soldier, who had lost his legs to an artillery attack. He was very dark-skinned. His hair was black and curly and his eyes were black and warm. His face was covered with bright tattoos.

94   "Are you Maori?" he asked my grandmother.

95   "No," she said. "I'm Spokane Indian. From the United States."

96   "Ah, yes," he said. "I have heard of your tribes. But you are the first American Indian I have ever met."

97   "There's a lot of Indian soldiers fighting for the United States," she said. "I have a brother fighting in Germany, and I lost another brother on Okinawa."

98   "I am sorry," he said. "I was on Okinawa as well. It was terrible."

99   "I am sorry about your legs," my grandmother said.

100   "It's funny, isn't it?" he said.

101   "What's funny?"

102   "How we brown people are killing other brown people so white people will remain free."

103   "I hadn't thought of it that way."

104   "Well, sometimes I think of it that way. And other times I think of it the way they want me to think of it. I get confused."

105   She fed him morphine.

106   "Do you believe in Heaven?" he asked.

107   "Which Heaven?" she asked.

NOTE

Maori (par. 93): Polynesian people native to New Zealand

108 "I'm talking about the Heaven where my legs are waiting for me."

109 They laughed.

110 "Of course," he said, "my legs will probably run away from me when I get to Heaven. And how will I ever catch them?"

111 "You have to get your arms strong," my grandmother said. "So you can run on your hands."

112 They laughed again.

113 Sitting beside Junior, I laughed at the memory of my grandmother's story. I put my hand close to Junior's mouth to make sure he was still breathing. Yes, Junior was alive, so I took my two dollars and fifty cents and walked to the Korean grocery store in Pioneer Square.

7 P.M.

114 At the Korean grocery store, I bought a fifty-cent cigar and two scratch lottery tickets for a dollar each. The maximum cash prize was five hundred dollars a ticket. If I won both, I would have enough money to buy back the regalia.

115 I loved Mary, the young Korean woman who worked the register. She was the daughter of the owners, and she sang all day.

116 "I love you," I said when I handed her the money.

117 "You always say you love me," she said.

118 "That's because I will always love you."

119 "You are a sentimental fool."

120 "I'm a romantic old man."

121 "Too old for me."

122 "I know I'm too old for you, but I can dream."

123 "O.K.," she said. "I agree to be a part of your dreams, but I will only hold your hand in your dreams. No kissing and no sex. Not even in your dreams."

124 "O.K.," I said. "No sex. Just romance."

125 "Goodbye, Jackson Jackson, my love. I will see you soon."

126 I left the store, walked over to Occidental Park, sat on a bench, and smoked my cigar all the way down.

127 Ten minutes after I finished the cigar, I scratched my first lottery ticket and won nothing. I could only win five hundred dollars now, and that would only be half of what I needed.

128 Ten minutes after I lost, I scratched the other ticket and won a free ticket—a small consolation and one more chance to win some money.

129 I walked back to Mary.

130 "Jackson Jackson," she said. "Have you come back to claim my heart?"

131 "I won a free ticket," I said.

132 "Just like a man," she said. "You love money and power more than you love me."

133 "It's true," I said. "And I'm sorry it's true."

134 She gave me another scratch ticket, and I took it outside. I like to scratch my tickets in private. Hopeful and sad, I scratched that third ticket and won real money. I carried it back inside to Mary.

135 "I won a hundred dollars," I said.

136 She examined the ticket and laughed.

137   "That's a fortune," she said, and counted out five twenties. Our fingertips touched as she handed me the money. I felt electric and constant.

138   "Thank you," I said, and gave her one of the bills.

139   "I can't take that," she said. "It's your money."

140   "No, it's tribal. It's an Indian thing. When you win, you're supposed to share with your family."

141   "I'm not your family."

142   "Yes, you are."

143   She smiled. She kept the money. With eighty dollars in my pocket, I said goodbye to my dear Mary and walked out into the cold night air.

8 P.M.

144   I wanted to share the good news with Junior. I walked back to him, but he was gone. I heard later that he had hitchhiked down to Portland, Oregon, and died of exposure in an alley behind the Hilton Hotel.

9 P.M.

145   Lonesome for Indians, I carried my eighty dollars over to Big Heart's in South Downtown. Big Heart's is an all-Indian bar. Nobody knows how or why Indians migrate to one bar and turn it into an official Indian bar. But Big Heart's has been an Indian bar for twenty-three years. It used to be way up on Aurora Avenue, but a crazy Lummi Indian burned that one down, and the owners moved to the new location, a few blocks south of Safeco Field.

146   I walked into Big Heart's and counted fifteen Indians—eight men and seven women. I didn't know any of them, but Indians like to belong, so we all pretended to be cousins.

147   "How much for whiskey shots?" I asked the bartender, a fat white guy.

148   "You want the bad stuff or the badder stuff?"

149   "As bad as you got."

150   "One dollar a shot."

151   I laid my eighty dollars on the bar top.

152   "All right," I said. "Me and all my cousins here are going to be drinking eighty shots. How many is that apiece?"

153   "Counting you," a woman shouted from behind me, "that's five shots for everybody."

154   I turned to look at her. She was a chubby and pale Indian woman, sitting with a tall and skinny Indian man.

155   "All right, math genius," I said to her, and then shouted for the whole bar to hear. "Five drinks for everybody!"

156   All the other Indians rushed the bar, but I sat with the mathematician and her skinny friend. We took our time with our whiskey shots.

157   "What's your tribe?" I asked.

NOTES

migrate (par. 145): move to

Lummi (par. 145): Native American tribe from the west coast of Washington

158   "I'm Duwamish," she said. "And he's Crow."

159   "You're a long way from Montana," I said to him.

160   "I'm Crow," he said. "I flew here."

161   "What's your name?" I asked them.

162   "I'm Irene Muse," she said. "And this is Honey Boy."

163   She shook my hand hard, but he offered his hand as if I was supposed to kiss it. So I did. He giggled and blushed, as much as a dark-skinned Crow can blush.

164   "You're one of them two-spirits, aren't you?" I asked him.

165   "I love women," he said. "And I love men."

166   "Sometimes both at the same time," Irene said.

167   We laughed.

168   "Man," I said to Honey Boy. "So you must have about eight or nine spirits going on inside you, enit?"

169   "Sweetie," he said. "I'll be whatever you want me to be."

170   "Oh, no," Irene said. "Honey Boy is falling in love."

171   "It has nothing to do with love," he said.

172   We laughed.

173   "Wow," I said. "I'm flattered, Honey Boy, but I don't play on your team."

174   "Never say never," he said.

175   "You better be careful," Irene said. "Honey Boy knows all sorts of magic."

176   "Honey Boy," I said, "you can try to seduce me, but my heart belongs to a woman named Mary."

177   "Is your Mary a virgin?" Honey Boy asked.

178   We laughed.

179   And we drank our whiskey shots until they were gone. But the other Indians bought me more whiskey shots, because I'd been so generous with my money. And Honey Boy pulled out his credit card, and I drank and sailed on that plastic boat.

180   After a dozen shots, I asked Irene to dance. She refused. But Honey Boy shuffled over to the jukebox, dropped in a quarter, and selected Willie Nelson's "Help Me Make It Through the Night." As Irene and I sat at the table and laughed and drank more whiskey, Honey Boy danced a slow circle around us and sang along with Willie.

181   "Are you serenading me?" I asked him.

182   He kept singing and dancing.

183   "Are you serenading me?" I asked him again.

184   "He's going to put a spell on you," Irene said.

185   I leaned over the table, spilling a few drinks, and kissed Irene hard. She kissed me back.

NOTES

Duwamish (par. 158): a Native American tribe from the eastern coast of Puget Sound, where present-day Seattle is located

Crow (par. 158): Native American tribe from southeastern Montana

enit (par. 168): Native American slang word meaning "isn't it," "sure enough"

10 P.M.

186   Irene pushed me into the women's bathroom, into a stall, shut the door behind us, and shoved her hand down my pants. She was short, so I had to lean over to kiss her. I grabbed and squeezed her everywhere I could reach, and she was wonderfully fat, and every part of her body felt like a large, warm, soft breast.

MIDNIGHT

187   Nearly blind with alcohol, I stood alone at the bar and swore I had been standing in the bathroom with Irene only a minute ago.

188   "One more shot!" I yelled at the bartender.

189   "You've got no more money!" he yelled back.

190   "Somebody buy me a drink!" I shouted.

191   "They've got no more money!"

192   "Where are Irene and Honey Boy?"

193   "Long gone!"

2 A.M.

194   "Closing time!" the bartender shouted at the three or four Indians who were still drinking hard after a long, hard day of drinking. Indian alcoholics are either sprinters or marathoners.

195   "Where are Irene and Honey Boy?" I asked.

196   "They've been gone for hours," the bartender said.

197   "Where'd they go?"

198   "I told you a hundred times, I don't know."

199   "What am I supposed to do?"

200   "It's closing time. I don't care where you go, but you're not staying here."

201   "You are an ungrateful bastard. I've been good to you."

202   "You don't leave right now, I'm going to kick your ass."

203   "Come on, I know how to fight."

204   He came at me. I don't remember what happened after that.

4 A.M.

205   I emerged from the blackness and discovered myself walking behind a big warehouse. I didn't know where I was. My face hurt. I felt my nose and decided that it might be broken. Exhausted and cold, I pulled a plastic tarp from a truck bed, wrapped it around me like a faithful lover, and fell asleep in the dirt.

6 A.M.

206   Somebody kicked me in the ribs. I opened my eyes and looked up at a white cop.

207   "Jackson," the cop said. "Is that you?"

208   "Officer Williams," I said. He was a good cop with a sweet tooth. He'd given me hundreds of candy bars over the years. I wonder if he knew I was diabetic.

209   "What the hell are you doing here?" he asked.

210   "I was cold and sleepy," I said. "So I lay down."

211   "You dumb-ass, you passed out on the railroad tracks."

212   I sat up and looked around. I was lying on the railroad tracks. Dockworkers stared at me. I should have been a railroad-track pizza, a double Indian pepperoni with extra cheese. Sick and scared, I leaned over and puked whiskey.

213   "What the hell's wrong with you?" Officer Williams asked. "You've never been this stupid."

214   "It's my grandmother," I said. "She died."

215   "I'm sorry, man. When did she die?"

216   "Nineteen seventy-two."

217   "And you're killing yourself now?"

218   "I've been killing myself ever since she died."

219   He shook his head. He was sad for me. Like I said, he was a good cop.

220   "And somebody beat the hell out of you," he said. "You remember who?"

221   "Mr. Grief and I went a few rounds."

222   "It looks like Mr. Grief knocked you out."

223   "Mr. Grief always wins."

224   "Come on," he said. "Let's get you out of here."

225   He helped me up and led me over to his squad car. He put me in the back. "You throw up in there and you're cleaning it up," he said.

226   "That's fair."

227   He walked around the car and sat in the driver's seat. "I'm taking you over to detox," he said.

228   "No, man, that place is awful," I said. "It's full of drunk Indians."

229   We laughed. He drove away from the docks.

230   "I don't know how you guys do it," he said.

231   "What guys?" I asked.

232   "You Indians. How the hell do you laugh so much? I just picked your ass off the railroad tracks, and you're making jokes. Why the hell do you do that?"

233   "The two funniest tribes I've ever been around are Indians and Jews, so I guess that says something about the inherent humor of genocide."

234   We laughed.

235   "Listen to you, Jackson. You're so smart. Why the hell are you on the street?"

236   "Give me a thousand dollars and I'll tell you."

237   "You bet I'd give you a thousand dollars if I knew you'd straighten up your life."

238   He meant it. He was the second-best cop I'd ever known.

239   "You're a good cop," I said.

240   "Come on, Jackson," he said. "Don't blow smoke up my ass."

241   "No, really, you remind me of my grandfather."

242   "Yeah, that's what you Indians always tell me."

243   "No, man, my grandfather was a tribal cop. He was a good cop. He never arrested people. He took care of them. Just like you."

244   "I've arrested hundreds of scumbags, Jackson. And I've shot a couple in the ass."

245   "It don't matter. You're not a killer."

246   "I didn't kill them. I killed their asses. I'm an ass-killer."

247   We drove through downtown. The missions and shelters had already released their overnighters. Sleepy homeless men and women stood on street corners and stared up at a gray sky. It was the morning after the night of the living dead.

248   "Do you ever get scared?" I asked Officer Williams.

249   "What do you mean?"

250   "I mean, being a cop, is it scary?"

251   He thought about that for a while. He contemplated it. I liked that about him.

252   "I guess I try not to think too much about being afraid," he said. "If you think about fear, then you'll be afraid. The job is boring most of the time. Just driving and looking into dark corners, you know, and seeing nothing. But then things get heavy. You're chasing somebody, or fighting them or walking around a dark house, and you just know some crazy guy is hiding around a corner, and hell, yes, it's scary."

253   "My grandfather was killed in the line of duty," I said.

254   "I'm sorry. How'd it happen?"

255   I knew he'd listen closely to my story.

256   "He worked on the reservation. Everybody knew everybody. It was safe. We aren't like those crazy Sioux or Apache or any of those other warrior tribes. There've only been three murders on my reservation in the last hundred years."

257   "That is safe."

258   "Yeah, we Spokane, we're passive, you know. We're mean with words. And we'll cuss out anybody. But we don't shoot people. Or stab them. Not much, anyway."

259   "So what happened to your grandfather?"

260   "This man and his girlfriend were fighting down by Little Falls."

261   "Domestic dispute. Those are the worst."

262   "Yeah, but this guy was my grandfather's brother. My great-uncle."

263   "Oh, no."

264   "Yeah, it was awful. My grandfather just strolled into the house. He'd been there a thousand times. And his brother and his girlfriend were drunk and beating on each other. And my grandfather stepped between them, just as he'd done a hundred times before. And the girlfriend tripped or something. She fell down and hit her head and started crying. And my grandfather kneeled down beside her to make sure she was all right. And for some reason my great-uncle reached down, pulled my grandfather's pistol out of the holster, and shot him in the head."

265   "That's terrible. I'm sorry."

266   "Yeah, my great-uncle could never figure out why he did it. He went to prison forever, you know, and he always wrote these long letters. Like fifty pages of tiny little handwriting. And he was always trying to figure out why he did it. He'd write and write and write and try to figure it out. He never did. It's a great big mystery."

267   "Do you remember your grandfather?"

268   "A little bit. I remember the funeral. My grandmother wouldn't let them bury him. My father had to drag her away from the grave."

269   "I don't know what to say."

270   "I don't, either."

271   We stopped in front of the detox center.

272   "We're here," Officer Williams said.

273   "I can't go in there," I said.

274   "You have to."

275   "Please, no. They'll keep me for twenty-four hours. And then it will be too late."

276   "Too late for what?"

277   I told him about my grandmother's regalia and the deadline for buying it back.

278   "If it was stolen, you need to file a report," he said. "I'll investigate it myself. If that thing is really your grandmother's, I'll get it back for you. Legally."

279   "No," I said. "That's not fair. The pawnbroker didn't know it was stolen. And, besides, I'm on a mission here. I want to be a hero, you know? I want to win it back, like a knight."

280   "That's romantic crap."

281   "That may be. But I care about it. It's been a long time since I really cared about something."

282   Officer Williams turned around in his seat and stared at me. He studied me.

283   "I'll give you some money," he said. "I don't have much. Only thirty bucks. I'm short until payday. And it's not enough to get back the regalia. But it's something."

284   "I'll take it," I said.

285   "I'm giving it to you because I believe in what you believe. I'm hoping, and I don't know why I'm hoping it, but I hope you can turn thirty bucks into a thousand somehow."

286   "I believe in magic."

287   "I believe you'll take my money and get drunk on it."

288   "Then why are you giving it to me?"

289   "There ain't no such thing as an atheist cop."

290   "Sure, there is."

291   "Yeah, well, I'm not an atheist cop."

292   He let me out of the car, handed me two fivers and a twenty, and shook my hand.

293   "Take care of yourself, Jackson," he said. "Stay off the railroad tracks."

294   "I'll try," I said.

295   He drove away. Carrying my money, I headed back toward the water.

NOTES

detox (par. 271): a hospital or clinic where patients are detoxified (treated for alcohol or drug dependence)

inherent (par. 233): intrinsic, essential

genocide (par. 233): systematic killing of a racial or ethnic group

missions and shelters (par. 247): places where the poor or homeless receive assistance

Sioux or Apache (par. 256): North American tribes widely considered to be warlike or aggressive because they fought white settlers who tried to take their tribal land

atheist (par. 289): someone who believes God does not exist

8 A.M.

296   On the wharf, those three Aleuts still waited on the wooden bench.

297   "Have you seen your ship?" I asked.

298   "Seen a lot of ships," the elder Aleut said. "But not our ship."

299   I sat on the bench with them. We sat in silence for a long time. I wondered if we would fossilize if we sat there long enough.

300   I thought about my grandmother. I'd never seen her dance in her regalia. And, more than anything, I wished I'd seen her dance at a pow-wow.

301   "Do you guys know any songs?" I asked the Aleuts.

302   "I know all of Hank Williams," the elder Aleut said.

303   "How about Indian songs?"

304   "Hank Williams is Indian."

305   "How about sacred songs?"

306   "Hank Williams is sacred."

307   "I'm talking about ceremonial songs. You know, religious ones. The songs you sing back home when you're wishing and hoping."

308   "What are you wishing and hoping for?"

309   "I'm wishing my grandmother was still alive."

310   "Every song I know is about that."

311   "Well, sing me as many as you can."

312   The Aleuts sang their strange and beautiful songs. I listened. They sang about my grandmother and about their grandmothers. They were lonesome for the cold and the snow. I was lonesome for everything.

10 A.M.

313   After the Aleuts finished their last song, we sat in silence for a while. Indians are good at silence.

314   "Was that the last song?" I asked.

315   "We sang all the ones we could," the elder Aleut said. "The others are just for our people."

316   I understood. We Indians have to keep our secrets. And these Aleuts were so secretive they didn't refer to themselves as Indians.

317   "Are you guys hungry?" I asked.

318   They looked at one another and communicated without talking.

319   "We could eat," the elder Aleut said.

11 A.M.

320   The Aleuts and I walked over to the Big Kitchen, a greasy diner in the International District. I knew they served homeless Indians who'd lucked into money.

321   "Four for breakfast?" the waitress asked when we stepped inside.

322   "Yes, we're very hungry," the elder Aleut said.

323   She took us to a booth near the kitchen. I could smell the food cooking. My stomach growled.

324   "You guys want separate checks?" the waitress asked.

325   "No, I'm paying," I said.

326   "Aren't you the generous one," she said.

327   "Don't do that," I said.

328   "Do what?" she asked.

329   "Don't ask me rhetorical questions. They scare me."

330   She looked puzzled, and then she laughed.

331   "O.K., Professor," she said. "I'll only ask you real questions from now on."

332   "Thank you."

333   "What do you guys want to eat?"

334   "That's the best question anybody can ask anybody," I said. "What have you got?"

335   "How much money you got?" she asked.

336   "Another good question," I said. "I've got twenty-five dollars I can spend. Bring us all the breakfast you can, plus your tip."

337   She knew the math.

338   "All right, that's four specials and four coffees and fifteen per cent for me."

339   The Aleuts and I waited in silence. Soon enough, the waitress returned and poured us four coffees, and we sipped at them until she returned again, with four plates of food. Eggs, bacon, toast, hash-brown potatoes. It's amazing how much food you can buy for so little money.

340   Grateful, we feasted.

NOON

341   I said farewell to the Aleuts and walked toward the pawnshop. I heard later that the Aleuts had waded into the salt water near Dock 47 and disappeared. Some Indians swore they had walked on the water and headed north. Other Indians saw the Aleuts drown. I don't know what happened to them.

342   I looked for the pawnshop and couldn't find it. I swear it wasn't in the place where it had been before. I walked twenty or thirty blocks looking for the pawnshop, turned corners and bisected intersections, and looked up its name in the phone books and asked people walking past me if they'd ever heard of it. But that pawnshop seemed to have sailed away like a ghost ship. I wanted to cry. And just when I'd given up, when I turned one last corner and thought I might die if I didn't find that pawnshop, there it was, in a space I swear it hadn't occupied a few minutes ago.

343   I walked inside and greeted the pawnbroker, who looked a little younger than he had before.

344   "It's you," he said.

345   "Yes, it's me," I said.

346   "Jackson Jackson."

347   "That is my name."

348   "Where are your friends?"

349   "They went traveling. But it's O.K. Indians are everywhere."

350   "Do you have the money?"

351   "How much do you need again?" I asked, and hoped the price had changed.

NOTES

rhetorical question (par. 329): a question to which no answer is expected

bisected (par. 342): literally, cut in half; here, crossed through the middle, by walking corner to corner

352   "Nine hundred and ninety-nine dollars."

353   It was still the same price. Of course, it was the same price. Why would it change?

354   "I don't have that," I said.

355   "What do you have?"

356   "Five dollars."

357   I set the crumpled Lincoln on the countertop. The pawnbroker studied it.

358   "Is that the same five dollars from yesterday?"

359   "No, it's different."

360   He thought about the possibilities.

361   "Did you work hard for this money?" he asked.

362   "Yes," I said.

363   He closed his eyes and thought harder about the possibilities. Then he stepped into the back room and returned with my grandmother's regalia.

364   "Take it," he said, and held it out to me.

365   "I don't have the money."

366   "I don't want your money."

367   "But I wanted to win it."

368   "You did win it. Now take it before I change my mind."

369   Do you know how many good men live in this world? Too many to count!

370   I took my grandmother's regalia and walked outside. I knew that solitary yellow bead was part of me. I knew I was that yellow bead in part. Outside, I wrapped myself in my grandmother's regalia and breathed her in. I stepped off the sidewalk and into the intersection. Pedestrians stopped. Cars stopped. The city stopped. They all watched me dance with my grandmother. I was my grandmother, dancing.

What Means Switch

Gish Jen

1   Here we are, nice Chinese family—father, mother, two born-here girls. Where should we live next? My parents slide the question back and forth like a cup of ginseng neither one wants to drink. Until finally it comes to them, what they really want is a milkshake (chocolate) and to go with it a house in Scarsdale. What else? The broker tries to hint: the neighborhood, she says. Moneyed. Many delis. Meaning rich and Jewish. But someone has sent my parents a list of the top ten schools nationwide (based on the opinion of selected educators "and others"), and so, many-deli or not, we nestle into a Dutch colonial on the Bronx River Parkway. The road is winding where we are, very charming; drivers miss their turns, plow up our flowerbeds, then want to use our telephone. "Of course," my mom tells them, like it's no big deal, we can replant. We're the type to adjust. You know—the lady drivers weep, my mom

NOTE

ginseng (par. 1): in other words, ginseng tea. Ginseng is an Asian plant.

gets out the Kleenex for them. We're a bit down the hill from the private-plane set. In other words, only in our dreams do our parka zippers jam, what with all the lift tickets we have stapled to them, Killington on top of Sugarbush on top of Stowe, and we don't even know where the Virgin Islands are—although certain of us do know that virgins are like priests and nuns, which there were a lot more of in Yonkers, where we just moved from, than there are here.

2   This is my first understanding of class. In our old neighborhood everybody knew everything about virgins and nonvirgins, not to say the technicalities of staying in between. Or almost everybody, I should say; in Yonkers I was the laugh-along type. Here I'm an expert.

3   "You mean the man . . . ?" Pigtailed Barbara Gugelstein spits a mouthful of Coke back into her can. "That is *so* gross!"

4   Pretty soon I'm getting popular for a new girl. The only problem is Danielle Meyers, who wears blue mascara and has gone steady with two boys. "How do *you* know," she starts to ask, and proceeds to edify us all with how she French-kissed one boyfriend and just regular kissed another. ("Because, you know, he had braces.") We hear about his rubber bands, how once one popped right into her mouth; I realize I need to find somebody to kiss too. But how? I can't do mascara—my eyelashes stick together. Plus, as Danielle the Great Educator points out, I'm *Chinese*.

5   Luckily, I just about then happen to tell Barbara Gugelstein I know karate. I don't know why I tell her this. My sister, Callie, is the liar in the family; ask anybody. I'm the one who doesn't see why we should have to hold our heads up. But for some reason I tell Barbara Gugelstein I can make my hands like steel by thinking hard. "I'm not supposed to tell anyone," I say.

6   She backs away, blinking. I could be the burning bush.

7   "I can't do bricks," I say—a bit of expectation management. "But I can do your arm if you want." I set my hand in chop position.

8   "Uhh, it's okay," she says. "I know you can. I saw it on TV last night." That's when I recall that I, too, saw it on TV last night—in fact, at her house. I rush on to tell her I know how to get pregnant with tea.

9   "With tea?"

10   "That's how they do it in China."

11   She agrees that China is an ancient and great civilization that ought to be known for more than spaghetti and gunpowder. I tell her I know Chinese.

NOTES

burning bush (par. 6): According to the Old Testament, Moses saw a bush that was burning but was not being consumed by the fire. God spoke to Moses from inside the burning bush, and Moses hid his face, afraid to look upon God (Exodus 3: 1–6).

bar and bas mitzvahs (par. 11): Jewish ceremonies celebrating a 13-year-old's entry into religious adulthood. Bar mitzvahs are for boys; bas mitzvahs are for girls. As part of the religious ceremony, the boy or girl being honored *chants* (par. 11) passages from the Torah in Hebrew.

Seder (par. 11): the ceremonial meal taken on the first night of Passover, the Jewish holy days commemorating the delivery of the Jews from the bondage of the Egyptians.

mortar (par. 11): *Charoses*, one of the dishes on the Seder plate, symbolizes the ***mortar*** with which the enslaved Jews were forced to bake bricks. *Charoses* is a special mixture of apples, nuts, wine, and cinnamon.

schmaltz (par. 11): literally, liquefied chicken fat; figuratively, excessive sentimentality

goy (par. 11): non-Jew

"*Be-yeh-fa-foon,*" I say. "*Shee-veh. Ji nu.*" Meaning, "Stop acting crazy. Rice gruel. Soy sauce." She's impressed. At lunch the next day Danielle Meyers and Amy Weinstein and Barbara's crush, Andy Kaplan, are all impressed too. Scarsdale is a liberal town, not like Yonkers, where the Whitman Road gang used to throw crab-apple mash at Callie and me and tell us it would make our eyes stick shut. Here we're like permanent exchange students. In another ten years there'll be so many Orientals we'll turn into Asians; but for now, the mid-sixties, what with civil rights on TV, we're not so much accepted as embraced. Especially by the Jewish part of town—which, it turns out, is not all of town at all. That's just an idea people have, Callie says, and lots of them could take us or leave us, same as the Christians, who are nice too; I shouldn't generalize. So let me not generalize except to say that pretty soon I've been to so many bar and bas mitzvahs that I can almost say myself whether the kid chants like an angel or like a train conductor, maybe they could use him on the commuter line. At Seder I know to get a good pile of that mortar. Also, I know what is *schmaltz*. I know that I am a goy. This is not why people like me, though. People like me because I do not need to use deodorant, as I demonstrate in the locker room before and after gym. Also, I can explain to them, for example, what is tofu (*der-voo*, we say at home). Their mothers invite me to taste-test their Chinese cooking.

12   "Very authentic." I try to be reassuring. After all, they're nice people. "De-lish." I have seconds. On the question of what we eat, though, I have to admit, "Well, no, it's different from that." I have thirds. "What my mom makes is home style, it's not in the cookbooks."

13   *Not in the cookbooks*! Everyone's jealous. Meanwhile, the big deal at home is when we have turkey pot pie. Callie's the one who introduced them—Mrs. Wilder's, they come in this green-and-brown box—and when we have them, we both suddenly get interested in helping out in the kitchen. You know, we stand in front of the oven and help them bake. Twenty-five minutes. She and I have a deal, though, to keep it secret from school, since everybody else thinks they're gross. *We* think they're a big improvement over authentic Chinese home cooking. Ox tail soup—now, that's gross. Stir-fried beef with tomatoes. One day I say, "You know, Ma, I have never seen a stir-fried tomato in any Chinese restaurant we have ever been in, ever."

14   "In China," she says, pontifical, "we consider tomatoes a delicacy."

15   "Ma," I say. "Tomatoes are *Italian*."

16   "No respect for elders." She wags her finger at me, but I can tell it's just to try and shame me into believing her. "I'm tell you, tomatoes invented in China."

17   "*Ma.*"

18   "Is true. Like noodles. Invented in China."

19   "That's not what they said in school."

20   "*In China,*" my mother counters, "we also eat tomatoes uncooked, like apple. And in summertime we slice them, and put some sugar on top."

21   "Are you sure?"

NOTE

pontifical (par. 14): authoritative

22   My mom says of course she's sure, and in the end I give in, even though she once told me that China was such a long time ago, a lot of things she can hardly remember. She said sometimes she has trouble remembering her characters, that sometimes she'll be writing a letter, just writing along, and all of a sudden she won't be sure if she should put four dots or three.

23   "So what do you do then?"

24   "Oh, I just make a little sloppy."

25   "You mean you *fudge?*"

26   She laughed then, but another time, when she was showing me how to write my name, and I said, just kidding, "Are you sure that's the right number of dots, now?" she was hurt.

27   "I mean, of course you know," I said. "I mean, *oy*." Meanwhile, what *I* know is that in the eighth grade what people want to hear does not include the revelation that Chinese people eat sliced tomatoes with sugar on top. For a gross fact, it just isn't gross enough. On the other hand, the fact that somewhere in China somebody eats or has eaten or once ate living monkey brains—now that's conversation.

28   "They have these special tables," I say, "kind of like a giant collar. With a hole in the middle, for the monkey's neck. They put the monkey in the collar, and then they cut off the top of its head."

29   "Whadda they use for cutting?"

30   I think. "Scalpels."

31   "*Scalpels?*" Andy Kaplan says.

32   "Kaplan, don't be dense," Barbara Gugelstein says. "The Chinese invented scalpels."

33   Once a friend said to me, You know, everybody is valued for something. She explained how some people resented being valued for their looks; others resented being valued for their money. Wasn't it still better to be beautiful and rich than ugly and poor, though? You should just be glad, she said, that you have something people value. It's like having a special talent, like being good at ice-skating, or opera singing. She said, You could probably make a career out of it.

34   Here's the irony: I am.

35   Anyway. I am ad-libbing my way through eighth grade, as I've described. Until one bloomy spring day I come in late to homeroom, and to my chagrin discover there's a new kid in class.

36   Chinese.

37   So what should I do, pretend to have to go to the girls' room, like Barbara Gugelstein the day Andy Kaplan took his ID back? I sit down; I am so cool I remind myself of Paul Newman. First thing I realize, though, is that no one looking at me is thinking of Paul Newman. The notes fly:

NOTES

oy (par. 27): a Yiddish expression used to communicate annoyance, grief, dismay

ad-libbing (par. 35): improvising

chagrin (par. 35): annoyance

Paul Newman (par. 37): the actor who played Luke in the 1967 movie *Cool Hand Luke* (par. 52)

38   "*I* think he's cute."

39   "Who?" I write back. (I am still at an age, understand, when I believe a person can be saved by aplomb.)

40   "I don't think he talks English too good. Writes it either."

41   "Who?"

42   "They might have to put him behind a grade, so don't worry."

43   "He has a crush on you already, you could tell as soon as you walked in, he turned kind of orangish."

44   I hope I'm not turning orangish as I deal with my mail. I could use a secretary. The second round starts:

45   "What do you mean who? Don't be weird. Didn't you *see* him??? Straight back over your right shoulder!!!"

46   I have to look; what else can I do? I think of certain tips I learned in Girl Scouts about poise. I cross my ankles. I hold a pen in my hand. I sit up as though I have a crown on my head. I swivel my head slowly, repeating to myself, *I could be Miss America.*

47   "Miss Mona Chang."

48   Horror raises its hoary head.

49   "Notes, please."

50   Mrs. Mandeville's policy is to read all notes aloud.

51   I try to consider what Miss America would do and see myself: back straight, knees together, crying. Some inspiration. Cool Hand Luke, on the other hand, would, quick, eat the evidence. And why not? I should yawn as I stand up, and boom, the notes are gone. All that's left is to explain that it's an old Chinese reflex.

52   I shuffle up to the front of the room.

53   "One minute, please," Mrs. Mandeville says.

54   I wait, noticing how large and plastic her mouth is. She unfolds a piece of paper.

55   And I, Miss Mona Chang, who got almost straight A's her whole life except in math and conduct, am about to start crying in front of everyone. I am delivered out of hot Egypt by the bell. General pandemonium. Mrs. Mandeville still has her hand clamped on my shoulder, though; and the next thing I know, I'm holding the new boy's schedule. He's standing next to me like a big blank piece of paper. "This is Sherman," Mrs. Mandeville says.

56   "Hello," I say.

57   "*Non how a,*" I say.

58   I'm glad Barbara Gugelstein isn't there to see my Chinese in action. "*Ji nu,*" I say. "*Shee veh.*"

59   Later I find out that his mother asked if there were any other Orientals in our grade. She had him put in my class on purpose. For now, though, he looks at

NOTES

aplomb (par. 39): self-confidence

poise (par. 46): posture

hoary (par. 48): ancient

delivered out of hot Egypt (par. 55): a reference to the delivery of the Jews out of bondage in Egypt

pandemonium (par. 55): chaos

me as if I'm much stranger than anything else he's seen so far. Is this because he understands that I'm saying "soy sauce rice gruel" to him or because he doesn't?

60   "Sher-man," he says finally.

61   I look at his schedule card. Sherman Matsumoto. What kind of name is that for a nice Chinese boy?

62   (Later on, people ask me how I can tell Chinese from Japanese. I shrug. It's the kind of thing you just kind of know, I say. *Oy!*)

63   Sherman's got the sort of looks I think of as pretty-boy. Monsignor-black hair (not monk-brown, like mine), kind of bouncy. Crayola eyebrows, one with a round bald spot in the middle of it, like a golf hole. I don't know how anybody can think of him as orangish; his skin looks white to me, with pink triangles hanging down the front of his cheeks like flags. Kind of delicate-looking, but the only truly uncool thing about him is that his spiral notebook has a picture of a kitty cat on it. A big white fluffy one, with a blue ribbon above each perky little ear. I get much opportunity to view this, because all the poor kid understands about life in junior high school is that he should follow me everywhere. It's embarrassing. But he's obviously even more miserable than I am; so I try not to say anything. I decide to give him a chance to adjust. We communicate by sign language, and by drawing pictures, which he's better at than I am; he puts in every last detail, even if it takes forever. I try to be patient.

64   A week of this. Finally I enlighten him. "You should get a new notebook."

65   His cheeks turn a shade of pink you see mostly only in hyacinths.

66   "Notebook." I point to his. I show him mine, which is psychedelic, with purple and yellow stick-on flowers. I try to explain that he should have one like this, only without the flowers. He nods enigmatically, and the next day brings me a notebook just like his, except that this cat sports pink bows instead of blue.

67   "Pret-ty," he says. "You."

68   He speaks English! I'm dumbfounded. Has he spoken it all this time? I consider: Pretty. You. What does that mean? Plus actually he's said *"plit-ty,"* much as my parents would; I'm assuming he means pretty, but maybe he means pity. Pity. You.

69   "Jeez," I say finally.

70   "You are wel-come," he says.

71   I decorate the back of the notebook with stick-on flowers, and hold it so that they show when I walk through the halls. In class I keep my book open. After all, the kid's so new; I think I ought to have a heart. And for a livelong day nobody notices.

72   Then Barbara Gugelstein sidles up. "Matching notebooks, huh?"

73   I'm speechless.

74   "First comes love, then comes marriage, and then come chappies in a baby carriage."

NOTES

Monsignor (par. 63): a title bestowed by the Pope on clerics of his choosing to indicate that they are part of the Papal family

hyacinths (par. 65): a Mediterranean plants

75   "Barbara!"

76   "Get it?" she says. "Chinese Japs."

77   "Bar-*bra*," I say to get even.

78   "Just make sure he doesn't give you any *tea*," she says.

79   Are Sherman and I in love? Three days later I hazard that we are. My thinking proceeds this way: I think he's cute, and I think he thinks I'm cute. On the other hand, we don't kiss and we don't exactly have fantastic conversations. Our talks *are* getting better, though. We started out, "This is a book."

80   "Book."

81   "This is a chair."

82   "Chair."

83   Advancing to, "What is this?"

84   "This is a book."

85   Now, for fun, he tests me. " What is this?" he says. "This is a book," I say, as if I'm the one who has to learn how to talk.

86   He claps. "Good!"

87   Meanwhile, people ask me all about him. I could be his press agent.

88   "No, he doesn't eat raw fish."

89   "No, his father wasn't a kamikaze pilot."

90   "No, he can't do karate."

91   "Are you sure?" somebody asks.

92   Indeed he doesn't know karate, but judo he does. I am hurt that I'm not the one to find this out; the guys know from gym class. They line up to be flipped, he flips them all onto the floor, and after that he doesn't eat lunch at the girls' table with me anymore. I'm more or less glad. Meaning, when he was there, I never knew what to say. Now that he's gone, though, I seem to be stuck at the "This is a chair" level of conversation. Ancient Chinese eating habits have lost their cachet; all I get are more and more inquiries about me and Sherman. "I dunno," I'm saying all the time. *Are* we going out? We do stuff, it's true. For example, I take him to the department stores, explain to him who shops in Alexander's, who shops in Saks. I tell him my family's the type that shops in Alexander's. He says he's sorry. In Saks he gets lost, though maybe I'm the lost one. (It's true I find him calmly waiting at the front door, hands behind his back, like a guard.) I take him to the candy store. I take him to the bagel store. Sherman is crazy about bagels. I explain to him that Lender's is gross; he should get his bagels from the bagel store. He says thank you.

93   "Are you going steady?" people want to know.

94   How can we go steady when he doesn't have an ID bracelet? On the other hand, he brings me more presents than I think any girl's ever gotten before. Oranges. Flowers. A little bag of bagels. But what do they mean? Do they mean

NOTES

hazard (par. 79): guess

kamikaze pilot (par. 89): World War II Japanese pilots who were trained to intentionally crash their planes into enemy ships

cachet (par. 92): importance

Lender's (par. 92): a brand of store-bought bagels

thank you, I enjoyed our trip; do they mean I like you; do they mean I decided I liked the Lender's better even if they are gross, and you can have these? Sometimes I think he's acting on his mother's instructions. Also I know that at least a couple of items were supposed to go to our teachers. He told me that and turned red. I figured it still might mean something that he didn't throw them out.

95   More and more now, we joke. Like, instead of *I'm thinking,* he always says, "I'm sinking," which we both think is so funny that all either one of us has to do is pretend to be drowning and the other one cracks up. And he tells me things—for example, that electric lights are everywhere in Tokyo now.

96   "You mean you didn't have them before?"

97   "Everywhere now!" He's amazed too. "Since Olympics!"

98   "Olympics?"

99   He hums for me the Olympic theme song. "You know?" "Sure," I say, and hum with him happily. We could be a picture on a UNICEF poster. The only problem is that I don't really understand what the Olympics have to do with the modernization of Japan, any more than I get this other story he tells me, about that hole in his left eyebrow, which is from some time his father accidentally hit him with a lit cigarette. When Sherman was a baby, his father was drunk, having been out carousing; his mother was very mad but didn't say anything, just cleaned the whole house. Then his father was so ashamed he bowed to ask her forgiveness.

100   "Your mother cleaned the house?"

101   Sherman nods solemnly.

102   "And your father *bowed?*" I find this more astounding than anything I ever thought to make up. "That is so weird," I tell him.

103   "Weird," he agrees. "This I no forget, forever. *Father* bow to *mother!*"

104   We shake our heads.

105   As for the things he asks me, they're not topics I ever discussed before. Do I like it here? Of course I like it here, I was born here, I say. Am I Jewish? Jewish! I laugh. *Oy!* Am I American? "Sure I'm American," I say. "Everybody who's born here is American, and also some people who convert from what they were before. You could become American." But he says no, he could never. "Sure you could," I say. "You only have to learn some rules and speeches."

106   "But I Japanese," he says.

107   "You could become American anyway," I say. "Like I *could* become Jewish, if I wanted to. I'd just have to switch, that's all."

108   "But you Catholic," he says.

109   I think maybe he doesn't get what means switch.

110   I introduce him to Mrs. Wilder's turkey pot pies. "Gross?" he asks. I say they are, but we like them anyway. "Don't tell anybody." He promises. We bake them, eat them. While we're eating, he's drawing me pictures.

111   "This American," he says, and he draws something that looks like John Wayne. "This Jewish," he says, and draws something that looks like the Wicked Witch of the West, only male.

NOTES

UNICEF (par. 99): United Nations International Children's Emergency Fund
carousing (par. 99): partying

112　　"I don't think so," I say.

113　　He's undeterred. "This Japanese," he says, and draws a fair rendition of himself. "This Chinese," he says, and draws what looks to be another fair rendition of himself.

114　　"How can you tell them apart?"

115　　"This way," he says, and he puts the picture of the Chinese so that it faces the pictures of the American and the Jew. The Japanese faces the wall. Then he draws another picture, of a Japanese flag, so that the Japanese is looking at his flag. "Chinese lost in department store," he says. "Japanese know how go." For fun he draws another Japanese flag, a bigger one, which he attaches to the refrigerator with magnets. "In school, in ceremony, we this way," he explains, and bows to the picture.

116　　When my mother comes in, her face is so red that with the white wall behind her she looks a bit like the Japanese flag herself. Yet I get the feeling I better not say so. First she doesn't move. Then she snatches the flag off the refrigerator, so fast the magnets go flying. Two of them land on the stove. She crumples the paper. She hisses at Sherman, "*This is the U. S. of A., do you hear me!*"

117　　Sherman hears her.

118　　"You call your mother right now, tell her come pick you up."

119　　*He* understands perfectly. I, on the other hand, am buffaloed. How can two people who don't really speak English understand each other better than I can understand them? "But, Ma," I say.

120　　"Don't *Ma* me," she says.

121　　Later on she explains that the Second World War was in China, too. "Hitler," I say. "Nazis. Volkswagens." I know the Japanese were on the wrong side, because they bombed Pearl Harbor. My mother explains about before that. The Napkin Massacre. "*Nan*-king," she corrects me.

122　　"Are you sure?" I say. "In school they said the war was about putting the Jews in ovens."

123　　"Also about ovens."

124　　"About both?"

125　　"Both."

126　　"That's not what they said in school."

127　　"*Just forget about school.*"

128　　Forget about school? "I thought we moved here for the schools."

129　　"We moved here," she says, "for your education." Sometimes I have, no idea what she's talking about.

130　　"I like Sherman," I say after awhile.

131　　"He's nice boy," she agrees.

132　　Meaning what? I would ask, except that my dad's just come home, which means it's time to start talking about whether they should build a brick wall across the front of the lawn. Recently a car made it almost into our living

NOTES

undeterred (par. 113): not bothered

rendition (par. 113): representation

Nanking Massacre (par. 121): On December 13, 1937, the Japanese Imperial Army captured the Chinese city of Nanking. During the weeks that followed, Japanese troops ravaged the city, raped tens of thousands of women, and murdered between 100,000 and 300,000 Chinese citizens.

room, which was so scary that the driver fainted and an ambulance had to come. "We should have discussion," my dad said after that. It's what he says every time. And so for about a week, every night we have them.

133   "Are you just friends or more than just friends?" Barbara Gugelstein is giving me the cross-ex.

134   "Maybe," I say.

135   "Come on," she says. "I told you *everything* about me and Andy."

136   I actually *am* trying to tell Barbara everything about Sherman, but everything turns out to be nothing. Meaning I can't locate the conversation in what I have to say: Sherman and I go places, we talk, my mother once threw him out of the house because of the Second World War.

137   "I think we're just friends," I say.

138   "You think or you're sure?"

139   Now that I do less of the talking at lunch, I notice more what other people talk about—cheerleading, who likes who, this place in White Plains to get earrings. On none of these topics am I an expert. Of course, I'm still friends with Barbara Gugelstein, but I notice that Danielle Meyers has spun away to other groups.

140   Barbara's analysis goes this way: To be popular you have to have big boobs, a note from your mother that lets you use her Lord & Taylor credit card, and a boyfriend. On the other hand, what's so wrong with being unpopular? "We'll get them in the end," she says. It's what her dad tells her. "Like they'll turn out too dumb to do their own investing," she says, "and then they'll get killed in broker's fees and then they'll have to move to towns where the schools stink. And my dad should know," she winds up. "He's a broker."

141   "I guess," I say.

142   But the next thing I know, I have a true crush on Sherman Matsumoto. *Mis*ter Judo, the guys call him now, with real respect; and the more they call him that, the more I don't care that he carries a notebook with a cat on it.

143   I sigh. "Sherman."

144   "I thought you were just friends," Barbara Gugelstein says.

145   "We were," I say mysteriously. This, I've noticed, is how Danielle Meyers talks; everything's secret, she only lets out so much, it's apparent she didn't grow up with everybody telling her she had to share.

146   And here's the funny thing: The more I intimate that Sherman and I are hot and heavy, the more it seems we actually are. It's the old imagination giving reality a nudge. When I start to blush, he starts to blush; we reach a point where we can hardly talk at all.

147   "Well, there's first base with tongue, and first base without," I tell Barbara Gugelstein.

148   In fact, Sherman and I have brushed shoulders, and what actually happened was at least equivalent to first base, I was sure, maybe even second. I felt as though I'd turned into one huge shoulder; that's all I was, one huge shoulder. We not only didn't talk, we didn't breathe. But how can I tell Barbara Gugelstein that? So instead I say, "Well, there's second base and second base."

NOTE

intimate (par. 146): hint

149   Danielle Meyers is my friend again. She says, "I know exactly what you mean," just to make Barbara Gugelstein feel bad.

150   "Like *what* do I mean?" I say.

151   Danielle Meyers can't answer.

152   "You know what I think?" I tell Barbara the next day. "I think Danielle's giving us a line."

153   Barbara pulls thoughtfully on one of her pigtails.

154   If Sherman Matsumoto is never going give me an ID to wear, he should at least get up the nerve to hold my hand. I don't think he sees this. I think of the story he told about his parents, and in a synaptic firestorm realize we don't see the same things at all.

155   So one day, when we happen to brush shoulders again: I don't move away. He doesn't move away either. There we are. Like a pair of bleachers, pushed together but not quite matched up. After a while I have to breathe, I can't help it. I breathe in such a way that our elbows start to touch too. We are in a crowd, waiting for a bus. I crane my neck to look at the sign that says where the bus is going; now our wrists are touching. Then it happens: he links his pinky around mine.

156   Is that holding hands? Later, in bed, I wonder all night. One finger, and not even the biggest one.

157   Sherman is leaving in a month. Already! I think, well, I suppose he will leave and we'll never even kiss. I guess that's all right. Just when I've resigned myself to that, we hold hands all five fingers. Once when we are at the bagel shop, then again in my parents' kitchen. Then, when we are on the playground, he kisses the back of my hand.

158   He does it again not too long after that, in White Plains.

159   I invest in a bottle of mouthwash.

160   Instead of moving on, though, he kisses the back of my hand again. And again. I try raising my hand, hoping he'll make the jump from my hand to my cheek. It's like trying to wheedle an inchworm out the window. You know, *This way, this way.*

161   *All over the world people have their own cultures.* That's what we learned in social studies.

162   If we never kiss, I'm not going to take it personally.

163   It is the end of the school year. We've had parties. We've turned in our textbooks. Hooray! Outside, the asphalt already steams if you spit on it. Sherman isn't leaving for another couple of days, though, and he comes to visit every morning, staying until the afternoon, when Callie comes home from her big-deal job as a bank teller. We drink Kool-Aid in the back yard and hold hands until they are sweaty and make smacking noises coming apart. He tells me how busy his parents are, getting ready for the move. His mother, particularly, is very tired. Mostly we are mournful.

164   The very last day we hold hands and do not let go. Our palms fill up with water like a blister. We do not care. We talk more than usual. How much it will

NOTE

synaptic (par. 154): mental

cost to send an airmail letter to Japan, that kind of thing. Then suddenly he asks, will I marry him?

165   *I'm only thirteen.*

166   *But when old? Sixteen.*

167   *If you come back to get me.*

168   *I come. Or you can come to Japan, be Japanese.*

169   *How can I be Japanese?*

170   *Like you become American. Switch.*

171   He kisses me on the cheek, again and again and again.

172   His mother calls to say that she's coming to get him. I cry. I tell him how I've saved every present he's ever given me—the ruler, the pencils, the bags from the bagels, all the flower petals. I even have the orange peels from the oranges.

173   *All.*

174   *I put them in a jar.*

175   I'd show him, except that we're not allowed to go upstairs to my room. Anyway, something about the orange peels seems to choke him up too. *Mister judo,* but I've gotten him in a soft spot. We are going together to the bathroom to get some toilet paper to wipe our eyes when poor tired Mrs. Matsumoto, driving her family's car, skids up onto our lawn.

176   "Very sorry!"

177   We race outside.

178   "Very sorry!"

179   Mrs. Matsumoto is so short that all we can see of her is a green cotton sun hat, with a big brim. It's tied on. The brim is trembling.

180   I hope my mom's not going to start yelling about the Second World War.

181   "Is all right, no trouble," she says, materializing on the steps, behind me and Sherman. She's propped the screen door wide open; when I turn, I see she's waving. "No trouble, no trouble!"

182   "No trouble, no trouble!" I echo, twirling a few times with relief.

183   Mrs. Matsumoto keeps apologizing; my mom keeps insisting she shouldn't feel bad, it was only some grass and a small tree. Crossing the lawn, she insists that Mrs. Matsumoto get out of the car, even though it means trampling some lilies-of-the-valley. She insists that Mrs. Matsumoto come in for a cup of tea. Then she will not talk about anything unless Mrs. Matsumoto sits down, and unless she lets my mom prepare her a small snack. The coming in and the tea and the sitting down are settled pretty quickly, but they negotiate ferociously over the small snack, which Mrs. Matsumoto will not eat unless she can call Mr. Matsumoto. She makes the mistake of linking Mr. Matsumoto with a reparation of some sort, which my mom will not hear of.

184   "Please!"

185   "No no no no."

186   Back and forth it goes.

187   "'No no no no." "No no no no." "No no no no."

188   What kind of conversation is that? I look at Sherman, who shrugs. Finally, Mr. Matsumoto calls on his own, wondering where his wife is. He comes over

NOTE

reparation (par. 183): compensation (for damage)

in a taxi. He's a heavy-browed businessman, friendly but brisk—not at all a type you could imagine bowing to a lady with a taste for tie-on sun hats. My mom invites him in as if it's an idea she just this moment thought of. And would he maybe have some tea and a small snack?

189   Sherman and I sneak back outside for another farewell by the side of the house, behind the forsythia bushes. We hold hands. He kisses me on the cheek again, and then—just when I think he's finally going to kiss me on the lips—he kisses me on the neck.

190   Is this first base?

191   He does it more. Up and down, up and down. First it tickles, and then it doesn't. He has his eyes closed. I close my eyes too. He's hugging me. Up and down. Then down.

192   He's at my collarbone.

193   Still at my collarbone. Now his hand's on my ribs. So much for first base. More ribs. The idea of second base would probably make me nervous if he weren't on his way back to Japan and if I really thought we were going to get there. As it is, though, I'm not in much danger of wrecking my life on the shoals of passion; his unmoving hand feels more like a growth than a boyfriend. He has his whole face pressed to my neck skin so I can't tell his mouth from his nose. I think he may be licking me.

194   From indoors, a burst of adult laughter. My eyelids flutter. I start to try and wiggle such that his hand will maybe budge upward.

195   Do I mean for my top blouse button to come accidentally undone?

196   He clenches his jaw, and when he opens his eyes, they're fixed on that button like it's a gnat that's been bothering him for far too long. He mutters in Japanese. If later in life he were to describe this as a pivotal moment in his youth, I would not be surprised. Holding the material as far from my body as possible, he buttons the button. Somehow we've landed up too close to the bushes.

197   How to tell Barbara Gugelstein? She says, "Tell me what were his last words. He must have said something last."

198   "I don't want to talk about it."

199   "Maybe he said, 'Good-bye?'" she suggests. "'*Sayonara?*'" She means well.

200   "I don't want to talk about it."

201   "Aw, come on, I told you everything about . . ."

202   I say, "Because it's private, excuse me."

203   She stops, squints at me as though I were a far-off face she's trying to make out. Then she nods and very lightly places her hand on my forearm.

204   The forsythia seemed to be stabbing us in the eyes. Sherman said, more or less, *You will need to study how to switch.*

205   And I said, *I think you should switch.* The way you do everything is weird.

206   And he said, *You just want to tell everything to your friends. You just want to have boyfriend to become popular.*

NOTES

shoals (par. 193): literally, banks of sand that make the water shallow
pivotal moment (par. 196): turning point

207   Then he flipped me. Two swift moves, and I went sprawling through the air, a flailing confusion of soft human parts such as had no idea where the ground was, much less how hard it could be.

208   It is the fall, and I am in high school, and still he hasn't written, so finally I write him.

209   *I still have all your gifts, I write. I don't talk so much as I used to. Although I am not exactly a mouse either: I don't care about being popular anymore. I swear. Are you happy to be back in Japan? I know I ruined everything. I was just trying to be entertaining. I miss you with all my heart, and hope I didn't ruin everything.*

210   He writes back, *You will never be Japanese.*

211   I throw all the orange peels out that day. Some of them, it turns out, were moldy anyway. I tell my mother I want to move to Chinatown.

212   "Chinatown!" she says.

213   I don't know why I suggested it.

214   "What's the matter?" she says. "Still boy-crazy? That Sherman?"

215   "No."

216   "Too much homework?"

217   I don't answer.

218   "Forget about school."

219   Later she tells me that if I don't like school, I don't have to go every day. Some days I can stay home.

220   "Stay home?" In Yonkers, Callie and I used to stay home all the time, but that was because the schools there were *waste of time.*

221   "No good for a girl be too smart anyway."

222   For a long time I think about Sherman. But after a while I don't think about him as much as I just keep seeing myself flipped onto the ground, lying there shocked as the Matsumotos get ready to leave. My head has hit a rock; my brain aches as though it's been shoved to some new place in my skull. Otherwise I am okay. I see the forsythia, all those whippy branches, and can't believe how many leaves there are on a bush—every one green and perky and durably itself. And past them real sky. I try to remember why the sky's blue, even though this one's gone the kind of indescribable gray you associate with the inside of old shoes. I smell grass. Probably I have grass stains all over my back. I hear my mother calling through the back door, "Mona! Everyone leaving now," and "Not coming to say good-bye?" I hear Mr. and Mrs. Matsumoto bowing as they leave—or at least I hear the embarrassment in my mother's voice as they bow. I hear their car start. I hear Mrs. Matsumoto directing Mr. Matsumoto how to back off the lawn so as not to rip any more of it up. I feel the back of my head for blood—just a little. I hear their chug-chug grow fainter and fainter, until it has faded into the whuzz-whuzz of all the other cars. I hear my mom singing, "*Mon-a! Mon-a!*" until my dad comes home. Doors open and shut. I see myself standing up, brushing myself off so I'll have less explaining to do if she comes out to look for me. Grass stains—just like I thought.

223   I see myself walking around the house, going over to have a look at our churned-up yard. It looks pretty sad, two big brown tracks, right through the

NOTE

flailing (par. 207): thrashing

irises and the lilies of the valley, and that was a new dogwood we'd just planted. Lying there like that. I find myself thinking about my father, having to go dig it up all over again. Adjusting. I think how we probably ought to put up that brick wall. And sure enough, when I go inside, no one is worrying about me, or that little bit of blood at the back of my head, or the grass stains—that's what they're talking about: that wall. Again. My mom doesn't think it'll do any good, but my dad thinks we should give it a try. Should we or shouldn't we? How high? How thick? What will the neighbors say? I plop myself down on a hard chair. And all I can think is, we are the complete only family that has to worry about this. If I could, I'd switch everything to be different. But since I can't, I might as well sit here at the table for a while, discussing what I know how to discuss. I nod and listen to the rest.

A Rose for Emily

William Faulkner

I

1   When Miss Emily Grierson died, our whole town went to her funeral: the men through a sort of respectful affection for a fallen monument, the women mostly out of curiosity to see the inside of her house, which no one save an old man-servant—a combined gardener and cook—had seen in at least ten years.

2   It was a big, squarish frame house that had once been white, decorated with cupolas and spires and scrolled balconies in the heavily lightsome style of the seventies, set on what had once been our most select street. But garages and cotton gins had encroached and obliterated even the august names of that neighborhood; only Miss Emily's house was left, lifting its stubborn and co-quettish decay above the cotton wagons and the gasoline pumps—an eyesore among eyesores. And now Miss Emily had gone to join the representatives of those august names where they lay in the cedar-bemused cemetery among the ranked and anonymous graves of Union and Confederate soldiers who fell at the battle of Jefferson.

3   Alive, Miss Emily had been a tradition, a duty, and a care; a sort of heredi-tary obligation upon the town, dating from that day in 1894 when Colonel

NOTES

cupolas (par. 2): a rounded structure forming part of the roof of a house
spires (par. 2): small steeples
scrolled balconies (par. 2): balconies with fancy designs or "scrollwork"
lightsome (par. 2): graceful
encroached (par. 2): moved in
obliterated (par. 2): destroyed
august (par. 2): grand
coquettish (par. 2): literally, flirtatious
cedar-bemused (par. 2): overgrown with cedars
hereditary (par. 3): inherited
remitted (par. 3): cancelled

Sartoris, the mayor—he who fathered the edict that no Negro woman should appear on the street without an apron—remitted her taxes, the dispensation dating from the death of her father on into perpetuity. Not that Miss Emily would have accepted charity. Colonel Sartoris invented an involved tale to the effect that Miss Emily's father had loaned money to the town, which the town, as a matter of business, preferred this way of repaying. Only a man of Colonel Sartoris' generation and thought could have invented it, and only a woman could have believed it.

4   When the next generation, with its more modern ideas, became mayors and aldermen, this arrangement created some little dissatisfaction. On the first of the year they mailed her a tax notice. February came, and there was no reply. They wrote her a formal letter, asking her to call at the sheriff's office at her convenience. A week later the mayor wrote her himself, offering to call or to send his car for her, and received in reply a note on paper of an archaic shape, in a thin, flowing calligraphy in faded ink, to the effect that she no longer went out at all. The tax notice was also enclosed, without comment.

5   They called a special meeting of the Board of Aldermen. A deputation waited upon her, knocked at the door through which no visitor had passed since she ceased giving china-painting lessons eight or ten years earlier. They were admitted by the old Negro into a dim hall from which a stairway mounted into still more shadow. It smelled of dust and disuse—a close, dank smell. The Negro led them into the parlor. It was furnished in heavy, leather-covered furniture. When the Negro opened the blinds of one window, they could see that the leather was cracked; and when they sat down, a faint dust rose sluggishly about their thighs, spinning with slow motes in the single sun-ray. On a tarnished gilt easel before the fireplace stood a crayon portrait of Miss Emily's father.

6   They rose when she entered—a small, fat woman in black, with a thin gold chain descending to her waist and vanishing into her belt, leaning on an ebony cane with a tarnished gold head. Her skeleton was small and spare; perhaps that was why what would have been merely plumpness in another was obesity in her. She looked bloated, like a body long submerged in motionless water, and of that pallid hue. Her eyes, lost in the fatty ridges of her face, looked like two small pieces of coal pressed into a lump of dough as they moved from one face to another while the visitors stated their errand.

7   She did not ask them to sit. She just stood in the door and listened quietly until the spokesman came to a stumbling halt. Then they could hear the invisible watch ticking at the end of the gold chain.

NOTES

dispensation (par. 3): exemption

perpetuity (par. 3): eternity

archaic (par. 4): old-fashioned

calligraphy (par. 4): fancy writing

deputation (par. 5): a group of citizens that represents others

dank (par. 5): damp

motes (par. 5): specks

gilt (par. 5): a gold coating

ebony (par. 6): a black wood

pallid hue (par. 6): pale color

8   Her voice was dry and cold. "I have no taxes in Jefferson. Colonel Sartoris explained it to me. Perhaps one of you can gain access to the city records and satisfy yourselves."

9   "But we have. We are the city authorities, Miss Emily. Didn't you get a notice from the sheriff, signed by him?"

10   "I received a paper, yes," Miss Emily said. "Perhaps he considers himself the sheriff . . . I have no taxes in Jefferson."

11   "But there is nothing on the books to show that, you see. We must go by the—"

12   "See Colonel Sartoris. I have no taxes in Jefferson."

13   "But, Miss Emily—"

14   "See Colonel Sartoris." (Colonel Sartoris had been dead almost ten years.) "I have no taxes in Jefferson. Tobe!" The Negro appeared. "Show these gentlemen out."

II

15   So she vanquished them, horse and foot, just as she had vanquished their fathers thirty years before about the smell. That was two years after her father's death and a short time after her sweetheart—the one we believed would marry her—had deserted her. After her father's death she went out very little; after her sweetheart went away, people hardly saw her at all. A few of the ladies had the temerity to call, but were not received, and the only sign of life about the place was the Negro man—a young man then—going in and out with a market basket.

16   "Just as if a man—any man—could keep a kitchen properly," the ladies said; so they were not surprised when the smell developed. It was another link between the gross, teeming world and the high and mighty Griersons.

17   A neighbor, a woman, complained to the mayor, Judge Stevens, eighty years old.

18   "But what will you have me to do about it, madam?" he said.

19   "Why, send her word to stop it," the woman said. "Isn't there a law?"

20   "I'm sure that won't be necessary," Judge Stevens said. "It's probably just a snake or a rat that nigger of hers killed in the yard. I'll speak to him about it."

21   The next day he received two more complaints, one from a man who came in diffident deprecation. "We really must do something about it, Judge. I'd be the last one in the world to bother Miss Emily, but we've got to do something." That night the Board of Aldermen met—three graybeards and one younger man, a member of the rising generation.

22   "It's simple enough," he said. "Send her word to have her place cleaned up. Give her a certain time to do it in, and if she don't . . . "

NOTES

vanquished (par. 15): defeated
temerity (par. 15): nerve
teeming (par. 16): crowded
diffident (par. 21): hesitant
deprecation (par. 21): mild disapproval

23   "Dammit, sir," Judge Stevens said, "will you accuse a lady to her face of smelling bad?"

24   So the next night, after midnight, four men crossed Miss Emily's lawn and slunk about the house like burglars, sniffing along the base of the brickwork and at the cellar openings while one of them performed a regular sowing motion with his hand out of a sack slung from his shoulder. They broke open the cellar door and sprinkled lime there, and in all the outbuildings. As they recrossed the lawn, a window that had been dark was lighted and Miss Emily sat in it, the light behind her, and her upright torso motionless as that of an idol. They crept quietly across the lawn and into the shadow of the locusts that lined the street. After a week or two the smell went away.

25   That was when people had begun to feel really sorry for her. People in our town, remembering how old lady Wyatt, her great-aunt, had gone completely crazy at last, believed that the Griersons held themselves a little too high for what they really were. None of the young men were quite good enough for Miss Emily and such. We had long thought of them as a tableau, Miss Emily a slender figure in white in the background, her father a spraddled silhouette in the foreground, his back to her and clutching a horsewhip, the two of them framed by the back-flung front door. So when she got to be thirty and was still single, we were not pleased exactly, but vindicated; even with insanity in the family she wouldn't have turned down all of her chances if they had really materialized.

26   When her father died, it got about that the house was all that was left to her, and in a way, people were glad. At last they could pity Miss Emily. Being left alone, and a pauper, she had become humanized. Now she too would know the old thrill and the old despair of a penny more or less.

27   The day after his death all the ladies prepared to call at the house and offer condolence and aid, as is our custom. Miss Emily met them at the door, dressed as usual and with no trace of grief on her face. She told them that her father was not dead. She did that for three days, with the ministers calling on her, and the doctors, trying to persuade her to let them dispose of the body. Just as they were about to resort to law and force, she broke down, and they buried her father quickly.

28   We did not say she was crazy then. We believed she had to do that. We remembered all the young men her father had driven away, and we knew that with nothing left, she would have to cling to that which had robbed her, as people will.

NOTES

sowing (par. 24): scattering

torso (par. 24): upper body

tableau (par. 25): like a posed picture

spraddled (par. 25): spread out

silhouette (par. 25): literally, the outline of some figure

vindicated (par. 25): proven correct

materialized (par. 25): occurred

pauper (par. 26): a very poor person

condolence (par. 27): sympathy

III

29   She was sick for a long time. When we saw her again, her hair was cut short, making her look like a girl, with a vague resemblance to those angels in colored church windows—sort of tragic and serene.

30   The town had just let the contracts for paving the sidewalks, and in the summer after her father's death they began the work. The construction company came with niggers and mules and machinery, and a foreman named Homer Barron, a Yankee—a big, dark, ready man, with a big voice and eyes lighter than his face. The little boys would follow in groups to hear him cuss the niggers, and the niggers singing in time to the rise and fall of picks. Pretty soon he knew everybody in town. Whenever you heard a lot of laughing anywhere about the square, Homer Barron would be in the center of the group. Presently, we began to see him and Miss Emily on Sunday afternoons driving in the yellow-wheeled buggy and the matched team of bays from the livery stable.

31   At first we were glad that Miss Emily would have an interest, because the ladies all said, "Of course a Grierson would not think seriously of a Northerner, a day laborer." But there were still others, older people, who said that even grief could not cause a real lady to forget *noblesse oblige*—without calling it *noblesse oblige*. They just said, "Poor Emily. Her kinsfolk should come to her." She had some kin in Alabama; but years ago her father had fallen out with them over the estate of old lady Wyatt, the crazy woman, and there was no communication between the two families. They had not even been represented at the funeral.

32   And as soon as the old people said, "Poor Emily," the whispering began. "Do you suppose it's really so?" they said to one another. "Of course it is. What else could . . . " This behind their hands; rustling of craned silk and satin behind jalousies closed upon the sun of Sunday afternoon as the thin, swift clop-clop-clop of the matched team passed: "Poor Emily."

33   She carried her head high enough—even when we believed that she was fallen. It was as if she demanded more than ever the recognition of her dignity as the last Grierson; as if it had wanted that touch of earthiness to reaffirm her imperviousness. Like when she bought the rat poison, the arsenic. That was over a year after they had begun to say "Poor Emily," and while the two female cousins were visiting her.

34   "I want some poison," she said to the druggist. She was over thirty then, still a slight woman, though thinner than usual, with cold, haughty black eyes in a face the flesh of which was strained across the temples and about the eye-sockets as you imagine a lighthouse-keeper's face ought to look. "I want some poison," she said.

NOTES

serene (par. 29): peaceful

let (par. 30): issued

noblesse oblige (par. 31): Literally, "nobility obligates." The term refers to the obligation of a person of high standing to be honorable and generous.

jalousies (par. 32): blinds

reaffirm (par. 33): prove again

imperviousness (par. 33): ability to be affected by nothing

35   "Yes, Miss Emily. What kind? For rats and such? I'd recom—"

36   "I want the best you have. I don't care what kind."

37   The druggist named several. "They'll kill anything up to an elephant. But what you want is—"

38   "Arsenic," Miss Emily said. "Is that a good one?"

39   "Is . . . arsenic? Yes, ma'am. But what you want—"

40   "I want arsenic."

41   The druggist looked down at her. She looked back at him, erect, her face like a strained flag. "Why, of course," the druggist said. "If that's what you want. But the law requires you to tell what you are going to use it for."

42   Miss Emily just stared at him, her head tilted back in order to look him eye for eye, until he looked away and went and got the arsenic and wrapped it up. The Negro delivery boy brought her the package; the druggist didn't come back. When she opened the package at home there was written on the box, under the skull and bones: "For rats."

IV

43   So the next day we all said, "She will kill herself"; and we said it would be the best thing. When she had first begun to be seen with Homer Barron, we had said, "She will marry him." Then we said, "She will persuade him yet," because Homer himself had remarked—he liked men, and it was known that he drank with the younger men in the Elks' Club—that he was not a marrying man. Later we said, "Poor Emily" behind the jalousies as they passed on Sunday afternoon in the glittering buggy, Miss Emily with her head high and Homer Barron with his hat cocked and a cigar in his teeth, reins and whip in a yellow glove.

44   Then some of the ladies began to say that it was a disgrace to the town and a bad example to the young people. The men did not want to interfere, but at last the ladies forced the Baptist minister—Miss Emily's people were Episcopal—to call upon her. He would never divulge what happened during that interview, but he refused to go back again. The next Sunday they again drove about the streets, and the following day the minister's wife wrote to Miss Emily's relations in Alabama.

45   So she had blood-kin under her roof again and we sat back to watch developments. At first nothing happened. Then we were sure that they were to be married. We learned that Miss Emily had been to the jeweler's and ordered a man's toilet set in silver, with the letters H. B. on each piece. Two days later we learned that she had bought a complete outfit of men's clothing, including a nightshirt, and we said, "They are married." We were really glad. We were glad because the two female cousins were even more Grierson than Miss Emily had ever been.

46   So we were not surprised when Homer Barron—the streets had been finished some time since—was gone. We were a little disappointed that there was not a public blowing-off, but we believed that he had gone on to prepare for

NOTES

divulge (par. 44): reveal

a man's toilet set (par. 45): personal items such as a hairbrush, a razor, and so on

cabal (par. 46): a group of people united to bring about a certain result

circumvent (par. 46): outsmart

Miss Emily's coming, or to give her a chance to get rid of the cousins. (By that time it was a cabal, and we were all Miss Emily's allies to help circumvent the cousins.) Sure enough, after another week they departed. And, as we had expected all along, within three days Homer Barron was back in town. A neighbor saw the Negro man admit him at the kitchen door at dusk one evening.

47   And that was the last we saw of Homer Barron. And of Miss Emily for some time. The Negro man went in and out with the market basket, but the front door remained closed. Now and then we would see her at the window for a moment, as the men did that night when they sprinkled the lime, but for almost six months she did not appear on the streets. Then we knew that this was to be expected too; as if that quality of her father which had thwarted her woman's life so many times had been too virulent and too furious to die.

48   When we next saw Miss Emily, she had grown fat and her hair was turning gray. During the next few years it grew grayer and grayer until it attained an even pepper-and-salt iron-gray, when it ceased turning. Up to the day of her death at seventy-four it was still that vigorous iron-gray, like the hair of an active man.

49   From that time on her front door remained closed, save for a period of six or seven years, when she was about forty, during which she gave lessons in china-painting. She fitted up a studio in one of the downstairs rooms, where the daughters and granddaughters of Colonel Sartoris' contemporaries were sent to her with the same regularity and in the same spirit that they were sent to church on Sundays with a twenty-five-cent piece for the collection plate. Meanwhile her taxes had been remitted.

50   Then the newer generation became the backbone and the spirit of the town, and the painting pupils grew up and fell away and did not send their children to her with boxes of color and tedious brushes and pictures cut from the ladies' magazines. The front door closed upon the last one and remained closed for good. When the town got free postal delivery, Miss Emily alone refused to let them fasten the metal numbers above her door and attach a mailbox to it. She would not listen to them.

51   Daily, monthly, yearly we watched the Negro grow grayer and more stooped, going in and out with the market basket. Each December we sent her a tax notice, which would be returned by the post office a week later, unclaimed. Now and then we would see her in one of the downstairs windows—she had evidently shut up the top floor of the house—like the carven torso of an idol in a niche, looking or not looking at us, we could never tell which. Thus, she passed from generation to generation—dear, inescapable, impervious, tranquil, and perverse.

52   And so she died. Fell ill in the house filled with dust and shadows, with only a doddering Negro man to wait on her. We did not even know she was

NOTES

thwarted (par. 47): frustrated
virulent (par. 47): poisonous
tedious (par 50): tiresome
niche (par. 51): literally, a recess in a wall in which a statue is usually placed
tranquil (par. 51): calm
perverse (par. 51): extremely strange

sick; we had long since given up trying to get any information from the Negro. He talked to no one, probably not even to her, for his voice had grown harsh and rusty, as if from disuse.

53   She died in one of the downstairs rooms, in a heavy walnut bed with a curtain, her gray head propped on a pillow yellow and moldy with age and lack of sunlight.

V

54   The Negro met the first of the ladies at the front door and let them in, with their hushed, sibilant voices and their quick, curious glances, and then he disappeared. He walked right through the house and out the back and was not seen again.

55   The two female cousins came at once. They held the funeral on the second day, with the town coming to look at Miss Emily beneath a mass of bought flowers, with the crayon face of her father musing profoundly above the bier and the ladies sibilant and macabre; and the very old men—some in their brushed Confederate uniforms—on the porch and the lawn, talking of Miss Emily as if she had been a contemporary of theirs, believing that they had danced with her and courted her perhaps, confusing time with its mathematical progression, as the old do, to whom all the past is not a diminished road but, instead, a huge meadow which no winter ever quite touches, divided from them now by the narrow bottleneck of the most recent decade of years.

56   Already we knew that there was one room in that region above stairs which no one had seen in forty years, and which would have to be forced. They waited until Miss Emily was decently in the ground before they opened it.

57   The violence of breaking down the door seemed to fill this room with pervading dust. A thin, acrid pall as of the tomb seemed to lie everywhere upon this room decked and furnished as for a bridal: upon the valance curtains of faded rose color, upon the rose-shaded lights, upon the dressing table, upon the delicate array of crystal and the man's toilet things backed with tarnished silver, silver so tarnished that the monogram was obscured. Among them lay a collar and tie, as if they had just been removed, which lifted, left upon the surface a pale crescent in the dust. Upon a chair hung the suit, carefully folded; beneath it the two mute shoes and the discarded socks.

58   The man himself lay in the bed.

59   For a long while we just stood there, looking down at the profound and fleshless grin. The body had apparently once lain in the attitude of an embrace,

NOTES

sibilant (par. 54): hissing

bier (par. 55): a stand upon which a coffin is placed

macabre (par. 55): fascinated with death

a contemporary (par. 55): a person of approximately the same age

acrid (par. 57): harsh, irritating

pall (par. 57): atmosphere of gloom

profound (par. 59): difficult to understand

grimace (par. 59): a facial expression

cuckolded (par. 59): literally, a cuckhold is a man whose wife is unfaithful to him

inextricable (par. 59): inseparable

but now the long sleep that outlasts love, that conquers even the grimace of love, had cuckolded him. What was left of him, rotted beneath what was left of the nightshirt, had become inextricable from the bed in which he lay; and upon him and upon the pillow beside him lay that even coating of the patient and bidding dust.

60   Then we noticed that in the second pillow was the indentation of a head. One of us lifted something from it, and leaning forward, that faint and invisible dust dry and acrid in the nostrils, we saw a long strand of iron-gray hair.

The Chrysanthemums

John Steinbeck

1   The high grey-flannel fog of winter closed off the Salinas Valley from the sky and from all the rest of the world. On every side it sat like a lid on the mountains and made of the great valley a closed pot. On the broad, level land floor the gang plows bit deep and left the black earth shining like metal where the shares had cut. On the foothill ranches across the Salinas River, the yellow stubble fields seemed to be bathed in pale cold sunshine, but there was no sunshine in the valley now in December. The thick willow scrub along the river flamed with sharp and positive yellow leaves.

2   It was a time of quiet and of waiting. The air was cold and tender. A light wind blew up from the southwest so that the farmers were mildly hopeful of a good rain before long; but fog and rain do not go together.

3   Across the river, on Henry Allen's foothill ranch there was little work to be done, for the hay was cut and stored and the orchards were plowed up to receive the rain deeply when it should come. The cattle on the higher slopes were becoming shaggy and rough-coated.

4   Elisa Allen, working in her flower garden, looked down across the yard and saw Henry, her husband, talking to two men in business suits. The three of them stood by the tractor shed, each man with one foot on the side of the little Fordson. They smoked cigarettes and studied the machine as they talked.

5   Elisa watched them for a moment and then went back to her work. She was thirty-five. Her face was lean and strong and her eyes were as clear as water. Her figure looked blocked and heavy in her gardening costume, a man's black hat pulled low down over her eyes, clodhopper shoes, a figured print dress almost completely covered by a big corduroy apron with four big pockets to hold the snips, the trowel and scratcher, the seeds and the knife she worked with. She wore heavy leather gloves to protect her hands while she worked.

NOTES

gang plows (par. 1): plows that turn more than one furrow (row) at a time
scrub (par. 1): underdeveloped shrubs and trees
clodhopper shoes (par. 5): large work shoes
snips, trowel, scratcher (par. 5): gardening tools

6   She was cutting down the old year's chrysanthemum stalks with a pair of short and powerful scissors. She looked down toward the men by the tractor shed now and then. Her face was eager and mature and handsome; even her work with the scissors was overeager, overpowerful. The chrysanthemum stems seemed too small and easy for her energy.

7   She brushed a cloud of hair out of her eyes with the back of her glove, and left a smudge of earth on the cheek in doing it. Behind her stood the neat white farm house with red geraniums close-banked around it as high as the windows. It was a hard-swept looking little house, with hard-polished windows, and a clean mud-mat on the front steps.

8   Elisa cast another glance toward the tractor shed. The strangers were getting into their Ford coupe. She took off a glove and put her strong fingers down into the forest of new green chrysanthemum sprouts that were growing around the old roots. She spread the leaves and looked down among the close-growing stems. No aphids were there, no sowbugs or snails or cutworms. Her terrier fingers destroyed such pests before they could get started.

9   Elisa started at the sound of her husband's voice. He had come near quietly, and he leaned over the wire fence that protected her flower garden from cattle and dogs and chickens.

10   "At it again," he said. "You've got a strong new crop coming."

11   Elisa straightened her back and pulled on the gardening glove again. "Yes. They'll be strong this coming year." In her tone and on her face there was a little smugness.

12   "You've got a gift with things," Henry observed. "Some of those yellow chrysanthemums you had this year were ten inches across. I wish you'd work out in the orchard and raise some apples that big."

13   Her eyes sharpened. "Maybe I could do it, too. I've a gift with things, all right. My mother had it. She could stick anything in the ground and make it grow. She said it was having planters' hands that knew how to do it."

14   "Well, it sure works with flowers," he said.

15   "Henry, who were those men you were talking to?"

16   "Why, sure, that's what I came to tell you. They were from the Western Meat Company. I sold those thirty head of three-year old steers. Got nearly my own price, too."

17   "Good," she said. "Good for you."

18   "And I thought," he continued, "I thought how it's Saturday afternoon, and we might go to Salinas for dinner at a restaurant, and then to a picture show to celebrate, you see."

19   "Good," she repeated. "Oh, yes. That will be good."

20   Henry put on his joking tone. "There's fights tonight. How'd you like to go to the fights?"

NOTES

coupe (par. 8): a two-door automobile

aphids, sowbugs, snails, cutworms (par. 8): garden pests

terrier fingers (par. 8): Fingers that work like a terrier's claws. A terrier is known for its digging ability.

smugness (par. 11): self-satisfaction

21 "Oh, no," she said breathlessly. "No, I wouldn't like fights."

22 "Just fooling, Elisa. We'll go to a movie. Let's see. It's two now. I'm going to take Scotty and bring down those steers from the hill. It'll take us maybe two hours. We'll go in town about five and have dinner at the Cominos Hotel. Like that?"

23 "Of course, I'll like it. It's good to eat away from home."

24 "All right, then. I'll go get up a couple of horses."

25 She said, "I'll have plenty of time to transplant some of these sets, I guess."

26 She heard her husband calling Scotty down by the barn. And a little later she saw the two men ride up the pale yellow hillside in search of the steers.

27 There was a little square sandy bed kept for rooting the chrysanthemums. With her trowel she turned the soil over and over, and smoothed it and patted it firm. Then she dug ten parallel trenches to receive the sets. Back at the chrysanthemum bed she pulled out the little crisp shoots, trimmed off the leaves of each one with her scissors and laid it on a small orderly pile.

28 A squeak of wheels and plod of hoofs came from the road. Elisa looked up. The country road ran along the dense bank of willows and cottonwoods that bordered the river, and up this road came a curious vehicle, curiously drawn. It was an old spring-wagon, with a round canvas top on it like the cover of a prairie schooner. It was drawn by an old bay horse and a little grey-and-white burro. A big stubble-bearded man sat between the cover flaps and drove the crawling team. Underneath the wagon, between the hind wheels, a lean and rangy mongrel dog walked sedately. Words were painted on the canvas in clumsy, crooked letters. "Pots, pans, knives, sisors, lawn mores. Fixed." Two rows of articles and the triumphantly definitive "Fixed" below. The black paint had run down in little sharp points beneath each letter.

29 Elisa, squatting on the ground, watched to see the crazy, loose-jointed wagon pass by. But it didn't pass. It turned into the farm road in front of her house, crooked old wheels skirling and squeaking. The rangy dog darted from between the wheels and ran ahead. Instantly the two ranch shepherds flew out at him. Then all three stopped, and with stiff and quivering tails, with taut straight legs, with ambassadorial dignity, they slowly circled, sniffing daintily. The caravan pulled up to Elisa's wire fence and stopped. Now the newcomer dog, feeling outnumbered, lowered his tail and retired under the wagon with raised hackles and bared teeth.

30 The man on the wagon seat called out. "That's a bad dog in a fight when he gets started."

NOTES

spring-wagon (par. 28): a farm wagon equipped with springs

prairie schooner (par. 28): a covered wagon

rangy (par. 28): long-limbed

mongrel dog (par. 28): a mutt

sedately (par. 28): calmly

skirling (par. 29): squealing

quivering (par. 29): trembling

taut (par. 29): tight

caravan (par. 29): a travelling group

hackles (par. 29): hair on the neck and back of a dog

31   Elisa laughed. "I see he is. How soon does he generally get started?"

32   The man caught up her laughter and echoed it heartily. "Sometimes not for weeks and weeks," he said. He climbed stiffly down, over the wheel. The horse and the donkey drooped like unwatered flowers.

33   Elisa saw that he was a very big man. Although his hair and beard were greying, he did not look old. His worn black suit was wrinkled and spotted with grease. The laughter had disappeared from his face and eyes the moment his laughing voice ceased. His eyes were dark and they were full of the brooding that gets in the eyes of teamsters and of sailors. The calloused hands he rested on the wire fence were cracked, and every crack was a black line. He took off his battered hat.

34   "I'm off my general road, ma'am," he said. "Does this dirt road cut over across the river to the Los Angeles highway?"

35   Elisa stood up and shoved the thick scissors in her apron pocket. "Well, yes, it does, but it winds around and then fords the river. I don't think your team could pull through the sand."

36   He replied with some asperity, "It might surprise you what them beasts can pull through."

37   "When they get started?" she asked.

38   He smiled for a second. "Yes. When they get started."

39   "Well," said Elisa, "I think you'll save time if you go back to the Salinas road and pick up the highway there."

40   He drew a big finger down the chicken wire and made it sing. "I ain't in any hurry, ma'am. I go from Seattle to San Diego and back every year. Takes all my time. About six months each way. I aim to follow nice weather."

41   Elisa took off her gloves and stuffed them in the apron pocket with the scissors. She touched the under edge of her man's hat, searching for fugitive hairs. "That sounds like a nice kind of a way to live," she said.

42   He leaned confidentially over the fence. "Maybe you noticed the writing on my wagon. I mend pots and sharpen knives and scissors. You got any of them things to do?"

43   "Oh, no," she said quickly. "Nothing like that." Her eyes hardened with resistance.

44   "Scissors is the worst thing," he explained. "Most people just ruin scissors trying to sharpen 'em, but I know how. I got a special tool. It's a little bobbit kind of thing, and patented. But it sure does the trick."

45   "No. My scissors are all sharp."

46   "All right, then. Take a pot," he continued earnestly, " a bent pot, or a pot with a hole. I can make it like new so you don't have to buy no new ones. That's a saving for you."

47   "No," she said shortly. "I tell you I have nothing like that for you to do."

NOTES

brooding (par. 33): serious

teamsters (par. 33): people who drive teams or trucks as an occupation

fords (par. 35): crosses

asperity (par. 36): harshness

48   His face fell to an exaggerated sadness. His voice took on a whining under-tone. "I ain't had a thing to do today. Maybe I won't have no supper tonight. You see I'm off my regular road. I know folks on the highway clear from Seattle to San Diego. They save their things for me to sharpen up because they know I do it so good and save them money."

49   "I'm sorry," Elisa said irritably. "I haven't anything for you to do."

50   His eyes left her face and fell to searching the ground. They roamed about until they came to the chrysanthemum bed where she had been working. "What's them plants, ma'am?"

51   The irritation and resistance melted from Elisa's face. "Oh, those are chrysanthemums, giant whites and yellows. I raise them every year, bigger than anybody around here."

52   "Kind of a long-stemmed flower? Looks like a quick puff of colored smoke?" he asked.

53   "That's it. What a nice way to describe them."

54   "They smell kind of nasty till you get used to them," he said.

55   "It's a good bitter smell," she retorted, "not nasty at all."

56   He changed his tone quickly. "I like the smell myself."

57   "I had ten-inch blooms this year," she said.

58   The man leaned farther over the fence. "Look. I know a lady down the road a piece, has got the nicest garden you ever seen. Got nearly every kind of flower but no chrysanthemums. Last time I was mending a copper-bottom washtub for her (that's a hard job but I do it good), she said to me, 'If you ever run acrost some nice chrysanthemums I wish you'd try to get me a few seeds.' That's what she told me."

59   Elisa's eyes grew alert and eager. "She couldn't have known much about chrysanthemums. You can raise them from seed, but it's much easier to root the little sprouts you see there."

60   "Oh," he said. "I s'pose I can't take none to her, then."

61   "Why yes you can," Elisa cried. "I can put some in damp sand, and you can carry them right along with you. They'll take root in the pot if you keep them damp. And then she can transplant them."

62   "She'd sure like to have some, ma'am. You say they're nice ones?"

63   "Beautiful," she said. "Oh, beautiful." Her eyes shone. She tore off the bat-tered hat and shook out her dark pretty hair. "I'll put them in a flower pot, and you can take them right with you. Come into the yard."

64   While the man came through the picket gate Elisa ran excitedly along the geranium-bordered path to the back of the house. And she returned carrying a big red flower pot. The gloves were forgotten now. She kneeled on the ground by the starting bed and dug up the sandy soil with her fingers and scooped it into the bright new flower pot. Then she picked up the little pile of shoots she had prepared. With her strong fingers she pressed them into the sand and tamped around them with her knuckles. The man stood over her. "I'll tell you what to do," she said. "You remember so you can tell the lady."

65   "Yes, I'll try to remember."

66   "Well, look. These will take root in about a month. Then she must set them out, about a foot apart in good rich earth like this, see?" She lifted a handful of dark soil for him to look at. "They'll grow fast and tall. Now

remember this. In July tell her to cut them down, about eight inches from the ground."

67   "Before they bloom?" he asked.

68   "Yes, before they bloom." Her face was tight with eagerness. "They'll grow right up again. About the last of September the buds will start."

69   She stopped and seemed perplexed. "It's the budding that takes the most care," she said hesitantly. "I don't know how to tell you." She looked deep into his eyes, searchingly. Her mouth opened a little, and she seemed to be listening. "I'll try to tell you," she said. "Did you ever hear of planting hands?"

70   "Can't say I have, ma'am."

71   "Well, I can only tell you what it feels like. It's when you're picking off the buds you don't want. Everything goes right down into your fingertips. You watch your fingers work. They do it themselves. You can feel how it is. They pick and pick the buds. They never make a mistake. They're with the plant. Do you see? Your fingers and the plant. You can feel that, right up your arm. They know. They never make a mistake. You can feel it. When you're like that you can't do anything wrong. Do you see that? Can you understand that?"

72   She was kneeling on the ground looking up at him. Her breast swelled passionately.

73   The man's eyes narrowed. He looked away self-consciously. "Maybe I know," he said. "Sometimes in the night in the wagon there—"

74   Elisa's voice grew husky. She broke in on him. "I've never lived as you do, but I know what you mean. When the night is dark—why, the stars are sharp-pointed, and there's a quiet. Why, you rise up and up! Every pointed star gets driven into your body. It's like that. Hot and sharp and—lovely."

75   Kneeling there, her hand went out toward his legs in the greasy black trousers. Her hesitant fingers almost touched the cloth. Then her hand dropped to the ground. She crouched low like a fawning dog.

76   He said, "It's nice, just like you say. Only when you don't have no dinner, it ain't."

77   She stood up then, very straight, and her face was ashamed. She held the flower pot out to him and placed it gently in his arms. "Here. Put it in your wagon, on the seat, where you can watch it. Maybe I can find something for you to do."

78   At the back of the house she dug in the can pile and found two old and battered aluminum saucepans. She carried them back and gave them to him. "Here, maybe you can fix these."

79   His manner changed. He became professional. "Good as new I can fix them." At the back of his wagon he set a little anvil, and out of an oily tool box dug a small machine hammer. Elisa came through the gate to watch him while he pounded out the dents in the kettles. His mouth grew sure and knowing. At a difficult part of the work he sucked his underlip.

80   "You sleep right in the wagon?" Elisa asked.

81   "Right in the wagon, ma'am. Rain or shine I'm dry as a cow in there."

NOTE

fawning (par. 75): timid

82   "It must be nice" she said. "It must be very nice. I wish women could do such things."

83   "It ain't the right kind of a life for a woman."

84   Her upper lip raised a little, showing her teeth. "How do you know? How can you tell?" she said.

85   "I don't know ma'am," he protested. "Of course I don't know. Now here's your kettles, done. You don't have to buy no new ones."

86   "How much?"

87   "Oh, fifty cents'll do. I keep my prices down and my work good. That's why I have all them satisfied customers up and down the highway."

88   Elisa brought him a fifty-cent piece from the house and dropped it in his hand. "You might be surprised to have a rival some time. I can sharpen scissors, too. And I can beat the dents out of little pots. I could show you what a woman might do."

89   He put his hammer back in the oily box and shoved the little anvil out of sight. "It would be a lonely life for a woman, ma'am, and a scarey life, too, with animals creeping under the wagon all night." He climbed over the single tree, steadying himself with a hand on the burro's white rump. He settled himself in the seat, picked up the lines. "Thank you kindly, ma'am," he said. "I'll do like you told me; I'll go back and catch the Salinas road."

90   "Mind," she called, "if you're long in getting there, keep the sand damp."

91   "Sand, ma'am? . . . Sand? Oh, sure. You mean round the chrysanthemums. Sure I will." He clucked his tongue. The beasts leaned luxuriously into their collars. The mongrel dog took his place between the back wheels. The wagon turned and crawled out the entrance road and back the way it had come, along the river.

92   Elisa stood in front of her wire fence watching the slow progress of the caravan. Her shoulders were straight, her head thrown back, her eyes half-closed, so that the scene came vaguely into them. Her lips moved silently forming the words "Good-bye—good-bye." Then she whispered, "That's a bright direction. There's a glowing there." The sound of her whisper startled her. She shook herself free and looked about to see whether anyone had been listening. Only the dogs had heard. They lifted their heads toward her from their sleeping in the dust, and then stretched out their chins and settled asleep again. Elisa turned and ran hurriedly into the house.

93   In the kitchen she reached behind the stove and felt the water tank. It was full of hot water from the noonday cooking. In the bathroom she tore off her soiled clothes and flung them into the corner. And then she scrubbed herself with a little block of pumice, legs and thighs, loins and chest and arms, until her skin was scratched and red. When she had dried herself she stood in front of a mirror in her bedroom and looked at her body. She tightened her stomach and threw out her chest. She turned and looked over her shoulder at her back.

94   After a while she began to dress, slowly. She put on her newest underclothing and her nicest stockings and the dress which was the symbol of her

NOTES

pumice (par. 93): a rough, lightweight stone
rouged (par. 94): reddened

prettiness. She worked carefully on her hair, pencilled her eyebrows and rouged her lips.

95   Before she was finished she heard the little thunder of hoofs and the shouts of Henry and his helper as they drove the red steers into the corral. She heard the gate bang shut and set herself for Henry's arrival.

96   His steps sounded on the porch. He entered the house calling, "Elisa, where are you?"

97   "In my room, dressing. I'm not ready. There's hot water for your bath. Hurry up. It's getting late."

98   When she heard him splashing in the tub, Elisa laid his dark suit on the bed, and shirt and socks and tie beside it. She stood his polished shoes on the floor beside the bed. Then she went to the porch and sat primly and stiffly down. She looked toward the river road where the willow-line was still yellow with frosted leaves so that under the high grey fog they seemed a thin band of sunshine. This was the only color in the grey afternoon. She sat unmoving for a long time. Her eyes blinked rarely.

99   Henry came banging out of the door, shoving his tie inside his vest as he came. Elisa stiffened and her face grew tight. Henry stopped short and looked at her. "Why—why, Elisa. You look so nice!"

100   "Nice? You think I look nice? What do you mean by 'nice'?"

101   Henry blundered on. "I don't know. I mean you look different, strong and happy."

102   "I am strong? Yes, strong. What do you mean 'strong'?"

103   He looked bewildered. "You're playing some kind of a game," he said helplessly. "It's a kind of a play. You look strong enough to break a calf over your knee, happy enough to eat it like watermelon."

104   For a second she lost her rigidity. "Henry! Don't talk like that. You didn't know what you said." She grew complete again. "I'm strong," she boasted. "I never knew before how strong."

105   Henry looked down toward the tractor shed, and when he brought his eyes back to her, they were his own again. "I'll get out the car. You can put on your coat while I'm starting."

106   Elisa went into the house. She heard him drive to the gate and idle down his motor, and then she took a long time to put on her hat. She pulled it here and pressed it there. When Henry turned the motor off she slipped into her coat and went out.

107   The little roadster bounced along on the dirt road by the river, raising the birds and driving the rabbits into the brush. Two cranes flapped heavily over the willow-line and dropped into the riverbed.

108   Far ahead on the road Elisa saw a dark speck. She knew.

109   She tried not to look as they passed it, but her eyes would not obey. She whispered to herself sadly. "He might have thrown them off the road. That wouldn't have been much trouble, not very much. But he kept the pot," she explained. "He had to keep the pot. That's why he couldn't get them off the road."

NOTE

bewildered (par. 103): confused

110   The roadster turned a bend and she saw the caravan ahead. She swung full around toward her husband so she could not see the little covered wagon and the mismatched team as the car passed them.

111   In a moment it was over. The thing was done. She did not look back. She said loudly, to be heard above the motor, "It will be good, tonight, a good dinner."

112   "Now you're changed again," Henry complained. He took one hand from the wheel and patted her knee. "I ought to take you in to dinner oftener. It would be good for both of us. We get so heavy out on the ranch."

113   "Henry," she asked, "could we have wine at dinner?"

114   "Sure we could. Say! That will be fine."

115   She was silent for a little while; then she said, "Henry, at those prize fights, do the men hurt each other very much?"

116   "Sometimes a little, not often. Why?"

117   "Well, I've read how they break noses, and blood runs down their chests. I've read how the fighting gloves get heavy and soggy with blood."

118   He looked around at her. "What's the matter, Elisa? I didn't know you read things like that." He brought the car to a stop then turned to the right over the Salinas River bridge.

119   "Do any women ever go to the fights?" she asked.

120   "Oh, sure, some. What's the matter, Elisa? Do you want to go? I don't think you'd like it, but I'll take you if you really want to go."

121   She relaxed limply in the seat. "Oh, no. No. I don't want to go. I'm sure I don't." Her face was turned away from him. "It will be enough if we can have wine. It will be plenty." She turned up her coat collar so he could not see that she was crying weakly—like an old woman.

Essays

Shame

Dick Gregory

1   I never learned hate at home, or shame. I had to go to school for that. I was about seven years old when I got my first big lesson. I was in love with a little girl named Helene Tucker, a light-complexioned little girl with pigtails and nice manners. She was always clean and she was smart in school. I think I went to school mostly to look at her. I brushed my hair and even got me a little old handkerchief. It was a lady's handkerchief, but I didn't want Helene to see me wipe my nose on my hand. The pipes were frozen again, there was no water in the house, but I washed my socks and shirt every night. I'd get a pot, and go over to Mr. Ben's grocery store, and stick my pot down into his soda machine. Scoop out some chopped ice. By evening the ice melted to water for washing. I got sick a lot that winter because the fire would go out at night before the clothes were dry. In the morning I'd put them on, wet or dry, because they were the only clothes I had.

2   Everybody's got a Helene Tucker, a symbol of everything you want. I loved her for her goodness, her cleanness, her popularity. She'd walk down my street and my brothers and sisters would yell, "Here comes Helene," and I'd rub my tennis sneakers on the back of my pants and wish my hair wasn't so nappy and the white folk's shirt fit me better. I'd run out on the street. If I knew my place and didn't come too close, she'd wink at me and say hello. That was a good feeling. Sometimes I'd follow her all the way home, and shovel the snow off her walk and try to make friends with her Momma and her aunts. I'd drop money on her stoop late at night on my way back from shining shoes in the taverns. And she had a Daddy, and he had a good job. He was a paper hanger.

3   I guess I would have gotten over Helene by summertime, but something happened in that classroom that made her face hang in front of me for the next twenty-two years. When I played the drums in high school it was for Helene and when I broke track records in college it was for Helene and when I started standing behind microphones and heard applause I wished Helene could hear it, too. It wasn't until I was twenty-nine years old and married and making money that I really got her out of my system. Helene was sitting in that classroom when I learned to be ashamed of myself.

4   It was on a Thursday. I was sitting in the back of the room, in a seat with a chalk circle drawn around it. The idiot's seat, the troublemaker's seat.

5   The teacher thought I was stupid. Couldn't spell, couldn't read, couldn't do arithmetic. Just stupid. Teachers were never interested in finding out that you couldn't concentrate because you were so hungry, because you hadn't had any breakfast. All you could think about was noontime, would it ever come? Maybe you could sneak in to the cloakroom and steal a bite of some kid's lunch out of a coat pocket. A bite of something. Paste. You can't really make a meal of paste, or put it on bread for a sandwich, but sometimes I'd scoop a few spoonfuls out of the paste jar in the back of the room. Pregnant people get strange tastes. I was pregnant with poverty. Pregnant with dirt and pregnant with smells that made people turn away, pregnant with cold and pregnant

with shoes that were never bought for me, pregnant with five other people in my bed and no Daddy in the next room, and pregnant with hunger. Paste doesn't taste too bad when you're hungry.

6   The teacher thought I was a troublemaker. All she saw from the front of the room was a little black boy who squirmed in his idiot's seat and made noises and poked the kids around him. I guess she couldn't see a kid who made noises because he wanted someone to know he was there.

7   It was on a Thursday, the day before the Negro payday. The eagle always flew on Friday. The teacher was asking each student how much his father would give to the Community Chest. On Friday night, each kid would get the money from his father, and on Monday he would bring it to the school. I decided I was going to buy me a Daddy right then. I had money in my pocket from shining shoes and selling papers, and whatever Helene Tucker pledged for her Daddy I was going to top it. And I'd hand the money right in. I wasn't going to wait until Monday to buy me a Daddy.

8   I was shaking, scared to death. The teacher opened her book and started calling out names alphabetically.

9   "Helene Tucker?"

10   "My Daddy said he'd give two dollars and fifty cents."

11   "That's very nice, Helene. Very, very nice indeed."

12   That made me feel pretty good. It wouldn't take too much to top that. I had almost three dollars in dimes and quarters in my pocket. I stuck my hand in my pocket and held onto the money, waiting for her to call my name. But the teacher closed her book after she called everybody else in the class.

13   I stood up and raised my hand.

14   "What is it now?"

15   "You forgot me."

16   She turned toward the blackboard. "I don't have time to be playing with you, Richard."

17   "My Daddy said he'd . . ."

18   "Sit down, Richard, you're disturbing the class."

19   "My Daddy said he'd give . . . fifteen dollars."

20   She turned and looked mad. "We are collecting this money for you and your kind, Richard Gregory. If your Daddy can give fifteen dollars you have no business being on relief."

21   "I got it right now, I got it right now, my Daddy gave it to me to turn in today, my Daddy said . . ."

22   "And furthermore," she said, looking right at me, her nostrils getting big and her lips getting thin and her eyes opening wide, "we know you don't have a Daddy."

23   Helene Tucker turned around, her eyes full of tears. She felt sorry for me. Then I couldn't see her too well because I was crying, too.

24   "Sit down, Richard."

NOTES

The eagle always flew on Friday (par. 7): Ten-dollar gold coins and, later, ten-dollar bills were called "eagles"; Friday was payday.

being on relief (par. 20): getting welfare

25   And I always thought the teacher kind of liked me. She always picked me to wash the blackboard on Friday, after school. That was a big thrill, it made me feel important. If I didn't wash it, come Monday the school might not function right.

26   "Where are you going, Richard?"

27   I walked out of school that day, and for a long time I didn't go back very often. There was shame there.

28   Now there was shame everywhere. It seemed like the whole world had been inside that classroom, everyone had heard what the teacher had said, everyone had turned around and felt sorry for me. There was shame in going to the Worthy Boys Annual Christmas Dinner for you and your kind, because everybody knew what a worthy boy was. Why couldn't they just call it the Boys Annual Dinner, why'd they have to give it a name? There was shame in wearing the brown and orange and white plaid mackinaw the welfare gave to three thousand boys. Why'd it have to be the same for everybody so when you walked down the street the people could see you were on relief? It was a nice warm mackinaw and it had a hood, and my Momma beat me and called me a little rat when she found out I stuffed it in the bottom of a pail full of garbage way over on Cottage Street. There was shame in running over to Mister Ben's at the end of the day and asking for his rotten peaches, there was shame in asking Mrs. Simmons for a spoonful of sugar, there was shame in running out to meet the relief truck. I hated that truck, full of food for you and your kind. I ran into the house and hid when it came. And then I started to sneak through alleys, to take the long way home so the people going into White's Eat Shop wouldn't see me. Yeah, the whole world heard the teacher that day, we all know you don't have a Daddy.

Daddy Tucked the Blanket

Randall Williams

1   About the time I turned 16, my folks began to wonder why I didn't stay home any more. I always had an excuse for them, but what I didn't say was that I had found my freedom and I was getting out.

2   I went through four years of high school in semirural Alabama and became active in clubs and sports; I made a lot of friends and became a regular guy, if you know what I mean. But one thing was irregular about me: I managed those four years without ever having a friend visit at my house.

3   I was ashamed of where I lived. I had been ashamed for as long as I had been conscious of class.

4   We had a big family. There were several of us sleeping in one room, but that's not so bad if you get along, and we always did. As you get older, though, it gets worse.

5   Being poor is a humiliating experience for a young person trying hard to be accepted. Even now—several years removed—it is hard to talk about. And I resent the weakness of these words to make you feel what it was really like.

6   We lived in a lot of old houses. We moved a lot because we were always looking for something just a little better than what we had. You have to understand

that my folks worked harder than most people. My mother was always at home, but for her that was a full-time job—and no fun, either. But my father worked his head off from the time I can remember in construction and shops. It was hard, physical work.

7   I tell you this to show that we weren't shiftless. No matter how much money Daddy made, we never made much progress up the social ladder. I got out thanks to a college scholarship and because I was a little more articulate than the average.

8   I have seen my Daddy wrap copper wire through the soles of his boots to keep them together in the wintertime. He couldn't buy new boots because he had used the money for food and shoes for us. We lived like hell, but we went to school well-clothed and with a full stomach.

9   It really is hell to live in a house that was in bad shape ten years before you moved in. And a big family puts a lot of wear and tear on a new house, too, so you can imagine how one goes downhill if it is teetering when you move in. But we lived in houses that were sweltering in summer and freezing in winter. I woke up every morning for a year and a half with plaster on my face where it had fallen out of the ceiling during the night.

10   This wasn't during the Depression; this was in the late '60s and early '70s.

11   When we boys got old enough to learn trades in school, we would try to fix up the old houses we lived in. But have you ever tried to paint a wall that crumbled when the roller went across it. And bright paint emphasized the holes in the wall. You end up more frustrated than when you began, especially when you know that at best you might come up with only enough money to improve one of the six rooms in the house. And we might move out soon after, anyway.

12   The same goes for keeping a house like that clean. If you have a house full of kids and the house is deteriorating, you'll never keep it clean. Daddy used to yell at Mama about that, but she couldn't do anything. I think Daddy knew it inside, but he had to have an outlet for his rage somewhere, and at least yelling isn't as bad as hitting, which they never did to each other.

13   But you have a kitchen which has no counter space and no hot water, and you will have dirty dishes stacked up. That sounds like an excuse, but try it. You'll go mad from the sheer sense of futility. It's the same thing in a house with no closets. You can't keep clothes clean and rooms in order if they have to be stacked up with things.

14   Living in a bad house is generally worse on girls. For one thing, they traditionally help their mother with the housework. We boys could get outside and work in the field or cut wood or even play ball and forget about living conditions. The sky was still pretty.

NOTES

shiftless (par. 7): lazy, irresponsible
teetering (par. 9): on the brink of going downhill
the Depression (par. 10): a time of terrible economic conditions, beginning with the great stock market crash of 1929 and lasting until about 1940
deteriorating (par. 12): decaying, falling apart
futility (par. 13): uselessness

Old House, Clayton, Alabama

—*Leah McCraney*

15   But the girls got the pressure, and as they got older it became worse. Would they accept dates knowing they had to "receive" the young man in a dirty hallway with broken windows, peeling wallpaper, and a cracked ceiling? You have to live it to understand it, but it creates a shame which drives the soul of a young person inward.

16   I'm thankful none of us ever blamed our parents for this, because it would have crippled our relationships. As it worked out, only the relationship between our parents was damaged. And I think the harshness which they expressed to each other was just an outlet to get rid of their anger at the trap their lives were in. It ruined their marriage because they had no one to yell at but each other. I knew other families where the kids got the abuse, but we were too much loved for that.

17   Once I was about sixteen and Mama and Daddy had a particularly violent argument about the washing machine, which had broken down. Daddy was on the back porch—that's where the only water faucet was—trying to fix it and Mama had a washtub out there washing school clothes for the next day and they were screaming at each other.

18   Later that night everyone was in bed and I heard Daddy get up from the couch where he was reading. I looked out from my bed across the hall into their room. He was standing right over Mama and she was already asleep. He pulled the blanket up and tucked it around her shoulders and just stood there and tears were dropping off his cheeks and I thought I could faintly hear them splashing against the linoleum rug.

19   Now they're divorced.

20   I had courses in college where housing was discussed, but the sociologists never put enough emphasis on the impact living in substandard housing has on a person's psyche. Especially children's.

21   Small children have a hard time understanding poverty. They want the same things children from more affluent families have. They want the same things they see advertised on television, and they don't understand why they can't have them.

22   Other children can be incredibly cruel. I was in elementary school in Georgia—and this is interesting because it is the only thing I remember about that particular school—when I was about eight or nine.

23   After Christmas vacation had ended, my teacher made each student describe all his or her Christmas presents. I became more and more uncomfortable as the privilege passed around the room towards me. Other children were reciting the names of the dolls they had been given, the kinds of bicycles and the grandeur of their games and toys. Some had lists which seemed to go on and on for hours.

24   It took me only a few seconds to tell the class that I had gotten for Christmas a belt and a pair of gloves. And then I was laughed at—because I cried—by a roomful of children and a teacher. I never forgave them, and that night I made my mother cry when I told her about it.

25   In retrospect, I am grateful for that moment, but I remember wanting to die at the time.

NOTES

psyche (par. 20): soul, spirit
affluent (par. 21): wealthy
grandeur (par. 23): greatness

A Hanging

George Orwell

1   It was in Burma, a sodden morning of the rains. A sickly light, like yellow tinfoil, was slanting over the high walls into the jail yard. We were waiting outside the condemned cells, a row of sheds fronted with double bars, like small animal cages. Each cell measured about ten feet by ten and was quite bare within except for a plank bed and a pot for drinking water. In some of them brown silent men were squatting at the inner bars, with their blankets draped around them. These were the condemned men, due to be hanged within the next week or two.

2   One prisoner had been brought out of his cell. He was a Hindu, a puny wisp of a man, with a shaven head and vague liquid eyes. He had a thick, sprouting moustache, absurdly too big for his body, rather like the moustache of a comic man of the films. Six tall Indian warders were guarding him and getting him ready for the gallows. Two of them stood by with rifles with fixed bayonets, while the other handcuffed him, passed a chain through his handcuffs and fixed it to their belts, and lashed his arms tight to his sides. They crowded very close about him, with their hands always on him in a careful, caressing grip, as though all the while feeling him to make sure he was there. It was like men handling a fish which is still alive and may jump back into the water. But he stood quite unresisting, yielding his arms limply to the ropes, as though he hardly noticed what was happening.

3   Eight o'clock struck and a bugle call, desolately thin in the wet air, floated from the distant barracks. The superintendent of the jail, who was standing apart from the rest of us, moodily prodding the gravel with his stick, raised his head at the sound. He was an army doctor, with a grey toothbrush moustache and a gruff voice. "For God's sake hurry up, Francis," he said irritably. "The man ought to have been dead by this time. Aren't you ready yet?"

4   Francis, the head jailer, a fat Dravidian in a white drill suit and gold spectacles, waved his black hand. "Yes sir, yes sir," he bubbled. "All iss satisfactorily prepared. The hangman iss waiting. We shall proceed."

5   "Well, quick march, then. The prisoners can't get their breakfast till this job's over."

6   We set out for the gallows. Two warders marched on either side of the prisoner, with their rifles at the slope; two others marched close against him, gripping him by arm and shoulder, as though at once pushing and supporting him. The rest of us, magistrates and the like, followed behind. Suddenly, when we had gone ten yards, the procession stopped short without any order or warning. A dreadful thing had happened—a dog, come goodness knows whence, had appeared in the yard. It came bounding among us with a loud

NOTES

sodden (par. 1): soaked
desolately (par. 3): gloomily
Dravidian (par. 4): a member of the original native population of Southern India
magistrates (par. 6): officials who have the authority to enforce the law
pariah (par. 6): literally, an outcast

volley of barks, and leapt round us wagging its whole body, wild with glee at finding so many human beings together. It was a large wooly dog, half Airedale, half pariah. For a moment it pranced round us, and then, before anyone could stop it, it had made a dash for the prisoner, and jumping up, tried to lick his face. Everyone stood aghast, too taken aback even to grab at the dog.

7   "Who let that bloody brute in here?" said the superintendent angrily. "Catch it, someone!"

8   A warder, detached from the escort, charged clumsily after the dog, but it danced and gambolled just out of his reach, taking everything as part of the game. A young Eurasian jailer picked up a handful of gravel and tried to stone the dog away, but it dodged the stones and came after us again. Its yaps echoed from the jail walls. The prisoner, in the grasp of the two warders, looked on incuriously, as though this was another formality of the hanging. It was several minutes before someone managed to catch the dog. Then we put my handkerchief through its collar and moved off once more, with the dog still straining and whimpering.

9   It was about forty yards to the gallows. I watched the bare brown back of the prisoner marching in front of me. He walked clumsily with his bound arms, but quite steadily, with the bobbing gait of the Indian who never straightens his knees. At each step his muscles slid neatly into place, the lock of hair on his scalp danced up and down, his feet printed themselves on the wet gravel. And once, in spite of the men who gripped him by each shoulder, he stepped slightly aside to avoid a puddle on the path.

10   It is curious, but till that moment I had never realized what it means to destroy a healthy, conscious man. When I saw the prisoner step aside to avoid the puddle, I saw the mystery, the unspeakable wrongness, of cutting a life short when it is in full tide. This man was not dying, he was alive just as we are alive. All the organs of his body were working—bowels digesting food, skin renewing itself, nails growing, tissues forming—all toiling away in solemn foolery. His nails would still be growing when he stood on the drop, when he was falling through the air with a tenth-of-a-second to live. His eyes saw the yellow gravel and the grey walls, and his brain still remembered, foresaw, reasoned—reasoned even about puddles. He and we were a party of men walking together, seeing, hearing, feeling, understanding the same world; and in two minutes, with a sudden snap, one of us would be gone—one mind less, one world less.

11   The gallows stood in a small yard, separate from the main grounds of the prison, and overgrown with tall prickly weeds. It was a brick erection like three sides of a shed, with planking on top, and above that two beams and a crossbar with the rope dangling. The hangman, a grey-haired convict in the white uniform of the prison, was waiting beside his machine. He greeted us with a servile crouch as we entered. At a word from Francis the two warders, gripping

NOTES

aghast (par. 6): shocked

gambolled (par. 8): leaped playfully

Eurasian (par. 8): one who is of European and Asian descent

gait (par. 9): walk

servile crouch (par. 11): bending like an obedient servant

the prisoner more closely than ever, half led, half pushed him to the gallows and helped him clumsily up the ladder. Then the hangman climbed up and fixed the rope round the prisoner's neck.

12   We stood waiting, five yards away. The warders had formed in a rough circle round the gallows. And then, when the noose was fixed, the prisoner began crying out to his god. It was a high, reiterated cry of "Ram! Ram! Ram! Ram!" not urgent and fearful like a prayer or cry for help, but steady, rhythmical, almost like the tolling of a bell. The dog answered the sound with a whine. The hangman, still standing on the gallows, produced a small cotton bag like a flour bag and drew it down over the prisoner's face. But the sound, muffled by the cloth, still persisted, over and over again: "Ram! Ram! Ram! Ram! Ram!"

13   The hangman climbed down and stood ready, holding the lever. Minutes seemed to pass. The steady, muffled crying from the prisoner went on and on "Ram! Ram! Ram!" never faltering for an instant. The superintendent, his head on his chest, was slowly poking the ground with his stick; perhaps he was counting the cries, allowing the prisoner a fixed number—fifty, perhaps, or a hundred. Everyone had changed color. The Indians had gone grey like bad coffee, and one or two of the bayonets were wavering. We looked at the lashed, hooked man on the drop, and listened to his cries—each cry another second of life; the same thought was in all our minds: oh, kill him quickly, get it over, stop that abominable noise!

14   Suddenly the superintendent made up his mind. Throwing up his head he made a swift motion with his stick. "Chalo!" he shouted almost fiercely.

15   There was a clanking noise, and then dead silence. The prisoner had vanished, and the rope was twisted on itself. I let go of the dog, and it galloped immediately to the back of the gallows; but when it got there it stopped short, barked, and then retreated into a corner of the yard, where it stood among the weeds, looking timorously out at us. We went round the gallows to inspect the prisoner's body. He was dangling with his toes pointed straight downwards, very slowly revolving, as dead as a stone.

16   The superintendent reached out with his stick and poked the bare body; it oscillated, slightly. "*He's* all right," said the superintendent. He backed out from under the gallows, and blew out a deep breath. The moody look had gone out of his face quite suddenly. He glanced at his wristwatch. "Eight minutes past eight. Well, that's all for this morning, thank God."

17   The warders unfixed bayonets and marched away. The dog, sobered and conscious of having misbehaved itself, slipped after them. We walked out of the gallows yard, past the condemned cells with their waiting prisoners, into the big central yard of the prison. The convicts, under the command of warders armed with lathis, were already receiving their breakfast. They squatted

NOTES

reiterated (par. 12): repeated

abominable (par. 13): awful

"Chalo" (par. 14): start

timorously (par. 15): timidly, shyly

oscillated (par. 16): moved back and forth

lathis (par. 17): clubs

in long rows, each man holding a tin pannikin, while two warders with buckets marched round ladling out rice; it seemed quite a homely, jolly scene, after the hanging. An enormous relief had come upon us now that the job was done. One felt an impulse to sing, to break into a run, to snigger. All at once everyone began chattering gaily.

18   The Eurasian boy walking beside me nodded towards the way we had come, with a knowing smile: "Do you know, sir, our friend (he meant the dead man), when he heard his appeal had been dismissed, he pissed on the floor of his cell. From fright. Kindly take one of my cigarettes, sir. Do you not admire my new silver case, sir? From the boxwallah, two rupees eight annas. Classy European style."

19   Several people laughed—at what, nobody seemed certain.

20   Francis was walking by the superintendent, talking garrulously: "Well, sir, all hass passed off with the utmost satisfactoriness. It wass all finished—flick! like that. It iss not always so—oah, no! I have known cases where the doctor wass obliged to go beneath the gallows and pull the prisoner's legs to ensure decease. Most disagreeable!"

21   "Wriggling about, eh? That's bad," said the superintendent.

22   "Ach, sir, it iss worse when they become refractory! One man, I recall, clung to the bars of hiss cage when we went to take him out. You will scarcely credit, sir, that it took six warders to dislodge him, three pulling at each leg. We reasoned with him. 'My dear fellow,' we said, 'think of all the pain and trouble you are causing to us!' But no, he would not listen! Ach, he was very troublesome!"

23   I found that I was laughing quite loudly. Everyone was laughing. Even the superintendent grinned in a tolerant way. "You'd better all come out and have a drink," he said quite genially. "I've got a bottle of whisky in the car. We could do with it."

24   We went through the big double gates of the prison, into the road. "Pulling at his legs!" exclaimed a Burmese magistrate suddenly, and burst into a loud chuckling. We all began laughing again. At that moment Francis's anecdote seemed extraordinarily funny. We all had a drink together, native and European alike, quite amicably. The dead man was a hundred yards away.

NOTES

pannikin (par. 17): cup

boxwallah (par. 18): peddler

rupees and annas (par. 18): Rupees are the basic monetary unit of India; annas are equal to one-sixteenth of a rupee.

talking garrulously (par. 20): talking in a rambling manner, babbling

refractory (par. 22): stubborn

genially (par. 23): pleasantly

amicably (par. 24): friendly

Death and Justice

Edward Koch

1   Last December a man named Robert Lee Willie, who had been convicted of raping and murdering an eighteen-year-old woman, was executed in a Louisiana state prison. In a statement issued several minutes before his death,

Mr. Willie said: "Killing people is wrong. . . . It makes no difference whether it's citizens, countries, or governments. Killing is wrong." Two weeks later in South Carolina, an admitted killer named Joseph Carl Shaw was put to death for murdering two teenagers. In an appeal to the governor for clemency, Mr. Shaw wrote: "Killing was wrong when I did it. Killing is wrong when you do it. I hope you have the courage and the moral strength to stop the killing."

2   It is a curiosity of modern life that we find ourselves being lectured on morality by cold-blooded killers. Mr. Willie previously had been convicted of aggravated rape, aggravated kidnapping, and the murders of a Louisiana deputy and a man from Missouri. Mr. Shaw committed another murder a week before the two for which he was executed, and admitted mutilating the body of a fourteen-year-old girl he killed. I can't help wondering what prompted these murderers to speak out against killing as they entered the death-house door. Did their newfound reverence for life stem from the realization that they were about to lose their own?

3   Life is indeed precious, and I believe the death penalty helps to affirm this fact. Had the death penalty been a real possibility in the minds of these murderers, they might well have stayed their hand. They might have shown moral awareness before their victims died, and not after. Consider the tragic death of Rosa Velez, who happened to be home when a man named Luis Vera burglarized her apartment in Brooklyn. "Yeah, I shot her," Vera admitted. "She knew me, and I knew I wouldn't go to the chair."

4   During my twenty-two years in public service, I have heard the pros and cons of capital punishment expressed with special intensity. As a district leader, councilman, congressman, and mayor, I have represented constituencies generally thought of as liberal. Because I support the death penalty for heinous crimes of murder, I have sometimes been the subject of emotional and outraged attacks by voters who find my position reprehensible or worse. I have listened to their ideas. I have weighed their objections carefully. I still support the death penalty. The reasons I maintain my position can be best understood by examining the arguments most frequently heard in opposition.

5   1. *The death penalty is "barbaric."* Sometimes opponents of capital punishment horrify with tales of lingering death on the gallows, of faulty electric chairs, or of agony in the gas chamber. Partly in response to such protests, several states such as North Carolina and Texas switched to death by lethal injection. The condemned person is put to death painlessly, without ropes, voltage, bullets,

NOTES

clemency (par. 1): a reduction of the sentence given a criminal

affirm (par. 3): confirm, support

stayed (par. 3): stopped

the chair (par. 3): that is, the electric chair

constituencies (par. 4): groups of voters

liberal (par. 4): One who tends to favor social or political reform. A conservative is one who tends to favor the preservation of existing social or political systems.

heinous (par. 4): horribly evil

reprehensible (par. 4): deserving of strong criticism

"barbaric" (par. 5): brutal, uncivilized

lethal (par. 5): deadly

"hygienic" (par. 5): clean, neat

or gas. Did this answer the objections of death penalty opponents? Of course not. On June 22, 1984, *The New York Times* published an editorial that sarcastically attacked the new "hygienic" method of death by injection, and stated that "execution can never be made humane through science." So it's not the method that really troubles opponents. It's the death itself they consider barbaric.

6   Admittedly, capital punishment is not a pleasant topic. However, one does not have to like the death penalty in order to support it any more than one must like radical surgery, radiation, or chemotherapy in order to find necessary these attempts at curing cancer. Ultimately we may learn how to cure cancer with a simple pill. Unfortunately, that day has not yet arrived. Today we are faced with the choice of letting the cancer spread or trying to cure it with the methods available, methods that one day will almost certainly be considered barbaric. But to give up and do nothing would be far more barbaric and would certainly delay the discovery of an eventual cure. The analogy between cancer and murder is imperfect, because murder is not the "disease" we are trying to cure. The disease is injustice. We may not like the death penalty, but it must be available to punish crimes of cold-blooded murder, cases in which any other form of punishment would be inadequate and, therefore, unjust. If we create a society in which injustice is not tolerated, incidents of murder—the most flagrant form of injustice—will diminish.

7   *2. No other major democracy uses the death penalty.* No other major democracy—in fact, few other countries of any description—is plagued by a murder rate such as that in the United States. Fewer and fewer Americans can remember the days when unlocked doors were the norm and murder was a rare and terrible offense. In America the murder rate climbed 122 percent between 1963 and 1980. During that same period, the murder rate in New York City increased by almost 400 percent, and the statistics are even worse in many other cities. A study at M.I.T. showed that based on 1970 homicide rates a person who lived in a large American city ran a greater risk of being murdered than an American soldier in World War II ran of being killed in combat. It is not surprising that the laws of each country differ according to differing conditions and traditions. If other countries had our murder problem, the cry for capital punishment would be just as loud as it is here. And I dare say that any other major democracy where 75 percent of the people supported the death penalty would soon enact it into law.

8   *3. An innocent person might be executed by mistake.* Consider the work of Adam Bedau, one of the most implacable foes of capital punishment in this country. According to Mr. Bedau, it is "false sentimentality to argue that the death penalty should be abolished because of the abstract possibility that an innocent person might be executed." He cites a study of the 7,000 executions

NOTES

humane (par. 5): compassionate
analogy (par. 6): comparison
flagrant (par. 6): obvious
M.I.T. (par. 7): Massachusetts Institute of Technology
implacable (par. 8): unchanging
dismembered (par. 8): cut the limbs off

in this country from 1893 to 1971, and concludes that the record fails to show that such cases occur. The main point, however, is this. If government functioned only when the possibility of error didn't exist, government wouldn't function at all. Human life deserves special protection, and one of the best ways to guarantee that protection is to assure that convicted murderers do not kill again. Only the death penalty can accomplish this end. In a recent case in New Jersey, a man named Richard Biegenwald was freed from prison after serving eighteen years for murder; since his release he has been convicted of committing four murders. A prisoner named Lemuel Smith, who, while serving four life sentences for murder (plus two life sentences for kidnapping and robbery) in New York's Green Haven Prison, lured a woman corrections officer into the chaplain's office and strangled her. He then mutilated and dismembered her body. An additional life sentence for Smith is meaningless. Because New York has no death penalty statute, Smith has effectively been given a license to kill.

9   But the problem of multiple murder is not confined to the nation's penitentiaries. In 1981, ninety-one police officers were killed in the line of duty in this country. Seven percent of those arrested in the cases that have been solved had a previous arrest for murder. In New York City in 1976 and 1977, 85 persons arrested for homicide had a previous arrest for murder. Six of these individuals had two previous arrests for murder, and one had four previous murder arrests. During those two years the New York police were arresting for murder persons with a previous arrest for murder on the average of one every 8.5 days. This is not surprising when we learn that in 1975, for example, the median time served in Massachusetts for homicide was less than two-and-a-half years. In 1976, a study sponsored by the Twentieth Century Fund found the average time served in the United States for first degree murder is ten years. The median time served may be considerably lower.

10   4. *Capital punishment cheapens the value of human life.* On the contrary, it can be easily demonstrated that the death penalty strengthens the value of human life. If the penalty for rape were lowered, clearly it would signal a lessened regard for the victims' suffering, humiliation, and personal integrity. It would cheapen their horrible experience, and expose them to an increased danger of recurrence. When we lower the penalty for murder, it signals a lessened regard for the value of the victim's life. Some critics of capital punishment, such as columnist Jimmy Breslin, have suggested that a life sentence is actually a harsher penalty for murder than death. This is sophistic nonsense. A few killers may decide not to appeal a death sentence, but the overwhelming majority make every effort to stay alive. It is by exacting the highest penalty for the taking of human life that we affirm the highest value of human life.

11   5. *The death penalty is applied in a discriminatory manner.* This factor no longer seems to be the problem it once was. The appeals process for a condemned prisoner is lengthy and painstaking. Every effort is made to see that

NOTES

statute (par. 8): law
sophistic (par. 10): clever
assertions (par. 11): claims

the verdict and sentence were fairly arrived at. However, assertions of discrimination are not an argument for ending the death penalty but for extending it. It is not justice to exclude everyone from the penalty of the law if a few are found to be so favored. Justice requires that the law be applied equally to all.

12   6. *Thou Shalt Not Kill.* The Bible is our greatest source of moral inspiration. Opponents of the death penalty frequently cite the sixth of the Ten Commandments in an attempt to prove that capital punishment is divinely proscribed. In the original Hebrew, however, the Sixth Commandment reads, "Thou Shall Not Commit Murder," and the Torah specifies capital punishment for a variety of offenses. The biblical viewpoint has been upheld by philosophers throughout history. The greatest thinkers of the nineteenth century—Kant, Locke, Hobbes, Rousseau, Montesquieu, and Mill—agreed that natural law properly authorizes the sovereign to take life in order to vindicate justice. Only Jeremy Bentham was ambivalent. Washington, Jefferson, and Franklin endorsed it. Abraham Lincoln authorized executions for deserters in wartime. Alexis de Tocqueville, who expressed profound respect for American institutions, believed that the death penalty was indispensable to the support of social order. The United States Constitution, widely admired as one of the seminal achievements in the history of humanity, condemns cruel and inhuman punishment, but does not condemn capital punishment.

13   7. *The death penalty is state-sanctioned murder.* This is the defense with which Messrs. Willie and Shaw hoped to soften the resolve of those who sentenced them to death. By saying in effect, "You're no better than I am," the murderer seeks to bring his accusers down to his own level. It is also a popular argument among opponents of capital punishment, but a transparently false one. Simply put, the state has rights that the private individual does not. In a democracy, those rights are given to the state by the electorate. The execution of a lawfully condemned killer is no more an act of murder than is legal imprisonment an act of kidnapping. If an individual forces a neighbor to pay him money under a threat of punishment, it's called extortion. If the state does it, it's called taxation. Rights and responsibilities surrendered by the individual are what give the state its power to govern. This contract is the foundation of civilization itself.

14   Everyone wants his or her rights, and will defend them zealously. Not everyone, however, wants responsibilities, especially the painful responsibilities that come with law enforcement. Twenty-one years ago a woman named Kitty

NOTES

proscribed (par. 12): forbidden

Torah (par. 12): sacred law of Judaism; first five books of the Old Testament

sovereign (par. 12): ruler

vindicate (par. 12): defend

ambivalent (par. 12): unsure

indispensable (par. 12): necessary

seminal (par. 12): ground-breaking

sanctioned (par. 13): approved

resolve (par. 13): determination

transparently (par. 13): obviously

electorate (par. 13): voters

Genovese was assaulted and murdered on a street in New York. Dozens of neighbors heard her cries for help but did nothing to assist her. They didn't even call the police. In such a climate the criminal understandably grows bolder. In the presence of moral cowardice, he lectures us on our supposed failings and tries to equate his crimes with our quest for justice.

15   The death of anyone—even a convicted killer—diminishes us all. But we are diminished even more by a justice system that fails to function. It is an illusion to let ourselves believe that doing away with capital punishment removes the murderer's deed from our conscience. The rights of society are paramount. When we protect guilty lives, we give up innocent lives in exchange. When opponents of capital punishment say to the state: "I will not let you kill in my name," they are also saying to murderers: "You can kill in your own name as long as I have an excuse for not getting involved."

16   It is hard to imagine anything worse than being murdered while neighbors do nothing. But something worse exists. When those neighbors shrink back from justly punishing the murderer, the victim dies twice.

NOTES

zealously (par. 14): passionately

diminishes (par. 15): lessens

paramount (par. 15): most important

Mother Tongue

Amy Tan

1   I am not a scholar of English or literature. I cannot give you much more than personal opinions on the English language and its variations in this country or others.

2   I am a writer. And by that definition, I am someone who has always loved language. I am fascinated by language in daily life. I spend a great deal of my time thinking about the power of language—the way it can evoke an emotion, a visual image, a complex idea, or a simple truth. Language is the tool of my trade. And I use them all—all the Englishes I grew up with.

3   Recently, I was made keenly aware of the different Englishes I do use. I was giving a talk to a large group of people, the same talk I had already given to half a dozen other groups. The nature of the talk was about my writing, my life, and my book, *The Joy Luck Club*. The talk was going along well enough, until I remembered one major difference that made the whole talk sound wrong. My mother was in the room. And it was perhaps the first time she had heard me give a lengthy speech, using the kind of English I have never used with her. I was saying things like, "The intersection of memory upon imagination" and

NOTES

evoke (par. 2): call forth

wrought (par. 3): constructed

nominalized (par. 3): referring to nouns

"There is an aspect of my fiction that relates to thus-and-thus"—a speech filled with carefully wrought grammatical phrases, burdened, it suddenly seemed to me, with nominalized forms, past perfect tenses, conditional phrases, all the forms of standard English that I had learned in school and through books, the forms of English I did not use at home with my mother.

4   Just last week, I was walking down the street with my mother, and I again found myself conscious of the English I was using, the English I do use with her. We were talking about the price of new and used furniture and I heard myself saying this: "Not waste money that way." My husband was with us as well, and he didn't notice any switch in my English. And then I realized why. It's because over the twenty years we've been together I've often used that same kind of English with him, and sometimes he even uses it with me. It has become our language of intimacy, a different sort of English that relates to family talk, the language I grew up with.

5   So you'll have some idea of what this family talk I heard sounds like, I'll quote what my mother said during a recent conversation which I videotaped and then transcribed. During this conversation, my mother was talking about a political gangster in Shanghai who had the same last name as her family's, Du, and how the gangster in his early years wanted to be adopted by her family, which was rich by comparison. Later, the gangster became more powerful, far richer than my mother's family, and one day showed up at my mother's wedding to pay his respects. Here's what she said in part:

6   "Du Yusong having business like fruit stand. Like off the street kind. He is Du like Du Zong—but not Tsung-ming Island people. The local people call putong, the river east side, he belong to that side local people. That man want to ask Du Zong father take him in like become own family. Du Zong father wasn't look down on him, but didn't take seriously, until that man big like become a mafia. Now important person, very hard to inviting him. Chinese way, came only to show respect, don't stay for dinner. Respect for making big celebration, he shows up. Mean gives lots of respect. Chinese custom. Chinese social life that way. If too important won't have to stay too long. He come to my wedding. I didn't see, I heard it. I gone to boy's side, they have YMCA dinner. Chinese age I was nineteen."

7   You should know that my mother's expressive command of English belies how much she actually understands. She reads the *Forbes* report, listens to *Wall Street Week,* converses daily with her stockbroker, reads all of Shirley MacLaine's books with ease—all kinds of things I can't begin to understand. Yet some of my friends tell me they understand 50 percent of what my mother says. Some say they understand 80 to 90 percent. But to me, my mother's English is perfectly clear, perfectly natural. It's my mother tongue. Her language, as I hear it, is vivid, direct, full of observation and imagery. That was the language that helped shape the way I saw things, expressed things, made sense of the world.

NOTES

intimacy (par. 4): closeness

belies (par. 7): disguises

vivid (par. 7): lively

8   Lately, I've been giving more thought to the kind of English my mother speaks. Like others, I have described it to people as "broken" or "fractured" English. But I wince when I say that. It has always bothered me that I can think of no way to describe it other than "broken," as if it were damaged and needed to be fixed, as if it lacked a certain wholeness and soundness. I've heard other terms used, "limited English," for example. But they seem just as bad, as if everything is limited, including people's perceptions of the limited English speaker.

9   I know this for a fact, because when I was growing up, my mother's "limited" English limited *my* perception of her. I was ashamed of her English. I believed that her English reflected the quality of what she had to say. That is, because she expressed them imperfectly her thoughts were imperfect. And I had plenty of empirical evidence to support me: the fact that people in department stores, at banks, and at restaurants did not take her seriously, did not give her good service, pretended not to understand her, or even acted as if they did not hear her.

10   My mother has long realized the limitations of her English as well. When I was fifteen, she used to have me call people on the phone to pretend I was she. In this guise, I was forced to ask for information or even to complain and yell at people who had been rude to her. One time it was a call to her stockbroker in New York. She had cashed out her small portfolio and it just so happened we were going to go to New York the next week, our very first trip outside California. I had to get on the phone and say in an adolescent voice that was not very convincing, "This is Mrs. Tan."

11   And my mother was standing in the back whispering loudly, "Why he don't send me check, already two weeks late. So mad he lie to me, losing me money."

12   And then I said in perfect English, "Yes, I'm getting rather concerned. You had agreed to send the check two weeks ago, but it hasn't arrived."

13   Then she began to talk more loudly. "What he want, I come to New York tell him front of his boss, you cheating me?" And I was trying to calm her down, make her be quiet, while telling the stockbroker, "I can't tolerate any more excuses. If I don't receive the check immediately, I am going to have to speak to your manager when I'm in New York next week." And sure enough, the following week there we were in front of this astonished stockbroker, and I was sitting there red-faced and quiet, and my mother, the real Mrs. Tan, was shouting at his boss in her impeccable broken English.

14   We used a similar routine just five days ago, for a situation that was far less humorous. My mother had gone to the hospital for an appointment, to find out about a benign brain tumor a CAT scan had revealed a month ago. She said she had spoken very good English, her best English, no mistakes. Still, she said, the hospital did not apologize when they said they had lost the CAT scan and she had come for nothing. She said they did not seem to have any sympathy

NOTES

wince (par. 8): react with discomfort
empirical evidence (par. 9): evidence gathered from one's observations
portfolio (par. 10): collection of stocks
impeccable (par. 13): flawless
benign (par. 14): noncancerous

when she told them she was anxious to know the exact diagnosis, since her husband and son had both died of brain tumors. She said they would not give her any more information until the next time and she would have to make another appointment for that. So she said she would not leave until the doctor called her daughter. She wouldn't budge. And when the doctor finally called her daughter, me, who spoke in perfect English—lo and behold—we had assurances the CAT scan would be found, promises that a conference call on Monday would be held, and apologies for any suffering my mother had gone through for a most regrettable mistake.

15   I think my mother's English almost had an effect on limiting my possibilities in life as well. Sociologists and linguists probably will tell you that a person's developing language skills are more influenced by peers. But I do think that the language spoken in the family, especially in immigrant families which are more insular, plays a large role in shaping the language of the child. And I believe that it affected my results on achievement tests, IQ tests, and the SAT. While my English skills were never judged as poor, compared to math, English could not be considered my strong suit. In grade school I did moderately well, getting perhaps B's, sometimes B-pluses, in English and scoring perhaps in the sixtieth or seventieth percentile on achievement tests. But those scores were not good enough to override the opinion that my true abilities lay in math and science, because in those areas I achieved A's and scored in the ninetieth percentile or higher.

16   This was understandable. Math is precise; there is only one correct answer. Whereas, for me at least, the answers on English tests were always a judgment call, a matter of opinion and personal experience. Those tests were constructed around items like fill-in-the-blank sentence completion, such as, "Even though Tom was ____, Mary thought he was ____." And the correct answer always seemed to be the most bland combinations of thoughts, for example, "Even though Tom was shy, Mary thought he was charming," with the grammatical structure "even though" limiting the correct answer to some sort of semantic opposites, so you wouldn't get answers like, "Even though Tom was foolish, Mary thought he was ridiculous." Well, according to my mother, there were very few limitations as to what Tom could have been and what Mary might have thought of him. So I never did well on tests like that.

17   The same was true with word analogies, pairs of words in which you were supposed to find some sort of logical, semantic relationship—for example, "*Sunset* is to *nightfall* as ____ is to ____." And here you would be presented with a list of four possible pairs, one of which showed the same kind of relationship: *red* is to *stoplight, bus* is to *arrival, chills* is to *fever, yawn* is to *boring*. Well, I could never think that way. I knew what the tests were asking, but I could not block out of my mind the images already created by the first pair, "*sunset* is to *nightfall*"—and I would see a burst of colors against a darkening sky, the moon rising, the lowering of a curtain of stars. And all the other pairs of words—red, bus, stoplight, boring—just threw up a mass of confusing images,

NOTES

linguists (par. 15): specialists in language studies
insular (par. 15): isolated
semantic opposites (par. 16): terms opposite in meaning

making it impossible for me to sort out something as logical as saying: "A sunset precedes nightfall" is the same as "a chill precedes a fever." The only way I would have gotten that answer right would have been to imagine an associative situation, for example, my being disobedient and staying out past sunset, catching a chill at night, which turns into feverish pneumonia as punishment, which indeed did happen to me.

18   I have been thinking about all this lately, about my mother's English, about achievement tests. Because lately I've been asked, as a writer, why there are not more Asian-Americans represented in American literature. Why are there few Asian-Americans enrolled in creative writing programs? Why do so many Chinese students go into engineering? Well, these are broad sociological questions I can't begin to answer. But I have noticed in surveys—in fact, just last week—that Asian students, as a whole, always do significantly better on math achievement tests than in English. And this makes me think that there are other Asian-American students whose English spoken in the home might also be described as "broken" or "limited." And perhaps they also have teachers who are steering them away from writing and into math and science, which is what happened to me.

19   Fortunately, I happen to be rebellious in nature and enjoy the challenge of disproving assumptions made about me. I became an English major my first year in college, after being enrolled as pre-med. I started writing nonfiction as a freelancer the week after I was told by my former boss that writing was my worst skill and I should hone my talents toward account management.

20   But it wasn't until 1985 that I finally began to write fiction. And at first I wrote using what I thought to be wittily crafted sentences, sentences that would finally prove I had mastery over the English language. Here's an example from the first draft of a story that later made its way into *The Joy Luck Club*, but without this line: "That was my mental quandary in its nascent state." A terrible line, which I can barely pronounce.

21   Fortunately, for reasons I won't get into today, I later decided I should envision a reader for the stories I would write. And the reader I decided upon was my mother, because these were stories about mothers. So with this reader in mind—and in fact she did read my early drafts—I began to write stories using all the Englishes I grew up with: the English I spoke to my mother, which for lack of a better term might be described as "simple"; the English she used with me, which for lack of a better term might be described as "broken"; my translation of her Chinese, which could certainly be described as "watered down"; and what I imagined to be her translation of her Chinese if she could speak in perfect English, her internal language, and for that I sought to preserve the essence, but neither an English nor a Chinese structure. I wanted to

NOTES

freelancer (par. 19): someone who is self-employed

hone (par. 19): develop

quandary (par. 20): dilemma

nascent (par. 20): beginning

envision (par. 21): imagine

essence (par. 21): essential and distinct qualities

capture what language ability tests can never reveal: her intent, her passion, her imagery, the rhythms of her speech, and the nature of her thoughts.

22   Apart from what any critic had to say about my writing, I knew I had succeeded where it counted when my mother finished reading my book and gave me her verdict: "So easy to read."

The Myth of the Latin Woman: I Just Met a Girl Named Maria

Judith Ortiz Cofer

1   On a bus trip to London from Oxford University where I was earning some graduate credits one summer, a young man, obviously fresh from a pub, spotted me and as if struck by inspiration went down on his knees in the aisle. With both hands over his heart he broke into an Irish tenor's rendition of "Maria" from West Side Story. My politely amused fellow passengers gave his lovely voice the round of gentle applause it deserved. Though I was not quite as amused, I managed my version of an English smile: no show of teeth, no extreme contortions of the facial muscles—I was at this time of my life practicing reserve and cool. Oh, that British control, how I coveted it. But Maria had followed me to London, reminding me of a prime fact of my life: you can leave the Island, master the English language, and travel as far as you can, but if you are a Latina, especially one like me who so obviously belongs to Rita Moreno's gene pool, the Island travels with you.

2   This is sometimes a very good thing—it may win you that extra minute of someone's attention. But with some people, the same things can make you an island—not so much a tropical paradise as an Alcatraz, a place nobody wants to visit. As a Puerto Rican girl growing up in the United States and wanting like most children to "belong," I resented the stereotype that my Hispanic appearance called forth from many people I met.

NOTES

pub (par. 1): bar

rendition (par. 1): performance; artistic interpretation

West Side Story (par. 1): a 1957 musical about Tony and Maria, a boy and girl who meet and fall in love despite the fact that they are from rival New York City gangs, the Jets (a white gang) and the Sharks (a Puerto Rican gang). Tony is the founder of the Jets; Maria is the sister of Bernardo, the leader of the Sharks.

"Maria" (par. 1) is the song that Tony sings about his new love on his way home from the dance where they met.

contortions (par. 1): twisting

coveted (par. 1): wanted

the Island (par. 1): Puerto Rico

Rita Moreno (par. 1): A Puerto Rican actress and singer. For her portrayal of Anita (Bernardo's girlfriend) in the 1961 film version of *West Side Story*, she won the Academy Award for Best Supporting Actress. Moreno was the first Hispanic actress to win an Academy Award.

Gene pool (par. 1): a group of people who share a set of similar physical traits

Alcatraz (par. 2): a small rocky island in the San Francisco Bay where a military prison was located from 1859 to 1933 and a high security federal prison from 1933 to 1963.

3   Our family lived in a large urban center in New Jersey during the sixties, where life was designed as a microcosm of my parents' *casas* on the island. We spoke in Spanish, we ate Puerto Rican food bought at the *bodega*, and we practiced strict Catholicism complete with Saturday confession and Sunday mass at a church where our parents were accommodated into a one-hour Spanish mass slot, performed by a Chinese priest trained as a missionary for Latin America.

4   As a girl I was kept under strict surveillance, since virtue and modesty were, by cultural equation, the same as family honor. As a teenager I was instructed on how to behave as a proper *senorita*. But it was a conflicting message girls got, since the Puerto Rican mothers also encouraged their daughters to look and act like women and to dress in clothes our Anglo friends and their mothers found too "mature" for our age. It was, and is, cultural, yet I often felt humiliated when I appeared at an American friend's party wearing a dress more suitable to a semiformal than to a playroom birthday celebration. At Puerto Rican festivities, neither the music nor the colors we wore could be too loud. I still experience a vague sense of letdown when I'm invited to a "party" and it turns out to be a marathon conversation in hushed tones rather than a fiesta with salsa, laughter, and dancing—the kind of celebration I remember from my childhood.

5   I remember Career Day in our high school, when teachers told us to come dressed as if for a job interview. It quickly became obvious that to the barrio girls, "dressing up" sometimes meant wearing ornate jewelry and clothing that would be more appropriate (by mainstream standards) for the company Christmas party than as daily office attire. That morning I had agonized in front of my closet, trying to figure out what a "career girl" would wear because, essentially, except for Marlo Thomas on TV, I had no models on which to base my decision. I knew how to dress for school: at the Catholic school I attended we all wore uniforms; I knew how to dress for Sunday mass, and I knew what dresses to wear for parties at my relatives' homes. Though I do not recall the precise details of my Career Day outfit, it must have been a composite of the above choices. But I remember a comment my friend (an Italian-American) made in later years that coalesced my impressions of that day. She said that at the business school she was attending the Puerto Rican girls always

NOTES

microcosm (par. 3): miniature version

casas (par. 3): houses

bodega (par. 3): in Hispanic communities, a small grocery store and wine shop

senorita (par. 4): young lady

Anglo (par. 4): white, non-Hispanic

salsa (par. 4): a type of Latin-American dance music

barrio girls (par. 5): girls from the Hispanic neighborhood

Marlo Thomas on TV (par. 5): From 1966 to 1971, Marlo Thomas starred in *That Girl*, a TV comedy about a struggling actress who lives in New York City and tries to advance her acting and modeling career while finding time for her boyfriend and her father.

composite (par. 5): combination

coalesced (par. 5): united

credible (par. 5): reliable, trustworthy

stood out for wearing "everything at once." She meant, of course, too much jewelry, too many accessories. On that day at school, we were simply made the negative models by the nuns who were themselves not credible fashion experts to any of us. But it was painfully obvious to me that to the others, in their tailored skirts and silk blouses, we must have seemed "hopeless" and "vulgar." Though I now know that most adolescents feel out of step much of the time, I also know that for the Puerto Rican girls of my generation that sense was intensified. The way our teachers and classmates looked at us that day in school was just a taste of the culture clash that awaited us in the real world, where prospective employers and men on the street would often misinterpret our tight skirts and jingling bracelets as a come-on.

6   Mixed cultural signals have perpetuated certain stereotypes—for example, that of the Hispanic woman as the "Hot Tamale" or sexual firebrand. It is a one-dimensional view that the media have found easy to promote. In their special vocabulary, advertisers have "sizzling" and "smoldering" as the adjectives of choice for describing not only the foods but also the women of Latin America. From conversations in my house I recall hearing about the harassment that Puerto Rican women endured in factories where the "boss men" talked to them as if sexual innuendo was all they understood and, worse, often gave them the choice of submitting to advances or being fired.

7   It is custom, however, not chromosomes, that leads us to choose scarlet over pale pink. As young girls, we were influenced in our decisions about clothes and colors by the women—older sisters and mothers who had grown up on a tropical island where the natural environment was a riot of primary colors, where showing your skin was one way to keep cool as well as to look sexy. Most important of all, on the island, women perhaps felt freer to dress and move more provocatively, since, in most cases, they were protected by the traditions, mores, and laws of a Spanish/Catholic system of morality and machismo whose main rule was: You may look at my sister, but if you touch her I will kill you. The extended family and church structure could provide a young woman with a circle of safety in her small *pueblo* on the island; if a man "wronged" a girl, everyone would close in to save her family honor.

8   This is what I have gleaned from my discussions as an adult with older Puerto Rican women. They have told me about dressing in their best party clothes on Saturday nights and going to the town's plaza to promenade with their girlfriends in front of the boys they liked. The males were thus given an

NOTES

sexual innuendo (par. 6): remarks that indirectly suggest something sexual

chromosomes (par. 7): Chromosomes are strands of DNA that are found in cell nuclei; they contain the genes that determine the sex of an organism as well as the characteristics it inherits from its parents.

a riot (par. 7): an excess

primary colors (par. 7): The primary colors are red, yellow, and blue.

provocatively (par. 7): sexily

mores (par. 7): accepted moral standards

machismo (par. 7): exaggerated masculinity

pueblo (par. 7): village

gleaned (par. 8): gathered

promenade (par. 8): walk around

opportunity to admire the women and to express their admiration in the form of *piropos*: erotically charged street poems they composed on the spot. I have been subjected to a few *piropos* while visiting the Island, and they can be outrageous, although custom dictates that they must never cross into obscenity. This ritual, as I understand it, also entails a show of studied indifference on the woman's part; if she is "decent," she must not acknowledge the man's impassioned words. So I do understand how things can be lost in translation. When a Puerto Rican girl dressed in her idea of what is attractive meets a man from the mainstream culture who has been trained to react to certain types of clothing as a sexual signal, a clash is likely to take place. The line I first heard based on this aspect of the myth happened when the boy who took me to my first formal dance leaned over to plant a sloppy overeager kiss painfully on my mouth, and when I didn't respond with sufficient passion said in a resentful tone: "I thought you Latin girls were supposed to mature early"—my first instance of being thought of as a fruit or vegetable—I was supposed to ripen, not just grow into womanhood like other girls.

9   It is surprising to some of my professional friends that some people, including those who should know better, still put others "in their place." Though rarer, these incidents are still commonplace in my life. It happened to me most recently during a stay at a very classy metropolitan hotel favored by young professional couples for their weddings. Late one evening after the theater, as I walked toward my room with my new colleague (a woman with whom I was coordinating an arts program), a middle-aged man in a tuxedo, a young girl in satin and lace on his arm, stepped directly into our path. With his champagne glass extended toward me, he exclaimed, "Evita!" Our way blocked, my companion and I listened as the man half-recited, half-bellowed "Don't Cry for Me, Argentina." When he finished, the young girl said: "How about a round of applause for my daddy?" We complied, hoping this would bring the silly spectacle to a close. I was becoming aware that our little group was attracting the attention of the other guests. "Daddy" must have perceived this too, and he once more barred the way as we tried to walk past him. He began to shout-sing a ditty to the tune of "*La Bamba*"—except the lyrics were about a girl named Maria whose exploits all rhymed with her name and gonorrhea. The girl kept saying "Oh, Daddy" and looking at me with pleading eyes. She wanted me to laugh along with the others. My companion and I stood silently waiting for the man to end his offensive song. When he finished, I looked not at him but at his daughter. I advised her calmly never to ask her father what he had done in the army. Then I walked between them and to my room. My friend complimented me on my cool handling of the situation. I confessed to her that I really had wanted to push the jerk into the swimming pool. I knew

NOTES

metropolitan (par. 9): big city

Evita! (par. 9): Commonly known as "Evita," Eva Peron was the first lady of Argentina and a powerful political force from 1946 until her death in 1952. In *Evita*, a musical based on her life, the character of Eva Peron sings **"Don't Cry for Me, Argentina"** (par. 9).

"La Bamba" (par. 9): a song by Ritchie Valens (1941–1959), the first Hispanic rock and roll star

regale (par. 9): entertain

that this same man—probably a corporate executive, well educated, even worldly by most standards—would not have been likely to regale a white woman with a dirty song in public. He would perhaps have checked his impulse by assuming that she could be somebody's wife or mother, or at least somebody who might take offense. But to him, I was just an Evita or a Maria: merely a character in his cartoon-populated universe.

10   Because of my education and my proficiency with the English language I have acquired many mechanisms for dealing with the anger I experience. This was not true for my parents, nor is it true for the many Latin women working at menial jobs who must put up with stereotypes about our ethnic group such as: "They make good domestics." This is another facet of the myth of the Latin woman in the United States. Its origin is simple to deduce. Work as domestics, waitressing, and factory jobs are all that's available to women with little English and few skills. The myth of the Hispanic menial has been sustained by the same media phenomenon that made "Mammy" from *Gone with the Wind* America's idea of the black woman for generations; Maria, the housemaid or counter girl, is now indelibly etched into the national psyche. The big and the little screens have presented us with the picture of the funny Hispanic maid, mispronouncing words and cooking up a spicy storm in a shiny California kitchen.

11   This media-engendered image of the Latina in the United States has been documented by feminist Hispanic scholars, who claim that such portrayals are partially responsible for the denial of opportunities for upward mobility among Latinas in the professions. I have a Chicana friend working on a Ph.D. in philosophy at a major university. She says her doctor still shakes his head in puzzled amazement at all the "big words" she uses. Since I do not wear my diplomas around my neck for all to see, I too have on occasion been sent to that "kitchen," where some think I obviously belong.

12   One such incident that has stayed with me, though I recognize it as a minor offense, happened on the day of my first public poetry reading. It took place in Miami in a boat-restaurant where we were having lunch before the event. I was nervous and excited as I walked in with my notebook in my hand. An older woman motioned me to her table. Thinking (foolish me) that she wanted me to autograph a copy of my brand new slender volume of verse, I went over. She ordered a cup of coffee from me, assuming that I was the waitress. Easy enough to mistake my poems for menus, I suppose. I know that it wasn't an intentional act of cruelty, yet of all the good things that happened that day, I remember that scene most clearly, because it reminded me of what I had to overcome before anyone would take me seriously. In retrospect I understand

NOTES

proficiency (par. 10): great skill

menial (par. 10): unskilled

facet (par. 10): part

deduce (par. 10): figure out

indelibly (par. 10): permanently

psyche (par. 10): spirit or mind

media-engendered (par. 11): created and circulated by the media

Chicana (par. 11): a Mexican-American girl or woman

In retrospect (par. 12): looking back

faux pas (par. 12): social mistake

that my anger gave my reading fire, that I have almost always taken doubts in my abilities as a challenge—and that the result is, most times, a feeling of satisfaction at having won a convert when I see the cold, appraising eyes warm to my words, the body language change, the smile that indicates that I have opened some avenue for communication. That day I read to that woman and her lowered eyes told me that she was embarrassed at her little faux pas, and when I willed her to look up at me, it was my victory, and she graciously allowed me to punish her with my full attention. We shook hands at the end of the reading, and I never saw her again. She has probably forgotten the whole thing but maybe not.

13   Yet I am one of the lucky ones. My parents made it possible for me to acquire a stronger footing in the mainstream culture by giving me the chance at an education. And books and art have saved me from the harsher forms of ethnic and racial prejudice that many of my Hispanic *companeras* have had to endure. I travel a lot around the United States, reading from my books of poetry and my novel, and the reception I most often receive is one of positive interest by people who want to know more about my culture. There are, however, thousands of Latinas without the privilege of an education or the entrée into society that I have. For them life is a struggle against the misconceptions perpetuated by the myth of the Latina as whore, domestic, or criminal. We cannot change this by legislating the way people look at us. The transformation, as I see it, has to occur at a much more individual level. My personal goal in my public life is to try to replace the old pervasive stereotypes and myths about Latinas with a much more interesting set of realities. Every time I give a reading, I hope the stories I tell, the dreams and fears I examine in my work, can achieve some universal truth which will get my audience past the particulars of my skin color, my accent, or my clothes.

14   I once wrote a poem in which I called us Latinas "God's brown daughters." This poem is really a prayer of sorts, offered upward, but also, through the human-to-human channel of art, outward. It is a prayer for communication, and for respect. In it, Latin women pray "in Spanish to an Anglo God/with a Jewish heritage," and they are "fervently hoping/that if not omnipotent, at least He be bilingual."

NOTES

companeras (par. 13): allies

entrée (par. 13): power to enter

pervasive (par. 13): widespread

omnipotent (par. 14): all-powerful

bilingual (par. 14): able to speak two languages fluently

Making the Grade

Kurt Wiesenfeld

1   It was a rookie error. After 10 years I should have known better, but I went to my office the day after final grades were posted. There was a tentative knock on the door. "Professor Wiesenfeld? I took your Physics 2121 class? I flunked it? I wonder if there's anything I can do to improve my grade?"

I thought: "Why are you asking me? Isn't it too late to worry about it? Do you dislike making declarative statements?"

2   After the student gave his tale of woe and left, the phone rang. "I got a D in your class. Is there any way you can change it to 'Incomplete'?" Then the e-mail assault began: "I'm shy about coming in to talk to you, but I'm not shy about asking for a better grade. Anyway, it's worth a try." The next day I had three phone messages from students asking me to call them. I didn't.

3   Time was, when you received a grade, that was it. You might groan and moan but you accepted it as the outcome of your efforts or lack thereof (and, yes, sometimes a tough grader). In the last few years, however, some students have developed a disgruntled-consumer approach. If they don't like their grade, they go to the "return" counter to trade it in for something better.

4   What alarms me is their indifference toward grades as an indication of personal effort and performance. Many, when pressed about why they think they deserve a better grade, admit they don't deserve one but would like one anyway. Having been raised on gold stars for effort and smiley faces for self-esteem, they've learned that they can get by without hard work and real talent if they can talk the professor into giving them a break. This attitude is beyond cynicism. There's a weird innocence to the assumption that one expects (even deserves) a better grade simply by begging for it. With that outlook, I guess I shouldn't be as flabbergasted as I was that 12 students asked me to change their grades after final grades were posted.

5   That's 10 percent of my class who let three months of midterms, quizzes, and lab reports slide long past remedy. My graduate student calls it hyperrational thinking: if effort and intelligence don't matter, why should deadlines? What matters is getting a better grade through an unearned bonus, the academic equivalent of a freebie T-shirt or toaster giveaway. Rewards are disconnected from the quality of one's work. An act and its consequence are unrelated, random events.

6   Their arguments for wheedling better grades often ignore academic performance. Perhaps they feel it's not relevant. "If my grade isn't raised to a D I'll lose my scholarship." "If you don't give me a C, I'll flunk out." One sincerely overwrought student pleaded. "If I don't pass, my life is over." This is tough stuff to deal with. Apparently, I'm responsible for someone's losing a scholarship, flunking out or deciding whether life has meaning. Perhaps these students see me as a commodities broker with something they want—a grade. Though intrinsically worthless, grades, if properly manipulated, can be traded for what has value: a degree, which means a job, which means money. The one thing college actually offers—a chance to learn—is considered irrelevant, even less than worthless, because of the long hours and hard work required.

NOTES

tentative (par. 1): uncertain

woe (par. 2): suffering

cynicism (par. 4): scorn for the integrity of others

wheedling (par. 6): trying to persuade (by coaxing)

intrinsically (par. 6): essentially

7   In a society saturated with surface values, love of knowledge for its own sake does sound eccentric. The benefits of fame and wealth are more obvious. So is it right to blame students for reflecting the superficial values saturating our society?

8   Yes, of course it's right. These guys had better take themselves seriously now, because our country will be forced to take them seriously later, when the stakes are much higher. They must recognize that their attitude is not only self-destructive, but socially destructive. The erosion of quality control—giving appropriate grades for actual accomplishments—is a major concern in my department. One colleague noted that a physics major could obtain a degree without ever answering a written exam question completely. How? By pulling in enough partial credit and extra credit. And by getting breaks on grades.

9   But what happens once she or he graduates and gets a job? That's when the misfortunes of eroding academic standards multiply. We lament that school-children get "kicked upstairs" until they graduate from high school despite being illiterate and mathematically inept, but we seem unconcerned with college graduates whose less blatant deficiencies are far more harmful if their accreditation exceeds their qualifications.

10   Most of my students are science and engineering majors. If they're good at getting partial credit but not at getting the answer right, then the new bridge breaks or the new drug doesn't work. One finds examples here in Atlanta. Last year a light tower in the Olympic Stadium collapsed, killing a worker. It collapsed because an engineer miscalculated how much weight it could hold. A new 12-story dormitory could develop dangerous cracks due to a foundation that's uneven by more than six inches. The error resulted from incorrect data being fed into a computer. I drive past that dorm daily on my way to work, wondering if a foundation crushed under kilotons of weight is repairable or if this structure will have to be demolished. Two 10,000-pound steel beams at the new natatorium collapsed in March, crashing into the student athletic complex. (Should we give partial credit since no one was hurt?) Those are real-world consequences of errors and lack of expertise.

11   But the lesson is lost on the grade-grousing 10 percent. Say that you won't (not can't, but won't) change the grade they deserve to what they want, and they're frequently bewildered or angry. They don't think it's fair that they're judged according to their performance, not their desires or "potential." They don't think it's fair that they should jeopardize their scholarships or be in danger of flunking out simply because they could not or did not do their work. But it's more than fair; it's necessary to help preserve a minimum standard of quality that our society needs to maintain safety and integrity. I don't know if the 13th-hour students will learn the lesson, but I've learned mine. From now on, after final grades are posted, I'll lie low until the next quarter starts.

NOTES

saturated (par. 7): filled

eccentric (par. 7): strange

erosion (par. 8): wearing away; loss

lament (par. 9): express grief

inept (par. 9): unskilled

blatant (par. 9): obvious

accreditation (par. 9): credentials (degrees, certificates, and so forth)

natatorium (par. 10): indoor swimming pool

grousing (par. 11): complaining

bewildered (par. 11): puzzled

What Is Child Pornography?

George Will

1   Brian Dalton, 22, of Columbus, Ohio, will probably lower the moral tone of the prison if he serves the seven-year term—plus 18 months for violation of his probation—to which he recently was sentenced in Ohio. He seems to be an appalling person with ghastly tastes. But his conviction under a state statute concerning child pornography is puzzling. He was convicted for writing in his 14-page journal, for his private delectation, pornographic stories involving three fictional children, caged in a basement. The journal was found during a search of his home by his probation officer. Dalton was on probation after serving time in jail for a 1998 conviction involving pornographic photographs of children.

2   The Associated Press reports that Dalton's stories about the sexual abuse and torture of children were so lurid that grand jurors asked the detective reading them to stop almost as soon as he began. But Dalton is believed to be the first person ever convicted in any U.S. jurisdiction for child pornography involving writings rather than photographs, films, or other images of real children. A second problematic aspect of Dalton's case is that he evidently had no interest in disseminating his writings.

3   In 1969, in a case arising from Georgia, the Supreme Court ruled that "the mere private possession of obscene matter cannot constitutionally be made a crime." Here the court stepped back from an earlier ruling that seemed to assert categorically that obscenity is never constitutionally protected.

4   The court reasoned that, "Given the present state of knowledge, the state may no more prohibit mere possession of obscene matter on the grounds that it may lead to antisocial conduct than it may prohibit possession of chemistry books on the ground that they may lead to the manufacture of homemade spirits." The court grandly asserted that an American has a constitutional right "to read or observe what he pleases—the right to satisfy his intellectual and emotional needs in the privacy of his own home," and "the right to be free from state inquiry into the contents of his library" because, "if the First

NOTES

appalling (par. 1): frightful

ghastly (par. 1): horrible

delectation (par. 1): enjoyment

lurid (par. 2): shocking; graphic

disseminating (par. 2): distributing

In 1969, in a case arising from Georgia (par. 3): *Georgia v. Stanley* (1969)

an earlier ruling (par. 3): *Roth v. United States* (1957)

Amendment means anything, it means that a state has no business telling a man, sitting alone in the his own house, what books he may read or films he may watch."

5   Note the words "observe" and "films" and "watch."

6   However, in a 1982 case the Supreme Court upheld the constitutionality of a New York law that criminalized depicting sexual performances by children when the promotion involved materials depicting such performances. The court held that states have some leeway in regulating child pornography. This is so because, among other reasons, "the use" of children in pornography harms them.

7   Then in a 1990 case arising from Ohio the court held that the mere possession of child pornography can be proscribed. It had said that Georgia's justification for banning all obscenity, not just child pornography—the belief that obscenity could poison the minds of those exposed to it—was "inadequate" because it relied on a "paternalistic interest" in regulating minds. In contrast, Ohio's law proscribing even mere possession of child pornography was based on the state's "compelling interests in protecting the physical and psychological well-being of minors and in destroying the market for the exploitative use of children by penalizing those who possess and view the offending materials."

8   Note the word "view."

9   The court affirmed Ohio's right to attack child pornography "at all levels in the distribution chain" because the market for such materials "has been driven underground," making it difficult to suppress by attacking only production and distribution. Furthermore, "the materials produced by child pornographers permanently record the victim's abuse" and cause "continuing harm" by "haunting" real children for years.

10   The court added another justification for criminalizing mere possession of such material: "Evidence suggests that pedophiles use child pornography to seduce other children into sexual activity." Perhaps this is pertinent to Dalton's case, but, again, it seems to suggest that the problem is pornographic pictures or other images of real children. Are children apt to be seduced into sexual activity by written material?

11   The law under which Dalton was convicted criminalizes the creation of child pornography "material." It does not specify images. But, again, it is likely that the lawmakers were thinking of the making of pornographic photographs or film that require the participation of real children.

12   It is unclear why Dalton pleaded guilty, thereby discarding a chance to contest his conviction. Meanwhile, this autumn the Supreme Court will consider, in a California case, whether computer-generated images of children engaged in sexual activities is proscribable child pornography. The cumulative logic of past rulings, which stressed the involvement of real children, suggests it is not.

NOTES

in a 1982 case (par. 6): *New York v. Ferber* (1982)
leeway (par. 6): freedom to make decisions
a 1990 case arising from Ohio (par. 7): *Osborne v. Ohio* (1990)
proscribed (par. 7): prohibited
paternalistic (par. 7): fatherlike
exploitative (par. 7): selfish and unfair

pertinent (par. 10): relevant

apt (par. 10): likely

a California case (par. 12): *Ashcroft v. Free Speech Coalition* (2002). The Supreme Court ruled that key provisions of the Child Pornography Prevention Act of 1996 were unconstitutional.

Disgusting Doesn't Make It "Speech"

Ann Coulter

1   With even George Will and the Family Research Council predicting the child pornographer in Ohio will prevail on appeal, I am now officially The Only Person in America who says Ohio wins. (Other than, one hopes, the prosecutor.)

2   Convicted child pornographer Brian Dalton was charged with pandering child pornography on the basis of his private writings in a personal journal in his home. He pled guilty, which normally precludes appeal and may prevent me from collecting on my bets.

3   Point one: The states can do anything that isn't prohibited by the Constitution. (This elusive concept is admittedly difficult to grasp, especially if you are a Supreme Court justice and prefer to think of yourself as "Czar of the Universe.") If a state wants to outlaw artichokes, it can, unless the artichoke is actually, say, a gun, in which case it is constitutionally protected.

4   Thus, the only question is whether Dalton's private journal is protected by the First Amendment.

5   Dalton insists he had no intention of sharing his journal with his pederast friends. It was for his eyes only. This point has great emotional appeal, but throws into doubt whether Dalton's journal qualifies as "speech." To whom was he speaking? The reason burning an American flag is protected "speech" is that the First Amendment protects communication, not mere words.

6   If Dalton's journal was intended solely for his own individual pleasure, it's not apparent why it should have any greater constitutional significance than a blow-up doll. The whole point of the First Amendment is communication—expressive content, the marketplace of ideas, the government cannot distinguish truth from falsity, blah, blah, blah.

7   It may seem intuitively correct that you have a right to talk to yourself, but it also seems intuitively correct that you have a right to artichokes. Unless the

NOTES

prevail (par. 1): win

appeal (par. 1): a written request to a higher court to reverse or modify the judgment of a lower court

pandering (par. 2): supplying

precludes (par. 2): rules out

elusive (par. 3): mysterious

Czar (par. 3): ruler; the title of the emperors who ruled Russia prior to the 1917 Russian revolution

First Amendment (par. 4): The First Amendment to the U.S. Constitution states that "Congress shall make no law respecting an establishment of religion, or prohibiting the free exercise thereof; or abridging the freedom of speech, or of the press; or the right of the people peaceably to assemble, and to petition the government for a redress of grievances."

pederast (par. 5): a man who has sex with a boy

intuitively (par. 7): instinctively

Constitution protects it, states can ban it. Dalton was either pandering child pornography or he was talking to himself—which isn't obviously protected by the Constitution.

8   But let's say talking to oneself does constitute "speech." Not all speech is protected by the First Amendment. Obscenity, for example, is not protected.

9   After announcing various ridiculous definitions of "obscenity" over the years, the Supreme Court finally settled on this ridiculous definition: It must describe specific sexual acts in a patently offensive way; it must, taken as a whole, appeal to a prurient interest; and it must have no serious literary, artistic, political, or scientific value. (A later case clarified that "prurient interest" includes the narrow interests of deviants.)

10   You're probably thinking: Sexual acts, prurient interest, offensive content, and no serious literary value—that sounds like prime-time TV! I exaggerate. But approximately 90 percent of what Americans now think of as constitutionally protected pornography—the reason George Washington fought at Valley Forge, what separates us from the Communists—is technically unprotected "obscenity." The states could ban it if they wanted to.

11   Most state prosecutors don't bother prosecuting obscenity cases anymore because—well, first, they don't want to take on the entire Harvard Law School faculty. But also because smut just confuses the Supreme Court.

12   The septuagenarian justices spent most of the '60s watching porno on "movie day" at the court—a particular delight to Justice Thurgood Marshall, according to Bob Woodward's *The Brethren*. The constant sex flicks must have gotten to the old geezers. Every few years they would clean up and issue another incomprehensible, contradictory obscenity ruling.

13   William Brennan approved of all pornography that was degrading to women but voted against pornography that showed men in a state of arousal. Byron

NOTES

patently (par. 9): clearly

prurient (par. 9): lustful

deviants (par. 9): people whose behavior (especially sexual behavior) differs from what is socially acceptable

septuagenarian (par. 13): 70- to 80-year-old

Justice Thurgood Marshall (par. 12): Marshall (1908–1993) served as an associate justice of the U.S. Supreme Court from 1967 to 1991.

William Brennan (par. 13): Brennan (1906–1997) served as an associate justice of the U.S. Supreme Court from 1956 to 1990.

Byron White (par. 13): White (1917–2002) served as an associate justice of the U.S. Supreme Court from 1962 to 1993.

Potter Stewart (par. 13): Stewart (1915–1985) served as an associate justice of the U.S. Supreme Court from 1958 to 1981.

"I know it when I see it" (par. 13): Agreeing with the Supreme Court's decision in the case of *Jacobellis v. Ohio*, Justice Stewart wrote, "It is possible to read the Court's opinion in *Roth v. United States* and *Alberts v. California*, 354 U.S. 476, in a variety of ways. In saying this, I imply no criticism of the Court, which in those cases was faced with the task of trying to define what may be indefinable. I have reached the conclusion, which I think is confirmed at least by negative implication in the Court's decisions since *Roth* and *Alberts*, that under the First and Fourteenth Amendments criminal laws in this area are constitutionally limited to hardcore pornography. I shall not today attempt further to define the kinds of material I understand to be embraced within that shorthand description; and perhaps I could never succeed in intelligibly doing so. But I know it when I see it, and the motion picture involved in this case is not that." The movie Justice Stewart is referring to is *Les Amants* (*The Lovers*).

White protected all pornography unless it was "Blue Boy." Potter Stewart defined "obscenity" as "I know it when I see it"—but he never seemed to see it. William Douglas and Marshall viewed anything tenuously related to sex as "speech."

14 The one case in the midst of this idiocy that seems to support a right to possess even obscenity in the home is Justice Marshall's opinion in *Stanley v. Georgia*. Somehow bringing non-speech into the home suddenly made it "speech." On this theory, if an artichoke were used as a sexual aid in the home, it would be "speech."

15 That was too absurd even for the sex-addled justices. A few years later, in *United States v. Reidel*, the court quickly clarified that Stanley was a privacy case, not a First Amendment case at all. Then in *Bowers v. Hardwick* (no privacy right to engage in sodomy in the bedroom), the court claimed Stanley was a First Amendment case and not a "privacy" case. Stanley would be a great case for pornographers if the Supreme Court could ever find another case to which it applies.

16 Admittedly, it seems rather authoritarian for a government official to be reading any citizen's private journal. But the reason Dalton's journal was subject to review is that he is a convicted and paroled child pornographer. If you want to keep a journal private, here's a word to the wise: Try to avoid child-pornography convictions.

NOTES

William Douglas (par. 13): Douglas (1898–1980) served as an associate justice of the U.S. Supreme Court from 1939–1975.
tenuously (par. 13): vaguely
addled (par. 15): confused
sodomy (par. 15): anal intercourse

Should a Man Be Put in Jail for What He's Thinking?

Leonard Pitts, Jr.

1 A question.

2 Can a man be put in jail for what he's thinking?

3 Before you answer, you should know that what the man in question was thinking is about as repugnant as it gets.

4 Like child pornography. Twenty-two-year-old Brian Dalton, a Columbus, Ohio man, was convicted in 1998 of possessing sexually explicit photographs. He served a few months before being released on probation. And there the matter might have ended, except for what his probation officer found during a routine search of Dalton's home. Namely, Dalton's personal diary, which contained a 14-page story about three kids, ages 10 and 11, who are imprisoned, tortured, and molested.

NOTE

repugnant (par. 3): shocking

5   The story was wholly fictitious, the product of a diseased imagination. Yet it was said to be so vivid and vile that grand jurors who indicted Dalton asked a detective to stop reading from the diary after only two pages. Dalton wrote the tale for his personal use; there's no evidence he ever planned to disseminate it.

6   Not that this mattered when he was tried earlier this month under a state law allowing the prosecution of those found in possession of any pornographic material involving children. In other words, not just photos of real kids, but written fantasies, drawings, even, conceivably, computer-generated images, of children who do not exist. Under a plea bargain, Dalton will spend almost nine years in jail.

7   And that, friends and neighbors, is simply, frighteningly, wrong.

8   If you disagree, well, I can certainly understand. It's sickening to contemplate sympathy for a man like Dalton. But sympathy isn't the point. Dalton isn't even the point. Rather, the point is that what just happened in Ohio represents a clear and present danger to the rights you and I enjoy as United States citizens.

9   Funny thing about those rights. They are so much a part of us that we take them for granted. Indeed, sometimes our attitude toward them is downright cavalier—especially when we're talking about them in the context of odious others. It's hard to imagine, for instance, that many of us would countenance a government attempt to decide what we, personally, were allowed to see, say, or think. But some would willingly allow the same intrusion upon others— the Klansman, the rapper, the flag burner, the child pornographer—because we find them and their beliefs abhorrent. In allowing that intrusion, such people seldom see that they are betrayed by their own revulsion, induced to make a narrow argument and miss its broad implication:

10   If government is allowed to do it to "them," what stops government from doing it to you?

11   As a fan of the written word—and, not incidentally, as someone who makes his living from it—I find what just happened in the Buckeye State chilling. Under this broadly written statute, a serious writer who explores the subject of child pornography could be subject to the same fate that befell Dalton.

12   And how's this for paradox: the guy got probation after being convicted of possessing pornographic photos of real children. He's looking at almost nine years for writing private thoughts about fictitious ones.

13   No one would argue that the government doesn't have compelling reasons to keep tabs on Brian Dalton. He deserves punishment for his original crime. And treatment for his sickness. Children must be protected from him. But

NOTES

disseminate (par. 5): distribute
cavalier (par. 9): overconfident
odious (par. 9): detestable, hated
countenance (par. 9): support, encourage
abhorrent (par. 9): offensive
intrusion (par. 9): disturbance
induced (par. 9): persuaded
paradox (par. 12): contradiction
constitutionally (par. 13): legally

those goals could be accomplished without the constitutionally dubious means the state of Ohio has chosen.

14   Dalton's attorney, Isabella Dixon, says she may try to withdraw his guilty plea. He accepted the plea bargain, she has said, only because he "felt it was in his best interest at the time." So far, she has declined comment on her role in that decision.

15   So there the matter sits. I won't ask you to feel sorry for Dalton. I sure don't. But I will ask you to ponder the fact that there's nothing preordained about the rights we take for granted. That they can be nibbled away until they are gone.

16   And if you doubt that, you might want to consider again that question: Can a man be put in jail for what he's thinking?

17   He already has.

NOTES

dubious (par. 13): questionable, unclear
ponder (par. 15): consider
preordained (par. 15): certain, definite

Starved Out

Cynthia Fox

1   Crouching by a highway in 100 degree Kansas heat, Jayme Porter shivers in a cold that doesn't exist. She's nauseated, but because she's starving, she's too weak to throw up; she's dizzy, but because there's no fat padding her bones, it's too painful for her to sit on the ground. Sundae-colored cows graze alongside oil derricks, and excess-crop fires simmer on the horizon. But Jayme perches at the edge of this world of plenty, looking as if she's barely there, for her body is cannibalizing itself.

2   An hour later, Jayme, twenty, meets the Wichita hospital doctors she has traveled three hours from her home in Oklahoma to see. They make a surprising discovery. Since Wichita's eating disorders program reluctantly released her two months earlier—at a dangerous forty pounds underweight—because her insurance policy wouldn't cover the stay, no one has been providing her medical

NOTES

oil derricks (par. 1): wood or steel frame towers over oil wells
cannibalizing (par. 1): A cannibal is a person who eats human flesh. Here, Jayme's body is so starved for nourishment that it has begun to consume itself.
eating disorders (par. 2): A group of disorders involving rigid restriction or regulation of food intake. The most common of these disorders are anorexia nervosa and bulimia nervosa. Anorexia is characterized by an abnormal fear of being overweight, distorted self-image, extreme dieting, and severe weight loss. Essentially, *anorexics* (par. 2) will starve themselves to death. *Bulimia* (par. 12) is characterized by episodes of bingeing and purging: gross overeating followed by self-induced vomiting, laxative abuse, and/or excessive exercise. This behavior is often carried out in secret and causes a great deal of shame. A bulimic's body weight is often normal or near normal.
outpatient (par. 2): a person who receives treatment from a hospital or clinic without being hospitalized overnight

care, even on an outpatient basis. She weighs eighty-one pounds. She has trouble finding a job; some employers think she has AIDS. She has a handicapped-parking permit (her ravaged heart makes it difficult to walk), yet the parking space she uses most is at the gym where she works out obsessively. She's a severe anorexic, and the sister of a severe anorexic, yet because her insurance policy doesn't begin to meet her needs, she had been drifting from therapist to therapist, each assuming the others had been doing basic medical tests. None had.

3   Jayme is in for another surprise: Dr. Tamara Pryor, who has been treating her as an outpatient for one hour every two weeks, announces that even this may soon end. The Wichita program is about to go under for the second time in two years because so many patients lack adequate insurance. All studies indicate that the sicker Jayme gets, the more difficult it will be to cure her. Yet the sicker she's gotten, the less treatment she's received—and now she's faced with none. It's a situation her doctors understand, for in the past few years a bizarre paradox has emerged. Anorexia is the mental illness with the highest mortality rate—15 percent of the more than one million Americans who have it will die—yet it receives the least sufficient insurance reimbursement. But Jayme doesn't understand. "I'll still be able to see Dr. Pryor, right?" she asks. No one answers.

4   Managed care—the cost-cutting approach adopted by nearly all insurers—has gutted the eating disorders field in the past ten years. In the mid-1980s severe anorexics would stay two to seven months in hospitals until they reached ideal body weight. But stays for severe cases now range from two days to two weeks, with some insurers imposing a $10,000 lifetime cap, enough to cover about ten inpatient days, or, as in Jayme's case, a $30,000 lifetime limit. All this despite studies indicating that most patients released underweight need rehospitalization. Doctors now tell seventy-pound patients they must be sicker before they can be helped, the equivalent of "sending patients with strep throat away, saying they can't be treated until it causes kidney failure," says Dr. Walter Kaye, head of the University of Pittsburgh's eating disorders program. Adds Stanford's Dr. Regina Casper: "We actually convert people into chronic patients."

5   Some doctors spend more than ten hours a week arguing with insurers. "They wear you down with untrained reviewers, then make you go through three or four levels of appeals," says Dr. Arnold Andersen, who runs an eating disorders clinic at the University of Iowa. "It's like trying to stop the ocean." Insurers generally won't reveal their rejection criteria, never see patients and

NOTES

ravaged (par. 2): horribly damaged

obsessively (par. 2): excessively, irrationally

therapist (par. 2): psychiatrist, psychologist, or counselor (an individual whose work focuses on human behavior and mental disorders)

paradox (par. 3): seeming contradiction

reimbursement (par. 3): repayment

Managed care (par. 4): a health care system in which insurers limit the patient's choice of physicians and the physician's fees and determine the types of care the patient receives

gutted (par. 4): destroyed

chronic (par. 4): long-term

criteria (par. 5): standards

folded (par. 5): closed

make all judgments by phone. As a result, Andersen says, "every third case that needs hospitalization is not allowed in now." Dr. Elke Eckert, head of the University of Minnesota program, says that 40 percent of her patients are discharged before they should be. Adds Dr. Dean Krahn, who headed programs at the University of Michigan and the University of Wisconsin that folded because of insurance problems: "Patients gain five pounds and are discharged now. You get their anxiety up as high as it can be because they've gained weight, but you haven't had time to do anything that will help them accept it. It's torture rather than treatment." The prediction of many doctors: The 15 percent death rate will rise.

6   In recent months the problem has become even more urgent, as doctors have realized there are only a few top-notch programs left. If you have a severe eating disorder now, you may find not only that insurance won't pay for your care, you may find, as Jayme Porter did, that you have nowhere to go.

7   Back home in Stillwater, the day after she discovered the Wichita program might close, Jayme eats an apple for breakfast instead of the juice, yogurt, meat, cereal, milk, and two fruits prescribed. She heads for Oklahoma State University for the lab tests that should have been done months ago. Then she sets out on her daily walk wearing a twenty-pound knapsack that "helps me work out."

8   No one who spends a day with Jayme can wonder for long why severe anorexics need supervision. After her walk she returns to her trailer—the one her parents started out in and is now hers—parked outside the campus. She pours diet Mountain Dew into a forty-nine-ounce tumbler, explaining it has more caffeine than other sodas and gives her a buzz. She slips on a neon-orange minidress ("I get a rush seeing my skeleton") and checks, as she does every day, to make sure her forearm fits in a circle formed by her thumb and finger. Then she spends an hour in a ritual typical of anorexics. She puts a cup of broccoli on a plate—the same plate every day—and places it on the couch under her arm, out of view. She slowly eats while watching *One Life to Live*, her favorite soap. She ponders yogurt and retrieves one from the freezer ("it's harder frozen, so you eat less"). By day's end she should have eaten 2,800 calories. But no one is watching over her, so she'll eat just 500.

9   The trailer is devoid of personal effects, save pictures of her family in heart-shaped frames. She points out a stuffed bunny left at her door by a college friend "who won't come in anymore because he can't stand to look at me." She notes that Prozac has helped her divorce herself from some elements of her past—for example, an obsessive neatness that kept her from allowing people to sit on her couch because "the cushions got squashed." But she still talks to her mother, an administrator at the university, four times a day.

NOTES

knapsack (par. 7): backpack
buzz (par. 8): feeling of slight intoxication
rush (par. 8): thrill
devoid (par. 9): empty
Prozac (par. 9): an antidepressant drug

10   Jayme says she used to go drinking every night with boyfriends until late last year, "when I lost the last forty pounds and scared them all away." Doesn't she want to date? "One of my main goals is to get married and have babies," she says brightly. But she hasn't had her period in eleven months, which causes her mother to say angrily, "I've come to accept the fact that I may never have grandchildren." Jayme has starved herself back into childhood—her skin is covered with lanugo, the hair infants are born with—and forward into old age. Her hair is thinning, her teeth are rotting, and the longer she goes without menstruating the more she risks bone decay. She is trapped between her future and her past.

11   Jayme and her twenty-three-year-old sister, Julie, grew up in Agra, an Oklahoma town that once had high hopes. Agra expected to become the site of a large freight center, and in the 1920s, a town of banks, saloons, cotton gins, and 1,000 residents sprouted in the middle of nowhere. But the freight center was located elsewhere, and by the 1970s, when Julie and Jayme were born into what had become the typical Agra home—a trailer—all that was left was a blind man's concession stand, three churches, a school with ten children per grade, and a population of 336. The only nightlife could be found in tin-shack bars. It was the smallest of small towns, the last place some might expect to find eating disorders, which have been tagged "rich kids' diseases."

12   But studies indicate that bulimia is most common among the lower classes and that anorexia occurs all over the United States. The drive to succeed can play a more crucial role in the disorders than class or location, doctors think. Certainly, the Porters had drive. The girls' father, Galen Porter, a construction supervisor who raised livestock and prided himself on "always having fun," even during his tour in Vietnam, served on the local and state school boards. When Agra made national news after a parent demanded that the novel *The Color Purple* be taken off school shelves, Galen voted against censorship. He and his wife, Kay, sheltered their children from the more prohibitive local customs—which included a town church's demands that women stay at home, marry young, and never cut their hair—and encouraged them to succeed.

13   Succeed Julie and Jayme did. Agra's school had no arts and few sports programs, but it did have 4-H, Future Farmers of America, and Future Homemakers of America. Julie traveled the state with these organizations, winning speech contests while Jayme won sheep-showing contests. Both their bedrooms became shrines to achievement, their shelves stacked with trophies as tall as the pipes of a church organ. Both became one of only two in their grades to go to college.

14   Trouble hit when they were juniors in college. Their parents believe that for Julie, the discovery she wasn't going to be sorority president was the trigger: She lost forty pounds in two months and landed in a hospital weighing eighty-seven pounds. For Jayme, three years younger, her parents think it may have been the realization she hadn't excelled at anything since 4-H days. Both girls

NOTES

prohibitive (par. 12): restrictive
shrines (par. 13): monuments
trigger (par. 14): cause

describe that period simply: "I had to be thinnest." As the last of their high school friends married, it was clear the sisters' ambition had spun out of control.

15   Julie was lucky. Although her mother's insurance policy picked up only $10,500 of the $73,000 bill for her nine-month stay at nearby Laureate Hospital, she was able to continue treatment because a bureaucratic error led Laureate to believe that welfare had taken up the slack. Even after the error was realized, Laureate let her stay on, swallowing more than $20,000.

16   Jayme was not so lucky. When she hit ninety pounds last January, Laureate refused to take her unless her parents paid the $35,000 balance on Julie's bill. Hearing of a program in Arizona called Remuda Ranch, Kay and Galen say they checked with a benefits coordinator who told them their insurance company, American Fidelity Assurance, would not provide more than $10,000. So they re-mortgaged their house to come up with an extra $23,000 to pay for sixty days. But Jayme would stay in Arizona only thirty-five days. Remuda told the Porters Jayme had to leave immediately because she was considered "noncompliant."

17   At home over the next few weeks, Jayme lost more weight. "There was no place else to go," says Kay. Then, suddenly, hope: Wichita's Dr. Pryor consented to treat Jayme first and fight the insurance company later. Pryor, who had been cured of anorexia at age fifteen, took one look at Jayme and checked her into the hospital's intensive care unit.

18   Jayme continued her downward spiral. Her weight dropped to sixty pounds, and she was in a state of hypothermia with a body temperature below 92 degrees. Within days, Pryor, fearing Jayme would die, called the family to her bedside. "She couldn't lift the sheets over herself," Kay recalls. "If she sat up, her heart would go to 180, then would slow to thirty-two beats a minute, and when she tried to get out of bed, it went off the charts. The nurses said you could see the outlines of her organs through her skin. Galen or I would sleep with her every night. We were terrified that if we left her she would die." Julie says she could-n't look at her sister: "I thought I'd be sick. I've seen skinny, skinny girls but nothing like that. She said she wanted a Mr. Potato Head, so I brought her one, but she couldn't even stick the little pieces in him."

19   Jayme pulled through with feeding tubes and was admitted to the psychiatric ward. She began sessions with Pryor. But after three weeks hope fizzled again. "They couldn't afford us, and we couldn't afford them anymore," says Pryor. Having racked up a $50,000 bill in Wichita, none of which American Fidelity paid, Jayme was released on April 23 weighing seventy-nine pounds.

20   Insurance company officials would not comment on the adequacy of their policy, but they did provide records showing that American Fidelity paid only $30,000 of the $180,000 in psychiatric bills hospitals charged them. Pryor,

NOTES

bureaucratic (par. 15): administrative
remortgaged their house (par. 16): borrowed money, giving the lender a claim to their house until the loan is repaid
noncompliant (par. 16): not cooperative
hypothermia (par. 18): abnormally low body temperature
psychiatric ward (par. 19): unit of a hospital dedicated to helping people who are mentally ill
notorious (par. 20): well known (in an unfavorable way)

whose program has since closed, was upset she had to release Jayme. "We should be able to keep them in the hospital for weeks after they've achieved ideal body weight, so we can begin to control behavior," she says. "In 1994 the average inpatient stay of an anorexic here was twenty-one days—now it's two to four days. Patients are coming in so much sicker it's frightening. I've been notorious for forcing the hospital to swallow bills. That's no way to run a program. It's the craziest thing in the world."

21   In May, a month after Jayme was released, the nation's top eating disorders specialists gathered at the annual convention of the American Psychiatric Association in San Diego. They had a new problem. The National Alliance for the Mentally Ill was lobbying for bills in thirty-seven states that would require insurers to treat mental illnesses as seriously as physical illnesses. But NAMI hadn't recommended including eating disorders in any of the parity bills. So the doctors planned to take on both the insurance industry and their own profession. They would try to persuade NAMI to include eating disorders in its legislation.

22   "There's such bias," explained Illinois eating disorders expert Dr. Pat Santucci. "A congressman asked me, 'How am I supposed to convince a small-business man he has to pay for this girlie disease?'" NAMI postponed the meeting. About the bills, NAMI later explained, it can't risk combating the prejudices until the biology of these illnesses is better understood. Anorexia doctors can't afford many of their own patients, let alone their own lobbyists. They had to wait and watch as bills excluding eating disorders were passed in several states.

23   It's summer, and Jayme sits in her trailer, eyeing the clock like an alcoholic before cocktail hour. When it's time for her workout, she says, "Yes!" and leaps out of her slouch with arms and legs akimbo, like a puppet jerked to life.

24   No matter how anorexia begins, many doctors believe that starvation and compulsive exercising become addictive, and this is clearly true for Jayme. At the OSU gym, she sits in a machine that's twice as big as she is, working out with weights as heavy as she is, for nearly two hours. "I'm so strong," she says proudly.

25   Sixty miles away, in her Tulsa home, Julie flops into a chair, looking as puppetlike as her sister. But resemblances to Jayme end there. Julie received six months of intensive treatment—group therapy, psychotherapy, nutrition and body image class, AA, career counseling, twenty-four-hour monitoring—and it changed her life. She lost her rituals, lost her need to please the world. Her

NOTES

parity (par. 21): equivalency, equality

bias (par. 22): prejudice

akimbo (par. 23): bent

compulsive (par. 24): excessive

group therapy (par. 25): a form of therapy in which several clients, guided by a therapist (such as a psychologist or counselor), meet together to confront their personal difficulties

psychotherapy (par. 25): a form of therapy in which a therapist uses psychological methods to help a client overcome mental or emotional problems

nutrition and body image class (par. 25): a class designed to teach nutrition and develop an accurate and realistic image of what one's body is or should be like

AA (par. 25): Alcoholics Anonymous (a support group for people who wish to stop or have stopped drinking)

house is as cheerfully unkempt as Jayme's is spartan. She graduated from college in June and has developed a love she picked up at the hospital—art therapy. Now she's considering getting a master's.

26 Kay and Galen, $145,000 in debt, have seen strange times. They have lost faith in doctors, who keep telling them their daughters' health is a commodity they must purchase. "I'm scared stiff for any of us to get sick now," Kay says. Both shift from affection to disbelief when they speak of their girls, trying to recall which qualities which daughter has lost to her disease. The sisters say their parents can pretend their problems don't exist. And the family's dynamics have changed dramatically. Just when Julie and her parents should have been mending fences after her illness, Jayme began going through the same thing, distracting Kay and Galen's attention. Hurt, Julie rarely comes home. The lack of outside resources has made Jayme more dependent on her parents than ever, reflected in the sardonic tone she adopts when speaking to them. ("I'm just a manipulative little girl, aren't I, Mommy?" she says at one point, wrapping her arms around Kay's neck.) The girls, who have had to compete for attention and money, almost never speak to each other.

27 The Porters were once a family of go-getters who worked and played hard together. Now Kay and Galen sometimes act like kids wondering where the fun has gone. The sisters often act like parents exasperated with the children; the parents, who lie in bed every night wondering what they did wrong, have been rendered as emotionally and financially helpless as their girls. The Porters are as trapped in their love for one another as they are trapped in the clutches of a disease—and a flawed health care system—they don't understand.

28 Julie will likely survive, which becomes evident when she talks about her weight. "Ninety-eight pounds," she says, though she doesn't like to admit it "because it's still too thin." Jayme, too, is afraid to reveal her weight, eighty-one pounds, but for a different reason: "It's not thin enough."

NOTES

unkempt (par. 25): out of order
spartan (par. 25): rigidly ordered
commodity (par. 26): product
dynamics (par. 26): relationship
sardonic (par. 26): ironically humorous
exasperated (par. 27): out of patience

Heavy Judgment: A Sister Talks about the Pain of "Living Large"

Deborah Gregory

1 Thirteen years ago I was a model in Europe. I was cramped inside a tiny fitting room in Paris, and a couturier's purse-lipped assistant put a tape measure around my hips, then screamed, "Trop forte!" I didn't speak French, but I knew

NOTE

couturier's (par. 1): fashion designer's

Madame wasn't delighted with my curvy proportions. The next day another designer called my agency and told them he wouldn't book me because I was too fat. The evidence in question: At five feet eleven inches tall I had the audacity to tip the scales at 140 pounds. Scandalous! It has taken me many years to forgive myself for not maintaining the rigid 125- to 130-pound model mandate—and to forgive the fashion industry for requiring mannequins to be paper-thin.

2   "Sashaying," however, isn't the only business practicing fat-cell-count discrimination: Monitoring women's size has become a weighty issue in the workplace. My favorite rationale is the film industry's hocus-pocus excuse that actresses need to be skinny because celluloid automatically adds ten pounds to their image. But, mind you, it's okay for hefty actors like Forest Whitaker (*A Rage in Harlem* and *The Crying Game*) to bare it all in love scenes. I have painfully discovered the extent of fat discrimination over the last ten years as I have vacillated between 140 and 235 pounds. I currently weigh around 200. What has come with the extra pounds is blatant professional and social discrimination, both to my face and behind my back—the kind that routinely dismisses my skills, talents and God-given physical beauty.

3   The most recent example. A professional colleague, Tony J., was gracious enough to take a copy of my video reel to a television producer he knew at a network. Upon his return, Tony avoided my phone calls. When I finally reached him, he dillydallied before revealing, with much trepidation, that although the producer liked my "flavor" and was impressed with my journalistic credentials, he would only be interested in putting me on camera if I lost weight.

4   The toughest fact to swallow was that the producer in question is Black and the show is targeted to a Black audience. Has society's obsession with keeping women skinny bogarted its way into the Black community's psyche? The answer, painfully, is yes. Where once largeness was accepted—even revered—among Black folks, it now carries the same unmistakable stigma as it does among Whites.

Tipping the Scales of Equality

5   Since the 1960s, the Western standard of beauty for women has become drop-dead thin. Today the average American woman is five feet four inches tall

NOTES

audacity (par. 1): nerve
scandalous (par. 1): shocking
mandate (par. 1): rule
rationale (par. 2): reason
hocus-pocus (par. 2): nonsense
celluloid (par. 2): film
vacillated (par. 2): moved back and forth
blatant (par. 2): obvious
dillydallied (par. 3): hesitated
trepidation (par. 3): nervousness
obsession (par. 4): irrational, overwhelming concern
bogarted (par. 4): Literally, *to bogart* is to hoard, steal, borrow, or share something without asking permission.
psyche (par. 4): spirit
stigma (par. 4): disgrace

and 145 pounds, yet models are 23 percent below the average weight, compared with only 8 percent thirty-five years ago. Who's hit hardest by these waifishly slim media images? We are. Black and Latina women are twice as likely to be overweight as White women. Forty-eight percent of Black women and 30 percent of Latinas are overweight, as compared with 26 percent of White women, according to the National Center for Health Statistics.

6   Pound for pound, women suffer enormous social and professional consequences for heftier proportions. Consider these chilling statistics: Large women are 20 percent less likely to marry than their thinner counterparts. They also have household incomes that average $6,710 lower and are 10 percent more likely to be living in poverty, according to an eight-year study led by Steven L. Gortmaker, Ph.D., of the Harvard School of Public Health and published in the *New England Journal of Medicine.* (The typical obese woman in Gortmaker's study was five feet three inches tall and weighed 200 pounds.)

7   On the other hand, the same research revealed that obesity had less impact on men. Although heavy men are less likely to marry (only by 11 percent, however), they are just as well off financially as their thinner counterparts.

8   Many a large sister can attest to the consequences of society's "fat phobia." Reveals singer Annette Taylor, who has been a size 16 for the past two years and is now a size 14, "I haven't gotten jobs because of my size. For example, I was highly recommended to an A & R executive at a major record company who was searching for a female singer. The first question he asked me over the phone was 'What size are you?' Needless to say, I wasn't even asked to audition. Another time, I auditioned for the female spot in C & C Music Factory. Even though my vocal style was a perfect match for the group, it was clear that I didn't get the part because of my size." Laments Taylor: "The entertainment business is very discriminatory against larger women. My manager even told me that I have to lose weight so I can be video-ready."

9   Adds E. K. Daufin, another large sister and an assistant professor of English and communications at Fort Lewis College in Durango, Colorado, "I've had students in my class hand me diets." Milana Frank, a television producer in Miami, Florida, makes an observation that sums up the woes of large women best: "Because of my size, I have experienced oppression, depression, and recession."

A Pound of Flesh

10   Who determines obesity? Frankly, it appears to be society at large with its ever-so-skimpy standards of how much "fat" is acceptable on a woman. Even at my heaviest weight (235 pounds on my nearly six-foot frame), I have never appeared or defined myself as fat. Large, yes. Fat, no. Yet every day I have to listen

NOTES

waifishly (par. 5): A waif is an abandoned, neglected child.

phobia (par. 8): fear

laments (par. 8): mourns

oppression (par. 9): unjust treatment

depression (par. 9): extreme sadness

recession (par. 9): economic hardship

to people call me fat bitch, Fat Albert's wife, big-ass bitch, Heavy D, overweight lover. (At least Heavy D made money off the catchy tune of this same name!)

11   The medical community is currently involved in a "great weight debate," struggling to define obesity. Scientific surveys certainly don't tell the whole story; they usually deal in averages and don't reflect individual factors that influence a person's weight status.

12   Three years ago, the federal government took a stab at developing a more meaningful way to assess weight. *Dietary Guidelines for Americans* was produced jointly by the U.S. Department of Health and Human Services and the U.S. Department of Agriculture. The guidelines offer three criteria for determining the appropriateness of a person's weight: disease risk factors, weight tables (which group men and women together), and body-fat distribution. Of the three criteria, the government's weight tables have attracted the most attention by far, much to the frustration of C. Wayne Callaway, M.D., an associate clinical professor of medicine at George Washington University in Washington, DC, who was on the advisory committee that developed the criteria.

13   "The weight tables are only one factor in assessing a person's weight-related health risks," Callaway states firmly. "The most important factor is whether the person has a medical condition that would improve with weight loss, such as high blood pressure or borderline high blood sugar, an early sign of diabetes." Obviously someone with conditions like these who is on the middle to high end of the acceptable range of the weight tables should try to lose weight.

The Weight Scale: God or Guide?

14   It's sad but true that most of us determine our ideal size by the "a-woman-can-never-be-too-thin" mantra that has seized our society. And if we are the dreaded category—a large woman—we are constantly on a diet or, at the very least, profoundly ashamed of our size. I have never failed to notice that when a few women get together, sooner or later the conversation turns to pound-pondering, and inevitably even the thinnest in the group thinks she could stand to "lose a few pounds."

15   For too many women, the almighty scale rules our self-esteem. I used to weigh myself every morning—and I do mean before I drank any liquids, or even put on my perfume. In the final analysis, I found that I would be depressed no matter what the numbers were. Frustrated, I finally threw my scale out the window into the alley and heard it land with a resounding thud.

16   What is the root of society's obsession with women's body weight? In the PBS documentary *The Famine Within*, psychologist Catherine Steiner-Adair makes this astute observation: "I don't think it's a total coincidence that at exactly the same time women are being told they have equal rights and equal access to all professions and careers, there is a hidden clause that says, 'You can have

NOTES

criteria (par. 12): standards
mantra (par. 14): ritually recited phrase
profoundly (par. 14): deeply
psychologist (par. 16): an individual whose work focuses on human behavior and mental disorders
astute (par. 16): shrewd, insightful

equal opportunity as long as you have a body size that very few women can maintain.'"

17   You may be thinking, Oh, come on, we're much more accepting of large women in the Black community than Whites are. "Black women are just as concerned about weight as White women," explains Shiriki Kumanyika, Ph.D., a professor of epidemiology at Pennsylvania State University College of Medicine in Hershey. "The more we try to emulate the mainstream image, the more the desire to be thin is mimicked and the higher the risk of eating disorders in our community."

Whose Fault Is Fatness?

18   One of the most cherished assumptions that many people have is that body size and shape are under the complete control of the individual—and anyone who is heavy, plump, overweight, or fat is greasin' around the clock. "This is a complete misconception," explains Sally E. Smith, executive director of the National Association to Advance Fat Acceptance in Sacramento, California. "A person's weight is determined by a number of factors, including genetics, metabolism and dieting history." Our denial of these factors is what fuels the $33 billion dieting industry that urges us to believe only willpower stands between us and the body of a runway diva! On many occasions I've been out with friends (or even people I don't know) and my menu choices have been scrutinized: "Maybe you should get a salad." "You know fish is less fattening than chicken." "How much do you eat?" I've grown very careful about what I order in public and often feel self-conscious about eating, period.

19   The truth is, it has been a long time since I've overeaten compulsively. Due to a long history of dieting, I can no longer afford that luxury because I am one of the many victims of the pitfalls of dieting. "You can actually diet your way up to fatness," says Smith.

NOTES

epidemiology (par. 17): the branch of science that studies the cause, control, distribution, and prevention of disease

emulate (par. 17): imitate

mainstream (par. 17): majority

eating disorders (par. 17): A group of disorders involving rigid restriction or regulation of food intake. The most common of these disorders are anorexia nervosa and bulimia nervosa. Anorexia is characterized by an abnormal fear of being overweight, distorted self-image, extreme dieting, and severe weight loss. Essentially, anorexics will starve themselves to death. Bulimia is characterized by episodes of bingeing and purging: gross overeating followed by self-induced vomiting, laxative abuse, and/or extreme exercise. This behavior is often carried out in secret and causes a great deal of shame. A bulimic's body weight is often normal or near normal.

misconception (par. 18): misunderstanding

genetics (par. 18): heredity

metabolism (par. 18): the chemical processes that occur within cells to sustain life and provide energy

runway diva (par. 18): A model. A *runway* is a narrow platform that extends from a stage into an auditorium; a *diva* is a female star or lead performer.

scrutinized (par. 18): examined

compulsively (par. 19): excessively

pitfalls (par. 19): dangers

20   I know firsthand. When I originally reached my first high weight (which was 190 pounds), I went on a low-calorie diet and lost forty-five pounds in four months. After a few months at my lower weight, I went back to eating normally and not only gained the weight back but also reached a new high weight of 235 pounds. "With each period of low-calorie dieting, 95 to 98 percent of dieters can expect to gain back the weight and an additional 20 percent above that," claims Smith.

21   The question still remains: Why exactly are 48 percent of African-American women overweight? Part of it is genetics. "Black women have always been endowed with large hips, buttocks, legs, and breasts," explains Monica Dixon, a dietitian and image consultant in San Francisco. "This tendency dates back hundreds of years and is probably an adaptation to famine control. Historically, those who were able to maintain their adipose tissue were the ones who survived the periods of famine in African countries." Therefore, the genetic body type of women that prevailed in Africa became those with bigger hips and larger buttocks. "As a matter of fact, in some parts of Africa, women who are well endowed are considered of price," explains Mavis Thompson, M.D., a holistic practitioner in Brooklyn and author of *The Black Health Library Guide to Obesity* (Owl Books).

22   Another crucial factor: Black women may use food and body size to fight personal trauma. "When it comes to body weight, discrimination based on race, class, poverty, and sexual orientation affects African-American women tremendously," says Thompson. While men may act out their rage through violence, sex, alcohol, or drug addiction, women tend to eat as a way of coping— or to obliterate pain.

Used to Abuse

23   Some experts believe that discrimination against overweight individuals is so profound that Congress should consider extending legal protection to ensure their civil rights. "Discrimination against fat women seems to be the last fashionable form of overt prejudice people can safely indulge in without remorse," says Albert J. Stunkard, Ph.D., a professor of psychiatry at the University of Pennsylvania.

24   Last winter, in what could be a major legal precedent, an overweight Rhode Island State mental-institution attendant, Bonnie Cook, won back her

NOTES

endowed (par. 21): gifted

adipose tissue (par. 21): a layer of fat beneath the skin and around some internal organs

of price (par. 21): valuable

holistic practitioner (par. 21): a health-care provider who treats the whole person (mind, body, spirit, and emotions)

trauma (par. 22): suffering

to obliterate (par. 22): to get rid of

overt (par. 23): open

indulge (par. 23): participate

remorse (par. 23): regret, guilt

legal precedent (par. 24): a legal decision that serves as an example in future similar cases

position and $100,000 in damages when she was turned down for the job because of her weight.

25   There isn't a day that goes by that I don't have to endure comments about my weight from coworkers, people in elevators, and even my tax accountant ("Have you been to Weight Watchers yet?" he queried on my last visit). Brothers leer at me on the street and describe my proportions in exact detail. And well-meaning professional colleagues constantly make remarks about my appearance.

26   Fat-women jokes have also become the stock and trade of every stand-up comic's repertoire. On his album *Talkin' Shit,* comedian Martin Lawrence makes the timely observation that "women are always worrying about their weight!" But then the risqué Martin goes on to poke fun at us: "People make excuses for their weight. Ain't no excuses. 'It's my metabolism.' No, it's not. It's them Twizzlers in your goddamn back pocket! Let the Reese's cups go. Get out of the Haagen-Dazs line! If you are weighing over 250, stay the f—out of spandex!"

27   Why is it still okay to abuse large women? Explains Julia Boyd, a psychotherapist in Seattle and author of the book *In the Company of My Sisters: Black Women and Self-Esteem,* "We are very threatened by large-size women because they represent our worst fears—our own hidden fears of being overweight and rejected. They also disturb the status quo of the acceptable image that society has diligently enforced on women."

Living Large and Healthy

28   The real issue for large women is being healthy. Each of us must find our own body weight based on our genetics and height-body-mass index (small, medium, or large frame). We should feel fit and flexible and be able to run for buses and bound up flights of stairs. We must make the commitment (and stick to it!) to take care of ourselves by exercising and eating properly. If weight is really causing a health problem, we must address that. I exercise three to four times a week, am in excellent health (I visit my physician twice a year and have complete blood workups once a year), and adhere to a fairly healthy diet.

29   Basically, I feel great. What causes me a great deal of emotional anxiety is the glaring fact that society doesn't embrace women like me as readily as it

NOTES

queried (par. 25): asked

leer (par. 25): look lustfully and unpleasantly

repertoire (par. 26): collection of performance material

risqué (par. 26): somewhat vulgar

spandex (par. 26): elastic clothing

psychotherapist (par. 27): psychiatrist or psychologist

status quo (par. 27): usual state of affairs

height-body-mass index (par. 28): The body-mass index (BMI) uses the ratio of height to weight to determine the percentage of body fat: BMI = [(wt. in lbs) $\times$ 705)]/(height in inches)^2. For example, the BMI of a person who weighs 160 pounds and is 5′6″ (or 66″) tall would be calculated as follows: $(160 \times 705)/(66)^2$ = 112,800/4356 = 25.89. A BMI of less than 20 indicates a person may be underweight; of 20–25, healthy weight; 25–30, overweight; over 30, obese. The BMI is only a guideline. It does not take into account age, gender, frame, or physical fitness (athletics builds muscles, and muscles weigh more than fat).

adhere (par. 28): stick

does my thinner counterparts. All around me I see large women who are beautiful, stylish, glowing, healthy, and fit. But I also see too many who reject themselves, make themselves sick by dieting dangerously, and desperately try to live up to an impossible beauty ideal. Perhaps, most important, large women need to reject body size as the chief determinant of competence. We must spend time taking care of ourselves and developing professional and social skills that will offer true fulfillment. The bottom line: Any woman who relies solely on her looks for self-esteem will always be at someone else's mercy!

NOTE

competence (par. 29): ability

When Is It Rape?

Nancy Gibbs

1   A young man meets a young woman at a bar, invites her home late at night and apparently has sex with her on the lawn. Found shaking and curled up in the fetal position by a police investigator, she says it was rape. He says no—and his friends and family attest to his gentle nature and moral fiber. That tale of Good Friday in Palm Beach, Florida, landed in the news because it involved a Kennedy. But regardless of the judicial outcome, the case has shoved a much larger debate over rape into the minds of average American men and women. Plant the topic in a conversation, and chances are it will ripen into a bitter argument or a jittery sequence of pale jokes. Was it "really rape"? Was it "date rape"? Is there a difference?

2   What people think of as "real rape"—an assault by a monstrous stranger lurking in the shadows—accounts for only one out of five reported sexual attacks in the United States, so the phrase "acquaintance rape" was coined to describe the rest, all the cases of forced sex between people who already knew each other, however casually. But that was too clinical for headline writers, and so the popular term is the narrower "date rape," which suggests an ugly ending to a raucous night on the town.

3   These are not idle distinctions. Behind the research for labels is the central mythology about rape: that rapists are always strangers, and victims are women who ask for it. The mythology is hard to dispel because the crime is so rarely exposed. The experts guess—that is all they can do under the circumstances—that while one in four American women will be raped in her lifetime, less than 10 percent will report the assault, and less than 5 percent of the rapists will go to jail.

NOTES

in the fetal position (par. 1): with head, arms, and legs drawn in toward the chest
pale (par. 1): ineffective
raucous (par. 2): wild
idle (par. 3): useless
mythology (par. 3): untrue but widespread belief
dispel (par. 3): eliminate

4   Women charge that date rape is the hidden crime in the United States; men complain it is hard to prevent a crime they can't define. Women say it isn't taken seriously; men say it is a concept invented by women who like to tease but not take the consequences. Women say the date-rape debate is the first time the nation has talked frankly about sex; men say it is women's unconscious reaction to the excesses of the sexual revolution. Meanwhile, men and women argue among themselves about the "gray area" that surrounds the whole murky arena of sexual relations, and there is no consensus in sight.

5   In court, on campus, in conversation, the issue turns on the elasticity of the word rape, one of the few words in the language with the power to summon an image of a horrible crime.

6   At one extreme are those who argue that for the word to retain its impact, it must be strictly defined as forced sexual intercourse: a gang of thugs jumping a jogger, a psychopath preying on old women in a housing complex, a man with an ice pick on a side street. To stretch the definition of the word risks stripping away its power. In this view, if it happened on a date, it wasn't rape. A romantic encounter is a context in which sex could occur, and so what omniscient judge will decide whether there was genuine mutual consent?

7   Others are willing to concede that date rape sometimes occurs, that sometimes a man goes too far on a date without a woman's consent. But this infraction, they say, is not so ghastly a crime as street rape, and it should not be taken as seriously. This attitude sparks rage among women who carry scars received at the hands of men they knew. It makes no difference if the victim shared a drink or a moonlit walk or even a passionate kiss, they protest, if the encounter ended with her being thrown to the ground and forcibly violated. Date rape is not about a misunderstanding, they say. It is not a communications problem. It is not about a woman having regrets in the morning for a decision she made the night before. It is not about a "decision" at all. Rape is rape, and any form of forced sex—even between neighbors, coworkers, classmates, and casual friends—is a crime.

8   A more extreme form of that view comes from activists who see rape as a metaphor, its definition spreading to cover any kind of oppression of women. Rape, seen in this light, can occur not only on a date but also in a marriage, not only by violent assault but also by psychological pressure. A Swarthmore College pamphlet once explained that acquaintance rape "spans a spectrum of incidents and behaviors, ranging from crimes legally defined as rape to verbal

NOTES

"gray area" (par. 4): uncertainty

consensus (par. 4): agreement

elasticity (par. 5): adaptability

psychopath (par. 6): madman

omniscient (par. 6): all-knowing

concede (par. 7): admit

infraction (par. 7): offense

ghastly (par. 7): horrible

oppression (par. 8): unjust treatment

spectrum (par. 8): range

innuendo (par. 8): indirect suggestion

harassment and inappropriate innuendo." No wonder, then, that the battles become so heated. When innuendo qualifies as rape, the definitions have become so slippery that the entire subject sinks into a political swamp. The only way to capture the hard reality is to tell the story.

9   A thirty-two-year-old woman was on business in Tampa last year for the Florida supreme court. Stranded at the courthouse, she accepted a lift from a lawyer involved in her project. As they chatted on the ride home, she recalls, "he was saying all the right things, so I started to trust him." She agreed to have dinner, and afterward, at her hotel door, he persuaded her to let him come in to talk. "I went through the whole thing about being old-fashioned," she says. "I was a virgin until I was twenty-one. So I told him talk was all we were going to do."

10   But as they sat on the couch, she found herself asleep. "By now, I'm comfortable with him, and I put my head on his shoulder. He's not tried anything all evening, after all." Which is when the rape came. "I woke up to find him on top of me, forcing himself on me. I didn't scream or run. All I could think about was my business contacts and what if they saw me run out of my room screaming rape.

11   "I thought it was my fault. I felt so filthy, I washed myself over and over in hot water. 'Did he rape me?' I kept asking myself. I didn't consent. But who's gonna believe me? I had a man in my hotel room after midnight." More than a year later, she still can't tell the story without a visible struggle to maintain her composure. Although her attacker has admitted that he heard her say no, maintains the woman, "he says he didn't know that I meant no. He didn't feel he'd raped me, and he even wanted to see me again."

12   Her story is typical in many ways. The victim herself may not be sure right away that she had been raped, that she had said no and been physically forced into having sex. And the rapist commonly hears but does not heed the protest. "A date rapist will follow through no matter what the woman wants, because his agenda is to get laid," says Claire Walsh, a Florida-based consultant on sexual assaults. "First comes the dinner, then a dance, then a drink, then the coercion begins." Gentle persuasion gives way to physical intimidation, with alcohol as the ubiquitous lubricant. "When that fails, force is used," she says. "Real men don't take no for an answer."

13   Legally, it may be easier to prove a rape case now in the United States, but not by much. Survivors of rapes can expect to go on trial along with their attacker, if not in a courtroom then in the court of public opinion. *The New York Times* caused an uproar on its own staff not only for publishing the Palm Beach victim's name but also for laying out in detail her background, her high school grades and her driving record, along with an unattributed quote from a school official about her "little wild streak." A freshman at Carleton College

NOTES

her composure (par. 11): control of her emotions

agenda (par. 12): plan

coercion (par. 12): pressure, force

ubiquitous (par. 12): constantly encountered

an unattributed quote from a school official (par. 13): a quote from an unnamed school official

acquitted (par. 13): found not guilty and cleared

in Minnesota, who says she was repeatedly raped for four hours by a fellow student, claims that she was asked at an administrative hearing if she performed oral sex on dates. In 1989, a man charged with raping at knife point a woman he knew was acquitted in Florida because his victim had been wearing lace shorts and no underwear.

14   Susan Estrich, author of *Real Rape,* considers herself a lucky victim. This is not just because she survived an attack seventeen years ago by a stranger with an ice pick, one day before her graduation from Wellesley College. It's because police, and her friends, believed her. "The first thing the Boston police asked was whether it was a black guy," recalls Estrich, now a University of Southern California law professor. When she said yes and gave the details of the attack, their reaction was, "So, you were really raped." It was an instructive lesson, she says, in understanding how racism and sexism are factored into perceptions of the crime.

15   A new twist in society's sensibility came in 1975, when Susan Brownmiller published her book *Against Our Will: Men, Women and Rape.* In it she attacked the concept that rape was a sex crime, arguing instead that it was a crime of violence and power over women. Throughout history, she wrote, rape has played a critical function. "It is nothing more or less than a conscious process of intimidation, by which all men keep all women in a state of fear."

16   Out of this contention was born a set of arguments that have become politically correct wisdom on campus and in academic circles. This view holds that rape is a symbol of women's vulnerability to male institutions and attitudes. This line of reasoning has led some women, especially radicalized victims, to justify flinging around the term rape as a political weapon, referring to everything from violent sexual assaults to inappropriate innuendoes. Catherine Comins, assistant dean of student life at Vassar College, sees some value in this loose use of "rape": "To use the word carefully would be to be careful for the sake of the violator, and the survivors don't care a hoot about him." Comins argues that men who are unjustly accused can sometimes gain from the experience. "They have a lot of pain, but it is not a pain that I would necessarily have spared them. I think it ideally initiates a process of self-exploration. 'How do I see women?' 'If I didn't violate her, could I have?' 'Do I have the potential to do to her what they say I did?' Those are good questions."

17   Taken to extremes, there is an ugly element of vengeance at work here. Rape is an abuse of power. But so are false accusations of rape, and to suggest that men whose reputations are destroyed might benefit because it will make them more sensitive is an attitude that is sure to backfire on women who are seeking justice for all victims. On campuses where the issue is most inflamed, male students are outraged that their names can be scrawled on a bathroom-wall list of rapists and they have no chance to tell their side of the story.

NOTES

are factored into (par. 14): influence
radicalized victims (par. 16): victims whose trauma has caused them to take extreme positions
initiates (par. 16): begins
vengeance (par. 17): revenge

18   One male freshman at a liberal-arts college learned that he had been branded a rapist after a one-night stand with a friend. "I'm fighting against my hormonal instincts, and my moral instincts are saying, 'This is my friend and if I were sober, I wouldn't be doing this.'" But he went ahead anyway. "When you're drunk, and there are all sorts of ambiguity, and the woman says 'Please, please' and then she says no sometime later, even in the middle of the act, there still may very well be some kind of violation, but it's not the same thing. It's not rape." The morning after the encounter, he recalls, he and the woman woke up hung over and eager to put the memory behind them. Only months later did he learn that she had told a friend that he had torn her clothing and raped her. "I felt violated," he says. "I felt like she was taking advantage of me when she was very drunk. I never heard her say 'No!,' 'Stop!,' anything." He is angry and hurt at the charges, worried that they will get around, shatter his reputation and force him to leave the small campus.

19   So here, of course, is the heart of the debate. If rape is sex without consent, how exactly should consent be defined and communicated, when and by whom? Those who view rape through a political lens tend to place all responsibility on men to make sure that their partners are consenting at every point of a sexual encounter. At the extreme, sexual relations come to resemble major surgery, requiring a signed consent form. Historically, of course, this has never been the case, and there are some who argue that it shouldn't be—that women too must take responsibility for their behavior, and that the whole realm of intimate encounters defies regulation from on high.

20   What is lost in the ideological debate over date rape is the fact that men and women, especially when they are young, and drunk, and aroused, are not very good at communicating. "In many cases," says Estrich, "the man thought it was sex, and the woman thought it was rape, and they are both telling the truth." By the time they reach college, men and women are loaded with cultural baggage, drawn from movies, television, music videos, and "bodice ripper" romance novels. The messages come early and often, and nothing in the feminist revolution has been able to counter them. A recent survey of sixth- to ninth-graders in Rhode Island found that a fourth of the boys and a sixth of the girls said it was acceptable for a man to force a woman to kiss him or have sex if he has spent money on her. A third of the children said it would not be wrong for a man to rape a woman who had had previous sexual experiences.

NOTES

branded (par. 18): labeled
ambiguity (par. 18): unclearness
realm (par. 19): area
defies regulation (par. 19): is impossible to regulate
"bodice ripper" romance novels (par. 20): A bodice is the part of a woman's dress that extends from the waist to the neck, excluding the sleeves. A "bodice ripper" novel contains episodes in which the heroine is unable to resist the overpowering sexual advances of a man. While these are supposed to be scenes of passionate love, they are actually scenes of sexual assault.

21   The use of new terms, like acquaintance rape and date rape, while controversial, has given men and women the vocabulary they need to express their experiences with both force and precision. This dialogue will be useful if it helps strip away some of the dogmas, old and new, surrounding the issue. Those who hope to raise society's sensitivity to the problem of date rape would do well to concede that it is not precisely the same sort of crime as street rape, that there may be very murky issues of intent and degree involved.

22   On the other hand, those who downplay the problem should come to realize that date rape is a crime of uniquely intimate cruelty. While the body is violated, the spirit is maimed. How long will it take, once the wounds have healed, before it is possible to share a walk on a beach, a drive home from work or an evening's conversation without always listening for a quiet alarm to start ringing deep in the memory of a terrible crime?

NOTES

dogmas (par. 21): beliefs
concede (par. 21): acknowledge
maimed (par. 22): permanently wounded

Time for a Change on Drugs: Americans Are Ahead of the Politicians on This One

Molly Ivins

1   Heads up, team: I think we're starting to see a major change in the old Zeitgeist on the issue of drugs. This is one of those seismic shifts when the unsayable suddenly becomes sayable, when we notice that the emperor is wearing no clothes. The main problem with the war on drugs—you've probably noticed—is that we're losing. We're also seeing the start of a consensus that it's time to try something else. One way you can tell when one of these major shifts is happening is when some of those speaking out are so respected and respectable that they give cover to others who are more conformist.

2   The Lindesmith Centre in New York has marshaled an impeccable set of world citizens behind the simple proposition that the global war on drugs is

NOTES

Zeitgeist (par. 1): spirit of the times
seismic (par. 1): earthshaking
consensus (par. 1): agreement
conformist (par. 1): obedient
Lindesmith Centre (par. 2): an institute that focuses on issues related to drug policy
marshaled (par. 2): rallied, gathered
impeccable (par. 2): flawless
Walter Cronkite (par. 2): highly respected American broadcast journalist (b. 1916)

now causing more harm than drug abuse itself. Among those who signed that declaration are Walter Cronkite, former U.N. Secretary-General Javier Perez deCuellar, former U.S. Secretary of State George Shultz, Nobelist Oscar Arias, and on and on and on.

3   There are also several indications that the people are well ahead of the politicians on this one. On Election Day, medical marijuana initiatives passed in Washington state, Alaska, Arizona (second time), Oregon, and Nevada—this despite drug czar Barry McCaffrey and the rest of the drug war establishment swearing that this was tantamount to legalizing heroin. The people are perfectly capable of deciding that relieving the suffering of the dying is not the same as supporting the Medellin cartel. Notice, too, that Jesse "the Governor" Ventura, the crackerjack populist surprise in Minnesota, was elected in large part by young people who like his libertarian straight talk on drugs.

4   Of course, our normal politicians are frozen on this issue. Liberals have been drug-baited for so long that they live in terror of the dread accusation "soft on drugs." And the law-'n'-order conservatives have been making hay at the polls with this cheap scare stuff for so long that they're hooked on it. Fortunately, the libertarian wing of the right has made uncommon sense on the issue all along, and even establishment conservatives like William F. Buckley are open to reasonable discussion. There's a real chance here for conservatives to seize an important issue and do major public service at the same time.

5   Just to give you an idea how petrified the libs are on this issue, note President Clinton's performance—he fired Surgeon General Joycelyn Elders not for advocating *legalization* of drugs but for suggesting that it should be studied! And he stopped Donna Shalala, Secretary of Health and Human Services, from implementing a clean-needle program—an obviously sensible public health measure.

6   The liveliest recent polemic on the subject is Mike Gray's book *Drug Crazy: How We Got into This Mess and How We Can Get Out of It*. Gray has

NOTES

initiatives (par. 3): proposed laws

drug czar (par. 3): an official appointed to oversee the U.S. drug policy

tantamount to (par. 3): virtually the same as

Medellin cartel (par. 3): In the 1980s, Medellin, a city in northwestern Colombia (a country in South America), became the center of operations for Colombia's most powerful drug cartel, known as the Medellin cartel. A cartel is formed when a number of businesses unite in order to control the manufacture, distribution, and pricing of their products.

populist (par. 3): one who represents the views of the common people and supports their rights

libertarian (par. 3): Libertarians believe that an individual's freedom should be virtually unregulated by the state.

drug-baited (par. 4): harassed about drugs

right (par. 4): Those on the right (*conservatives*, par. 4) tend to favor the preservation of existing social or political systems; those on the left (*liberals*, par. 4) tend to favor social or political reform.

petrified (par. 5): terrified

libs (par. 5): liberals

implementing (par. 5): starting

a clean-needle program (par. 5): a program designed to slow the spread of AIDS by distributing clean needles to addicts

polemic (par. 6): controversial argument

some horrifying reports on how deeply the drug war has corrupted law enforcement across the country. He also makes a strong case that the war on drugs is just as disastrous a failure as was Prohibition, with exactly the same consequences in the growth of enormous criminal empires.

7   However, it may be that debating legalization will simply turn out to be polarizing and futile while it takes the focus off the need to at least reform drug regulation. For starters, we could consider decriminalizing marijuana, rethinking the mandatory minimum sentences that put small-time users in prison for years while leaving major dealers untouched. Another idiotic injustice that needs to be addressed immediately is the disparity in sentencing between crack cocaine—mostly used by inner-city blacks because of its cheap street price—and the powder cocaine favored by wealthy whites. Same drug, gross inequity in sentencing.

8   In-prison drug treatment programs make far more sense than the usual litany of more money, more cops, more prisons, longer sentences, etc. Well short of legalization, any fool can see how we could spend anti-drug money more effectively and fairly. That's a mandatory minimum in itself.

9   Our poor frozen political establishment does in fact replicate Prohibition. President Herbert Hoover appointed a commission to study Prohibition back in 1929, and after nineteen months of labor, the commission reported that it was a disaster area—and recommended no changes. A columnist known as F. P. A. summarized the finding in doggerel:

> Prohibition is an awful flop.
> We like it.
> It can't stop what it's meant to stop.
> We like it.
> It's left a trail of graft and slime.
> It's filled our land with vice and crime.
> It don't prohibit worth a dime.
> Nevertheless, we're for it.

Time for new tactics and strategy, and anyone who says so is not soft on drugs but strong on common sense.

NOTES

Prohibition (par. 6): The period from 1920 to 1933 during which the "the manufacture, sale, or transportation of intoxicating liquors" was forbidden by the Eighteenth Amendment to the U.S. Constitution. In 1933, Congress approved the Twenty-First Amendment, repealing the Eighteenth Amendment and ending Prohibition.

be polarizing (par. 7): cause people to divide themselves into two opposing groups

[be] futile (par. 7): be useless

mandatory (par. 7): required

disparity (par. 7): dissimilarity

gross (par. 7): obvious, enormous

inequity (par. 7): unfairness

litany (par. 8): chant

replicate (par. 9): repeat

doggerel (par. 9): satirical, often awkward verse

graft (par. 9): bribes

vice (par. 9): sin

Legalization of Narcotics: Myths and Reality

Joseph A. Califano

1   When the high priests of America's political right and left as articulate as the *National Review*'s William F. Buckley and *The New York Times*' Anthony Lewis peddle the same drug legalization line, it is time to shout *caveat emptor*—buyer beware. The boomlet to legalize drugs like heroin, cocaine, and marijuana that they, and magazines like *New York,* are trying to propagate is founded in myths, not realities, and it is the nation's children who could suffer long-lasting, permanent damage.

2   **Myth:** There has been no progress in the war on drugs.

3   **Reality:** The U.S. Department of Health and Human Services' National Household Drug Survey, the nation's most extensive assessment of drug usage, reports that, from 1979 to 1994, marijuana users dropped from 23,000,000 to 10,000,000, while cocaine users fell from 4,400,000 to 1,400,000. The drug-using segment of the population also is aging. In 1979, 10 percent were over age thirty-four; today, almost 30 percent are. The number of hardcore addicts has held steady at around 6,000,000, a situation most experts attribute to unavailability of treatment and the large number of addicts in the pipeline.

4   **Myth:** Whether to use drugs and become hooked is an adult decision.

5   **Reality:** It is children who choose. Hardly anyone in America begins drug use after age twenty-one. Based on everything known, an individual who does not smoke, use drugs, or abuse alcohol by twenty-one is virtually certain never to do so. The nicotine pushers understand this, which is why they fight so strenuously to kill efforts to keep their stuff away from kids.

6   **Myth:** Legalized drugs would be only for adults and not available to children.

7   **Reality:** Nothing in the American experience gives any credence to the ability to keep legal drugs out of the hands of children. It is illegal for them to purchase cigarettes, beer, and liquor. Nevertheless, 3,000,000 adolescents smoke an average of half a pack a day, constituting a $1,000,000,000-a-year market; and 12,000,000 underage Americans drink, a $10,000,000,000-a-year market.

8   **Myth:** Legalization would reduce crime and social problems.

9   **Reality:** Any short-term reduction in arrests from repealing drug laws would evaporate quickly as use increased and the criminal conduct—assault, murder, rape, child molestation, vandalism, and other violence—that drugs

NOTES

political right and left (par. 1): Those on the right (*conservatives*) tend to favor the preservation of existing social or political systems; those on the left (*liberals*) tend to favor social or political reform.

articulate (par. 1): well-spoken

peddle (par. 1): sell

propagate (par. 1): cultivate, grow

attribute (par. 3): credit

in the pipeline (par. 3): awaiting assistance

strenuously (par. 5): forcefully

gives any credence (par. 7): testifies

spawn (par. 9): produce

like cocaine and methamphetamines spawn exploded. The U.S. Department of Justice reports that criminals commit six times as many homicides, four times as many assaults, and almost one and a half times as many robberies under the influence of drugs as they do in order to get money to buy drugs.

10   **Myth:** The American experience with prohibition of alcohol supports drug legalization.

11   **Reality:** This ignores two important distinctions: Possession of alcohol for personal consumption was not illegal, and alcohol, unlike drugs such as heroin and cocaine, has a long history of broad social acceptance dating back to the Old Testament and ancient Greece. Largely because of this, the public and political consensus favoring Prohibition was short-lived. By the early 1930s, most Americans no longer supported it. Today, though, the public overwhelmingly favors keeping illegal drugs illegal. Despite these differences, which made Prohibition more difficult to enforce than the current drug laws, alcohol consumption dropped from 1.96 gallons per person in 1919 to .97 gallons per person in 1934, the first full year after Prohibition ended. Death rates from cirrhosis among men came down from 29.5 per 100,000 in 1911 to 10.7 per 100,000 in 1929. During Prohibition, admission to mental health institutions for alcohol psychosis dropped 60 percent; arrests for drunk and disorderly conduct went down 50 percent; welfare agencies reported significant declines in cases due to alcohol-related family problems; and the death rate from impure alcohol did not rise.

12   Neither did Prohibition generate a crime wave. Homicide increased at a higher rate between 1900 and 1910 than during Prohibition, and organized crime was well-established in the cities before 1920.

13   I put these facts on the record not to support a return to Prohibition, something I strongly oppose, but to set the historical record straight and temper the revisionist view of legalizers who take their history from celluloid images of 1930s gangster movies.

14   **Myth:** Greater availability and legal acceptability of drugs would not increase use.

15   **Reality:** This defies not only experience, but human nature. In the 1970s, the U.S. *de facto* decriminalized marijuana. The Shafer Commission appointed by President Richard Nixon recommended decriminalization, as did President

NOTES

consensus (par. 11): agreement

Prohibition (par. 11): The period from 1920–1933 during which the "the manufacture, sale, or transportation of intoxicating liquors" was forbidden by the Eighteenth Amendment to the U.S. Constitution. In 1933, Congress approved the Twenty-First Amendment, repealing the Eighteenth Amendment and ending Prohibition.

cirrhosis (par. 11): liver disease often caused by alcohol abuse

alcohol psychosis (par. 11): severe brain damage that is caused by alcohol abuse and results in a loss of contact with reality

temper (par. 13): modify

the revisionist view (par. 13): the view of those who support the revision of generally accepted views of historical events

celluloid (par. 13): film

de facto (par. 15): in reality although not officially

Jimmy Carter. The result was a soaring increase in marijuana use, particularly among youngsters. Today, just 11 percent of Americans report seeing drugs available in the area where they live; after legalization, there could be a place to purchase drugs in every neighborhood.

16   Today, the U.S. has 50,000,000 nicotine addicts, 18,000,000 alcoholics and alcohol abusers, and 6,000,000 illegal drug addicts. It is logical to conclude that, if drugs are easier to obtain, less expensive, and socially acceptable, more individuals will use them. Experts such as Columbia University's Herbert Kleber believe that, with legalization, the number of cocaine addicts alone would jump beyond the number of alcoholics.

17   **Myth:** Legalization will save money by allowing the government to spend less on law enforcement and permit taxation of drug sales.

18   **Reality:** While legalization temporarily might take some of the burden off the criminal justice system, such a policy would impose heavy additional costs on the health care and social service systems, schools, and the workplace. Like advocates of legalization today, opponents of alcohol prohibition claimed that taxes on the legal sale of alcohol would increase revenues dramatically and help erase the deficit. The real world result has been quite different.

19   **Myth:** Drug use is an issue of civil liberties.

20   **Reality:** This is a convenient misreading of John Stuart Mill's *On Liberty*. Legalizers cite Mill to argue that the state has no right to interfere in the private life of a citizen who uses drugs; only when an action harms someone else may the state take steps to prevent it. They ignore the fact that Mill's conception of freedom does not extend to the right of individuals to enslave themselves or to decide that they will give up their liberty. Mill wrote with blunt clarity: "The principle of freedom cannot require that he should be free not to be free. It is not freedom to be allowed to alienate his freedom."

21   Drug addiction is a form of enslavement. It "alters pathologically the nature and character of abusers," says Phoenix House president Mitchell Rosenthal. Even Mill at his most expansive would admit that the state can take action not just to free addicts from chains of chemical dependency that take away the freedom to be all that God meant them to be, but to prevent those bonds from shackling them. A nation devoted to individual freedom has an obligation to nourish a society and legal structure that protect people from the slavery of drug addiction.

22   Even Mill's most libertarian contention—that the state can regulate only those actions which directly affect others—does not support individual drug abuse and addiction. Such conduct does affect others directly, from the abused

NOTES

advocates (par. 18): supporters

civil liberties (par. 19): a citizen's fundamental freedoms

alienate (par. 20): give up

It "alters pathologically the nature and character of abusers" (par. 21): Drug addiction changes the structure and function of an abuser's tissues and organs; this change results in an alteration of the nature and character of abusers.

libertarian (par. 22): Libertarians believe that an individual's freedom should be virtually unregulated by the state.

contention (par. 22): argument

spouse and baby involuntarily addicted through the mother's umbilical cord to innocent bystanders injured or killed by adolescents high on crack cocaine. The drug abuser's conduct has a direct and substantial impact on every taxpayer who foots the bill for the criminal and health cost consequences of such actions.

23   Certainly a society that recognizes the state's compelling interest in banning (and stopping individuals from using) lead paint, asbestos insulation, unsafe toys, and flammable fabrics hardly can ignore its interest in banning cocaine, heroin, marijuana, methamphetamines, and hallucinogens. Indeed, refusing to include drug use in the right of privacy, the Supreme Court has approved state laws that prohibit even the sacramental use of peyote. With the exception of Alaska, state courts have held that possession of marijuana in the home is not protected by the right of privacy.

24   **Myth:** Legalization works well in European countries.

25   **Reality:** The ventures of Switzerland, England, the Netherlands, and Italy into drug legalization have had disastrous consequences. Switzerland's "Needle Park," touted as a way to restrict a few hundred heroin addicts to a small area, turned into a grotesque tourist attraction of 20,000 heroin addicts and junkies that had to be closed down before it infected the city of Zurich. England's foray into allowing any doctor to prescribe heroin quickly was curbed as heroin use increased.

26   In the Netherlands, anyone over age seventeen can drop into a marijuana "coffee shop" and pick types of marijuana like one might choose flavors of ice cream. Adolescent pot use there jumped nearly 200 percent while it was dropping by 66 percent in the United States. As crime and availability of drugs rose and complaints from city residents about the decline in their quality of life multiplied, the Dutch parliament moved to trim back the number of marijuana distribution shops in Amsterdam. Dutch persistence in selling pot has angered European neighbors because its wide-open attitude toward marijuana is believed to be spreading pot and other drugs beyond the Netherlands' borders.

27   Italy infrequently is mentioned by advocates of legalization, despite its lenient drug laws. Personal possession of small amounts of drugs has not been a crime in Italy since 1975, other than a brief period of recriminalization between 1990 and 1993. (Even then, Italy permitted an individual to possess one dose of a drug.) Under decriminalization, possession of two to three doses of drugs such as heroin generally was exempt from criminal sanction. Today, Italy has 300,000 addicts, the highest rate of heroin addiction in Europe. Seventy percent of all AIDS cases in Italy are attributable to drug use.

28   In contrast, Sweden offers an example of a successful restrictive drug policy. After a brief period of permitting doctors to give drugs to addicts, Sweden adopted the American policy of seeking a drug-free society in 1980. By 1988,

NOTES

compelling (par. 23): valid

sacramental use of peyote (par. 23): The top of the peyote cactus contains mescaline (a hallucinogenic drug) and is used by some Native Americans during religious rituals.

touted (par. 25): promoted

grotesque (par. 25): repulsive, bizarre

foray (par. 25): venture

sanction (par. 27): penalty

conscripts (par. 28): draftees

Sweden had seen drug use among young Army conscripts drop 75 percent and use by ninth-graders fall 66 percent.

29   What is most disturbing about the arguments for legalization is that they glide over the impact such a policy would have on American children. The United States assuredly is not the Garden of Eden of the Old Testament. Dealing with evil, including drugs, is part of the human experience. Nevertheless, there is a special obligation to protect youngsters from evil, and drugs are first and foremost an issue about children. It is adolescent experimentation that leads to abuse and addiction.

30   Today, most kids don't use illicit drugs, but all of them, particularly the poorest, are vulnerable to abuse and addiction. Russian roulette is not a game anyone should play. Legalizing drugs not only is playing Russian roulette with children, it is slipping a couple of extra bullets into the chamber.

NOTE

Russian roulette (par. 30): an often deadly game in which one chamber of a revolver's cylinder is loaded with a bullet, the cylinder is spun, the muzzle is pointed at one's own head, and the trigger is pulled

The Prisoner's Dilemma

Stephen Chapman

1   If the punitive laws of Islam were applied for only one year, all the devastating injustices would be uprooted. Misdeeds must be punished by the law of retaliation: cut off the hands of the thief; kill the murderers; flog the adulterous woman or man. Your concerns, your "humanitarian" scruples are more childish than reasonable. Under the terms of Koranic law, any judge fulfilling the seven requirements (that he have reached puberty, be a believer, know the Koranic laws perfectly, be just, and not be affected by amnesia, or be a bastard, or be of the female sex) is qualified to be a judge in any type of case. He can thus judge and dispose of twenty trials in a single day, whereas the Occidental justice might take years to argue them out.

–from *Sayings of the Ayatollah Khomeini*
(Bantam Books)

2   One of the amusements of life in the modern West is the opportunity to observe the barbaric rituals of countries that are attached to the customs of the dark ages. Take Pakistan, for example, our newest ally and client state in Asia. Last October President Zia, in harmony with the Islamic fervor that is

NOTES

punitive laws (par. 1): laws relating to punishment
Islam (par. 1): a religion founded by the prophet Mohammed (A.D. 570–632)
retaliation (par. 1): revenge
flog (par. 1): whip
Koranic (par. 1): pertaining to the Koran, the sacred book of Islam
Occidental (par. 1): Western
barbaric (par. 2): brutal, uncivilized
client state (par. 2): a country dependent on the economic support of another country

sweeping this part of the world, revived the traditional Moslem practice of flogging lawbreakers in public. In Pakistan, this qualified as mass entertainment, and no fewer than 10,000 law-abiding Pakistanis turned out to see justice done to twenty-six convicts. To Western sensibilities the spectacle seemed barbaric—both in the sense of cruel and in the sense of pre-civilized. In keeping with Islamic custom each of the unfortunates—who had been caught in prostitution raids the previous night and summarily convicted and sentenced—was stripped down to a pair of white shorts, which were painted with a red stripe across the buttocks (the target). Then he was shackled against an easel, with pads thoughtfully placed over the kidneys to prevent injury. The floggers were muscular, fierce-looking sorts—convicted murderers, as it happens—who paraded around the flogging platform in colorful loincloths. When the time for the ceremony began, one of the floggers took a running start and brought a five-foot stave down across the first victim's buttocks, eliciting screams from the convict and murmurs from the audience. Each of the twenty-six received from five to fifteen lashes. One had to be carried from the stage unconscious.

3   Flogging is one of the punishments stipulated by Koranic law, which has made it a popular penological device in several Moslem countries, including Pakistan, Saudi Arabia, and, most recently, the Ayatollah's Iran. Flogging, or *tázir,* is the general punishment prescribed for offenses that don't carry an explicit Koranic penalty. Some crimes carry automatic *hadd* punishments—stoning or scourging (a severe whipping) for illicit sex, scourging for drinking alcoholic beverages, amputation of the hands for theft. Other crimes—as varied as murder and abandoning Islam—carry the death penalty (usually carried out in public). Colorful practices like these have given the Islamic world an image in the West, as described by historian G. H. Jansen, "of blood dripping from the stumps of amputated hands and from the striped backs of malefactors, and piles of stones barely concealing the battered bodies of adulterous couples." Jansen, whose book *Militant Islam* is generally effusive in its praise of Islamic practices, grows squeamish when considering devices like flogging, amputation, and stoning. But they are given enthusiastic endorsement by the Koran itself.

4   Such traditions, we all must agree, are no sign of an advanced civilization. In the West, we have replaced these various punishments (including the death penalty in most cases) with a single device. Our custom is to confine criminals

NOTES

sensibilities (par. 2): emotions, reasoning
spectacle (par. 2): public display
summarily (par. 2): quickly and without formality
shackled (par. 2): chained
stave (par. 2): stick
eliciting (par. 2): causing
stipulated (par. 3): specified
penological (par. 3): relating to prisoners
malefactors (par. 3): lawbreakers
effusive (par. 3): excessive
endorsement (par. 3): approval
brazen (par. 4): excessively bold
genteel (par. 4): well bred

in prison for varying lengths of time. In Illinois, a reasonably typical state, grand theft carries a punishment of three to five years; armed robbery can get you from six to thirty. The lowest form of felony theft is punishable by one to three years in prison. Most states impose longer sentences on habitual offenders. In Kentucky, for example, habitual offenders can be sentenced to life in prison. Other states are less brazen, preferring the more genteel sounding "indeterminate sentence," which allows parole boards to keep inmates locked up for as long as life. It was under an indeterminate sentence of one to fourteen years that George Jackson served twelve years in California prisons for committing a $70 armed robbery. Under a Texas law imposing an automatic life sentence for a third felony conviction, a man was sent to jail for life last year because of three thefts adding up to less than $300 in property value. Texas also is famous for occasionally imposing extravagantly long sentences, often running into hundreds of thousands of years. This gives Texas a leg up on Maryland, which used to sentence some criminals to life plus a day—a distinctive if superfluous flourish.

5   The punishment *intended* by Western societies in sending their criminals to prison is the loss of freedom. But, as everyone knows, the actual punishment in most American prisons is of a wholly different order. The February 2 [1980] riot at New Mexico's state prison in Santa Fe, one of several bloody prison riots in the nine years since the Attica blood bath, once again dramatized the conditions of life in an American prison. Four hundred prisoners seized control of the prison before dawn. By sunset the next day thirty-three inmates had died at the hands of other convicts and another forty people (including five guards) had been seriously hurt. Macabre stories came out [about] prisoners being hanged, murdered with blowtorches, decapitated, tortured, and mutilated in a variety of gruesome ways by drug-crazed rioters.

6   The Santa Fe penitentiary was typical of most maximum-security facilities, with prisoners subject to overcrowding, filthy conditions, and routine violence. It also housed first-time, non-violent offenders, like check forgers and drug dealers, with murderers serving life sentences. In a recent lawsuit, the American Civil Liberties Union called the prison "totally unfit for human habitation." But the ACLU says New Mexico's penitentiary is far from the nation's worst.

7   That American prisons are a disgrace is taken for granted by experts of every ideological stripe. Conservative James Q. Wilson has criticized our "[c]rowded, antiquated prisons that require men and women to live in fear of

NOTES

indeterminate (par. 4): indefinite
superfluous flourish (par. 4): unnecessary addition
Attica (par. 5): prison in New York
macabre (par. 5): horror
decapitated (par. 5): beheaded
gruesome (par. 5): horrible, brutal
American Civil Liberties Union (par. 6): an organization that seeks to protect the civil rights of all Americans
habitation (par. 6): occupancy
ideological stripe (par. 7): political or philosophical position
Conservative (par. 7): one who tends to favor the preservation of existing social or political systems; considered a member of "the Right" (see "Leftist," below)

one another and to suffer not only deprivation of liberty but a brutalizing regimen." Leftist Jessica Mitford has called our prisons "the ultimate expression of injustice and inhumanity." In 1973 a national commission concluded that "the American correctional system today appears to offer minimum protection to the public and maximum harm to the offender." Federal courts have ruled that confinement in prisons in sixteen different states violates the constitutional ban on "cruel and unusual punishment."

8   What are the advantages of being a convicted criminal in an advanced culture? First there is the overcrowding in prisons. One Tennessee prison, for example, has a capacity of 806, according to accepted space standards, but it houses 2300 inmates. One Louisiana facility has confined four and five prisoners in a single six-foot-by-six-foot cell. Then there is the disease caused by overcrowding, unsanitary conditions, and poor or inadequate medical care. A federal appeals court noted that the Tennessee prison had suffered frequent outbreaks of infectious diseases like hepatitis and tuberculosis. But the most distinctive element of American prison life is its constant violence. In his book *Criminal Violence, Criminal Justice*, Charles Silberman noted that in one Louisiana prison, there were 211 stabbings in only three years, eleven of them fatal. There were fifteen slayings in a prison in Massachusetts between 1972 and 1975. According to a federal court, in Alabama's penitentiaries (as in many others), "robbery, rape, extortion, theft, and assault are everyday occurrences."

9   At least in regard to cruelty, it's not at all clear that the system of punishment that has evolved in the West is less barbaric than the grotesque practices of Islam. Skeptical? Ask yourself: would you rather be subjected to a few minutes of intense pain and considerable public humiliation, or be locked away for two or three years in a prison cell crowded with ill-tempered sociopaths? Would you rather lose a hand or spend ten years or more in a typical state prison? I have taken my own survey on this matter. I have found no one who does not find the Islamic system hideous. And I have found no one who, given the choices mentioned above, would not prefer its penalties to our own.

10   The great divergence between Western and Islamic fashions in punishment is relatively recent. Until roughly the end of the eighteenth century, criminals in Western countries rarely were sent to prison. Instead they were subject to an ingenious assortment of penalties. Many perpetrators of a variety of crimes simply were executed, usually by some imaginative and extremely unpleasant

NOTES

antiquated (par. 7): outdated

deprivation (par. 7): loss

regimen (par. 7): system

Leftist (par. 7): a liberal, or one who tends to favor social or political reform

grotesque (par. 9): hideous, horrible

skeptical (par. 9): doubting

sociopaths (par. 9): people whose behavior is antisocial

divergence (par. 10): difference

ingenious (par. 10): creative, clever

perpetrators (par. 10): those who are guilty

drawing and quartering (par. 10): the practice of tying each of a person's limbs to a different horse and having the four horses run in different directions so that the person was pulled into four pieces, or quartered

method involving prolonged torture, such as breaking on the wheel, burning at the stake, or drawing and quartering. Michael Foucault's book *Discipline and Punish: The Birth of the Prison* notes one form of capital punishment in which the condemned man's "belly was opened up, his entrails quickly ripped out, so that he had time to see them, with his own eyes, being thrown on the fire; in which he was finally decapitated and his body quartered." Some criminals were forced to serve on slave galleys. But in most cases various corporal measures such as pillorying, flogging, and branding sufficed.

11   In time, however, public sentiment recoiled against these measures. They were replaced by imprisonment, which was thought to have two advantages. First, it was considered to be more humane. Second, and more important, prison was supposed to hold out the possibility of rehabilitation—purging the criminal of his criminality—something that less civilized punishments did not even aspire to. An 1854 report by inspectors of the Pennsylvania prison system illustrates the hopes nurtured by humanitarian reformers:

> Depraved tendencies, characteristic of the convict, have been restrained by the absence of vicious association, and in the mild teaching of Christianity, the unhappy criminal finds a solace for an involuntary exile from the comforts of social life. If hungry, he is fed; if naked, he is clothed; if destitute of the first rudiments of education, he is taught to read and write; and if he has never been blessed with a means of livelihood, he is schooled in a mechanical art, which in after life may be to him the source of profit and respectability. Employment is not his toil nor labor, weariness. He embraces them with alacrity, as contributing to his moral and mental elevation.

12   Imprisonment is now the universal method of punishing criminals in the United States. It is thought to perform five functions, each of which has been given a label by criminologists. First, there is simple *retribution:* punishing the lawbreaker to serve society's sense of justice and to satisfy the victims' desire for revenge. Second, there is *specific deterrence:* discouraging the offender from misbehaving in the future. Third, *general deterrence:* using the offender as an example to discourage others from turning to crime. Fourth, *prevention:* at least during the time he is kept off the streets, the criminal cannot victimize other members of society. Finally, and most important, there is *rehabilitation:* reforming the criminal so that when he returns to society he will be inclined to obey the laws and able to make an honest living.

NOTES

entrails (par. 10): intestines
galleys (par. 10): ships
pillorying (par. 10): a type of punishment in which one's hands and head are placed within the holes of a stock or wooden frame
recoiled (par. 11): turned
purging (par. 11): ridding
aspire to (par. 11): attempt
depraved (par. 11): morally corrupt
solace (par. 11): comfort
destitute (par. 11): lacking
rudiments (par. 11): basics
alacrity (par. 11): eagerness
elevation (par. 11): improvement

13   How satisfactorily do American prisons perform by these criteria? Well, of course, they do punish. But on the other scores they don't do so well. Their effect in discouraging future criminality by the prisoner or others is the subject of much debate, but the soaring rates of the last twenty years suggest that prisons are not a dramatically effective deterrent to criminal behavior. Prisons do isolate convicted criminals, but only to divert crime from ordinary citizens to prison guards and fellow inmates. Almost no one contends any more that prisons rehabilitate their inmates. If anything, they probably impede rehabilitation by forcing inmates into prolonged and almost exclusive association with other criminals. And prisons cost a lot of money. Housing a typical prisoner in a typical prison costs far more than a stint at a top university. This cost would be justified if prisons did the job they were intended for. But it is clear to all that prisons fail on the very grounds—humanity and hope of rehabilitation—that caused them to replace earlier, cheaper forms of punishment.

14   The universal acknowledgment that prisons do not rehabilitate criminals has produced two responses. The first is to retain the hope of rehabilitation but do away with imprisonment as much as possible and replace it with various forms of "alternative treatment," such as psychotherapy, supervised probation, and vocational training. Psychiatrist Karl Menninger, one of the principal critics of American penology, has suggested even more unconventional approaches, such as "a new job opportunity or a vacation trip, a course of reducing exercises, a cosmetic surgical operation or a herniotomy, some night school courses, a wedding in the family (even one for the patient!), an inspiring sermon." The starry-eyed approach naturally has produced a backlash from critics on the right, who think that it's time to abandon the goal of rehabilitation. They argue that prisons perform an important service just by keeping criminals off the streets, and thus should be used with that purpose alone in mind.

15   So the debate continues to rage in all the same old ruts. No one, of course, would think of copying the medieval practices of Islamic nations and experimenting with punishments such as flogging and amputation. But let us consider them anyway. How do they compare with our American prison system in achieving the ostensible objectives of punishment? First, do they punish? Obviously they do, and in a uniquely painful and memorable way. Of course any sensible person, given the choice, would prefer suffering these punishments to years of incarceration in a typical American prison. But presumably no Western penologist would criticize Islamic punishments on the grounds that they are not barbaric enough. Do they deter crime? Yes, and probably more effectively than sending convicts off to prison. Now we read about a prison sentence in the newspaper, then think no more about the criminal's payment for his crimes until, perhaps, years later we read a small item reporting his release. By contrast,

NOTES

criteria (par. 13): a set of guidelines

contends (par. 13): argues

impede (par. 13): hinder

stint (par. 13): stay

herniotomy (par. 14): removal of a hernia

ostensible (par. 15): supposed

incarceration (par. 15): imprisonment

vivid (par. 15): sharp, lasting

one can easily imagine the vivid impression it would leave to be wandering through a local shopping center and to stumble onto the scene of some poor wretch being lustily flogged. And the occasional sight of an habitual offender walking around with a bloody stump at the end of his arm no doubt also would serve as a forceful reminder that crime does not pay.

16   Do flogging and amputation discourage recidivism? No one knows whether the scars on his back would dissuade a criminal from risking another crime, but it is hard to imagine that corporal measures could stimulate a higher rate of recidivism than already exists. Islamic forms of punishment do not serve the favorite new right goal of simply isolating criminals from the rest of society, but they may achieve the same purpose of making further crimes impossible. In the movie *Bonnie and Clyde,* Warren Beatty successfully robs a bank with his arm in a sling, but this must be dismissed as artistic license. It must be extraordinarily difficult, at the very least, to perform much violent crime with only one hand.

17   Do these medieval forms of punishment rehabilitate the criminal? Plainly not. But long prison terms do not rehabilitate either. And it is just as plain that typical Islamic punishments are no crueler to the convict than incarceration in the typical American state prison.

18   Of course there are other reasons besides its bizarre forms of punishment that the Islamic system of justice seems uncivilized to the Western mind. One is the absence of due process. Another is the long list of offenses—such as drinking, adultery, blasphemy, "profiteering," and so on—that can bring on conviction and punishment. A third is all the ritualistic mumbo-jumbo in pronouncements of Islamic law (like that talk about puberty and amnesia in the Ayatollah's quotation at the beginning of this article). Even in these matters, however, a little cultural modesty is called for. The vast majority of American criminals are convicted and sentenced as a result of plea bargaining, in which due process plays almost no role. It has been only half a century since a wave of religious fundamentalism stirred this country to outlaw the consumption of alcoholic beverages. Most states also still have laws imposing austere constraints on sexual conduct. Only two weeks ago the *Washington Post* reported that the FBI had spent two and a half years and untold amounts of money to break up a nationwide pornography ring. Flogging the clients of prostitutes, as the Pakistanis did, does seem silly. But only a few months ago Mayor Koch of New York was proposing that clients caught in his own city have their names broadcast by radio stations. We are not so far advanced on such matters as we often like to think. Finally, my lawyer friends assure me that the rules of jurisdiction for American courts contain plenty of

NOTES

recidivism (par. 16): return to criminal behavior

dissuade (par. 16): discourage

due process (par. 18): a set of procedures designed to protect the legal rights of citizens

blasphemy (par. 18): expressing lack of respect for God or anything considered sacred

profiteering (par. 18): making excessive profits

ritualistic (par. 18): ceremonial

pronouncements (par. 18): statements, declarations

plea bargaining (par. 18): a process in which a criminal agrees to plead guilty, thus avoiding a trial, in exchange for a reduced charge or sentence

austere (par. 18): severe

petty requirements and bizarre distinctions that would sound silly enough to foreign ears.

19 Perhaps it sounds barbaric to talk of flogging and amputation, and perhaps it is. But our system of punishment also is barbaric, and probably more so. Only cultural smugness about their system and willful ignorance about our own make it easy to regard the one as cruel and the other as civilized. We inflict our cruelties away from public view, while nations like Pakistan stage them in front of 10,000 onlookers. Their outrages are visible; ours are not. Most Americans can live their lives for years without having their peace of mind disturbed by the knowledge of what goes on in our prisons. To choose imprisonment over flogging and amputation is not to choose human kindness over cruelty, but merely to prefer that our cruelties be kept out of sight, and out of mind.

20 Public flogging and amputation may be more barbaric forms of punishment than imprisonment, even if they are not more cruel. Society may pay a higher price for them, even if the particular criminal does not. Revulsion against officially sanctioned violence and infliction of pain derives from something deeply ingrained in the Western conscience, and clearly it is something admirable. Grotesque displays of the sort that occur in Islamic countries probably breed a greater tolerance for physical cruelty, for example, which prisons do not do precisely because they conceal their cruelties. In fact it is our admirable intolerance for calculated violence that makes it necessary for us to conceal what we have not been able to do away with. In a way this is a good thing, since it holds out the hope that we may eventually find a way to do away with it. But in another way it is a bad thing, since it permits us to congratulate ourselves on our civilized humanitarianism while violating its norms in this one area of our national life.

NOTES

petty (par. 18): unimportant
smugness (par. 19): feeling of superiority
revulsion (par. 20): disgust
sanctioned (par. 20): approved
ingrained (par. 20): rooted
calculated (par. 20): planned, intended
humanitarianism (par. 20): respect for the rights and life of human beings
norms (par. 20): standards of behavior

Violent Crime:
Myths, Facts, and Solutions

The Conservative and Progressive Answers

D. Stanley Eitzen

Lecture delivered at the 1995 Symposium "The Shadow of Violence: Unconsidered Perspectives," Hastings College, Hastings, Nebraska, March 15, 1995

1   My remarks are limited to violent street crimes (assault, robbery, rape, and murder). We should not forget that there are other types of violent crimes that are just as violent and actually greater in magnitude than street crimes: corporate, political, organized, and white collar. But that is another subject for another time. Our attention this morning is on violent street crime, which has made our cities unsafe and our citizens extremely fearful. What are the facts about violent crime and violent criminals and what do we, as a society, do about them?

2   I am going to critique the prevailing thought about violent crime and its control because our perceptions about violent crime and much of what our government officials do about it is wrong. My discipline—sociology—knows a lot about crime but what we know does not seem to affect public perceptions and public policies. Not all of the answers, however, are always crystal clear. There are disagreements among reasonable and thoughtful people, coming from different theoretical and ideological perspectives. You may, difficult as it seems to me, actually disagree with my analysis. That's all right. The key is for us to address this serious problem, determine the facts, engage in dialogue, and then work toward logical and just solutions.

3   What do criminologists know about violent crime? Much of what we know is counterintuitive; it flies in the face of the public's understanding. So, let me begin with some demythologizing.

4   *Myth 1: As a Christian nation with high moral principles, we rank relatively low in the amount of violent crime.* Compared with the other industrialized nations of the world, we rank number one in belief in God, "the importance of God in our lives," and church attendance. We also rank first in murder rates, robbery rates, and rape rates. Take homicide, for example: the U.S. rate of ten per 100,000 is three times that of Finland, five times that of Canada, and nine times greater than found in Norway, the Netherlands, Germany, and Great Britain. In 1992, for example, Chicago, a city about one-fifth the population of the Netherlands had nine times more gun-related deaths than occurred in the Netherlands.

5   *Myth 2: We are in the midst of a crime wave.* When it comes to crime rates we are misled by our politicians, and the media. Government data indicate that between 1960 and 1970 crime rates doubled, then continued to climb through the 1970s. From 1970 to 1990 the rates remained about the same. The problem is with violent crime among youth, which has increased dramatically. Despite the rise in violent crime by youth, however, the *overall* violent crime rate actually has decreased in the 1990s.

6   Our perceptions are affected especially by the media. While crime rates have leveled and slightly declined during the 1990s, the media have given us a different picture. In 1993, for example, the three major networks doubled their crime stories and tripled their coverage of murders. This distortion of reality results, of course, in a general perception that we are in the midst of a crime wave.

NOTES

magnitude (par. 1): extent
critique (par. 2): review critically
perspectives (par. 2): mental outlooks
is counterintuitive (par. 3): contradicts instinct

7   *Myth 3: Serious violent crime is found throughout the age structure.* Crime is mainly a problem of male youths. Violent criminal behaviors peak at age seventeen and by age twenty-four it is one-half the rate. Young males have always posed a special crime problem. There are some differences now, however. Most significant, young males and the gangs to which they often belong now have much greater firepower. Alienated and angry youth once used clubs, knives, brass knuckles, and fists but now they use Uzis, AK47s, and "streetsweepers." The result is that since 1985, the murder rate for eighteen- to twenty-four-year-olds has risen 65 percent while the rate for fourteen to seventeen-year-olds has increased 165 percent.

8   The frightening demographic fact is that between now and the year 2005, the number of teenagers in the United States will grow by 23 percent. During the next ten years, black teenagers will increase by 28 percent and the Hispanic teenage population will grow by about 50 percent. The obvious prediction is that violent crime will increase dramatically over this period.

9   *Myth 4: The most dangerous place in America is in the streets where strangers threaten, hit, stab, or shoot each other.* The streets in our urban places are dangerous, as rival gangs fight, and drive-by shootings occur. But, statistically, the most dangerous place is in your own home, or when you are with a boyfriend or girlfriend, family member, or acquaintance.

10   *Myth 5: Violent criminals are born with certain predispositions toward violence.* Criminals are not born with a criminal gene. If crime were just a function of biology, then we would expect crime rates to be more or less the same for all social categories, times, and places. In fact, violent crime rates vary considerably by social class, race, unemployment, poverty, geographical place, and other social variables. Research on these variables is the special contribution of sociology to the understanding of criminal behavior.

11   Let's elaborate on these social variables because these have so much to do with solutions. Here is what we know about these social variables:

12   1. The more people in poverty, the higher the rate of street crime.

13   2. The higher the unemployment rate in an area, the higher the crime rate. Sociologist William J. Wilson says that black and white youths at age eleven are equally likely to commit violent crimes but by their late twenties, blacks are four times more likely to be violent offenders. However, when blacks and whites in their late twenties are employed, they differ hardly at all in violent behavior.

14   3. The greater the racial segregation in an area, the higher the crime rate. Sociologist Doug Massey argues that urban poverty and urban crime are the consequences of extremely high levels of black residential segregation and racial discrimination. Massey says,

> Take a group of people, segregate them, cut off their capital and guess what? The neighborhoods go downhill. There's no other outcome possible.

NOTES

"streetsweepers" (par. 7): twelve-gauge shotguns that can discharge the twelve rounds they hold in three seconds

demographic fact (par. 8): statistical fact about the population

predispositions (par. 10): tendencies

capital (par. 14): money for spending, lending, and investing

As these neighborhoods go downhill and economic opportunities evaporate, crimes go up.

15 4. The greater the family instability, the higher the probability of crimes by juveniles. Research is sketchy, but it appears that the following conditions are related to delinquent behaviors: (a) intense parental conflict; (b) lack of parental supervision; (c) parental neglect and abuse; and (d) failure of parents to discipline their children.

16 5. The greater the inequality in a neighborhood, city, region, or society, the higher the crime rate. In other words, the greater the disparities between rich and poor, the greater the probability of crime. Of all the industrialized nations, the United States has the greatest degree of inequality. For example, one percent of Americans own 40 percent of all the wealth. At the other extreme, $14\frac{1}{2}$ percent of all Americans live below the poverty line, and 5 percent of all Americans live below *one-half* of the poverty line.

17 When these social variables converge, they interact to increase crime rates. Thus, there is a relatively high probability of criminal behavior—violent criminal behavior—among young, black, impoverished males in inner cities where poverty, unemployment, and racial segregation are concentrated. There are about 5 million of these high-risk young men. In addition, we have other problem people. What do we do? How do we create a safer America?

18 To oversimplify a difficult and contentious debate, there are two answers—the conservative and progressive answers. The conservative answer has been to get tough with criminals. This involves mandatory sentences, longer sentences, putting more people in prison, and greater use of the death penalty. This strategy has accelerated with laws such as "three strikes and you're out (actually in)," and the passage of expensive prison building programs to house the new prisoners.

19 In my view, this approach is wrong-headed. Of course, some individuals must be put in prison to protect the members of society. Our policies, however, indiscriminately put too many people in prison at too high a cost. Here are some facts about prisons:

20 1. Our current incarceration rate is 455 per 100,000 (in 1971 it was 96 per 100,000). The rate in Japan and the Netherlands is one-tenth ours. Currently, there are 1.2 million Americans in prisons and jails (equivalent to the population of Philadelphia).

21 2. The cost is prohibitive, taking huge amounts of money that could be spent on other programs. It costs about $60,000 to build a prison cell and $20,000 to keep a prisoner for a year. Currently the overall cost of prisons and jails (federal, state, and local) is $29 billion annually. The willingness to spend for punishment reduces money that could be spent to alleviate other social problems. For example, eight years ago Texas spent $7 dollars on education for

NOTES

disparities (par. 16): differences

converge (par. 17): come together

contentious (par. 18): controversial

incarceration (par. 20): imprisonment

alleviate (par. 21): relieve

every dollar spent on prisons. Now the ratio is 4 to 1. Meanwhile, Texas ranks 37th among the states in per pupil spending.

22   3. As mentioned earlier, violent crimes tend to occur in the teenage years with a rapid drop-off afterwards. Often, for example, imprisonment under "three strikes and you're out" laws gives life imprisonment to many who are in the twilight of their criminal careers. We, and they, would be better off if we found alternatives to prison for them.

23   4. Prisons do not rehabilitate. Actually, prisons have the opposite effect. The prison experience tends to increase the likelihood of further criminal behavior. Prisons are overcrowded, mean, gloomy, brutal places that change people, but usually for the worse, not the better. Moreover, prisoners usually believe that their confinement is unjust because of the bias in the criminal justice system toward the poor and racial minorities. Finally, prisoners do not ever pay their debt to society. Rather they are forever stigmatized as "ex-cons" and, therefore, considered unreliable and dangerous by their neighbors, employers, fellow workers, and acquaintances. Also, they are harassed by the police as "likely suspects." The result is that they are often driven into a deviant subculture and eventually caught—about two-thirds are arrested within three years of leaving prison.

24   Progressives argue that conservative crime control measures are fundamentally flawed because they are "after the fact" solutions. Like a janitor mopping up the floor while the sink continues to overflow; he or she may even redouble the effort with some success but the source of the flooding has not been addressed. If I might mix metaphors here (although keeping with the aquatic theme), the obvious place to begin the attack on crime is *upstream,* before the criminal has been formed and the crimes have been committed.

25   We must concentrate our efforts on high-risk individuals before they become criminals (in particular, impoverished young inner-city males). These prevention proposals take time, are very costly, and out-of-favor politically but they are the only realistic solutions to reduce violent street crime.

26   The problem with the conservative "after the fact" crime fighting proposals is that while promoting criminal justice, these programs dismantle social justice. Thus, they enhance a criminogenic climate. During the Reagan years, for example, $51 billion dollars were removed from various poverty programs. Now, under the "Contract for America" the Republicans in Congress propose to reduce subsidized housing, to eliminate nutrition programs through WIC (Woman, Infants, and Children), to let the states take care of subsidized school lunches, and to eliminate welfare for unmarried mothers under eighteen who do not live with their parents or a responsible guardian.

NOTES

rehabilitate (par. 23): redirect prisoners so that they become law-abiding, productive citizens when they are released from prison

stigmatized (par. 23): labeled

deviant (par. 23): socially unacceptable

aquatic (par. 24): water related

criminogenic (par. 26): crime producing

subsidized (par. 26): partially or totally paid for by the government

27   Progressives argue that we abandon these children at our own peril. The current Republican proposals forsake the 26 percent of American children under six who live in poverty, including 54 percent of all African-American children and 44 percent of all Latino children under the age of six. Will we be safer as these millions of children in poverty grow to physical maturity?

28   Before I address specific solutions, I want to emphasize that sociologists examine the structural reasons for crime. This focus on factors outside the individual does not excuse criminal behavior, it tries to understand how certain structural factors *increase* the proportion of people who choose criminal options.

29   Knowing what we know about crime, the implications for policy are clear. These proposals, as you will note, are easy to suggest but they are very difficult to implement. I will divide my proposals into immediate actions to deal with crime now and long-term preventive measure[s]:

Measures to protect society immediately:

30   1. The first step is to protect society from predatory sociopaths. This does not mean imprisoning more people. We should, rather, only imprison the truly dangerous. The criminal law should be redrawn so that the list of crimes reflects the real dangers that individuals pose to society. Since prison does more harm than good, we should provide reasonable alternatives such as house arrest, half-way houses, boot camps, electronic surveillance, job corps, and drug/alcohol treatment.

31   2. We must reduce the number of handguns and assault weapons by enacting and vigorously enforcing stringent gun controls at the federal level. The United States is an armed camp with 210 million guns in circulation. Jeffrey Reiman has put it this way:

> Trying to fight crime while allowing such easy access to guns is like trying to teach a child to walk and tripping him each time he stands up. In its most charitable light, it is hypocrisy. Less charitably, it is complicity in murder.

32   3. We must make a special effort to get guns out of the hands of juveniles. Research by James Wright and his colleagues at Tulane University found that juveniles are much more likely to have guns for protection than for status and power. They suggest that we must restore order in the inner cities so that fewer young people do not feel the need to provide their own protection. They argue that a perceived sense of security by youth can be accomplished if there is a greater emphasis on community policing, more cooperation between police departments and inner city residents, and greater investment by businesses, banks, and cities in the inner city.

33   4. We must reinvent the criminal justice system so that it commands the respect of youth and adults. The obvious unfairness by race and social class must be

---

NOTES

peril (par. 27): risk

predatory sociopaths (par. 30): violent antisocial individuals

stringent (par. 31): rigorous, severe

hypocrisy (par. 31): saying one thing and doing the opposite

complicity (par. 31): criminal participation

addressed. Some laws are unfair. For example, the federal law requires a five-year, no-parole sentence for possession of five grams of crack cocaine, worth about $400. However, it takes 100 times as much powder cocaine—500 grams, worth $10,000—and a selling conviction to get the same sentence. Is this fair? Of course not. Is it racist? It is racist since crack is primarily used by African Americans while powder cocaine is more likely used by whites. There are also differences by race and social class in arrest patterns, plea bargain arrangements, sentencing, parole, and imposition of the death penalty. These differences provide convincing evidence that the poor and racial minorities are discriminated against in the criminal justice system. As long as the criminal justice system is perceived as unfair by the disadvantaged, that system will not exert any moral authority over them.

34   5. We must rehabilitate as many criminals as possible. Prisons should be more humane. Prisoners should leave prison with vocational skills useful in the real world. Prisoners should leave prison literate and with a high-school degree. And, society should formally adopt the concept of "forgiveness," saying to ex-prisoners, in effect, you have been punished for your crime, we want you to begin a new life with a "clean" record.

35   6. We must legalize the production and sale of "illicit drugs" and treat addiction as a medical problem rather than a criminal problem. If drugs were legalized or decriminalized, crimes would be reduced in several ways: (a) By eliminating drug use as a criminal problem, we would have 1.12 million *fewer* arrests each year. (b) There would be many *fewer* prisoners (currently about 60 percent of all federal prisoners and 25 percent of all state prisoners are incarcerated for drug offenses). (c) Money now spent on the drug war ($31 billion annually, not counting prison construction) could be spent for other crime control programs such as police patrols, treatment of drug users, and jobs programs. (d) Drugs could be regulated and taxed, generating revenues of about $5 billion a year. (e) It would end the illicit drug trade that provides tremendous profits to organized crime, violent gangs, and other traffickers. (f) It would eliminate considerable corruption of the police and other authorities. (g) There would be many fewer homicides. Somewhere between one-fourth and one-half of the killings in the inner cities are drug-related. (h) The lower cost of purchasing drugs reduces the need to commit crimes to pay for drug habits.

Long-term preventive measures to reduce violent crime:

36   1. The link between poverty and street crime is indisputable. In the long run, reducing poverty will be the most effective crime fighting tool. Thus, as a society, we need to intensify our efforts to break the cycle of poverty. This means providing a universal and comprehensive health-care system, low-cost housing, job training, and decent compensation for work. There must be pay equity for women. And, there must be an unwavering commitment to eradicate institutional sexism and racism. Among other benefits, such a strategy will strengthen families and give children resources, positive role models, and hope.

NOTES

vocational skills (par. 34): skills needed for occupations not requiring a college degree, such as plumbing and welding

illicit (par. 35): illegal

eradicate (par. 36): abolish

37   2. Families must be strengthened. Single-parent families and the working poor need subsidized child care, flexible work schedules, and leave for maternity and family emergencies at a reasonable proportion of their wages. Adolescent parents need the resources to stay in school. They need job training. We need to increase the commitment to family planning. This means providing contraceptives and birth control counseling to adolescents. This means using federal funds to pay for legal abortions when they are requested by poor women.

38   3. There must be a societal commitment to full and decent employment. Meaningful work at decent pay integrates individuals into society. It is a source of positive identity. Employed parents are respected by their children. Good paying jobs provide hope for the future. They also are essential to keep families together.

39   4. There must be a societal commitment to education. This requires two different programs. The first is to help at-risk children, beginning at an early age. As it is now, when poor children start school, they are already behind. As Sylvia Ann Hewlett has said:

> At age five, poor children are often less alert, less curious, and less effective at interacting with their peers than are more privileged youngsters.

This means that they are doomed to be underachievers. To overcome this we need intervention programs that prepare children for school. Research shows that Head Start and other programs can raise IQ scores significantly. There are two problems with Head Start, however. First, the current funding only covers 40 percent of eligible youngsters. And second, the positive effects from the Head Start program are sometimes short-lived because the children then attend schools that are poorly staffed, overcrowded, and ill-equipped.

40   This brings us to the second education program to help at-risk children. The government must equalize the resources of school districts, rather than the current situation where the wealth of school districts determines the amount spent per pupil. Actually, equalization is not the answer. I believe that there should be special commitment to invest *extra* resources in at-risk children. If we do, we will have a safer society in the long run.

41   These proposals seem laughable in the current political climate, where politicians—Republicans *and* Democrats—try to outdo each other in their toughness on crime and their disdain for preventive programs. They are wrong, however, and society is going to pay in higher crime rates in the future. I am convinced that the political agenda of the conservatives is absolutely heading us in the wrong direction—toward more violent crime rather than less.

42   The proposals that I have suggested are based on what we sociologists know about crime. They should be taken seriously, but they are not. The proposals are also based on the assumption that if we can give at-risk young people hope, they will become a part of the community rather than alienated from it. My premise is this: Everyone needs a dream. Without a dream, we become

NOTES

Head Start (par. 39): a federally funded program that provides preschool education for economically disadvantaged children

disdain (par. 41): contempt

agenda (par. 41): program

apathetic. Without a dream, we become fatalistic. Without a dream, and the hope of attaining it, society becomes our enemy. Many young people act in antisocial ways because they have lost their dream. These troubled and troublesome people are society's creations because we have not given them the opportunity to achieve their dreams—instead society has structured the situation so that they will fail. Until they feel that they have a stake in society, they will fail, and so will we.

NOTES

apathetic (par. 42): indifferent

fatalistic (par. 42): Fatalism is the belief that we have no control over our lives.

A Nasty Business

Bruce Hoffman

1   "Intelligence is capital," Colonel Yves Godard liked to say. And Godard undeniably knew what he was talking about. He had fought both as a guerrilla in the French Resistance during World War II and against guerrillas in Indochina, as the commander of a covert special-operations unit. As the chief of staff of the elite 10th Para Division, Godard was one of the architects of the French counter-terrorist strategy that won the Battle of Algiers, in 1957. To him, information was the *sine qua non* for victory. It had to be zealously collected, meticulously analyzed, rapidly disseminated, and efficaciously acted on. Without it, no anti-terrorist operation could succeed. As the United States prosecutes its global war against terrorism, Godard's dictum has acquired new relevance. Indeed, as is now constantly said, success in the struggle against Osama bin Laden

NOTES

Intelligence (par. 1): information gathered for the military from sympathizers, spies, prisoners, and so forth

capital (par. 1): a thing of value; an asset that can be used to produce future assets

guerrilla (par. 1): a member of a small, unconventional combat unit that uses methods such as sabotage, kidnapping, ambush, assassination, and bombing to achieve its political goals

French Resistance (par. 1): groups that forcefully opposed Nazi Germany's occupation of France

covert (par. 1): secret

special-operations unit (par. 1): a small group of military with specific training, designed to handle particularly difficult missions

elite (par. 1): highly regarded

Para (par. 1): Paratroop (Paratroopers are soldiers trained to parachute.)

Battle of Algiers (par. 1): The major battle of the Algerian War of Independence, the Battle of Algiers involved the extensive use of guerilla warfare, terrorism, and torture.

sine qua non (par. 1): the most essential thing

zealously (par. 1): passionately

meticulously (par. 1): carefully

disseminated (par. 1): distributed

efficaciously (par. 1): effectively

dictum (par. 1): pronouncement

minions (par. 1): followers, dependents

imperative (par. 1): essential and urgent duty

entails (par. 1): involves

and his minions will depend on good intelligence. But the experiences of other countries, fighting similar conflicts against similar enemies, suggest that Americans still do not appreciate the enormously difficult—and morally complex—problem that the imperative to gather "good intelligence" entails.

2   The challenge that security forces and militaries the world over have faced in countering terrorism is how to obtain information about an enigmatic enemy who fights unconventionally and operates in a highly amenable environment where he typically is indistinguishable from the civilian populace. The differences between police officers and soldiers in training and approach, coupled with the fact that most military forces are generally uncomfortable with, and inadequately prepared for, counterterrorist operations, strengthens this challenge. Military forces in such unfamiliar settings must learn to acquire intelligence by methods markedly different from those to which they are accustomed. The most "actionable," and therefore effective, information in this environment is discerned not from orders of battle, visual satellite transmissions of opposing force positions, or intercepted signals but from human intelligence gathered mostly from the indigenous population. The police, specifically trained to interact with the public, typically have better access than the military to what are called human intelligence sources. Indeed, good police work depends on informers, undercover agents, and the apprehension and interrogation of terrorists and suspected terrorists, who provide the additional information critical to destroying terrorist organizations. Many today who argue reflexively and sanctimoniously that the United States should not "overreact" by overmilitarizing the "war" against terrorism assert that such a conflict should be largely a police, not a military, endeavor. Although true, this line of argument usually overlooks the uncomfortable fact that, historically, "good" police work against terrorists has of necessity involved nasty and brutish means. Rarely have the importance of intelligence and the unpleasant ways in which it must often be obtained been better or more clearly elucidated than in the 1966 movie *The Battle of Algiers*. In an early scene in the film the main protagonist, the French paratroop commander, Lieutenant Colonel Mathieu (who is actually a composite of Yves Godard and two other senior French army officers who fought in the Battle of Algiers), explains to his men that the "military aspect is secondary." He says, "More

NOTES

countering (par. 2): working against

enigmatic (par. 2): mysterious

amenable (par. 2): agreeable

populace (par. 2): population, people

actionable (par. 2): able to lead to effective political or military action

discerned (par. 2): learned

indigenous (par. 2): native

apprehension (par. 2): arrest

interrogation (par. 2): questioning

sanctimoniously (par. 2): self-righteously

assert (par. 2): argue

elucidated (par. 2): demonstrated

protagonist (par. 2): hero

composite (par. 2): combination of personalities

immediate is the police work involved. I know you don't like hearing that, but it indicates exactly the kind of job we have to do."

3   I have long told soldiers, spies, and students to watch *The Battle of Algiers* if they want to understand how to fight terrorism. Indeed, the movie was required viewing for the graduate course I taught for five years on terrorism and the liberal state, which considered the difficulties democracies face in countering terrorism. The seminar at which the movie was shown regularly provoked the most intense and passionate discussions of the semester. To anyone who has seen *The Battle of Algiers*, this is not surprising. The late Pauline Kael, doyenne of American film critics, seemed still enraptured seven years after its original release when she described *The Battle of Algiers* in a 900-word review as "an epic in the form of a 'created documentary'"; "the one great revolutionary 'sell' of modern times"; and the "most impassioned, most astute call to revolution ever." The best reviews, however, have come from terrorists—members of the IRA; the Tamil Tigers, in Sri Lanka; and 1960s African-American revolutionaries—who have assiduously studied it. At a time when the U.S. Army has enlisted Hollywood screenwriters to help plot scenarios of future terrorist attacks, learning about the difficulties of fighting terrorism from a movie that terrorists themselves have studied doesn't seem farfetched.

4   In fact, the film represents the apotheosis of *cinéma vérité*. That it has a verisimilitude unique among onscreen portrayals of terrorism is a tribute to its director, Grilo Pontecorvo, and its cast—many of whose members reprised the real-life roles they had played actually fighting for the liberation of their country, a decade before. Pontecorvo, too, had personal experience with the kinds of situations he filmed: during World War II he had commanded a partisan brigade in Milan. Indeed, the Italian filmmaker was so concerned about not giving audiences a false impression of authenticity that he inserted a clarification in the movie's opening frames: "This dramatic reenactment of *The Battle of Algiers* contains NOT ONE FOOT of Newsreel or Documentary Film." The movie accordingly possesses an uncommon gravitas that immediately

NOTES

liberal state (par. 3): a government such as the U.S. that strives to protect the ideals of personal freedom through political, social, and economic reform

doyenne (par. 3): a woman who is the most experienced and respected person (in a particular field or industry)

enraptured (par. 3): deeply moved

astute (par. 3): insightful

IRA; Tamil Tigers, in Sri Lanka; and 1960s African-American revolutionaries (par. 3): The Irish Republican Army (*IRA*), the Liberation Tigers of Tamil Eelam (*Tamil Tigers*), and *1960s African-American revolutionaries* (such as the *Black Panthers*) believe that the only way for people to change the way their country is governed is through violence.

assiduously (par. 3): carefully and closely

scenarios (par. 3): an imagined sequence of possible events

apotheosis (par. 4): perfect example

cinéma vérité (par. 4): a style of filmmaking that emphasizes realism

verisimilitude (par. 4): appearance of truth or reality

reprised (par. 4): reenacted

partisan brigade (par. 4): band of guerilla fighters

Milan (par. 4): a city in Northern Italy

gravitas (par. 4): seriousness

draws viewers into the story. Like many of the best films, it is about a search—in this case for the intelligence on which French paratroops deployed in Algiers depended to defeat and destroy the terrorists of the National Liberation Front (FLN). "To know them means we can eliminate them" Mathieu explains to his men in the scene referred to above. "For this we need information. The method: interrogation." In Mathieu's universe there is no question of ends not justifying means: the Paras need intelligence, and they will obtain it however they can. "To succumb to humane considerations," he concludes, "only leads to hopeless chaos."

5   The events depicted on celluloid closely parallel those of history. In 1957, the city of Algiers was the center of a life-and-death struggle between the FLN and the French authorities. On one side were the terrorists, embodied both on screen and in real life in Ali La Pointe, a petty thief turned terrorist cell leader; on the other stood the army, specifically the elite 10th Para Division, under General Jacques Massu, another commander on whom the Mathieu composite was based. Veterans of the war to preserve France's control of Indochina, Massu and his senior officers—Godard included—prided themselves on having acquired a thorough understanding of terrorism and revolutionary warfare, and how to counter both. Victory, they were convinced, would depend on the acquisition of intelligence. Their method was to build a meticulously detailed picture of the FLN's apparatus in Algiers which would help the French home in on the terrorist campaign's masterminds—Ali La Pointe and his bin Laden, Saadi Yacef (who played himself in the film). This approach, which is explicated in one of the film's most riveting scenes, resulted in what the Francophile British historian Alistair Horne, in his masterpiece on the conflict, *A Savage War of Peace*, called a "complex organigramme [that] began to take shape on a large blackboard, a kind of skeleton pyramid in which, as each fresh piece of information came from the interrogation centres, another [terrorist] name (and not always necessarily the right name) would be entered." That this system proved tactically effective there is no doubt. The problem was that it thoroughly depended on, and therefore actively encouraged, widespread human rights abuses, including torture.

6   Massu and his men—like their celluloid counterparts—were not particularly concerned about this. They justified their means of obtaining intelligence with

NOTES

deployed (par. 4): sent into combat

succumb (par. 4): give into

celluloid (par. 5): film

embodied (par. 5): represented in the person of

acquisition (par. 5): collection

apparatus (par. 5): the organization of a political organization, particularly an underground political movement

explicated (par. 5): explained

riveting (par. 5): fascinating

Francophile (par. 5): one who admires France and the French

organigramme (par. 5): diagram of an organization

tactically effective (par. 5): effective in the pursuit of a particular goal

utilitarian (par. 6): practical

exculpatory (par. 6): guilt-clearing; blame-dodging

apathetic (par. 6): indifferent

utilitarian, cost-benefit arguments. Extraordinary measures were legitimized by extraordinary circumstances. The exculpatory philosophy embraced by the French Paras is best summed up by Massu's uncompromising belief that "the innocent [that is, the next victims of terrorist attacks] deserve more protection than the guilty." The approach, however, at least strategically, was counterproductive. Its sheer brutality alienated the native Algerian Muslim community. Hitherto mostly passive or apathetic, that community was now driven into the arms of the FLN, swelling the organization's ranks and increasing its popular support. Public opinion in France was similarly outraged, weakening support for the continuing struggle and creating profound fissures in French civil-military relations. The army's achievement in the city was therefore bought at the cost of eventual political defeat. Five years after victory in Algiers the French withdrew from Algeria and granted the country its independence. But Massu remained forever unrepentant: he insisted that the ends justified the means used to destroy the FLN's urban insurrection. The battle was won, lives were saved, and the indiscriminate bombing campaign that had terrorized the city was ended. To Massu, that was all that mattered. To his mind, respect for the rule of law and the niceties of legal procedure were irrelevant given the crisis situation enveloping Algeria in 1957. As anachronistic as France's attempt to hold on to this last vestige of its colonial past may now appear, its jettisoning of such long-standing and cherished notions as habeas corpus and due process, enshrined in the ethos of the liberal state, underscores how the intelligence requirements of counterterrorism can suddenly take precedence over democratic ideals.

7   Although it is tempting to dismiss the French army's resort to torture in Algeria as the desperate excess of a moribund colonial power, the fundamental message that only information can effectively counter terrorism is timeless. Equally disturbing and instructive, however, are the lengths to which security and military forces need often resort to get that information. I learned this

NOTES

fissures (par. 6): cracks

insurrection (par. 6): rebellion

indiscriminate (par. 6): widespread and devastating

anachronistic (par. 6): out of place in time and history

vestige (par. 6): trace, scrap, memento

jettisoning (par. 6): throwing away

habeas corpus (par. 6): a legal document that protects people from being falsely imprisoned by requiring that they be brought before a judge to assure that their detention is lawful

due process (par. 6): judicial proceedings that protect the rights of people accused of crimes

enshrined (par. 6): considered sacred

ethos (par. 6): cultural values

precedence (par. 6): priority

moribund (par. 7): dying

colonial power (par. 7): a country that maintains control over another, less powerful country

swank (par. 7): fancy

Colombo (par. 7): the largest city in Sri Lanka

carnage (par. 7): slaughter of large numbers of people

afflicted (par. 7): caused problems in

arrayed against (par. 7): arranged to oppose

some years ago, on a research trip to Sri Lanka. The setting—a swank ocean-front hotel in Colombo, a refreshingly cool breeze coming off the ocean, a magnificent sunset on the horizon—could not have been further removed from the carnage and destruction that have afflicted that island country for the past eighteen years and have claimed the lives of more than 60,000 people. Arrayed against the democratically elected Sri Lankan government and its armed forces is perhaps the most ruthlessly efficient terrorist organization-cum-insurgent force in the world today: the Liberation Tigers of Tamil Eelam, known also by the acronym LTTE or simply as the Tamil Tigers. The Tigers are unique in the annals of terrorism and arguably eclipse even bin Laden's al-Qaeda in professionalism, capability, and determination. They are believed to be the first nonstate group in history to stage a chemical-weapons attack when they deployed poison gas in a 1990 assault on a Sri Lankan military base—some five years before the nerve-gas attack on the Tokyo subway by the apocalyptic Japanese religious cult Aum Shinrikyo. Of greater relevance, perhaps, is the fact that at least a decade before the seaborne attack on the U.S.S. Cole, in Aden harbor, the LTTE's special suicide maritime unit, the Sea Tigers, had perfected the same tactics against the Sri Lankan navy. Moreover, the Tamil Tigers are believed to have developed their own embryonic air capability—designed to carry out attacks similar to those of September 11 (though with much smaller, noncommercial aircraft). The most feared Tiger unit, however, is the Black Tigers—the suicide cadre composed of the group's best-trained, most battle-hardened, and most zealous fighters. A partial list of their operations includes the assassination of the former Indian Prime Minister Rajiv Gandhi at a campaign stop in the Indian state of Tamil Nadu, in 1991; the assassination of Sri Lankan President Ranasinghe Premadasa, in 1993; the assassination of the presidential candidate Gamini Dissanayake, which also claimed the lives of fifty-four bystanders and injured about one hundred more, in 1994; the suicide truck bombing of the Central Bank of Sri Lanka, in 1996, which killed eighty-six people and wounded 1,400 others; and the attempt on the life of the current President of Sri Lanka, Chandrika Kumaratunga, in December of 1999. The powerful and much venerated leader of the LTTE is Velupillai Prabhakaran, who, like bin Laden, exercises a charismatic influence over his fighters. *The Battle of Algiers* is said to be one of Prabhakaran's favorite films.

NOTES

terrorist organization-cum-insurgent force (par. 7): terrorist organization that is also used as an insurgent force

annals (par. 7): historical records

eclipse (par. 7): surpass

the nerve-gas attack on the Tokyo subway by the apocalyptic Japanese religious cult Aum Shinrikyo (par. 7): Twelve people were killed and six thousand were injured during this 1995 attack, the largest attack within Japan since World War II.

the seaborne attack on the U.S.S. Cole (par. 7): During this 2000 attack masterminded by Osama Bin Laden and members of his al-Qaida network, two suicide bombers detonated their explosive-laden boat next to the ship, killing seventeen American soldiers and injuring thirty-nine others.

cadre (par. 7): core group

zealous (par. 7): fanatical

venerated (par. 7): revered, respected

charismatic (par. 7): captivating

8   I sat in that swank hotel drinking tea with a much decorated, battle-hardened Sri Lankan army officer charged with fighting the LTTE and protecting the lives of Colombo's citizens. I cannot use his real name, so I will call him Thomas. However, I had been told before our meeting, by the mutual friend—a former Sri Lankan intelligence officer who had also long fought the LTTE—who introduced us (and was present at our meeting), that Thomas had another name, one better known to his friends and enemies alike: Terminator. My friend explained how Thomas had acquired his sobriquet; it actually owed less to Arnold Schwarzenegger than to the merciless way in which he discharged his duties as an intelligence officer. This became clear to me during our conversation. "By going through the process of laws," Thomas patiently explained, as a parent or a teacher might speak to a bright yet uncomprehending child, "you cannot fight terrorism." Terrorism, he believed, could be fought only by thoroughly "terrorizing" the terrorists—that is, inflicting on them the same pain that they inflict on the innocent. Thomas had little confidence that I understood what he was saying. I was an academic, he said, with no actual experience of the life-and-death choices and the immense responsibility borne by those charged with protecting society from attack. Accordingly, he would give me an example of the split-second decisions he was called on to make. At the time, Colombo was on "code red" emergency status, because of intelligence that the LTTE was planning to embark on a campaign of bombing public gathering places and other civilian targets. Thomas's unit had apprehended three terrorists who, it suspected, had recently planted somewhere in the city a bomb that was then ticking away, the minutes counting down to catastrophe. The three men were brought before Thomas. He asked them where the bomb was. The terrorists—highly dedicated and steeled to resist interrogation—remained silent. Thomas asked the question again, advising them that if they did not tell him what he wanted to know, he would kill them. They were unmoved. So Thomas took his pistol from his gun belt, pointed it at the forehead of one of them, and shot him dead. The other two, he said, talked immediately; the bomb, which had been placed in a crowded railway station and set to explode during the evening rush hour, was found and defused, and countless lives were saved. On other occasions, Thomas said, similarly recalcitrant terrorists were brought before him. It was not surprising, he said, that they initially refused to talk; they were schooled to withstand harsh questioning and coercive pressure. No matter: a few drops of gasoline flicked into a plastic bag that is then placed over a terrorist's head and cinched tight around his neck with a web belt very quickly prompts a full explanation of the details of any planned attack.

9   I was looking pale and feeling a bit shaken as waiters in starched white jackets smartly cleared the china teapot and cups from the table, and Thomas

NOTES

sobriquet (par. 8): nickname

apprehended (par. 8): arrested

recalcitrant (par. 8): stubborn

coercive pressure (par. 8): forceful pressure to do something against one's will

exulted (par. 9): taken pride

rose to bid us good-bye and return to his work. He hadn't exulted in his explanations or revealed any joy or even a hint of pleasure in what he had to do. He had spoken throughout in a measured, somber, even reverential tone. He did not appear to be a sadist, or even manifestly homicidal. (And not a year has passed since our meeting when Thomas has failed to send me an unusually kind Christmas card.) In his view, as in Massu's, the innocent had more rights than the guilty. He, too, believed that extraordinary circumstances required extraordinary measures. Thomas didn't think I understood—or, more to the point, thought I never could understand. I am not fighting on the front lines of this battle; I don't have the responsibility for protecting society that he does. He was right: I couldn't possibly understand. But since September 11, and especially every morning after I read the "Portraits of Grief" page in *The New York Times*, I am constantly reminded of Thomas—of the difficulties of fighting terrorism and of the challenges of protecting not only the innocent but an entire society and way of life. I am never bidden to condone, much less advocate, torture. But as I look at the snapshots and the lives of the victims recounted each day, and think how it will take almost a year to profile the approximately 5,000 people who perished on September 11, I recall the ruthless enemy that America faces, and I wonder about the lengths to which we may yet have to go to vanquish him.

10   The moral question of lengths and the broader issue of ends versus means are, of course, neither new nor unique to rearguard colonial conflicts of the 1950s or to the unrelenting carnage that has more recently been inflicted on a beautiful tropical island in the Indian Ocean. They are arguably no different from the stark choices that eventually confront any society threatened by an enveloping violence unlike anything it has seen before. For a brief period in the early and middle 1970s Britain, for example, had something of this experience—which may be why, among other reasons, Prime Minister Tony Blair and his country today stand as America's staunchest ally. The sectarian terrorist violence in Northern Ireland was at its height, and had for the first time spilled into England in a particularly vicious and indiscriminate way. The views of a British army intelligence officer at the time, quoted by the journalist Desmond Hamill in his book *Pig in the Middle* (1985), reflect those of Thomas and Massu.

> Naturally one worries—after all, one is inflicting pain and discomfort and indignity on other human beings . . . [but] society has got to find a way of protecting itself . . . and it can only do so if it has good information. If you have a close-knit society which doesn't give information then you've got to find ways of getting it. Now the softies of the world

NOTES

sadist (par. 9): one who takes pleasure in causing other people pain

manifestly (par. 9): clearly, obviously

condone (par. 9): excuse

advocate (par. 9): argue for

rearguard (par. 10): troops assigned to protect the rear of a retreating army

a beautiful tropical island in the Indian Ocean (par. 10): Sri Lanka

Prime Minister Tony Blair (par. 10): the head of the British Government and an outspoken supporter of U.S. foreign policy

sectarian terrorist violence (par. 10): terrorist violence between religious groups

staunchest (par. 10): most loyal

exigent (par. 10): urgent; extraordinarily difficult

complain—but there is an awful lot of double talk about it. If there is to be discomfort and horror inflicted on a few, is this not preferred to the danger and horror being inflicted on perhaps a million people?

It is a question that even now, after September 11, many Americans would answer in the negative. But under extreme conditions and in desperate circumstances that, too, could dramatically change—much as everything else has so profoundly changed for us all since that morning. I recently discussed precisely this issue over the telephone with the same Sri Lankan friend who introduced me to Thomas years ago. I have never quite shaken my disquiet over my encounter with Thomas and over the issues he raised—issues that have now acquired an unsettling relevance. My friend sought to lend some perspective from his country's long experience in fighting terrorism. "There are not good people and bad people," he told me, "only good circumstances and bad circumstances. Sometimes in bad circumstances good people have to do bad things. I have done bad things, but these were in bad circumstances. I have no doubt that this was the right thing to do." In the quest for timely, "actionable" intelligence will the United States, too, have to do bad things—by resorting to measures that we would never have contemplated in a less exigent situation?

Torture's Allure and Effect

Darius Rejali

I

Torture's Dark Allure

1   Few things give a rush quite like having unlimited power over another human being. A sure sign the rush is coming is pasty saliva and a strange taste in one's mouth, according to a French soldier attached to a torture unit in Algeria. That powerful rush can be seen on the faces of some of the soldiers at Abu Ghraib, a rush that undoubtedly changed them forever. The history of slavery tells us that one can't feel such a rush without being corrupted by it. And the history of modern torture tells us that governments can't license this corruption—even in the cause of spreading democracy—without reducing the quality of their intelligence, compromising their allies and damaging their military and bureaucratic capabilities.

NOTES

Algeria (par. 1): a country in Northern Africa. France controlled Algeria from 1830 until the Algerian War of Independence (1954–1962). Guerilla warfare, terrorism, and torture were used extensively during the ***Battle of Algiers*** (1956–1957) (par. 39).

Abu Ghraib (par. 1): a prison located outside of Baghdad that attracted worldwide attention in April, 2004 after the publication of photographs showing U.S. military personnel abusing Iraqi prisoners

license (par. 1): authorize

intelligence (par. 1): information gathered for the military from sympathizers, spies, prisoners, and so forth

allies (par. 1): supporters

bureaucratic (par. 1): administrative

2   The abuse and torture at Abu Ghraib prison were originally blamed on a few American soldiers. Various investigations into the exact chain of command are underway, but they already point to policy decisions made at the highest levels of the U.S. government. Indeed, the recently revealed memos written by Justice Department lawyers in August 2002, at the request of the CIA and the White House, concerning treatment of al-Qaida suspects at Guantánamo Bay, Cuba, and by Pentagon lawyers in March 2003 (in which it was argued that the president and those he has empowered to conduct torture of foreign prisoners are immune from prosecution under international law) are evidence that the government was seeking ways to legally circumvent the Geneva Conventions. "The question put to lawyers was how the president and the others could commit war crimes and get away with it" is how Anne Applebaum put it in the *Washington Post* Wednesday. It turns out that many of the severest interrogation techniques used in Iraq were sanctioned by top military officials, including Secretary of Defense Donald Rumsfeld and the former commander in Iraq, Lt. Gen. Ricardo Sanchez. And this week, we learned that Rumsfeld had ordered a "high-value" detainee in Iraq held in secret, in part to keep him from being seen by the International Red Cross.

3   I learned how torture fit into modern life while growing up in Iran under Mohammad Reza Shah Pahlavi, whose government relied on Savak, a secret intelligence agency formed with the help of the CIA in 1957. Savak arrested and detained indefinitely people suspected of opposing the shah and tortured and executed thousands of political prisoners during his rule.

4   In the course of 20 years of research on modern torture and the bureaucracies that sponsored and practiced it in Germany, Japan, France, and Britain, I have studied the "stealthy" methods, those that leave few visible marks (i.e., blood or scars) on the victim. I noticed that stealthy techniques appeared more often in the wars of democracies than in those of dictatorships. Democratic states that use torture to gain intelligence or as punishment obviously

NOTES

the CIA (par. 2): the Central Intelligence Agency, the agency of the U.S. government that coordinates intelligence activities outside the country

al-Qaida (par. 2): a worldwide network of Islamic militants responsible for multiple terrorist attacks, most notably the 9/11/2001 attacks on the World Trade Center and the **Pentagon** (par. 2), the five-sided building that serves as the headquarters for the U.S. Department of Defense

Guantánamo Bay, Cuba (par. 2): location of a U.S. naval base where suspected al-Qaida members are being detained

circumvent (par. 2): go around

Geneva Conventions (par. 2): a series of treaties that govern various aspects of war, including the treatment of prisoners and civilians

sanctioned (par. 2): authorized

International Red Cross (par. 2): According to its own Mission Statement, the Red Cross is "an impartial, neutral and independent organization whose exclusively humanitarian mission is to protect the lives and dignity of victims of war and internal violence and to provide them with assistance."

Mohammad Reza Shah Pahlavi (par. 3): the last monarch of Iran, the shah reigned from 1941 to 1979. The last half of his rule was marked by corruption, intolerance, execution, and torture.

bureaucracies (par. 4): government agencies

stealthy (par. 4): secret; concealed

verified (par. 4): confirmed

prefer methods—such as electroshock, torture by water and ice, tying victims in agonizing postures, sonic devices and drugs—that cause pain but do not result in lasting injury, so that the torture cannot be verified by journalists, human rights monitors. or congressional committees. The advantage of stealth torture is that it reduces adverse publicity and finesses democratic oversight.

5   After 9/11, the warning signs of what the United States was up to were there, but then the events from Abu Ghraib brought all of it to the surface, revealing that the U.S. military was employing some of these stealthy techniques in Afghanistan and Iraq.

6   My research shows, however, that torture during interrogations rarely yields better information than traditional human intelligence, partly because no one has figured out a precise, reliable way to break human beings or any adequate method to evaluate whether what prisoners say when they do talk is true. Nor can torture be done in a professional way—anyone who tortures is necessarily corrupted by the experience and is often turned into a sadist. The psychic damage to the soldiers who conducted the torture at Abu Ghraib is likely to be permanent.

7   What's more, a democracy that legalizes the use of torture in its desperation to gain information loses something more important—the trust of its people, the foundation of a democracy. In Iraq, the United States was desperate as it sought to find and stop those responsible for the insurgency. When "intelligence" was not forthcoming from prisoners, senior U.S. Army officials decided to turn over interrogation to military intelligence personnel, who were instructed to use aggressive, even brutal techniques. These methods were rationalized as necessary in the overall global war on terrorism, but as my research has shown, institutionalizing torture in such a manner only ends up destroying all the individuals involved—and the military and political goals of the government in whose name torture is carried out.

8   Aside from its devastating effects and the wasted time and resources, does torture actually work? Organizations can certainly use torture to intimidate prisoners and to produce confessions (many of which turn out to be false). But the real question is whether organizations can apply torture scientifically and professionally to produce true information. Does this method yield better results than others at an army's disposal? The history of torture demonstrates that it does not—whether it is stealthy or not.

NOTES

human rights monitors (par. 4): people involved with humanitarian organizations like the International Red Cross who monitor the treatment of prisoners of war to prevent violation of the Geneva Conventions

adverse (par. 4): negative

finesses (par. 4): skillfully handles

yields (par. 6): produces

to break human beings (par. 6): to destroy a human being's will to resist

sadist (par. 6): one who takes pleasure in causing other people pain

psychic (par. 6): mental

the insurgency (par. 7): a group of people who attempt to overthrow a ruling authority (in this situation, the U.S.-backed Iraqi Coalition Government) through acts of violence and sabotage

rationalized (par. 7): justified

institutionalizing torture (par. 7): establishing torture as an accepted practice within an organization

intimidate (par. 8): frighten

9   Advocates of torture believe that more physical pain stimulates more compliance, but this view is not based on science; it is medical nonsense. Pain, as noted clinical psychologist Ron Melzack has shown, is far more complex than that. Injury does not always produce pain. In one study, 37 percent of people who arrived at an emergency ward with injuries such as amputated fingers, major skin lacerations, and fractured bones did not feel any pain until many minutes, even hours, after the injury. Similarly, soldiers with massive wounds sometimes do not feel their pain for a long time.

10   In addition, human beings differ widely in their ability to endure extreme pain. Clinical psychologists and some torturers in colonized nations agree that past experiences and cultural beliefs (for example, "suffering is divine") enable some human beings to endure pain others could not. People also vary in their ability to use psychological states like distraction or anxiety to reduce pain.

11   Moreover, pain, unlike heat, is not a single sensation but, as Melzack observes, can variously feel like burning, throbbing, or cutting. Victims can play these different sensations against each other, using one pain to distract themselves from another, much like a person might bite his hand as someone extracts a thorn.

12   Last, pain is not constant. As the body is damaged, its ability to sense pain declines. Torturers run out of places where they can apply pain effectively.

13   Unlike the physics of boiling water, in which one knows how much heat to apply, there is no way to calculate in advance how much torture is needed to obtain compliance from a prisoner. Science and technology can help with the conduct of torture: Modern instruments reduce the hard labor of torture, helping ensure that it is not lethal; and they guarantee that few marks will be left as evidence. But science and technology cannot predict the precise amount or kind of torture that will work with each human being. Opportunistic use of technology does not make torturers scientific any more than wearing a white lab coat makes torturers scientists.

14   If torture can't be scientific, can it at least be done professionally? To think that professionalism is a guard against causing excessive pain is an illusion. Instead, torture induces a dynamic that breaks down professionalism. Yale psychologist Stanley Milgram has shown that professionalism can serve to excuse ever more violent behavior. The myth of the professional torturer is also shattered in *Violence Workers: Police Torturers and Murderers Reconstruct Brazilian Atrocities*, by Martha K. Huggins, Philip G. Zimbardo, and Mika Haritos-Fatouros.

NOTES

Advocates (par. 9): those who support

compliance (par 9): cooperation

emergency ward (par. 9): Emergency Room

lacerations (par. 9): deep cuts

colonized nations (par. 10): nations under the political control of another, more powerful country

physics (par. 13): predictable laws of nature

lethal (par. 13): deadly

Opportunistic (par. 13): taking advantage of an opportunity with little concern about ethics or principles

dynamic (par. 14): motivating forces

myth (par. 14): false but commonly held belief

atrocities (par. 14): shockingly brutal acts

15 As a victim feels less pain, torturers have to push harder, using more severe methods to overtake the victim's maximal pain threshold. And because victims experience different types of pain, torturers have to use a scattershot approach. No matter how professional torturers may think they are, they have no choice but behaving like sadists. Even though many of the interrogators at Abu Ghraib were using techniques approved by their superiors, it is no surprise that they went far beyond these techniques, trying anything that worked.

16 Competition among torturers also drives brutality. As one torturer put it, each interrogator "thinks he is going to get the information at any minute and takes good care not to let the bird go to the next chap after he's softened him up nicely, when of course the other chap would get the honor and glory of it." Torture, as New York University economist Leonard Wantchekon has said, is a zero-sum game.

17 What's more, coercive interrogation undermines other professional policing skills: Why do fingerprinting when you've got a bat? Which means investigators rely on even more torture to get information, increasing the degree of brutality.

18 Finally, competition between intelligence agencies that conduct torture tears bureaucracies apart. Competition between intelligence agencies is a normal phenomenon, and usually a good one, producing multiple sources of information. But when agencies turn to torture, the competition to get first crack at the victim leads to unprofessional behavior and bureaucratic fragmentation. Brazilian police raided each other's prisons. The Nazi intelligence machine fragmented under the intense competition among the Kripo, Sipo, and regional Gestapos.

19 Is this way of applying pain more effective than other investigative methods? Torture is definitely inferior. The interrogation manual of Japanese fascists put it this way: "Care must be exercised when making use of rebukes, invectives, or torture as it will result in his telling falsehoods and making a fool of you." Torture "is only to be used when everything else has failed as it is the most clumsy [method]."

20 Since the 1970s, a large body of research has shown that unless the public specifically identifies suspects to the police, the chances that a crime will be solved falls to about 10 percent. Only a small percentage of crimes are discovered

NOTES

maximal (par. 15): ultimate

scattershot (par. 15): random

chap (par. 16): guy

zero-sum game (par. 16): a game or situation in which the winnings of some participants are exactly balanced by the losses of the other participants. When the total losses are subtracted from the total winnings, the sum is zero.

coercive (par. 17) threatening or forceful

phenomenon (par. 18) occurrence

Kripo, Sipo, and regional Gestapos (par. 18): various branches of the German secret police in charge of gathering information

fascists (par. 19): supporters of fascism (a system of government in which a dictator controls all aspects of national life)

rebukes (par. 19): criticisms

invectives (par. 19): abusive language

surveillance (par. 20): closely watching suspicious people or groups

or solved through surveillance, fingerprinting, DNA sampling, and offender profiling.

21   Police in long-term dictatorships like China and the Soviet Union also know the importance of public cooperation for solving crimes. Where they can't get public cooperation for certain crimes (such as against state property), they create an alternative human intelligence system—informants. Although such police states use torture for intimidation and false confessions, they also know that good intelligence requires humans willing to trust government enough to work with it.

22   Even guerrillas know this truth. An internal report from Iraq, quoted by Seymour Hersh in the May 24 *New Yorker*, states that the insurgents have depended mainly on "painstaking surveillance and reconnaissance" by the Iraqi police force, "which is rife with sympathy for the insurgents" and "proinsurgent individuals working within the (Coalition Provisional Authority's) so-called Green Zone." Not surprisingly, the insurgents' "strategic and operational intelligence has proven to be quite good."

23   Torture is a sign that a government either does not enjoy the trust of the people it governs or cannot recruit informers for a surveillance system. In both cases, torture to obtain information is a sign of institutional decay and desperation—as Saddam Hussein's Iraq clearly demonstrates. And torture accelerates this process, destroying the bonds of loyalty, respect, and trust that keep information flowing. As any remaining sources of intelligence dry up, governments have to torture even more.

24   But perhaps torture for something, anything, is better than sitting on one's hands. Maybe, somehow, one can retrieve a nugget of true information.

25   The problem is that "anything" needs to be verified, and as the Vietnam-era CIA Kubark manual explains, "a time-consuming delay results." In the meantime, the prisoner can think of new, more complex falsehoods. Intelligence gathering is especially vulnerable to this. In police work, the crime is already known; all one wants is the confession. But in intelligence, one must gather information about things that one does not know.

26   What's more, even prisoners who tell the truth under torture normally provide less detailed information than that obtainable through noncoercive interrogation. Damaged, sleep-deprived bodies remember information inaccurately, unable to make fine distinctions. Consider the case of a prisoner who wanted to tell the Chilean police an address: "Although I knew the street name, I had no idea of the number. Still furious, they realized that in truth I could not tell them where to go and once more they untied me."

NOTES

guerrillas (par. 22): members of small, unconventional combat units that use methods such as sabotage, kidnapping, ambush, assassination, and bombing to achieve their political goals

reconnaissance (par. 22): exploration of an area to gather military intelligence

rife with (par. 22): full of

Coalition Provisional Authority (par. 22): The government established by the United States after the end of Saddam Hussein's regime to maintain stability in Iraq until the establishment of an Iraqi civilian government.

Green Zone (par. 22): a four-mile zone in central Baghdad that is the main base for coalition authorities

27   Sometimes when prisoners provide true information, interrogators refuse to recognize it, since they assume most victims lie. So they continue torturing until they are satisfied. The notion that one will stop when one hears the right information presupposes that one has gathered circumstantial information that allows one to know the truth when one hears it. But that is precisely what does not happen with torture. Torturers spend so much time on torture that they have no time to gather supplementary evidence.

28   Finally, even when torturers think they know what they are looking for, they sometimes can't believe true information. One prisoner in Chile broke down several days into torture and revealed the names of the nuns and priests who had sheltered her. But the conservative and devout interrogators could not believe they were involved and continued torturing her.

29   What if time is short, as with a "ticking bomb"? Does torture offer a short-cut? Real torture—not the stuff of television—takes days, if not weeks. Even torturers know this. There are three things that limit torture's value in this context.

30   First, there is the medical limit. Physical methods, like psychological methods, take time. In the face of extreme pain, human beings faint and, as one French resistance fighter said, this "gives you a reprieve between blows" and delays interrogation. As the interrogation proceeds, victims become less sensitive to pain. After undergoing four torture sessions, a Norwegian resistance fighter concluded that "pain had reached its limit—when it could hurt no more, what did it matter how it was inflicted?" In addition, as torturers push harder, they sometimes cause inadvertent death. And dead men, like unconscious men, don't talk.

31   Second, there is the resource limit. For decades, guerrilla organizations have had "torture contracts" with their members: If you get arrested, keep the interrogators busy for 24 hours and let us change the passwords and locations. Give them false information mixed with half-truths. Make them waste their time and resources, and then after a day say whatever you want, since it will be useless then. Remember that you will become unconscious when the pain is extreme, and consider feigning unconsciousness.

32   Last, there's the psychological limit. The CIA Kubark manual notes that coercive investigation requires compiling a psychological profile, which can take days to write. Without a psychological profile, the manual says, torture is a "hit or miss" practice and "a waste of time and energy." Shot-in-the-dark torturing brings to mind the torturer's paradox. If he tortures first, he may be unable to get information by gentler means later. But if he tortures at the end, the prisoner may conclude that he is getting desperate and hold out longer.

NOTES

circumstantial (par. 27): detailed, specific

supplementary (par. 27): additional

"ticking bomb" (par. 29): a problem that will become dangerous if not addressed quickly

reprieve (par. 30): temporary relief

inflicted (par. 30): given out, administered

inadvertent (par. 30): unintended

feigning (par. 31): faking

paradox (par. 32): conflict between options

33   Hardcore believers, including presumably the common terrorist, don't break quickly. Torturing them just gives them an excuse to prove that they're stronger than you. Even the Gestapo discovered that with members of the resistance in World War II: Few resistance fighters gave accurate information.

34   In fact, as George Browder explains in his powerful book *Hitler's Enforcers,* "the Gestapo, like police anywhere, could not do its work without public support." The Gestapo's enormous success against the resistance, first in Germany and then elsewhere, depended heavily on bureaucratic files, police informants (G-men or V-men), and collaborators in foreign countries. "Increased reliance on interrogation through torture during the war years reflects the declining professionalism of an overextended staff much watered down with neophytes," Browder writes.

35   The priority in America's war on terror should be on developing human intelligence. Working one's way into a terror cell is not unlike working one's way into organized crime in the United States. One has to turn potential terrorists into double agents and to win the confidence and cooperation of the communities that shelter them. Technology is no substitute for this. Nor is torture.

36   Abu Ghraib should teach us what America's founders would have told us: that we are our own worst enemy. Leaders of dictatorships sign on to the Geneva Conventions only out of prudential fear of what other states might do to their POWs. Leaders of democracies sign on to them because they understand the evil that lurks in the heart of all human beings. Those who choose to abide by the rules do so not simply to restrain others but to restrain themselves.

37   Unrestrained power leaves behind a legacy of destruction that takes generations to undo. Torture, like incest, is the gift that keeps on giving. Democratic societies that legalized torture or tried to constrain its use have come to two ends. Some, like the Greeks and Romans, created tiered societies where authorities could torture whole classes of people (slaves or lesser citizens) and those who were beyond torture. Others, like the Italian city-states, were unable to prevent the executive branch from torturing more and more citizens and in the end fell to its dictatorial power.

38   The first result is hardly a model for modern democracies, and the second serves as a warning. In modern times, France routinized torture in Algeria, producing a racist, tiered society and an aggressive military government that almost overthrew French democracy. Proponents of torture would argue that destroying democratic institutions—and the individuals involved—is worth it if torture, as for the French in Algeria, succeeds in defeating terrorism.

NOTES

collaborators (par. 34): people who help an enemy force

neophytes (par. 34): beginners

double agents (par. 35): people who pretend to act as a spy for one group while actually acting as a spy for an opposing group

prudential (par. 36): sensible; reasonable

POWs (par. 36): Prisoners of War

lurks (par. 36): hides

legacy (par. 37): a tradition or belief handed down from generation to generation

constrain (par. 37): limit

II

Does Torture Work?

39   Torture apologists point to one powerful example to counter all the arguments against torture: the Battle of Algiers. In 1956, the Algerian FLN (National Liberation Front) began a terrorist bombing campaign in Algiers, the capital of Algeria, killing many innocent civilians. In 1957, Gen. Jacques Massu and the French government began a counterinsurgency campaign in Algiers using torture. As English military theorist Brian Crozier put it, "By such ruthless methods, Massu smashed the FLN organization in Algiers and re-established unchallenged French authority. And he did the job in seven months—from March to mid-October."

40   It is hard to argue with success. Here were professional torturers who produced consistently reliable information in a short time. It was a breathtaking military victory against terrorism by a democracy that used torture. Yet the French won by applying overwhelming force in an extremely constrained space, not by superior intelligence gathered through torture. As noted war historian John Keegan said in his recent study of military intelligence (*Intelligence in War: Knowledge of the Enemy from Napoleon to Al-Qaeda*), "it is force, not fraud or forethought, that counts" in modern wars.

41   The real significance of the Battle of Algiers, however, is the startling justification of torture by a democratic state. Algerian archives are now open, and many French torturers wrote their autobiographies in the 1990s. The story they tell will not comfort generals who tell self-serving stories of torture's success. In fact, the battle shows the devastating consequences of torture for any democracy foolish enough to institutionalize it.

42   Torture by the French failed miserably in Vietnam, and the French could never entirely secure the Algerian countryside, so either torture really did not work or there was some additional factor that made the difference in Algiers.

43   Among many torture apologists, only Gen. Massu, with characteristic frankness, identified the additional factor. In Vietnam, Massu said, the French posts were riddled with informants. Whatever the French found by torture, the Vietnamese opposition knew immediately. And long distances separated the posts. In Algiers, the casbah was a small space that could be cordoned off, and a determined settler population backed the army. The army was not riddled with informants, and the FLN never knew what the army was doing.

NOTES

Torture apologists (par. 39): people who defend or justify torture

counter (par. 39): oppose

counterinsurgency campaign (par. 39): military operations against an insurgency

fraud (par. 40): deception

archives (par. 41): historical records

casbah (par. 43): the Arab quarter of Algiers

cordoned off (par. 43): surrounded by the police or the military (in order to control movement in or out)

settler population (par. 43) Europeans who had themselves or whose ancestors had settled in Algeria during the period of French colonization and whose loyalties remained with France

44   And the French had an awesomely efficient informant system of their own. Massu took a census in the casbah and issued identity cards for the entire population. He ordered soldiers to paint numbers on each block of the casbah, and each block had a warden—usually a trustworthy Algerian—who reported all suspicious activities. Every morning, hooded informants controlled the exits to identify any suspects as they tried to leave. The FLN helped the French by calling a general strike, which revealed all its sympathizers. What made the difference for the French in Algiers was not torture, but the accurate intelligence obtained through public cooperation and informants.

45   In fact, no rank-and-file soldier has related a tale of how he personally, through timely interrogation, produced decisive information that stopped a ticking bomb. "As the pain of interrogation began," observed torturer Jean-Pierre Vittori, "they talked abundantly, citing the names of the dead or militants on the run, indicating locations of old hiding places in which we didn't find anything but some documents without interest." Detainees also provided names of their enemies—true information, but without utility to the French.

46   The FLN military men had also been told, when forced to talk, to give up the names of their counterparts in the rival organization, the more accommodationist MNA (National Algerian Movement). Not very knowledgeable in the subtleties of Algerian nationalism, the French soldiers helped the FLN liquidate the infrastructure of the more cooperative organization and tortured MNA members, driving them into extreme opposition.

47   Unlike in the famous movie, which portrays the Algerian population as united behind the FLN and assumes that torture is why the French won the battle, the real Battle of Algiers was a story of collaboration and betrayal by the local population. It was, as Alistair Horne describes in *A Savage War of Peace: Algeria 1954–1962*, a population that was cowed beyond belief and blamed the FLN leadership for having brought them to this pass.

48   Gen. Massu's strategy was not to go after the FLN bombers but to identify and disable anyone who was even remotely associated with the FLN. It was not a selective sweep. The smallest interrogation unit in Algiers possessed 100,000 files. Out of the casbah's total population of 80,000 citizens, Massu arrested 30 to 40 percent of all males.

49   Torture forced "loyal" Algerians to cooperate, but after the battle, they either ended their loyalty to France or were assassinated. Torture forced a politics of extremes, destroying the middle that had cooperated with the French. In the end,

NOTES

took a census (par. 44): recorded the name, gender, age, address, and so forth of each person

a warden (par. 44): an official

rank-and-file soldiers (par. 45): ordinary enlisted soldiers (as opposed to officers)

utility (par. 45): usefulness

accommodationist (par. 46): cooperative

subtleties (par. 46): the complicated and hidden nature

liquidate (par. 46): eliminate; kill

the infrastructure (par. 46): the basic organizational framework

cowed (par. 47): frightened

pass (par. 47): state of affairs

prefect (par. 49): head administrative official

there was no alternative to the FLN. As Paul Teitgin, the police prefect of Algiers, remarked, "Massu won the Battle of Algiers, but that meant losing the war."

50   The judicial system also collapsed under the weight of torture. Judges and prefects found themselves unable to deny warrants to armed men who tortured and killed for a living. Police records show that Teitgin issued 800 detention orders (*arrêtes d'assignation*) for eight months before the battle, 700 for the first three months of the battle, and then 4,000 a month for the remaining months. By the end of the battle, he had issued orders to detain 24,000, most of whom (80 percent of the men and 66 percent of the women) were routinely tortured.

51   And "what to do with these poor devils after their 'use'?" asked a French soldier. Many torturers preferred to kill them, though, one soldier conceded, genocide was difficult. "There isn't enough place in the prisons and one can't kill everyone . . ., so one releases them and they're going to tell others, and from mouth to mouth, the whole world knows." Then, he observed, their relatives and friends "join the resistance." By the end of the battle, about 13,000 Algerians (and some Frenchmen) were in detention camps and 3,000 "disappeared."

52   Doctors, whose task it was to monitor torture, were themselves corrupted by the torture. "Our problem is," remarked a doctor attached to a French torture unit, "should we heal this man who will again be tortured or let him die?" As oversight failed, the French military government arrested more people for flimsier reasons.

53   Use of torture also compromised the military. Lt. Col. Roger Trinquier, the famous French counterinsurgency expert, believed that torturers could act according to professional norms—applying only the pain necessary to get information and then stopping. But the stories of rank-and-file torturers confirm previous studies of the dynamics of torture. "I realized," remarked a French soldier, "that torture could become a drug. I understood then that it was useless to claim to establish limits and forbidden practices, i.e., yes to the electrotorture but without abusing it, any further no. In this domain also, it was all or nothing."

54   Torture drifted headlong into sadism, continuing long after valuable information could be retrieved. For example, soldiers arrested a locksmith and tortured him for three days. In his pocket, the locksmith had bomb blueprints with the address of an FLN bomb factory in Algiers. The locksmith bought time, the bombers relocated and the raid by the French three days later fell on open air. Had the soldiers been able to read Arabic, they would have found the bomb factory days earlier. But they were too busy torturing. As one would predict, engaging in torture prevented the use of ordinary—and more effective—policing skills. (Incidentally, the French could not believe that the most wanted man in the casbah had spent months only 200 yards from the headquarters of the army commandant.)

NOTES

warrants (par. 50): legal documents that authorize officials (usually police) to perform specific acts
conceded (par. 51): admitted
genocide (par. 51): the systematic elimination of an ethnic or racial group
compromised (par. 53): weakened the moral principles
domain (par. 53): situation

55   The French military also fragmented under the competition associated with torture. Parallel systems of administration emerged, and infighting occurred between the various intelligence agencies. Officers lost control of their charges, or the charges refused to follow higher command. And in the end, the soldiers blamed the generals for exposing them to torture, noting its pernicious effects on their lives, their families, and their friends—a sense of betrayal that has not diminished with the years.

56   Yves Godard, Massu's chief lieutenant, had insisted there was no need to torture. He suggested having the informant network identify operatives and then subject them to a simple draconian choice: Talk or die. This would have produced the same result as torture without damage to the army.

57   The British successfully used precisely this strategy with German spies during World War II. British counterespionage managed to identify almost every German spy without using torture—not just the 100 who hid among the 7,000 to 9,000 refugees coming to England to join their armies in exile each year, not just the 120 who arrived in similar fashion from friendly countries, but also the 70 sleeper cells that were in place before 1940. Only three agents eluded detection; five others refused to confess. Many Germans chose to become double agents rather than be tried and shot. They radioed incorrect coordinates for German V missiles, which landed harmlessly in farmers' fields. But for this misdirection, British historian Keegan concludes, in October 1944 alone close to 1,300 people would have died, with 10,000 more injured and 23,000 houses destroyed.

58   The U.S. Army's field manual for intelligence (FM34-52) notes that simple direct questioning of prisoners was 85 percent to 95 percent effective in World War II and 90 to 95 percent effective in the Vietnam War. What about those 5 percent at the margin? Couldn't savage, unprofessional, hit-or-miss torture yield some valuable information from them? Actually, there was one case in the Battle of Algiers in which torture did reveal important information.

59   In September 1957, in the last days of the battle, French soldiers detained a messenger known as "Djamal." Under torture, Djamal revealed where the last FLN leader in Algiers lay hidden. But that wasn't so important; informants had identified this location months before. The important information Djamal

NOTES

pernicious (par. 55): destructive

operatives (par. 56): people gathering intelligence

draconian (par. 56): extremely severe

counterespionage (par. 57): the part of the government dedicated to discovering enemy spies within the country

in exile (par. 57): living away from one's native country

sleeper cells (par. 57): a small group of people associated with an enemy who hide within an enemy population until they receive orders to take action against the foreign group

eluded (par. 57): escaped

coordinates (par. 57): a set of numbers that indicates a specific location

the Fourth Republic (par. 59): the period between 1946 and 1958, when France operated under its fourth constitution

coup (par. 59): government takeover by the military

President De Gaulle (par. 59): President of France from 1958–1969, De Gualle was a war hero from the Second World War and perhaps the most influential French politician of the 1900s.

revealed was that the French government had misled the military and was quietly negotiating a peace settlement with the FLN. This was shocking news. It deeply poisoned the military's relationship with the civilian government, a legacy that played no small part in the collapse of the Fourth Republic in May 1958 and in the attempted coup by some French military officers against President De Gaulle in April 1961.

60   The French won the Battle of Algiers primarily through force, not by superior intelligence gathered through torture. Whoever authorized torture in Iraq undermined the prospect of good human intelligence. Even if the torture at Abu Ghraib served to produce more names ("actionable intelligence") and recruit informants, torture in the end polarized the population, eliminating the middle that might cooperate. Dividing the world into "friends" and "enemies," those who are with us or against us, meant that we lost the cooperation of those who wished to be neither or who were enemies of our enemies.

61   Whoever authorized torture in Afghanistan and Iraq also destroyed the soldiers who were ordered to perform it. Studies of torturers show that they would rather work as killers on death squads, where the work is easier. Torture is hard, stressful work. Many torturers develop emotional problems, become alcoholics, beat their families, and harbor a deep sense of betrayal toward the military brass that hangs them out to twist in the wind. The soldiers at Abu Ghraib had dreams, dreams that democracy promised to fulfill, dreams that now may never be fulfilled thanks to the arrogance of their superiors.

62   Those who authorize torture need to remember that it isn't something that simply happens in some other country. Soldiers trained in stealthy techniques of torture take these techniques back into civilian life as policemen and private security guards. It takes years to discover the effects of having tortured. Americans' use of electric torture in Vietnam appeared in Arkansas prisons in the 1960s and in Chicago squad rooms in the 1970s and 1980s.

63   Likewise, the excruciating water tortures U.S. soldiers used in the Spanish-American War appeared in American policing in the next two decades. For those who had been tortured, it was small comfort when, on Memorial Day 1902, President Roosevelt regretted the "few acts of cruelty" American troops had performed.

64   Some believe that judges can issue selective torture warrants to security officers in important cases. But the rapid increase in the number of torture warrants issued during the Battle of Algiers is evidence enough that civil servants can exercise little selective control once they have licensed unlimited power.

65   Others believe that torture occasionally is necessary and that when it is, one should have to answer for one's actions before the law. But "morally justified"

NOTES

polarized (par. 60): caused everyone to take sides

hangs them out to twist in the wind (par. 61): abandons them (The expression is a reference to the corpse of a hanged person left dangling and turning in the air.)

excruciating (par. 63): extremely painful

Spanish-American War (par. 63): War between the U.S. and Spain, which occurred in 1898 and resulted in the U.S. receiving several Spanish colonies

scrutiny (par. 65): close examination

torture does not resemble morally justified civil disobedience. Civil rights protesters break the law in public and then submit their behavior to juries and
courts. But I know of no modern torturer who voluntarily submitted to public
scrutiny and took the heat. Like boasts of bravery, this opinion is too easy to
hold when there is no danger of it being tested. Modern torturers operate in
secrecy and specialize in techniques that leave no marks. What would we really
know of Abu Ghraib in the absence of the photographs?

66   And once soldiers get away with torture, they repeat it. Few things predict
future torture as much as past impunity.

67   It is easy to criticize the leaders and torture apologists who misled us and
continue to do so. What is harder is to determine how to repair the damage.
One crazy man can block the well, but it takes the whole village to remove the
stone, an Iranian proverb says.

68   We can learn from the mistakes of other democracies that have tortured.
These democracies lost their wars because the brutality they licensed reduced
their intelligence, compromised their allies and corrupted their military and
government, and they could not come to terms with that.

69   When the politicians first heard of the torture, they denied it happened,
minimized the violence, and called it ill treatment. When the evidence
mounted, they tried a few bad apples, disparaged the prisoners, and observed
that terrorists had done worse things. They justified the torture as effective
and necessary for the extreme circumstances and countercharged that critics
were aiding the enemy. As time passed, they offered apologies but accepted no
consequences and argued that there was no point in dwelling on past events.

70   The torture continued because these democrats could not institutionally
recommit themselves to limited power at home or abroad. The torture interrogations yielded the predictable results, and the democracies remained mired
in their wars despite overwhelming military superiority against a far smaller
enemy. Soon the politicians had to choose between losing their democracy
and losing their war. That is how democracies lose wars.

NOTES

impunity (par. 66): lack of punishment
disparaged (par. 69): spoke negatively about
mired (par. 70): trapped

Textbook
Chapters

Presidency in Crisis

Policies of the Nixon, Ford, and Carter Administrations 1968–1980

Joseph R. Conlin

from
**The American Past:
A Survey of American History**

Seventh Edition

PRESIDENCY IN CRISIS

The Nixon, Ford, and Carter Administrations 1968–1980

Official White House Photo

In a country where there is no hereditary throne nor hereditary aristocracy, an office raised far above all other offices offers too great a stimulus to ambition. This glittering prize, always dangling before the eyes of prominent statesmen, has a power stronger than any dignity under a European crown to lure them from the path of straightforward consistency.

James Lord Bryce

Americans expect their presidents to do what no monarch by Divine Right could ever do—resolve for them all the contradictions and complexities of life.

Robert T. Hartmann

THE HEROES OF Greek myth were constantly pursuing Proteus, the herdsman of the seas, for he could foresee the future and, if captured, had to reveal what he knew. Proteus was rarely caught. He also had the power to assume the shape of any creature, enabling him to wriggle out of his pursuers' grasp.

Richard Milhous Nixon, his enemies said, was never quite captured because he was always changing his shape. John Kennedy said that Nixon pretended to be so many different people that he had forgotten who he was. Liberals called him "Tricky Dicky." At several turns of his career, even his Republican boosters were constrained to assure Americans that the "Old Nixon" was no more; it was a "New Nixon" who was running for office.

The "Real Nixon," like the real Proteus, remained elusive and enigmatic to the end. Senator Barry Goldwater said that Richard Nixon was "the most complete loner I've ever known."

THE NIXON PRESIDENCY

Nixon is a compelling historical figure. He lacked the personal qualities thought essential to success in late-twentieth-century politics: He was not physically attractive; he lacked social grace, wit, and "charisma." No one ever said of him, "He's a nice guy." Nixon was shy; his manner was furtive. He disguised his discomfort in front of a crowd by willing it, by changing his shape.

Odd Duck

The liberals' dislike of Nixon had the intensity of a hatred, but those who hated the liberals did not love Nixon. President

Affirmative Action

Originally, as Lyndon Johnson defined it in coining the phrase, "affirmative action" was an admonition to employers and universities to be aggressive in recruiting members of racial minorities and women as a way of righting past wrongs. By the 1980s, affirmative action had come to mean giving preference in employment and admission to educational institutions to women, African Americans, Hispanics, Indians, and Pacific Islanders. As such, by 1990 it was a defining position of the "politically correct," especially academics and university administrators. They were so determined to preserve preferences in admissions policies that when courts and referenda struck down their affirmative action programs, they contrived convoluted schemes by which to preserve racial preferences while adhering to the letter of the law. (Before 2000, the numbers of white women in virtually all educational programs made them victims, rather than beneficiaries, of affirmative action.)

Affirmative action never had widespread support. Public opinion polls revealed that a majority of every group affected by it, both groups discriminated against (whites, Asian Americans, males) and those that benefited (African Americans, Hispanics, women) opposed race- or gender-based preferences. Because Democratic candidates for public office could not afford to oppose affirmative action vigorously (they needed the "politically correct" voters), the issue probably contributed to the decline of the party at the turn of the century.

Ironically, Republicans, not Democrats, were responsible for the reinterpretation of affirmative action to mean preferential treatment. In the Nixon administration, federal agencies were instructed that they were to favor businesses owned by members of minority groups when doling out federal contracts. Republican political strategists understood that in helping to create more wealthy African American and Hispanic businesspeople, they were creating voters and campaign contributors for whom Republican probusiness policies trumped Democratic sentiments based on race and gender. The percentage of African Americans voting Republican remained small during the 1990s but grew annually as the numbers of wealthy and middle-class black people increased. Affirmative action never affected voting patterns among women; women remained just about evenly divided between the two major parties, as they had been since 1920.

Eisenhower came within a hair of dumping him as his running mate in 1952 and considered replacing him in 1956. In 1960, when Nixon was running for president by emphasizing his experience, Ike humiliated him by saying he was unable to recall an instance in which Nixon contributed to an important decision.

The right-wing Republicans Nixon served well for two decades accepted his leadership without trusting him. When Nixon faced the premature end of his presidency, aides who owed their careers to him stumbled over one another in their haste to turn on him. All was forgiven at his funeral in 1994: Eulogists focused on his achievements, which were numerous, one momentous. Aside from his daughters, however, no one at the memorial ceremonies at Nixon's boyhood home in Whittier, California, spoke of him with affection.

Richard Nixon clawed his way from a middle-class background in southern California to the top of the heap through hard work and the tenacious bite of a pit bull. Although he overstated it in his autobiographical *Six Crises,* he overcame formidable obstacles. If the self-made Horatio Alger boy is an American hero, Nixon belongs in the pantheon, for he was all pluck and little luck. Whatever else historians may say of Richard Nixon, he earned everything he ever got.

Political Savvy

President Nixon had little interest in domestic matters. He believed that "the country could run itself domestically without a president." He left all but the most important decisions to two young White House aides, H. R. Haldeman and John Ehrlichman. With a studied arrogance that amused them, Haldeman and Ehrlichman insulated Nixon from Congress and sometimes from his cabinet. They were themselves unpopular. Like Nixon, they would have few friends when the roof collapsed on the administration.

Politicking, which Nixon never enjoyed, he left to Vice President Spiro T. Agnew, a former governor of Maryland whom Nixon named to the ticket to attract the blue-collar and ethnic voters whom third-party George Wallace was trying to seduce. Agnew was an energetic campaigner and relished his role as Nixon's hit man. He stormed around the country delighting Republican conservatives by flailing antiwar students and the weak-willed, overpaid educators who indulged them in their disruptive activities. He excoriated liberal Supreme Court justices and the news media. Agnew was fond of tongue-twisting alliteration. His masterpiece was "nattering nabobs of negativism," that is, journalists.

Agnew's liberal baiting provided Nixon with a superb smoke screen, for, despite his many denunciations of big-spending liberal government, the president had no interest in dismantling the bureaucracies the Great Society had created. His only major modification of Lyndon Johnson's welfare state was the "New Federalism": turning federal revenues over to the states so that they could run social programs. The New Federalism actually increased the overall size of the nation's government bureaucracies and the inefficiency and waste inevitable in large organizations.

On other fronts, Nixon might as well have been a Democrat. He sponsored a scheme for welfare reform, the Family Assistance Plan, that was to provide a flat annual payment to poor households if their breadwinners registered with employment agencies. (It failed in Congress.) When, in 1971, Nixon worried that a jump in inflation might threaten his reelection the following year, he slapped on wage and price controls, a Republican anathema since World War II.

And yet, Democrats could not gloat, and few Republicans yelped. Nixon understood that the people who ran his party cared only about power and business-friendly government. The grassroots "conservatives" he called the "silent majority" were largely indifferent, or even favorable, toward liberal economic policies. They were repelled by the social

Official White House Photo

▲ *President Nixon in the Oval Office with his young aides, H. R. Haldeman (foreground) and John Ehrlichman (seated, rear). Nixon secretly recorded his conversations in his inner sanctum. His decision to do so was curious, if for no other reason than because the tapes revealed him to be foul mouthed. In the end, proof on the recordings of his implication in criminal activities destroyed him.*

and cultural causes that 1970s liberals embraced; by what they considered kid-gloves treatment of African Americans; by assaults on traditional moral codes by feminists and gay rights activists; by the anti-Americanism prominent in the antiwar movement and, increasingly, preached by liberal academics; and by Supreme Court decisions they said hobbled police in dealing with criminals.

The Warren Court

Fourteen associate justices served with Chief Justice Earl Warren between 1953 and 1969, many of them at odds with him. Nevertheless, the label "Warren Court" had some justification. Under Warren, the Supreme Court practiced "judicial activism" (reading new meanings into the Constitution in order to ensure justice and fairness by contemporary standards) as opposed to "judicial restraint" (adhering strictly to the meaning of those who wrote the Constitution and its amendments). Judicial activism, its critics said, turned the Court into a legislative body serving political ends. Judicial restraint required the justices to refuse to hear cases involving political issues and to apply the letter of the law to the cases they judged.

The first important decision of the Supreme Court under Warren, *Brown v. Board of Education of Topeka* (1954), faintly presaged the Warren Court's character. In ruling that

segregation of public schools by race was unconstitutional, *Brown* drew on contemporary sociological and psychological sources to interpret the equality clause of the Fourteenth Amendment. Putting African Americans in separate schools, the Court said, was unequal treatment because, no matter how well funded their schools were, segregation fixed in black pupils a sense of their inferior status in society.

Segregationists (and some legal experts who abhorred segregation) said that, in *Brown,* the Court was making law,

Griswold and Roe

A Warren Court decision that was to open a can of political worms only after Warren's retirement was Griswold v. Connecticut (1965). It asserted an individual's right to privacy, a very broad reading of the Constitution, on the grounds that the enumerated rights in the Bill of Rights had "penumbras" that provided constitutional standing to practices not mentioned in the Constitution.

In Roe v. Wade (1973), four years after Warren retired, the Court drew on Griswold (and other precedents) to rule that state legislatures could not deny a woman's right to an abortion. Ironically, the opinion was written by a justice Nixon had appointed to bring judicial restraint to the Supreme Court, with the concurrence of Warren Burger, whom Nixon named to replace Earl Warren.

infringing on powers the Constitution reserved to legislative bodies. The complaint was not new. In 1905, progressives had protested when a pro-employer Supreme Court struck down a New York law forbidding child labor. Liberals howled in 1935 when business-minded justices declared two New Deal programs unconstitutional. The new twist after 1954 was that progressives and liberals celebrated the Warren Court's judicial activism, whereas conservatives (soon mostly Republicans) wrung their hands in dismay.

A series of Warren Court decisions concerning the rights of people accused of crimes caused another uproar. Culminating in *Miranda v. Arizona* (1966), the Warren Court ruled that evidence of a crime seized in a search could not be used against a defendant unless it had been specifically described in the search warrant; that even an obviously guilty criminal had to be freed if police, while questioning him, denied him access to a lawyer; and that, when making an arrest, police were required to explain that the Fifth Amendment protection against self-incrimination permitted the accused criminal to refuse to answer any questions put to him. The Court's decisions were based more on the questions "Is it fair?" and "Does it protect the individual?" than "Does the Constitution explicitly forbid it?" *Miranda,* for example, discarded the principle taught schoolchildren for a generation that "ignorance of the law is no excuse."

When, in 1968, Chief Justice Warren feared that Nixon (whom he despised) would win the presidential election, he resigned so that President Johnson could name his successor. Johnson blundered. He promoted a Texas crony already on the Court, Abe Fortas, to the chief justiceship. Republicans almost immediately discredited Fortas by revealing that he had accepted fees for public appearances that were, at best, dubious. Warren remained to preside at Nixon's inauguration and was only then replaced by Warren Burger, a proponent of judicial restraint.

NIXON AND VIETNAM

Nixon had watched the Vietnam War prematurely terminate Lyndon Johnson's political career. "The damned fool" Johnson had, in the words of a protest song, mired the country "hip deep in the Big Muddy" and was helpless to do anything but to tell the nation to "push on." Nixon had bigger fish to fry. He wanted out of the war. But how? The North Vietnamese refused to negotiate.

Vietnamization

Nixon's objection to the war was political. By sending a huge army to Vietnam, which sustained high casualties without making discernible progress, Johnson had transformed an annoying but marginal antiwar movement into massive disillusionment with the adventure. In order to isolate the hard-core protesters from the majority of the population, he assigned Spiro Agnew the job of smearing the militants as anti-American, while he reduced American casualties by turning the war over to the South Vietnamese.

> **Cleanup**
> In 1912, the Chicago Sanitation Department cleared the streets of the carcasses of 10,000 dead horses. In 1968, the Chicago Police Department cleared the streets of 24,500 carcasses of dead automobiles.

The United States would "participate in the defense and development of allies and friends," he said, but Americans would no longer "undertake all the defense of the free nations of the world." Nixon opted for "Vietnamization" of the war. "In the previous administration," he explained, "we Americanized the war in Vietnam. In this administration we are Vietnamizing the search for peace."

The large but unreliable Army of the Republic of Vietnam (ARVN) was retrained to replace Americans on the bloody front lines. As South Vietnamese units were deemed ready for combat, American troops came home. At about the same rate that LBJ had escalated the American presence, Nixon de-escalated it. From a high of 541,000 American soldiers in South Vietnam when Nixon took office, the American force declined to 335,000 in 1970 and 24,000 in 1972.

Nixon returned the American role in the war to where it had been in 1964. The trouble was that, in 1964, North Vietnamese troops in South Vietnam had been minimal; by 1970, they were the enemy. As Nixon hoped, the influence of the student antiwar movement declined. What he did not anticipate was that another less theatrical, but far more formidable, opposition emerged. Mainstream Democrats who had dutifully supported Johnson's war, including congressmen and senators, now demanded that the Republican Nixon make more serious efforts to negotiate an end to it.

Expansion of the War

Even Republican senator George Aiken suggested that the United States simply declare victory and pull out of Vietnam. Nixon could not go as far as that. He was beholden for his election to "hawks" who believed that Johnson failed in Vietnam because he had not been tough enough. Nixon reassured them: "We will not be humiliated. We will not be defeated." As much as he and his personal foreign policy guru, Henry A. Kissinger, wanted done with the war, they believed they had to salvage the independence of South Vietnam in order to save face.

So, while Nixon reduced the American presence in Vietnam, he tried to bludgeon North Vietnam into negotiations by expanding the scope of the war with low-casualty air attacks. In the spring of 1969, he sent bombers over neutral Cambodia to destroy sanctuaries where about 50,000 North Vietnamese troops rested between battles. For a year, the American people knew nothing of this new war. Then, in 1970, Nixon sent ground forces into Cambodia, an action that could not be concealed.

The result was renewed uproar. Critics condemned the president for attacking a neutral nation. Several hundred university presidents closed their campuses for fear of student violence. Events at two colleges proved their wisdom. At Kent State University in Ohio, the National Guard opened fire on demonstrators, killing four and wounding eleven. Ten days later, although the issue was not clearly the war, two students demonstrating at Jackson State College in Mississippi were killed by police.

Congress reacted to the widening of the war by repealing the Gulf of Tonkin Resolution. Nixon responded that repeal was immaterial. As commander in chief, he had the right to take whatever military action he believed necessary. Nonetheless, when the war was further expanded into Laos in February 1971, ARVN troops carried the burden of the fighting.

Falling Dominoes

Vietnamization did not work. Without American troops by their side, the ARVN was humiliated in Laos. The Communist organization in that country, the Pathet Lao, grew in strength until, in 1975, it seized control of the country. Tens of thousands of refugees fled.

In Cambodia, the consequences were worse. Many young Cambodians were so angered by the American bombing that they flocked to join the Khmer Rouge, which increased in size from 3,000 in 1970 to 30,000 in a few years. In 1976, the commander, Pol Pot, came to power with a regime as criminal as the Nazi government of Germany. In three years, Pol Pot's fanatical followers murdered 3 million people in a population of 7.2 million!

Eisenhower's Asian dominoes had fallen not because the United States was weak in the face of a military threat but because the United States had endlessly expanded a war that, in 1963, was little more than a brawl. In the process, Indochinese neutrals like Cambodia's Prince Sihanouk were undercut. By the mid-1970s, North Vietnam was dominated by militarists; Laos, by a small Communist organization; and Cambodia, by a monster.

In South Vietnam, the fighting dragged on until the fall of 1972, when, after suffering 12 days of earthshaking bombing, the North Vietnamese finally agreed to meet with Kissinger and arrange a cease-fire. They signed the Paris Accords, which went into effect in January 1973. The treaty required the United States to withdraw all troops from Vietnam within 60 days and the North Vietnamese to release the prisoners of war they held. Until free elections were held, North Vietnamese troops could remain in South Vietnam.

South Vietnamese president Nguyen Van Thieu believed he had been sold out. Nixon had left him facing a massive enemy force. For two years, the country simmered. In April 1975, the ARVN collapsed, and the North Vietnamese moved on a virtually undefended Saigon. North and South Vietnam were united, Saigon renamed Ho Chi Minh City. Ironically, Cambodia's nightmare ended only when the North Vietnamese invaded the country, overthrew Pol Pot, and installed a puppet regime.

The Bottom Line

America's longest war ravaged a prosperous country. Once an exporter of rice, Vietnam was short of food through the 1980s. About a million ARVN soldiers lost their lives, the Vietcong and North Vietnamese about the same number. Estimates of civilian dead ran as high as 3.5 million. About 5.2 million acres of jungle and farmland were ruined by defoliation. American bombing also devastated hundreds of cities, towns, bridges, and highways. The air force dropped more bombs on Vietnam than on Europe during World War II.

The vengeance of the victors (and Pol Pot) caused a massive flight of refugees. About 10 percent of the people of Southeast Asia fled after the war. Some spent everything they owned to bribe venal North Vietnamese officials to let them go. Others piled into leaky boats and cast off into open waters, unknown numbers to drown. To the credit of the United States, some 600,000 Vietnamese, Laotians, Cambodians, and ethnic minorities like the Hmong and Mien (whom every government in Southeast Asia mistreated) were admitted to the United States.

The war cost the United States $150 billion, more than any other American conflict except World War II. Some 2.7 million American men and women served in the conflict; 57,000 of them were killed, and 300,000 were wounded. Many men were disabled for life. Some lost limbs; others were poisoned by Agent Orange, the toxic defoliant the army used to clear jungle. Yet others were addicted to drugs or alcohol. Mental disturbances and violent crime were alarmingly common among Vietnam veterans.

And yet, for 10 years, Vietnam veterans were ignored and shunned. Politicians, not only liberals who opposed the war but also the superpatriotic hawks who wanted the troops to fight on indefinitely, neglected to vote money for government programs to help them. Only in 1982, almost a decade after the war ended, was a monument to the soldiers erected in Washington, D.C.

Principled Foreign Policy

So bitter was the American defeat in Vietnam that, as late as 1990, the United States officially insisted that Pol Pot was the legal ruler of Cambodia. In 1991, the United States engineered a settlement in which the murderous Khmer Rouge shared in the government of the nation.

NIXON-KISSINGER FOREIGN POLICY

Nixon called the Vietnam war a "sideshow." Henry A. Kissinger said that it was a mere "footnote to history." Both men wanted to bring the conflict to an end so that they could bring about a complete reordering of relations among the world's great powers.

▲ *Vietnamese refugees fleeing Hue during the final victory of the Vietcong and North Vietnamese in 1975. Ten percent of the population eventually fled the country. The United States admitted 600,000 refugees as immigrants.*

The Long Crusade

For more than 20 years before the Nixon presidency, virtually all American policy makers divided the world into two hostile camps and a "Third World" of unaligned, mostly undeveloped states. Nuclear weapons made all-out conflict between the United States and the Soviet Union unthinkable except if the only alternative was the annihilation of just one of them. Ideology made antagonism and mistrust inevitable. The only prospect for change was the peaceful internal collapse of one of the superpowers.

Before he was elected president, Nixon expressed nothing to indicate that he imagined another possibility, but when the opportunity for a revolution in American foreign policy presented itself, he seized it.

Premises of Détente

Nixon recognized that the world had changed significantly since the beginning of the Cold War and his political career. The bipolar view of geopolitics had become obsolete with Japan, once a docile American dependency, now the world's third largest economic power; the nations of western Europe groping their way toward unity and an independent economic, political, and military role; and the People's Republic of China, if it was ever subservient to the Soviet Union, no longer so. Reports had reached the West of Chinese-Soviet battles on their 2,000-mile border.

Nixon meant to win his niche in history by effecting a diplomatic reshuffling after which the *five* centers of power dealt with one another rationally and, therefore, with a modicum of confidence. In 1971, he said, "It will be a safer world and a better world, if we have a strong and healthy United States, Europe, Soviet Union, China, Japan—each balancing the other, not playing one against the other, an even balance."

There was no idealism in Nixon's goal of détente (relaxation of tensions). He prided himself on being a hardheaded realist and chose another, Henry Kissinger, as his in-house adviser on foreign policy, who probably introduced the president to the French word that he attached to his policy.

Kissinger on the Cold War

Commenting on relations between the United States and the Soviet Union, Henry Kissinger said:

The superpowers often behave like two heavily armed blind men feeling their way around a room, each believing himself in mortal peril from the other whom he assumes to have perfect vision. . . . Each tends to ascribe to the other side a consistency, foresight and coherence that its own experience belies. Of course, over time even two blind men can do enormous damage to each other, not to speak of the room.

▲ *Henry Kissinger, President Nixon's foreign policy advisor and then his Secretary of State, cultivated the image of a ladies' man on the Washington social scene. His escorts were inevitably glamorous like actress Shirley MacLaine.*

Kissinger was a witty, urbane, brilliant, and cheerfully conceited refugee from Nazism. Although he had lived in the United States for 30 years, his German accent was as thick as if he had just flown in from Frankfurt, which led some of his critics to see it as just another of his many affectations. There was nothing affected in his dedication to *Realpolitik*—the amoral, opportunistic approach to diplomacy associated with Kissinger's historical idol, Count Otto von Bismarck. Kissinger believed that the leaders of the Soviet Union and China were as little concerned with ideals and sentiments as he and Nixon were. They only needed encouragement to launch a new era. His calculation was dramatically confirmed in 1971, when the Vietnam War was still raging and the ripest of denunciations were still flying among Chinese, Russians, and Americans.

Rapprochement with China

Once the Korean War was concluded, the only contacts between China and the United States had been mutual imprecations. Then, in 1971, an American table-tennis team touring Japan received an invitation from the People's Republic to fly over and play a few games before returning home. Thus were diplomatic signals conveyed in the East.

Kissinger virtually commanded the Ping-Pong players to go (they were trounced—the Chinese could not have been expected to pick basketball) and opened talks with Chinese diplomats. He flew secretly to Beijing, where he arranged for a goodwill tour of China by Nixon himself. Only then was the astonishing news released: The lifelong scourge of Red China would tour the Forbidden City, view the Great Wall, and sit down with chopsticks at a Mandarin banquet with Chairman Mao Zedong and Chou En-lai, drinking toasts to Chinese-American amity with fiery Chinese spirits.

In fact, Nixon's meeting with Mao was ceremonial; the chairman was senile. However, Chou (who, it turned out, had long advocated better relations with the United States) was still alert and active. His protégés, Hua Kuo-feng (who succeeded Mao in 1976) and Deng Xiaoping (who had done time for advocating quasi-capitalist economic reforms) reassured Nixon that he had calculated correctly in coming to China.

Chinese students were invited to study at American universities, and China opened its doors to American tourists, who came by the tens of thousands, clambering up the Great Wall and buying red-ribboned trinkets by the ton. American businessmen involved in everything from oil exploration to the bottling of soft drinks flew to China, anxious to sell American technology and consumer goods in the market that had long symbolized the traveling salesman's ultimate territory. The United States dropped its veto of Communist China's claim to a seat in the United Nations (an absurd position from the start) and established a legation in Beijing. In 1979, the two countries established full diplomatic relations.

Soviet Policy

China did not prove much of a customer. Japan grabbed the market in electronic consumer baubles; Japan already owned the American market! Before long, the Chinese were cutting into America's sales elsewhere of films, recordings, and other popular entertainments by making unauthorized "bootleg" copies. The impelling motive of the Chinese in courting the United States was not economic exchange but China's chilly relations with the Soviet Union. They were "playing the America card."

That was all right with Nixon and Kissinger. They were "playing the China card," putting the fear of a cozy Chinese-American relationship into the Soviets. The gambit worked. In June 1972, just months after his China trip, Nixon flew to Moscow and signed an agreement to open what came to be called the Strategic Arms Limitation Talks (usually known as "SALT"), the first significant step toward slowing down the arms race since the Kennedy administration.

At home, the photos of Nixon clinking champagne glasses with Mao and hugging Brezhnev bewildered right-wing Republicans and flummoxed Nixon's liberal critics. In fact, as Nixon understood, only a Republican like himself with impeccable Cold Warrior credentials could have accomplished what he did.

Shuttle Diplomacy

Nixon was grateful to Kissinger and, in 1973, named him secretary of state. For a year, Kissinger's diplomatic successes piled up. His greatest triumph came in the Middle East after the Yom Kippur War of 1973, in which Egypt and Syria attacked Israel and, for the first time in the long Arab-Israeli conflict, fought the Israelis to a draw.

▲ *President and Mrs. Nixon at the Great Wall of China. All Americans were astonished by such photographs. Hard-line Republican Cold Warriors were flabbergasted. For more than a quarter century, Americans had been told that Communist China was an outlaw nation.*

Knowing that the Israelis were not inclined to accept less than victory and fearing what a prolonged war in the oil-rich Middle East would mean for the United States, Kissinger shuttled, seemingly without sleep, between Syria, Egypt, and Israel, carrying proposal and counterproposal for a settlement. Unlike Dulles, who had also represented American interests on the fly, Kissinger was an ingratiating diplomat. He ended the war, winning the gratitude of Egyptian president Anwar Sadat while not alienating Israel.

After 1974, Kissinger lost his magic touch, in part because of revived world tensions that were not his doing. Soviet premier Leonid Brezhnev may have wanted to reduce the chance of a direct conflict between Russia and the United States. However, he was enough of an old Bolshevik to continue aiding guerrilla movements in Africa and Latin America. Cuba's Fidel Castro, with a large army to keep in trim, loaned combat troops to several countries, notably Angola in southwestern Africa.

Nixon and Kissinger were also willing to fight the Cold War by proxy in the Third World, competing with the Soviets for spheres of influence. Although right-wing Republicans opposed to détente stepped up their attacks on Kissinger, he was actually pursuing their kind of confrontational policies in strife-torn countries like Angola.

The most damaging mark on Kissinger's record as the diplomat in chief of a democratic country was revealed in 1974. The previous year, he had covertly aided, and may have

instigated, a coup by the military in Chile that overthrew and murdered the president, Salvador Allende. Allende was a championship-caliber bungler; but he was also Chile's democratically elected leader, and his American-backed successor, Augusto Pinochet, instituted a barbaric and brutal regime marked by torture and murder of opponents.

WATERGATE AND GERALD FORD

By 1974, when news of the Pinochet connection broke in the United States, Kissinger was no longer serving Richard Nixon. The crisis of the presidency that began when Lyndon Johnson was repudiated became graver when Nixon was forced to resign in disgrace. The debacle had its beginnings in the election campaign of 1972, in which, thanks to the transformation of the Democratic party, victory was in Nixon's pocket from the start.

A New Definition of Liberalism

Between 1968 and 1972, privileged "New Age" liberals, dedicated to the antiwar movement, sympathetic to minorities, and enthusiastic about women's liberation, gay rights, and other lifestyle issues, rather than New Deal concerns for working people, won control of several key Democratic party

■ **HOW THEY LIVED** ■

Sex: From No-No to Obsession

The traditional American code of sexual morality—a middle-class code—was Christian sexual morality plus the prohibition, in polite society, of talking about sex in any way but with euphemisms. Nineteenth-century bowdlerizers deleted the earthiness from Shakespeare and published Bibles heavily edited for the abstemious.

Total ignorance of sexual mechanics was not uncommon among the daughters of the hyperrespectable "Victorian" middle and upper classes. Diaries and memoirs reveal that many a bride was shocked on her wedding night. Some brides-to-be who were taken aside by an older sister before the nuptials and informed of what the honeymoon held in store thought that they were the victims of a crude joke. The "double standard" allowed young men to be better educated. Thought to be slaves of irresistible urges, men were not "ruined" by "sowing wild oats."

The traditional sexual code forbade masturbation, fornication, adultery, and, within marriage, oral and anal sex. Homosexuality was "the sin that dare not speak its name." By 1900, most states had laws making these acts and pornography criminal as well as immoral. Anthony Comstock, head of the New York Society for the Suppression of Vice, was pathologically obsessed with sex. In 1873, he succeeded in promoting a federal law that, on the face of it, forbade mailing information about contraception but that was employed against anything sexual of which "Comstockery" disapproved.

The code was no more a reflection of actual practice than laws forbidding theft meant there was no embezzlement, robbery, or burglary in America. Some daughters of the middle class had illegitimate babies, although they were kept secret if the family could afford to send the mother to be on an extended visit with "an aunt." It is impossible to know how widespread adultery was. It made the newspapers only when an irate husband killed the man who had cuckolded him, the lovers did away with the superfluous husband, or adultery was cited as grounds in a celebrated divorce.

The code began to totter at the turn of the twentieth century, when jobs and bright lights attracted respectable young women to the big city. Freed from family supervision, they "dated" young men without chaperones, and some, the sexual urge being what it is, experimented. American women born after 1900, maturing during the Roaring '20s, indulged in premarital sex far more often than their mothers had. If traditional sexual morals did not restrain a woman, the only powerful deterrent to enjoying a "liberated" sex life was the fear of pregnancy. Margaret Sanger, who devoted her life to disseminating information about birth control and contraceptive devices, was harassed not so much because she wanted to spare married women the constant pregnancies that impoverished them and ruined their health—which was Sanger's goal—but because of the (justified) belief that knowledge of contraception encouraged unmarried women and girls to tread where they should not.

The "sexual revolution"—anything goes—began in 1960, when an oral contraceptive was marketed by G. D. Searle Pharmaceuticals. Efforts to keep "the pill" out of the hands of unmarried girls and young women were, of course, doomed from the start. The flower children, in their determination to defy their parents in every way, defined the "love" on which the counterculture was based primarily as promiscuous sex: sex on a whim with anyone because it was pleasurable and natural, which was what counted. The hippies shocked people by talking

---

committees through which they retooled the party machinery. The new procedures and standards for selecting convention delegates penalized longtime party stalwarts: labor unions, big-city machines, those southern "good old boys" who had not already gone Republican, and other political professionals. The McGovern reforms (named for the liberal, antiwar senator from South Dakota, George McGovern) guaranteed representation to party conventions on the basis of gender and race.

The Election of 1972

Consequently, the Democratic convention that met in Miami in the summer of 1972 was the youngest convention ever. There were far more women, blacks, Hispanics, and Indians on the floor than ever before, and most were militantly antiwar. They nominated Senator McGovern and adopted a platform calling for a negotiated end to the Southeast Asian war (then Vietnamized but expanded) and supporting the demands of feminist organizations that abortions be available to women who wanted them.

A decent man profoundly grieved by the war, McGovern tried to distance himself from the most extreme proposals his supporters put before the convention, notably the demand that homosexuality be accepted as an alternative lifestyle. McGovern understood that such a plank was unlikely to win the favor of blue-collar workers who traditionally voted Democratic. The gay rights debate was scheduled for late at night, when few were watching the convention on television, and quietly shelved. McGovern emphasized his pledge to bring peace in Vietnam, tax reforms to benefit middle- and lower-income people, and his record of integrity as compared with Nixon's reputation for deviousness.

But Vietnamization had reduced the arguments of the antiwar movement to pleas for morality. Virtually no labor unions supported McGovern, and most of the old Democratic pros sat on their hands. McGovern had moderated the demands of the lifestyle liberals, but he could not repudiate them any more than Goldwater could have repudiated the John Birch Society in 1964. But the cold fact was, the Miami convention did not represent the views of the electorate.

Nixon won 60.8 percent of the popular vote, a swing of 20 million votes in eight years. He carried every state but Massachusetts (and the District of Columbia). The fact that he was a shoo-in from the beginning of the campaign makes

about sex too—endlessly—but that taboo had already been felled. A series of court decisions put books that had long been banned into the bookshops. In 1959, D. H. Lawrence's *Lady Chatterley's Lover,* long suppressed because of its explicitly sexual passages, was cleared for sale in the United States. In 1966, the Supreme Court approved publication of an eighteenth-century pornographic classic, *Fanny Hill.* In 1969, the Court said that, because of the "right of privacy," it was not illegal merely to possess obscene or pornographic material.

During the 1970s, casual sex and pornography went bigtime. Languishing cinemas ran nothing but pornographic films and tried, with some success, to attract women as dates or in groups. "Singles bars," explicitly advertised as places where one could meet a sexual partner for a "one-night stand," were fixtures in every city and many towns. "Adult motels" suspended mirrors on ceilings and pumped pornographic movies to TV sets in perfumed rooms. Apartment complexes were retooled with party rooms, saunas, and hot tubs to accommodate "swinging singles." Marriage practices could hardly remain unaffected. The divorce rate soared from 2.5 divorces per 1,000 marriages in 1965 to 5.3 per 1,000 in 1979. The rate of illegitimate births tripled during the 1960s and 1970s, and the number of abortions increased at an equal rate.

Homosexuals benefited from the new openness and relaxation of sexual attitudes. They began "coming out of the closet," proclaiming that their sexuality was an important part of their individual identity and nothing of which to be ashamed. Hundreds of gay and lesbian groups took to the streets in colorful parades. They formed lobbies, soon supported by the "politically correct," to push for laws preventing discrimination against homosexuals in housing and employment. The din was such that someone remarked, "The sin that dare not speak its name cannot sit down and shut up."

"Swinging" on a mass scale proved to be a fad among heterosexuals. Singles bars and singles apartments lost their panache. Pornographic movie theaters closed by the hundreds, in part because, except to aficionados of the genre, the films were dreary and boring—when you've seen one, you've seen them all—but mostly because the Internet brought porn into homes.

Venereal disease caused a decline in casual sex from the frenzy of the 1970s. A penicillin-resistant strain of gonorrhea made the rounds among "swingers"; chlamydia and herpes, relatively innocuous venereal infections, reached epidemic proportions. Rather more serious was a new affliction, Acquired Immune Deficiency Syndrome—AIDS—which slowly and agonizingly killed most of its victims. In developed countries like the United States (although not in the Third World), AIDS was largely a disease of homosexuals and intravenous drug users (it is transmitted only by contact with blood). But, into the 1990s, it was not described as threatening only gays and junkies, in part because it was not politically correct to do so, in part because researchers would have had great difficulty getting funds to research a disease thought to be the exclusive problem of groups on which conventional Americans looked with distaste.

It is difficult to imagine a reversal of the sexual revolution short of a totalitarian government that would make the Taliban's Afghanistan look like a permissive regime. The human sex drive is overwhelming, something that traditional moralists obviously understood, judging by the zeal with which they attempted to repress it.

the surreptitious activities of his Committee to Reelect the President (an unwisely selected name—it abbreviated as "CREEP"), and Nixon's approval of them, impossible to explain except as a reflection of an abnormal psychology.

The Watergate Cover-Up

On June 17, 1972, early in the presidential campaign, Washington police arrested five men who were trying to plant electronic eavesdropping devices in Democratic party headquarters in an upscale apartment and office complex called the Watergate. Three of the suspects were on CREEP's payroll. McGovern tried to exploit the incident as part of his integrity campaign but got nowhere when Nixon and his campaign manager, Attorney General John Mitchell, denied any knowledge of the incident and denounced the burglars as common criminals.

Nixon may have known nothing about the break-in in advance. However, he learned shortly thereafter that the burglars acted on orders from aides close to him. He never considered reporting or disciplining his men. Instead, he instructed his staff to find money to hush up the men in jail. Two of them, however, James E. McCord and Howard Hunt, refused to take the fall. They informed Judge John Sirica that they had taken orders from highly placed administration officials.

Rumors flew. Two reporters for the *Washington Post,* Robert Woodward and Carl Bernstein, made contact with an anonymous informant, still identified only as "Deep Throat" (the title of a pornographic movie), who fed them inside information. A special Senate investigating committee headed by Sam Ervin of North Carolina picked away at the tangle from yet another direction, slowly tracing not only the Watergate break-in and cover-up but other illegal acts and "dirty tricks" to the White House.

The Imperial Presidency

Each month brought new, dismaying insights into the inner workings of the Nixon presidency. On Nixon's personal command, an "enemies list" had been compiled. On it were journalists, politicians, intellectuals, and even movie stars who criticized Nixon. One Donald Segretti was put in charge of spreading half-truths and lies to discredit critics of the administration. G. Gordon Liddy, who was involved in the

Watergate break-in, proposed fantastic schemes involving yachts and prostitutes to entrap political enemies in career-ending scandals. The dirty-tricks campaign grew so foul that not even J. Edgar Hoover, the never squeamish head of the FBI, would touch it.

Watergate was just one of several illegal break-ins sponsored by the administration. Nixon's aides engineered the burglary of a Los Angeles psychiatrist's office to secure information about his patient, Daniel Ellsberg, a Defense Department employee who published confidential information about the prosecution of the war in Vietnam.

Observers spoke of an "imperial presidency." Nixon and his coterie had become so arrogant in the possession of power that they believed they were above the law. Indeed, several years later, Nixon was to tell an interviewer on television, "When the president does it, that means it is not illegal."

If imperial in their pretensions, however, "all the president's men" were singularly lacking in a sense of nobility. One by one, Nixon's aides abandoned ship, each convinced that he was being set up as the fall guy for his colleagues. The deserters described their roles in the Watergate cover-up and dirty-tricks campaign, and named others higher up who told them what to do. In the midst of the scandal, Vice President Spiro Agnew pleaded no-contest to income tax evasion and charges that he accepted bribes when he was governor of Maryland. Agnew was forced to resign in October 1973. He was replaced under the Twenty-Fifth Amendment by Congressman Gerald Ford of Michigan.

Resignation

Then came Nixon's turn, and he was, as the old saw has it, hoisted on his own petard. He had recorded conversations in the Oval Office that clearly implicated him in the Watergate cover-up. (These recordings also revealed him to use the language of a sailor: The public transcripts of the tapes were peppered with "expletive deleted.") After long wrangles in

---

Persistence

When Nixon ran for reelection in 1972, he became the seventh person to run for president three times as the nominee of a major party. These were the seven and the dates of their nominations (the years they won are in boldface):

Thomas Jefferson: 1796, **1800, 1804**
Andrew Jackson: 1824, **1828, 1832**
Henry Clay: 1824, 1832, 1844
Grover Cleveland: **1884,** 1888, **1892**
William Jennings Bryan: 1896, 1900, 1908
Franklin D. Roosevelt: **1932, 1936, 1940, 1944**
Richard M. Nixon: 1960, **1968, 1972**

Technically, John Adams, like FDR, ran for president four times. That is, although it was intended he be elected as George Washington's vice president in 1788 and 1792, constitutionally, he was, like Washington, a candidate for president. Before 1804, there were no vice presidential candidates; the presidential candidate who finished second in the electoral college became vice president.

Eugene V. Debs was the Socialist party presidential candidate five times: 1900, 1904, 1908, 1912, and 1920. Norman Thomas was the Socialist party candidate six times: 1928, 1932, 1936, 1940, 1944, and 1948.

---

the courts, the president was ordered to surrender the tapes to the courts.

That Nixon did not destroy the tapes early in the crisis, before destruction was itself a criminal offense, is difficult to understand. Some insiders said he intended to make money by selling them after he retired. Others said that, like Lyndon Johnson, his mind cracked during the crisis. Nixon had, for some years, been medicating himself with illegally acquired Dilantin, a drug that alleviates anxiety. Secretary of State Kissinger was startled when Nixon asked him to kneel with him and pray. (Neither was a religious man.) Secretary of Defense Schlesinger quietly informed the Joint Chiefs of Staff not to carry out any orders from the White House until they were cleared with him or Kissinger.

After the House of Representatives Judiciary Committee recommended impeaching Nixon, he threw in the towel. On August 9, 1974, on national television, he resigned the presidency and flew to his home in San Clemente, California.

A Ford, Not a Lincoln

Gerald Ford had held a safe seat in the House from Michigan. He rose to be minority leader on the basis of seniority and party loyalty. His ambition was to be Speaker of the House before he retired; events made him vice president and, quickly, president.

Ford was an object of some ridicule. Lyndon Johnson told reporters that Ford's problem dated from the days when he played center on the University of Michigan football team without a helmet. Others quipped that he could not walk and chew gum at the same time. Newspaper photographers laid in

---

Constitutional Contradiction?

Gerald Ford was appointed to the vice presidency under the provisions of the Twenty-Fifth Amendment, which was ratified in 1967. It stipulates that "whenever there is a vacancy in the office of the Vice President, the President shall nominate a Vice President." When Ford succeeded to the presidency, he appointed Nelson A. Rockefeller to the vice presidency. Neither the president nor the vice president held office by virtue of election. However, as some constitutional experts were quick to point out, Article 2, Section 1 of the Constitution provides that the president and vice president are to "be elected."

In fact, the contradiction was always there, if never put to the test. The Constitution and laws hold that the secretary of state and the Speaker of the House are next in line to the presidency after the vice president. A case could be made that the Speaker is elected, but not the secretary of state.

Official White House Photo

▲ *Gerald Ford, the "accidental president" who won widespread affection by not pretending to be anything but the forthright and hardworking public servant he had been in Congress. Despite serious economic problems, he was defeated only narrowly in 1976, when he ran in his only national election.*

wait to snap shots of him bumping his head on door frames, tumbling down the slopes of the Rockies on everything but his skis, and slicing golf balls into crowds of spectators.

And yet, Ford's simplicity and forthrightness were a relief after Nixon's squirming and deceptions. He told the American people that fate had given them "a Ford, not a Lincoln." Democrats howled "deal" when Ford pardoned Nixon of all crimes he may have committed, but Ford's explanation—that the American people needed to put Watergate behind them—was plausible and in character. Two attempts to shoot him by deranged women in California helped to win sympathy for the first president who had not been elected to any national office.

Despite his unusual route to the White House, Gerald Ford had no more intention of being a caretaker president than John Tyler had when he became the first president to succeed to the office by reason of death. But it was Ford's misfortune, as it had been Tyler's, to face serious problems without the support of an important segment of his party. The Republican party's right wing, now led by former California governor Ronald Reagan, did not like détente or

Nixon's (now Ford's) refusal to launch a frontal attack on government regulation and the liberal welfare state.

A Tank Half Empty

The most serious of the woes facing Ford struck at one of the basic assumptions of twentieth-century American life: that cheap energy was available in unlimited quantities to fuel the economy and support the freewheeling lifestyle of the middle class.

By the mid-1970s, 90 percent of the American economy was generated by the burning of fossil fuels: coal, natural gas, and especially petroleum. Fossil fuels are nonrenewable sources of energy. Unlike food crops, lumber, and water—or, for that matter, a horse and a pair of sturdy legs—they cannot be called on again once they have been used. The supply of them is finite. Although experts disagreed about the extent of the world's reserves of coal, gas, and oil, no one challenged the obvious fact that one day they would be no more.

The United States was by far the world's biggest user of nonrenewable sources of energy. In 1975, while comprising about 6 percent of the world's population, Americans consumed a third of the world's annual production of oil. Much of it was burned to less-than-basic ends. Americans overheated and overcooled their offices and houses. They pumped gasoline into a dizzying variety of purely recreational vehicles, some of which brought the roar of the freeway to the wilderness and devastated fragile land. Their worship of the private automobile meant that little tax money was spent on public mass transit. They packaged their consumer goods in throwaway containers of glass, metal, paper, and petroleum-based plastics; supermarkets wrapped lemons individually in transparent plastic and fast-food cheeseburgers were cradled in Styrofoam caskets to be discarded within seconds of being handed over the counter. The bill of indictment, drawn up by conservationists, went on, but, resisting criticism and satire alike, American consumption increased.

OPEC and the Energy Crisis

About 61 percent of the oil that Americans consumed in the 1970s was produced at home, and large reserves remained under native ground. But the nation also imported huge quantities of crude oil. In October 1973, Americans discovered just how little control they had over the 39 percent of their oil that came from abroad.

In that month, the Organization of Petroleum Exporting Countries (OPEC) temporarily halted oil shipments and announced the first of a series of big jumps in the price of their product. One of their justifications was that the irresponsible consumption habits of the advanced Western nations, particularly the United States, jeopardized their future. That is, if countries like Saudi Arabia and Nigeria continued to supply oil cheaply, consuming nations would continue to burn it profligately, thus hastening the day when the wells ran dry. On that day, if the oil-exporting nations had not laid

▲ *Several times during the 1970s, gasoline was in such short supply Americans had to wait in lines, often for hours, to fill up. Some cities had no gasoline for sale for days at a time. The entire state of Hawaii was brought nearly to a halt awaiting tankers from California.*

the basis for another kind of economy, they would be destitute. Particularly in the Middle East, there were few alternative resources to support fast-growing populations. By raising prices, OPEC said, the oil producing nations would earn capital with which to build for a future without petroleum, while encouraging the consuming nations to conserve, thus lengthening the era when oil would be available.

From a geopolitical perspective, there was much to be said for the argument, but few ordinary Americans (and few greedy dissolutes in the OPEC countries) thought geopolitically. Arab sheiks and Nigerian generals grew rich, and American motorists were stunned when they had to wait in long lines in order to pay unprecedented prices for gasoline. In some big cities and Hawaii, gasoline for private cars was hardly to be had for weeks.

The price of gasoline never climbed to Japanese or European levels, but it was shock enough for people who were accustomed to buying "two dollars' worth" to discover that two dollars bought a little more than enough to drive home. Moreover, the prices of goods that required oil in their production climbed too. Inflation, already 9 percent during Nixon's last year, rose to 12 percent a year when Ford was president.

Whip Inflation Now!

Opposed to wage and price controls such as Nixon employed, Ford launched a campaign called WIN! (short for

"Whip Inflation Now!"). He urged Americans to deter inflation by refusing to buy exorbitantly priced goods and by ceasing to demand higher wages. The campaign was ridiculed from the start, and, within a few weeks, Ford quietly retired the WIN! button that he was wearing on his lapel. He had seen few others in his travels around the country and began to feel like a man in a funny hat.

Instead, Ford tightened the money supply in order to slow down the economy, which resulted in the most serious recession since 1937, with unemployment climbing to 9 percent. Ford was stymied by a vicious circle: Slowing inflation meant throwing people out of work; fighting unemployment meant inflation; trying to steer a middle course meant "stagflation"—mild recession plus inflation.

Early in 1976, polls showed Ford losing to most of the likely Democratic candidates. Capitalizing on this news, Ronald Reagan, the sweetheart of right-wing Republicans, launched a well-financed campaign to replace him as the party's candidate. Using his control of the party organization, Ford beat Reagan at the convention, but the travails of his two years in office took their toll. He could not overcome the image that he was the most accidental of presidents, never elected to national office. His full pardon of Nixon came back to haunt him. In November 1976, he lost narrowly to a most unlikely Democratic candidate, James Earl Carter of Georgia, who called himself "Jimmy." The Democrats were back, but the decline in the prestige of the presidency continued.

QUIET CRISIS

Since Eisenhower, every president had been identified closely with Congress. Kennedy, Johnson, Nixon, and their defeated opponents had all been senators. The day of the governor candidate seemed to have ended with FDR. Governors did not get the national publicity that senators did. Then, Jimmy Carter came out of nowhere to win the Democratic nomination in 1976. His political career consisted of one term in the Georgia assembly and one term as governor.

Indeed, it was Carter's lack of association with the federal government that helped him win the nomination and, by a slim margin, the presidency. Without a real animus for Gerald Ford, many Americans were attracted to the idea of an "outsider," which is how Carter presented himself. "Hello, my name is Jimmy Carter, and I'm running for president," he told thousands of people face to face in his softly musical Georgia accent. Once he started winning primaries, the media did the rest. When television commentators said that there was a bandwagon rolling, voters dutifully responded by jumping on it.

Inauguration day, when Carter and his shrewd but uningratiating wife, Rosalynn, walked the length of Pennsylvania Avenue, was very nearly the last entirely satisfactory day of the Carter presidency. Whether the perspective of time will attribute his failure as chief executive to his unsuitability to the office or to the massiveness of the problems he faced, it is difficult to imagine historians of the future looking at the Carter era other than as it is now remembered, dolefully.

Peacemaking

Carter had his successes. He defused an explosive situation in Central America, where Panamanians were protesting American sovereignty over the Panama Canal Zone. The narrow strip of United States territory bisected the small republic and seemed to be an insult in an age when nationalist sensibilities in small countries were as touchy as boils.

Most policy makers saw no need to hold on to the Canal Zone in the face of the protests. The United States would be able to occupy the canal within hours in the case of an international crisis. In 1978, the Senate narrowly ratified an agreement with Panama to guarantee the permanent neutrality of the canal itself while gradually transferring sovereignty over it to Panama, culminating on December 31, 1999. Ronald Reagan, who began to campaign for the presidency as soon as Carter was inaugurated, denounced the treaty, but widespread protest dissipated quickly.

Carter's greatest achievement was to save the rapprochement between Israel and Egypt that began to take shape in November 1977 when Egyptian president Anwar

▲ *Jimmy Carter's finest day as president. In 1978, he managed to persuade (or threaten) Israeli prime minister Menachem Begin (right) to sign the Camp David Accords with Egyptian president Anwar Sadat. Carter should have been awarded the Nobel Peace Prize. He was awarded the prize in 2002, but for his humanitarian work after leaving the presidency.*

Sadat risked the enmity of the Arab world by calling for a permanent peace in the Middle East before the Israeli Knesset, or parliament. Rather than cooperate with Sadat, Israeli prime minister Menachem Begin, himself a former terrorist, refused to make concessions commensurate with the Egyptian president's high-stakes gamble.

In 1978, Carter brought Sadat and Begin to meet with him at Camp David, the presidential retreat in the Maryland woods outside Washington. There, Sadat grew so angry with Begin's refusal to compromise that he actually packed his suitcases. Although Carter was unable to persuade Begin to agree that the west bank of the Jordan River, which Israel had occupied in 1967, must eventually be returned to Arab rule, he did bring the two men together. In March 1979, Israel and Egypt signed a treaty.

The End of Détente

Whereas Carter advanced the cause of peace in the Middle East, he shattered the détente that Nixon, Kissinger, and Ford had nurtured. Like Nixon, Carter virtually ignored his first secretary of state, a professional diplomat, Cyrus Vance, and depended on a White House adviser, Zbigniew Brzezinski, for advice.

Unlike the flexible and opportunistic Kissinger, Brzezinski, a Polish refugee from Communism, was an anti-Soviet ideologue. Brzezinski's hatred of the Soviet Union blinded him to opportunities to improve relations between the nuclear superpowers. Moreover, whereas Kissinger had been a charmer, Brzezinski was tactless and crude in a world in which protocol and manners could be as important as substance. The foreign ministers of several of America's allies discreetly informed the State Department that they would not deal with him under any circumstances.

Carter's hostility toward the Soviet Union had different origins. A deeply religious man, moralistic to the point of sanctimony, he denounced the Soviet Union for trampling on human rights. In March 1977, Carter interrupted and set back the Strategic Arms Limitation Talks with completely new proposals. Eventually, a new SALT-II treaty was negotiated and signed, but Carter withdrew it from Senate consideration in December 1979 when the Soviet Union invaded Afghanistan to prop up a client government there. Détente was dead.

The Economy Under Carter: More of the Same

Inflation reached new heights under Carter, almost 20 percent during 1980. By the end of the year, one dollar was worth only 15 cents in 1940 values. That is, on average, it took one dollar in 1980 to purchase what in 1940 cost 15 cents. The dollar had suffered fully half of this loss during the 1970s.

Carter could not be faulted for the energy crisis. After the crunch of 1974, Americans became more energy conscious, replacing their big "gas guzzlers" with more efficient smaller cars. Even this sensible turn contributed to the

Carter and the Segregationists

Jimmy Carter had an unusual record on the segregation issue for a white southerner of his era. In the 1950s, as a successful businessman in Plains, Georgia, he had been asked to join the racist White Citizens' Council, the annual dues of which were $5. Carter replied, "I've got $5 but I'd flush it down the toilet before I'd give it to you."

nation's economic malaise, however. American automobile manufacturers had repeatedly refused to develop small, energy-efficient cars. For a time during the 1960s, after the success of the Germans' Volkswagen Beetle, Ford, General Motors, and Chrysler made compact cars. But within a few years, compacts had miraculously grown to be nearly as large as the road monsters of the 1950s. In the energy crunch of the 1970s, American automakers had nothing to compete with a flood of Japanese imports: Toyotas, Datsuns, and Hondas. The automobile buyer's dollars sailed across the Pacific.

Even then, by 1979, oil consumption was higher than ever, and an even higher proportion of it was imported than in 1976. American oil refiners actually cut back on domestic production, which led many people to wonder if the crisis was genuine or just a cover while the refiners reaped windfall profits—which they did. As prices soared, the oil companies paid dividends such as the always healthy industry had never known.

The price of electricity rose by 200 percent. Utility companies called for the construction of more nuclear power plants in anticipation of even higher rate increases. But Americans had become apprehensive about nuclear energy as an alternative to fossil fuels, following an accident and near catastrophe at the Three Mile Island nuclear plant near Harrisburg, Pennsylvania; the release, at about the same time, of *The China Syndrome,* a film that portrayed a disconcertingly similar accident; and the revelation that a big California reactor about to go online was crisscrossed with construction flaws and built over a major earthquake fault. Was anything in America going right?

Malaise

Carter was repeatedly embarrassed by his aides and family, and himself had a talent for blunders. Genuinely suspicious of the Washington establishment, he surrounded himself with cronies from Georgia who did not, or would not, understand the etiquette and rituals of the capital. Banker Bert Lance, whom Carter wanted as budget director, was tainted by petty, unacceptable loan scams; Ambassador to the United Nations Andrew Young met secretly with leaders of the terrorist Palestine Liberation Organization, which the United States did not recognize as a legitimate representative of the Palestinians. Carter had to fire Young.

The national press, stimulated by the role of journalists in exposing the Watergate scandal, leaped on every trivial incident—a Carter aide tipsy in a cocktail lounge or the president's "down-home" brother Billy's ridiculous opinions—to embarrass the president. Carter honestly but foolishly told an interviewer for *Playboy* magazine, "I've looked on a lot of women with lust. I've committed adultery in my heart many times." In 1980, when Carter's presidency was on the line, his mother told a reporter, "Sometimes when I look at all my children, I say to myself, 'Lillian, you should have stayed a virgin.'"

The Carter administration lacked direction. "Carter believes fifty things," one of his advisers said, "but no one thing. He holds explicit, thorough positions on every issue under the sun, but he has no large view of relations between them." Carter was not unlike most Americans in his engineer mentality. He believed it best to face each specific problem as it arose, working out a specific solution for each.

Such pragmatism had worked for Franklin D. Roosevelt. It did not work for Jimmy Carter. With him at the helm, government resembled a ship without a rudder, drifting aimlessly. Carter was sensitive to what journalists called a national "malaise," but he only embarrassed himself when he tried to address the amorphous problem. He called 130 prominent men and women from every sector of American life to Washington; having listened to them, he was able to announce only that there was "a crisis of the American spirit"—right back where he started from.

for FURTHER READING

James Gilbert, *Another Chance: America Since 1945,* 1984, provides a general overview of this period; Godfrey Hodgson, *America in Our Time,* 1976, deals with the first part of it. However, we are too close to the 1970s to expect too dependable a narrative history of the decade. Many contemporary historians were themselves participants and partisans during these years. Many of the major players are still around, trying to shape their posterity.

Some have written memoirs, perhaps as much for monstrous advances from publishers as for self-justification. These accounts can, nevertheless, be useful and are valuable sources. See Richard M. Nixon, *RN: The Memoirs of Richard Nixon,* 1978; George McGovern, *Grassroots,* 1977; Gerald R. Ford, *A Time to Heal: The Autobiography of Gerald R. Ford,* 1979; Henry A. Kissinger, *White House Years,* 1979, and *Years of Upheaval,* 1982; Jimmy Carter, *Keeping Faith,* 1982; and Rosalynn Carter, *First Lady from Plains,* 1984. A fascinating study of Nixon written before his fall is Garry Wills, *Nixon Agonistes,* 1970. On Kissinger, see Robert Morris, *Uncertain Greatness: Henry Kissinger and American Foreign Policy,* 1977.

Carl Bernstein and Robert Woodward, *All the President's Men,* 1974, is by the two reporters for the *Washington Post* who doggedly investigated the Watergate affair and helped bring about Nixon's fall. Perhaps the most insightful analysis of what happened is Arthur M. Schlesinger Jr., *The Imperial Presidency,* 1973. See also T. H. White, *Breach of Faith,* 1975; Leon Jaworski, *The Right and the Power,* 1976; and Sam Ervin, *The Whole Truth: The Watergate Conspiracy,* 1980.

On national politics and policy during the 1970s, see David Broder, *The Party's Over,* 1972; Samuel Lubell, *The Hidden Crisis in American Politics,* 1970; A. J. Reichley, *Conservatives in an Age of Change: The Nixon and Ford Administrations,* 1981; and Theodore H. White, *The Making of a President, 1972,* 1973. For foreign policy, see Henry Kissinger's memoirs listed above. On specific issues, see R. L. Garthoff, *Détente and Confrontation,* 1985; A. E. Goodman, *The Lost Peace: America's Search for a Negotiated Settlement of the Vietnam War,* 1978; R. A. Pastor, *Condemned to Repetition,* 1987 (on Central America); W. B. Quandt, *Decade of Decision: American Foreign Policy Toward the Arab-Israeli Conflict,* 1978; and G. Sick, *All Fall Down: America's Tragic Encounter with Iran,* 1985.

AMERICAN JOURNEY ONLINE AND INFOTRAC COLLEGE EDITION

Visit the source collections at http://ajaccess.wadsworth.com and http://infotrac.thomsonlearning.com, and use the Search function with the following key terms to explore documents, images, audio and video clips, articles, and commentary related to the material in this chapter:

Détente

Earl Warren

H. R. Haldeman

Henry Kissinger

John Ehrlichman

Kent State

Richard Nixon

Vietnamization

Watergate

Additional resources, exercises, and Internet links related to this chapter are available on *The American Past* Web site: http://history.wadsworth.com/americanpast7e.

HISTORY ONLINE

Nixon White House Phone Calls
www.c-span.org/executive/presidential/nixon.asp
Audio extracts from the tape recordings that brought President Nixon down.

Iranian Hostage Crisis
www.louisville.edu/library/ekstrom/govpubs/subjects/hist/iranhostage.html
Documents of the Iranian hostage crisis of 1979–1981, including excerpts from a hostage's diary.

Social Responsibility
and
Business Ethics

Louis E. Boone
and
David L. Kurtz

from
Contemporary
Business

Eleventh Edition

Chapter 2
Business Ethics and
Social Responsibility

Learning Goals

1 Explain the concepts of business ethics and social responsibility.

2 Describe the factors that influence business ethics.

3 List the stages in the development of ethical standards.

4 Identify common ethical dilemmas in the workplace.

5 Discuss how organizations shape ethical behavior.

6 Describe how businesses' social responsibility is measured.

7 Summarize the responsibilities of business to the general public, customers, and employees.

8 Explain why investors and the financial community are concerned with business ethics and social responsibility.

Tyco Takes a Dive

Whatever the outcome of Dennis Kozlowski's state and federal felony trials, the former chief executive of Tyco International is likely to be long remembered for the sheer size and scale of his alleged misdeeds. With the company's chief financial officer Mark Swartz, Kozlowski faces 38 felony counts of stealing

$170 million from the company and profiting by an additional $430 million acquired through illegal stock sales. Former chief corporate counsel Mark Belnick was also indicted for taking improper loans from the firm.

How did Kozlowski's ethical judgment lapse so badly that, according to *Business-Week,* the more he made, the more he spent and the more he stole? And how did those who were responsible to Tyco's shareholders allow it to happen? According to Manhattan District Attorney Robert Morgenthau, who brought the first of many charges against Kozlowski, today's corporate wrongdoers have a harder time acting alone. "Now, you've got a lot of people involved, and that's the lawyers, accountants, executives, the board of directors. The whole system seemed to have broken down," he says.

Kozlowski began his long career at Tyco as an exceptional manager and worked his way quickly through the corporate ranks. By the time he became CEO in 1992, the company, which makes security systems, electrical and electronic components, and undersea fiber-optic cable, was worth about $3 billion. Then Kozlowski embarked on a rapid-fire expansion program in which he acquired as many as 200 companies a year—nearly one every busi-

© AP/Wide World Photos

ness day. Annual revenues multiplied fivefold during the 1990s, ultimately reaching $36 billion in 2001, and the company and its CEO were widely admired.

Kozlowksi began to make large corporate donations, reportedly giving millions of dollars of Tyco's money to educational and charitable organizations, sometimes in his own name. But he also began to spend wildly—on luxurious homes, art, yachts, sailboats, lavish parties, and such extravagant purchases as a $6,000 shower curtain. Most of these expenses were also paid for with Tyco's money.

In the wake of the indictments and the plunge in its share value, Tyco, under a new CEO and an entirely new board of directors, is struggling to recover. Whether he was motivated by boredom as some suggest, by a feeling that he had earned what he considered the "perks" of his office, or by simple greed, Kozlowski remains a unique example of a CEO whose personal desires apparently outran his sense of responsibility to his firm. But what of those charged with overseeing and controlling his behavior? The board of directors at Tyco, like the board of any corporation, is charged with selecting the CEO, whom they can also fire, and with reviewing company performance, approving all major decisions that affect the corporation, and authorizing compensation, including salaries, bonuses, and perks. Kozlowski apparently undermined much of the board's oversight role. As a member of the board with the best access to corporate information, he heavily filtered the information that reached board members. He negotiated his own near immunity from firing as well as generous retirement benefits. He made sure that nearly $96 million in unapproved bonuses for Swartz and himself were authorized, and he established financial ties with many board members who later failed to protest his actions or regain their authority. Nor did the board alert Tyco's shareholders to the improper loans, bonuses, and stock sales that enriched the executives. One of the board members has pleaded guilty to securities fraud, but many observers find the entire board guilty of a serious breach of their financial responsibility. The Tyco board could serve as the poster child for corporate governance failure. Not surprisingly, new CEO Edward D. Breen, Jr., hired away from his position as Motorola president to right the Tyco ship, secured resignations from most members, and the firm's shareholders elected a new board in 2003.

As one associate director of the Securities and Exchange Commission said of the Tyco case, "It's important that outside directors remember they've got responsibilities and jobs to do and that they should not be co-opted by the executive suite."[1]

Chapter Overview

The dark cloud of scandal visited the boardrooms of dozens of U.S. corporations during the first years of the 21st century. Tyco International was not alone in experiencing ethical failures that led to lawsuits, indictments, fines, guilty pleas, jail sentences for high-profile executives, the financial failures of several well-known American businesses, job losses for thousands of former employees at these firms, and the loss of billions in savings by investors who held stocks in these companies. Also included were well-known companies like Adelphia Communications, Enron, Global Crossing, HealthSouth, ImClone, and WorldCom. Enron's auditor, highly respected public accountant giant Arthur Andersen, declared bankruptcy after information spread about its failure to disclose accurate information to shareholders and regulatory officials—to say nothing of its shredding of Enron documents. The image of the CEO—and business in general—suffered as the evening news carried dramatic pictures of the so-called *perp walk*—parading indicted—and handcuffed—corporate executives before the media in an exercise previously applied to local criminals. Following a series of disclosures in congressional investigations and from civil and criminal investigations by state attorneys general, in 2002 Congress enacted the **Sarbanes-Oxley Act** to correct these abuses by adding oversight for the nation's major companies and a special oversight board to regulate public accounting firms that audit the financial records of these corporations.

As we discussed in Chapter 1, the underlying aim of business is to serve customers at a profit. But most companies try to do more than that, looking for ways to give back to customers, society, and the environment. When does a company's self-interest conflict with society's and customers' well-being? And must the goal of seeking profits conflict with upholding high principles of right and wrong? In response to the second question, a growing number of businesses of all sizes are answering no.

Concern for Ethical and Societal Issues

An organization that wants to prosper over the long term cannot do so without considering **business ethics,** the standards of conduct and moral values governing actions and decisions in the work environment. Businesses also must take into account a wide range of social issues, including how a decision will affect the environment, employees, and customers. These issues are at the heart of social responsibility, the philosophies, policies, procedures, and actions directed toward the enhancement of society's welfare as a primary objective. In short, businesses must find the delicate balance between doing what is right and doing what is profitable.

In business, as in life, deciding what is right or wrong in a given situation does not always involve a clear-cut choice. As Figure 2.1 shows, businesses have many responsibilities—to customers, to employees, to investors, and to society as a whole. Sometimes conflicts can arise in trying to serve the different needs of these separate constituencies. The ethical values of executives and individual employees at all levels can influence the decisions and actions a business takes. Throughout your own business career, you will encounter many situations in which you will need to weigh right and wrong before making a decision or taking action. So, we begin our discussion of business ethics by focusing on individual ethics.

business ethics
standards of business conduct and moral values.

FIGURE 2.1
Constituencies to Which Businesses Are Responsible

Business ethics are also shaped by the ethical climate within an organization. Codes of conduct and ethical standards play increasingly significant roles in businesses in which doing the right thing is both supported and applauded. This chapter demonstrates how a firm can create a framework to encourage—and even demand—high standards of ethical behavior and social responsibility from its employees. The chapter also considers the complex question of what business owes to society and how societal forces mold the actions of businesses. Finally, it examines the influence of business ethics and social responsibility on global business.

 Concept Check

1. To whom do businesses have responsibilities?
2. If a firm is meeting all its responsibilities to others, why do ethical conflicts arise?

The New Ethical Environment

Over the past five years, business ethics have been in the spotlight as never before. High-profile investigations, lawsuits, arrests, and even convictions, as well as business failures due to fraud and corruption, have created a long string of headline news. While these events have brought about rapid change in many areas and new laws to prevent them from happening again, they have also obscured for many people the fact that most companies and their leaders are highly ethical.[2] A recent CNN/USA Today/Gallup poll found that only 17 percent of U.S. respondents rated business executives highly, down from 25 percent a year earlier.[3] And 94 percent of respondents to a *BusinessWeek Online* survey felt that misdeeds by companies such as Enron and WorldCom were a "very serious" or "somewhat serious" problem.[4]

Our Credo

We believe our first responsibility is to the doctors, nurses and patients, to mothers and fathers and all others who use our products and services. In meeting their needs everything we do must be of high quality. We must constantly strive to reduce our costs in order to maintain reasonable prices. Customers' orders must be serviced promptly and accurately. Our suppliers and distributors must have an opportunity to make a fair profit.

We are responsible to our employees, the men and women who work with us throughout the world. Everyone must be considered as an individual. We must respect their dignity and recognize their merit. They must have a sense of security in their jobs. Compensation must be fair and adequate, and working conditions clean, orderly and safe. We must be mindful of ways to help our employees fulfill their family responsibilities. Employees must feel free to make suggestions and complaints. There must be equal opportunity for employment, development and advancement for those qualified. We must provide competent management, and their actions must be just and ethical.

We are responsible to the communities in which we live and work and to the world community as well. We must be good citizens – support good works and charities and bear our fair share of taxes. We must encourage civic improvements and better health and education. We must maintain in good order the property we are privileged to use, protecting the environment and natural resources.

Our final responsibility is to our stockholders. Business must make a sound profit. We must experiment with new ideas. Research must be carried on, innovative programs developed and mistakes paid for. New equipment must be purchased, new facilities provided and new products launched. Reserves must be created to provide for adverse times. When we operate according to these principles, the stockholders should realize a fair return.

FIGURE 2.2

Johnson & Johnson's Credo

Source: "Our Company: Our Credo," Johnson & Johnson Web site, **http://www.jnj.com**.

Yet the vast majority of business owners and managers have built and maintained enduring companies without breaking the rules. As Joseph Neubauer, CEO of Aramark Worldwide Corp., points out and most executives are aware, "It takes a lifetime to build a reputation, and only a short time to lose it all." Companies that show high earnings and steady sales growth over time were led by CEOs who personified the best in management practices. These leaders may not be household names, but they and hundreds of other mainstream business executives are highly respected for their integrity, honesty, and business ethics. One example of a firm with a longstanding commitment to ethical practice is Johnson & Johnson, the giant multinational manufacturer of health-care products. The sixth most admired company in the world, according to *Fortune*, Johnson & Johnson has abided by the same basic code of ethics, its well-known Credo, for more than 50 years. The Credo, reproduced in Figure 2.2, remains the ethical standard against which the company's employees periodically evaluate how well their firm is performing. Management is pledged to address any lapses that are reported.[5]

It is clear, though, that not all companies successfully set and meet high ethical standards. Thousands of employees who lost their jobs due to management misdeeds and millions of investors who saw their savings melt away as the value of their investments in these rogue companies either plummeted or vanished entirely felt betrayed lately, spurring Congress, regulatory agencies, and businesses everywhere to take new steps to rectify problems and prevent them from occurring in the future. A survey of about 125 companies in 22 countries found, for instance, that more than three out of four are setting up ethics standards and codes, up from less than half in 1991. Cropping up more frequently in such ethical guidelines are not just issues already covered by law, such as contracts, employment discrimination, and safety, but also broader ethical concerns about the environment, child labor, and human rights.[6] With passage of the Sarbanes-Oxley Act of 2002, which establishes new rules and regulations for securities trading and accounting practices, a company is also required to publish its code of ethics, if it has one, and inform the public of any changes made to it. The new law may actually motivate even more firms to develop written codes and guidelines for ethical business behavior.

In addition to the growing number of firms currently creating their own ethical codes, others have proceeded to implement them through the seven steps specified during the 1990s when the federal government created the U.S. Sentencing Commission to institutionalize ethics compliance programs that would establish high ethical standards and end corporate misconduct.[7] The requirements for such programs are shown in Table 2.1.

The current ethical environment of business also includes the appointment of new corporate officers specifically charged with deterring wrongdoing and ensuring that ethical standards are met. These ethics compliance officers, whose numbers are rapidly rising, are responsible for conducting employee training programs that help spot potential fraud and abuse within the firm, investigating sexual harassment and discrimination charges, and monitoring any potential conflicts of interest. Some also ensure that financial reporting of the financial statements is accurate.[8] This last responsibility is more important

BUSINESS TOOL KIT

The Basics of Business Ethics

Business ethics are big business these days. The downfall of such corporate giants as Enron, World-Com, and Global Crossing demonstrates the power of decisions made *not* based on ethical values. Doing the right thing still matters in business, so developing your own personal arsenal of ethics before facing sticky situations at work can go a long way. Knowing your limitations of what you will and won't do in any certain situation helps both your decision making and your value as an employee. Here are a few tips on developing your own personal code of ethics at work:

1. Evaluate your personal moral and/or religious system for absolutes. Oftentimes, what you've been taught at home about ethics and fair play will resonate in the business world as well.
2. Role-play iffy ethical situations and gauge your response. If asked by a manager to shred documents after hours, what would you do? If offered a job at a company that has sweatshops in Malaysia, would you take the job? Realize that right and wrong in the business world are not always clear-cut, so it's best to evaluate a situation before you respond to it.
3. Today's headlines illustrate that ethics come from the top. If your company's top management or CEO doesn't place an obvious emphasis on ethics, seek out their position on the subject. If one is not

already in place, use your own personal set of ethics to encourage your department in developing a professional set of ethics for the company.
4. When you are faced with an ethical dilemma, there are three questions you should ask yourself, according to the authors of *The Power of Ethical Management:* Is it legal? Is it balanced? How will it make me feel about myself? Authors Kenneth Blanchard and Norman Vincent Peale believe that asking these three questions gives you a more balanced approach to the dilemma, especially if it falls into that "gray" area.
5. If one is offered at your school, consider taking a business ethics course. Many colleges and businesses schools are now offering a required class on the legal, ethical, and political aspects of business. If you are a business major, it would be wise for you to take a course in ethics before you graduate to the "real world" of right and wrong.

Sources: Matthew Phillips, "College Courses Offer Basics for Dealing Ethically in Business," *The Business Review: Albany Edition,* accessed February 23, 2003; Paul Singer, "Business Schools Add Ethics in Wake of Corporate Scandals," *Associated Press State & Local Wire,* August 16, 2002, accessed at **http://www.kellogg.northwestern.edu/news/hits/ 020816ap.htm**; "Business Ethics: The Foundation of Effective Leadership," **http://www.onlinewbc.gov/docs/manage/ethics.html**, accessed August 10, 2001.

Table 2.1	Minimum Requirements for Ethics Compliance Programs

- Standards and procedures, such as codes of ethics, capable of detecting and preventing misconduct
- High-level personnel responsible for ethics compliance programs
- No substantial discretionary authority given to individuals with a propensity for misconduct
- Effective communication of ethical code requirements through ethics training programs
- Establishment of systems to monitor, audit, and report misconduct
- Consistent enforcement of ethical codes and punishment
- Continuous improvement of the ethics compliance program

Source: U.S. Sentencing Commission, *Federal Sentencing Guidelines Manual.* St. Paul, MN: West Publishing, 1984, Ch. 8.

Stage 1: Preconventional

Individual is mainly looking out for his or her own interests. Rules are followed only out of fear of punishment or hope of reward.

↓

Stage 2: Conventional

Individual considers the interests and expectations of others in making decisions. Rules are followed because it is a part of belonging to the group.

↓

Stage 3: Postconventional

Individual follows personal principles for resolving ethical dilemmas. He or she considers personal, group, and societal interests.

FIGURE 2.3
Stages of Moral and Ethical Development

than ever, now that the Sarbanes-Oxley Act requires financial officers and CEOs to personally certify the validity of companies' financial statements.

Individuals Make a Difference

In today's business environment, individuals can make the difference in ethical expectations and behavior. As executives, managers, and employees demonstrate their personal ethical principles—or lack of ethical principles—the expectations and actions of those who work for and with them can change.

What is the current status of individual business ethics in the U.S.? Although ethical behavior can be difficult to track or even define in all circumstances, evidence suggests that some individuals act unethically or illegally on the job. A poll of U.S. employees found that 30 percent knew of or suspected unethical behavior in their companies. In another poll, the main types of unethical behavior observed by employees were lying, withholding information, abusing or intimidating employees, inaccurately reporting the amount of time worked, and discrimination. Each year, U.S. organizations lose more than $400 billion to fraud, or an average of $9 per day per employee.[9]

Technology seems to have expanded the range and impact of unethical behavior. For example, anyone with computer access to data has the potential to steal or manipulate the data or to shut down the system, even from a remote location. Often, the people who hack into a company's computers are employees, and some observers consider employee attacks to be the most expensive. They often result in the theft of intellectual property, such as patented or copyrighted information. Computer technology also helps people at one company attack another. Steven Cade, whose business, La Jolla Club Golf Co., specializes in child-sized golf clubs, recently admitted to using the Internet to spread deceptive messages about a much larger competitor, Callaway Golf Co. Cade admitted he used 27 different false names to post these messages online.

Nearly every employee, at every level, wrestles with ethical questions at some point or another. Some rationalize questionable behavior by saying, "Everybody's doing it." Others act unethically because they feel pressured on their jobs or have to meet performance quotas. Yet, some avoid unethical acts that don't mesh with their personal values and morals. To help you understand the differences in the ways individuals arrive at ethical choices, the next section focuses on how personal ethics and morals develop.

Development of Individual Ethics

Individuals typically develop ethical standards in the three stages shown in Figure 2.3: the preconventional, conventional, and postconventional stages. In the preconventional stage, individuals primarily consider their own needs and desires in making decisions. They obey external rules only because they are afraid of punishment or hope to receive rewards if they comply.

In the second stage, the conventional stage, individuals are aware of and act in response to their duty to others, including their obligations to their family members, coworkers, and organizations. The expectations of these groups influence how they choose between what is acceptable and unacceptable in certain situations. Self-interest, however, continues to play a role in decisions.

The postconventional stage, the final stage, represents the highest level of ethical and moral behavior. The individual is able to move beyond mere self-interest and duty and take the larger needs of society into account as well. He or she has developed personal ethical principles for determining what is right and can apply those principles in a wide variety of situations.

An individual's stage in moral and ethical development is determined by a huge number of factors. Experiences help to shape responses to different situations. A person's family, educational, cultural, and religious backgrounds can also play a role, as can the environment within the firm. Individuals can also have different styles of deciding ethical dilemmas, no matter what their stage of moral development.

> *They Said It*
>
> I would rather be the man who bought the Brooklyn Bridge than the one who sold it.
>
> —*Will Rogers (1879–1935)*
> *American humorist*

To help you understand and prepare for the ethical dilemmas you may confront in your career, let's take a closer look at some of the factors involved in solving ethical questions on the job.

On-the-Job Ethical Dilemmas

In the fast-paced world of business, you will sometimes be called on to weigh the ethics of decisions that can affect not just your own future but possibly the futures of your fellow workers, your company, and its customers. As already noted, it's not always easy to distinguish between what is right and wrong in many business situations, especially when the needs and concerns of various parties conflict.

Consider the situation decision makers at pharmaceutical companies face. Under worldwide pressure to make life-saving drugs affordable in developing countries, the drug industry faces the possibility that it might have to drastically lower prices on expensive new drugs. Or under a "health care crisis" trade rule set by the World Trade Organization, drug makers might have to allow countries to develop their own cheap generic versions of drugs that are legally still under patent protection. During the anthrax scare that followed the 9/11 terrorist

FIGURE 2.4
Common Business Ethical Challenges

attacks, the U.S. and Canadian governments threatened to violate drug makers' patents themselves to make an anthrax antidote affordable. While they are still conscious of their responsibility to shareholders who expect the companies to be profitable, some drug firms are now taking the initiative to act against diseases. Merck has been treating 25 million people a year for river blindness at no cost, and after years of such efforts, it may soon eradicate this debilitating disease. Five drug companies have joined with United Nations agencies to cut the prices of HIV drugs. Aventis and Bristol-Myers Squibb are working with the World Health Organization to distribute a drug that failed to treat cancer but is a powerful antidote to sleeping sickness. The Swiss firm Novartis is giving away a drug combination that could eradicate leprosy and is selling a new malaria drug to developing countries at cost. But says Novartis CEO Daniel Vasella, "I need to justify what I am doing to my shareholders."[10]

As these examples illustrate, solving ethical dilemmas is not easy. In many cases, each possible decision can have unpleasant consequences and positive benefits that must be evaluated. The ethical issues that confront managers of drug companies are just one example of many different types of ethical questions encountered in the workplace. Figure 2.4 identifies four of the most common ethical challenges that businesspeople face: conflict of interest, honesty and integrity, loyalty versus truth, and whistleblowing.

Conflict of Interest   A **conflict of interest** exists when a businessperson is faced with a situation in which an action benefiting one person or group has the potential to harm another. Conflicts of interest may pose ethical challenges when they involve the businessperson's own interests and those of someone to whom he or she has a duty or when they involve two parties to whom the businessperson has a duty. Lawyers, business consultants, or advertising agencies would face a conflict of interest if they represented two competing companies: A strategy that would most benefit one of the client companies might harm the other client. Similarly, a real estate agent would face an ethical conflict if he or she represented both the buyer and seller in a transaction. In general, the buyer benefits from a low price, and the seller benefits from a high price. Handling the situation responsibly would be possible, but it would also be difficult. A conflict may also exist between someone's personal interests and those of an organization or its customers. An offer of gifts or bribes for special treatment creates a situation in which the buyer, but not necessarily his or her company, may benefit personally.

conflict of interest
situation in which a business decision may be influenced by the potential for personal gain.

Ethical ways to handle conflicts of interest include (1) avoiding them and (2) disclosing them. Some companies have policies against taking on clients who are competitors of existing clients. Most businesses and government agencies have written policies prohibiting employees from accepting gifts or specifying a maximum gift value of, say, $50. Or a member of a board of directors or committee might abstain from voting on a decision in which he or she has a personal interest. In other situations, people state their potential conflict of interest so that the people affected can decide whether to get information or help they need from another source instead.

Honesty and Integrity   Employers highly value honesty and integrity. An employee who is honest can be counted on to tell the truth. An employee with **integrity** goes beyond truthfulness. Having integrity means adhering to deeply felt ethical principles in business situations. It includes doing what you say you will do and accepting responsibility for mistakes. Behaving with honesty and integrity inspires trust, and as a result, it can help build long-term relationships with customers, employers, suppliers, and the public. Employees, in turn, want their managers and the company as a whole to treat them honestly and with integrity. One ethical issue concerning employees that has surfaced recently involves insurance policies. Many companies, especially banks, have built up huge tax-free investments by taking out life insurance policies on employees without their knowledge. When an employee or retiree died, the company collected the insurance, and that person's survivors never knew about it. New rules require firms to obtain employee permission, however, and employees are winning more lawsuits in so-called "janitor's insurance" cases.[11]

Unfortunately, violations of honesty and integrity are widespread. Some people misrepresent their academic credentials and previous work experience on their résumés or job applications. Others steal from their employers by taking home supplies or products without permission or by carrying out personal business during the time they are being paid to work. Many employees lie to protect themselves from punishment or to make their performance look better than it really is. Following the merger of CUC International and HFS to form Cendant, a major provider of travel (trip.com and CheapTickets), auto rentals (Avis and Budget), and real estate (Century 21, Coldwell Banker, ERA) services, managers from HFS began to find financial discrepancies. They discovered that the top managers at CUC had for years been reporting incorrect financial data about the company, claiming $500 million in profits that were purely fictional. CUC's former head, Walter Forbes, said he didn't know about the misbehavior and wasn't responsible for it. He resigned in exchange for a severance package worth $47.5 million. Others have challenged Forbes's statements of ignorance, and Cendant has taken Forbes to court in an attempt to force him to repay the entire amount.[12]

> ## They Said It
>
> I can't remember a time that I've seen lawyers be perceived as more trustworthy than accountants.
>
> —*Marty McGough (b. 1960)*
> *vice president of research, Widmeyer Communications, on the results of a new poll on trustworthiness*

Loyalty versus Truth   Businesspeople expect their employees to be loyal and to act in the best interests of the company. But when the truth about a company is not favorable, an ethical conflict can arise. Individuals may have to decide between loyalty to the company and truthfulness in business relationships. People resolve such dilemmas in various ways. Some place the highest value on loyalty, even at the expense of truth. Others avoid volunteering negative information but answer truthfully if someone asks them a specific question. People may emphasize truthfulness and actively disclose negative information, especially if the cost of silence is high, as in the case of operating a malfunctioning aircraft or selling tainted medicine. Two investigators for Los Alamos National Laboratory in New Mexico, home of some of the U.S.'s most sensitive defense secrets, reported the loss of $2.7 million worth of missing computers and other property and the abuse of lab-issued credit cards (with which one employee had tried to buy a car). An investigation by the Department of Energy found that even if the lab was not guilty of covering up such "blatant acts of criminality," it had at least subjected the two men to intimidation and pressure to keep quiet, including issuing a series of memos urging employees to "resist the temptation to 'spill your guts.'" "I believe in being dedicated to your boss," said one of the two men, "but there's a line you don't cross, and they crossed that line and began to perceive wrong as right."[13]

Whistleblowing   When an individual does encounter unethical or illegal actions at work, the person must decide what action to take. Sometimes it is possible to resolve the problem by working through channels within the organization. If that fails, the person should weigh the potential damages to the greater public good. If the damage is significant, a person who places ethical standards above personal well-being may conclude that the only solution is to blow the whistle. **Whistleblowing** is an employee's disclosure to government authorities or the media of illegal, immoral, or unethical practices of the organization. The two men who reported the theft of property at Los Alamos were whistleblowers, as were the three women profiled in the Hits and Misses box.

whistleblowing
employee's disclosure to government authorities or the media of illegal, immoral, or unethical practices committed by an organization.

HITS & MISSES

The Year of the Whistleblower

As extraordinary as the wrongdoing at Enron and WorldCom, and indifference at the FBI, was the courage of whistleblowers who spoke up. Sherron Watkins, former vice president at Enron, Cynthia Cooper, vice president at WorldCom, and Colleen Rowley, staff attorney for the FBI, each came forward about problems they uncovered on the job.

Profiteering and improper accounting made Enron the largest corporate bankruptcy in U.S. history at the time. A cover-up of billion-dollar losses left WorldCom in a life-and-death struggle to emerge from bankruptcy. Failure to heed Rowley's warnings about Zacarias Moussaoui allowed his activities to go unwatched; Moussaoui was later indicted as a coconspirator in the September 11 terrorist attacks.

Like whistleblowers before them, Watkins, Cooper, and Rowley suffered repercussions. Rowley's actions were compared to those of a spy, and she was harassed by calls to resign and rumors that the FBI might file criminal charges against her. Cooper is trying to help WorldCom recover despite being screamed at and patronized. Watkins was relegated to overseeing make-work projects until she finally resigned from Enron. Yet all say they would do it again.

Thanks to the Sarbanes-Oxley Act of 2002, whistleblowers now have added protection. Bosses who retaliate against a whistleblower face prison, and fired workers can be rehired more easily. Companies might no longer be able to require employees to obtain permission before speaking to the media. Corporate lawyers who see wrongdoing must report it to management and then to the company's board.

While blowing the whistle may still make a person unpopular, companies must learn what Colleen Rowley already knows. "Loyalty to whoever you work for is extremely important. The only problem is, it's not *the* most important thing."

QUESTIONS FOR CRITICAL THINKING

1. Do you agree with Rowley's statement that loyalty to a boss is not the most important factor for any employee?

2. What impact do you think the Sarbanes-Oxley provisions will have on employees' willingness to speak out?

Sources: Jodie T. Allen, "Women Who Blow Whistles," *U.S. News & World Report,* January 6, 2003, p. 48; Richard Lacayo and Amanda Ripley, "Persons of the Year," *Time,* December 30, 2002–January 6, 2003, pp. 30–59; Paul Dwyer et al., "Year of the Whistleblowers," *BusinessWeek,* December 16, 2002, pp. 107–110.

A whistleblower must weigh a number of issues in deciding whether to come forward. Resolving an ethical problem within the organization can be more effective, assuming higher level managers cooperate. A company that values ethics will try to correct a problem, and staying at a company that does not value ethics may not be worthwhile. In some cases, however, people resort to whistleblowing because they believe the unethical behavior is causing significant damage that outweighs the risk that the company will retaliate against the whistleblower. Those risks have been real in the past. About half of whistleblowers who responded to a survey by the National Whistleblower Center said they were fired for reporting illegal conduct, and most of the other respondents said they had been harassed or unfairly disciplined at work after reporting wrongdoing at their firms.[14] The two men who blew the whistle at Los Alamos were fired, though they have since been rehired to help in the investigation at the lab.

State and federal laws protect whistleblowers in certain situations, such as reports of discrimination, and the Sarbanes-Oxley Act of 2002 now requires that firms in the private sector provide procedures for anonymous reporting of accusations of fraud. Under the act, anyone who retaliates against an employee for taking concerns of unlawful conduct to a public official can be

They Said It

The fact is that the improper shredding of documents took place on my watch—and I believe it is now in the best interest of the firm for me to step down.

—Joseph Berardino (b. 1951) former Arthur Andersen CEO upon resigning his post

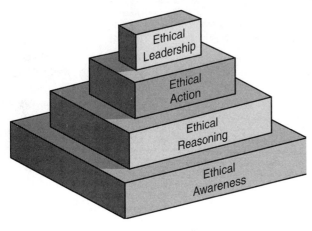
prosecuted. Whistleblowers who still experience dramatic retribution for their actions have recourse thanks to the act—those who have been fired, demoted, threatened, or harassed have 90 days to file a complaint with the U.S. Department of Labor.

Obviously, whistleblowing and other ethical issues arise relatively infrequently in firms with strong organizational climates of ethical behavior. The next section examines how a business can develop an environment that discourages unethical behavior among individuals.

FIGURE 2.5
Structure of an Ethical Environment

How Organizations Shape Ethical Conduct

No individual makes decisions in a vacuum. Choices are strongly influenced by the standards of conduct established within the organizations where people work. Most ethical lapses in business reflect the values of the firms' corporate cultures.

As shown in Figure 2.5, development of a corporate culture to support business ethics happens on four levels: ethical awareness, ethical reasoning, ethical action, and ethical leadership. If any of these four factors is missing, the ethical climate in an organization will weaken.

Ethical Awareness

The foundation of an ethical climate is ethical awareness. As we have already seen, ethical dilemmas occur frequently in the workplace. So, employees need help in identifying ethical problems when they occur. Workers also need guidance about how the firm expects them to respond.

code of conduct formal statement that defines how the organization expects and requires employees to resolve ethical issues.

One way for a firm to provide this support is to develop a **code of conduct,** a formal statement that defines how the organization expects and requires employees to resolve ethical questions. Johnson & Johnson's Credo, presented earlier, is such a code. At the most basic level, a code of conduct may simply specify ground rules for acceptable behavior, such as

Citibank encourages consumers to use their credit wisely. The company uses its Web site to educate credit card users about the "rules" of credit and ways to spend responsibly, prevent fraud, protect their identity, understand different types of credit, apply for credit, budget wisely, and use credit bureau reports.

identifying the laws and regulations that employees must obey. Other companies use their codes of conduct to identify key corporate values and provide frameworks that guide employees as they resolve moral and ethical dilemmas.

Canada-based Nortel Networks, an international telecommunications giant with customers in 150 countries, uses a code of conduct to define its values and help employees put them into practice. The code of conduct defines seven core values that Nortel requires as it strives to become known as a company of integrity. The code also defines standards for conduct among employees and between employees and the company's shareholders, customers, suppliers, and communities. Employees are expected to treat one another with respect, including respect for individual and cultural differences, protect the company's assets, and fulfill whatever commitments they make. The code of conduct also states that each employee is responsible for behaving consistently with its standards and for reporting possible violations of the code. Nortel provides each employee with a copy of this code of conduct and also posts it on its Web site.[15]

Other firms incorporate similar codes in their policy manuals or mission statements; some issue a code of conduct or statement of values in the form of a small card that employees and managers can carry with them. Harley-Davidson has developed a brief code of ethics that employees can apply both at work and in their personal lives. It reads: "Tell the truth, keep your promises, be fair, respect the individual and encourage intellectual curiosity."

Sometimes companies can express ethical awareness through their advertising, as in the Citibank ad shown here.

Ethical Reasoning

Although a code of conduct can provide an overall framework, it cannot detail a solution for every ethical situation. Some ethical questions have black-and-white answers, but others do not. Businesses must provide the tools employees need to evaluate the options and arrive at suitable decisions.

Many firms have instituted ethics training programs. More than 50 percent of the employees surveyed in one study reported that their companies provide training in the subject. Lockheed Martin Corp. has developed a training program in the form of interactive lessons that employees can access online. The sessions include cases performed by actors, plus tests in the form of multiple-choice questions. They cover a variety of business-related topics, from security to sexual harassment. The company also keeps tabs on which employees have completed which training sessions. In addition, Lockheed Martin uses a game called the Ethics Challenge, in which the players use cards and tokens to read about and resolve ethical quandaries based on real-life situations. Everyone in the company, from hourly workers to the chairman, is required to play the Ethics Challenge once per year.

Many authorities debate whether ethics can actually be taught, and one recent study suggests that a corporate ethics program to deter theft had the greatest impact on employees least likely to steal from the company in the first place.[16] But training can give employees an opportunity to practice applying ethical values to hypothetical situations as a prelude to applying the same standards to real-world situations.

Ethical Action

Codes of conduct and ethics training help employees to recognize and reason through ethical problems. In addition, firms must also provide structures and approaches that allow decisions to be turned into ethical actions. Texas Instruments gives its employees a reference card to help them make ethical decisions on the job. The size of a standard business card, it lists the following guidelines:

- Does it comply with our values?
- If you do it, will you feel bad?
- How will it look in the newspaper?
- If you know it's wrong, don't do it!
- If you're not sure, ask.
- Keep asking until you get an answer.

Goals set for the business as a whole and for individual departments and employees can affect ethical behavior. A firm whose managers set unrealistic goals for employee performance may find an increase in cheating, lying, and other misdeeds, as employees attempt to protect themselves. In today's Internet economy, the high value placed on speed can create a climate in which ethical behavior is sometimes challenged. Ethical decisions often require careful and quiet thought, and such thought seems to be nearly impossible in a business that is moving at warp speed.

Some companies encourage ethical action by providing support for employees faced with dilemmas. One common tool is an employee hotline, a telephone number that employees can call, often anonymously, for advice or to report unethical behavior they have witnessed. Nortel Networks, for example, operates a Business Ethics Advice Line. Employees from around the world can contact the advice line via phone or e-mail to ask for advice in applying the code of conduct in specific situations. Ethics compliance officers at some firms, as mentioned previously, are responsible for guiding employees through ethical minefields.

Ethical Leadership

Executives must not only talk about ethical behavior but also demonstrate it in their actions. This principle requires employees to be personally committed to the company's core values and be willing to base their actions on them. In a recent survey, employees questioned about ethical leadership said they felt less pressure to commit misconduct in their organizations when leaders and managers behaved ethically. They also reported being more satisfied with their organizations overall. Consistent with these findings, another large-scale study found that when employees think their employer's ethics program was designed primarily to protect upper management from being blamed for misconduct, the program actually promotes unethical behavior.[17]

One important way for business leaders to model ethical behavior is to admit when they are wrong and correct their organization's mistakes and problems. The Red Cross, already under scrutiny for its use of funds, was widely criticized for announcing plans to divert some of the nearly $1 billion raised under the auspices of a special 9/11 Liberty Fund. The charity said it would create a blood bank and upgrade its telecommunications equipment with some of the money. The fund had been created for the aid of victims of the 9/11 terrorist attacks, and most people made donations to it for that specific purpose. When the public protested, the Red Cross abandoned plans to divert the money and pledged to use all of the Liberty Fund for its original purpose, as well as to revamp its fund-raising practices so that such problems do not recur. "We made some large mistakes," said chairman David McLaughlin at a news conference.[18]

However, ethical leadership should also go one step further and charge each employee at every level with the responsibility to be an ethical leader. Everyone should be aware of transgressions and be willing to defend the organization's standards. The Nortel Networks guidelines specifically communicate these responsibilities. The company tells employees, "You have a responsibility to ask questions when you have doubts about the ethical implications of any given situation or proposed course of action" and "You have a responsibility to report any concerns about business practices within the corporation that may violate this Code of Business Conduct."[19] As noted earlier, Nortel also provides employees with the tools for carrying out these responsibilities.

Perhaps one of the best measures of ethical leadership is whether a company focuses on the welfare of its customers and investors and how well it can perform in the long run. Jack Welch, former CEO of General Electric, well known for his business successes, continues to be highly regarded for his leadership and for leaving his company thriving, as the Best Business Practices box discusses.

Unfortunately, not all organizations are able to build a solid framework of business ethics. Because the damage from ethical misconduct can powerfully affect a firm's stakeholders—customers, investors, employees, and the public—pressure is exerted on businesses to act in acceptable ways. But when businesses fail, the law must step in to enforce good business practices. Many of the laws that affect specific industries or individuals are described in other chapters in this book. For example, legislation affecting international business operations is discussed in Chapter 4. Laws designed to assist small businesses are examined in Chapter 5. Laws related to labor unions are described in Chapter 9. Legislation related to banking and the securities markets is discussed in Chapters 17 and 18. Finally, for an examination of the legal and governmental forces designed to safeguard society's interests when businesses fail at self-regulation, see the Appendix to Part 1, "The Legal Framework for Business," beginning on page 138.

Concept Check

1. What is a code of conduct?
2. How does ethical leadership contribute to ethical standards throughout a company?

BEST BUSINESS PRACTICES

GE's Former Chief Leaves Trail of Profits

Jack Welch was CEO of General Electric for 21 years. His goal, to make GE the most competitive enterprise in the world, sometimes meant making difficult decisions, like letting about 100,000 employees go during his early years at the helm when the company was struggling. Although the huge job cuts earned him the title Neutron Jack, Welch never shrank from his duties. The CEO's goal was always to produce high-quality products for his customers and superior company performance for his investors. He succeeded admirably on both counts.

Under his leadership, GE not only became an aggressive, adaptable, and successful firm but also has consistently ranked among the world's most respected companies, admired for its customer orientation and integrity. The company has ranked at the top of the *Financial Times*'s list of the World's Most Respected Companies for the past five years. Contributing to this success is the company's Six Sigma quality program, begun under Welch's reign, which focuses on reducing production errors to minimal levels and is discussed in more detail in Chapter 11. The company is also widely respected for its customer-oriented mindset. As the Web site says, "Customers are at the center of GE's universe; they define quality."

Welch's success resulted in his becoming one of the world's most highly regarded corporate CEOs of the past 50 years. In fact, despite his retirement, he still ranks No. 2 on the list of most respected business leaders—right behind Bill Gates. That doesn't mean Welch didn't attract controversy over some of his management practices. He established a rigorous—and sometimes criticized—annual evaluation process in which the lowest-rated performers were dismissed. His philosophy about employees was clear, however: "They have to constantly demonstrate that they deserve to be there." But during Welch's tenure, the company's stock price rose by a jaw-dropping 2,800+ percent and GE's value increased to $450 billion.

On the heels of his departure, information divulged during his messy divorce case raised questions about Welch's spectacular retirement package. GE had agreed to pay for a luxury apartment in New York, tickets to the opera and sports events, satellite hookups for each of his four homes, limo service, laptops, printers, software, and many other perks. Criticism of the package was swift, and accusations of greed followed. Welch eventually agreed to pay for between $2 and $2.5 million of these promised company benefits each year. Yet unlike other disgraced CEOs who took their companies into financial ruin, Welch's legacy still shines. GE's most recent earnings achieved a record $15.1 billion, and that despite an economic downturn.

QUESTIONS FOR CRITICAL THINKING

1. Discuss Jack Welch's ethical leadership style in terms of three main constituents: customers, investors, and employees.

2. Do you think Welch's end results—a successful company—justified his actions? Why or why not?

Sources: General Electric Web site, **http://www.ge.com**, accessed February 3, 2004; Michael Skapinker, "Different Game, Same Winners," *Financial Times*, January 17, 2003, **http://www.ft.com**; Philip Kennicott, "Rich with Irony," *The Washington Post*, October 14, 2002, p. C01; Richard Cohen and David Gow, "SEC Inquiry as Jack Welch Gives Up Freebies," *The Guardian*, September 17, 2002, **http://www.guardian.co.uk**.

Acting Responsibly to Satisfy Society

A second major issue affecting business is the question of social responsibility. In a general sense, **social responsibility** is management's acceptance of the obligation to consider profit, consumer satisfaction, and societal well-being of equal value in evaluating the firm's performance. It is the recognition that business must be concerned with the qualitative dimensions of consumer, employee, and societal benefits as well as the quantitative measures of sales and profits, by which business performance is traditionally measured. Businesses may exercise social responsibility because such behavior is required by law, because it enhances the company's image, or because management believes it is the ethical course of action.

Historically, a company's social performance has been measured by its contribution to the overall economy and the employment opportunities it provides. Variables such as wage payments often serve

social responsibility
management's acceptance of the obligation to consider profit, consumer satisfaction, and societal well-being of equal value in evaluating the firm's performance.

to indicate social performance. Although profits and employment remain important, today many factors contribute to an assessment of a firm's social performance, including providing equal employment opportunities; respecting the cultural diversity of employees; responding to environmental concerns; providing a safe, healthy workplace; and producing high-quality products that are safe to use.

A business is also judged by its interactions with the community. To demonstrate their social responsibility, many corporations highlight charitable contributions and community service in their annual reports and on their Web site. Procter & Gamble, for instance, contributes millions of dollars through the Procter & Gamble Fund, corporate contributions, product donations, individual facilities' gifts, and other types of giving. The company donates products to America's Second Harvest, a network of food banks. It donates to universities and research organizations patents that do not fit the company's strategic plans but may offer commercial potential, thereby providing revenue to the organizations that apply the patents.[20]

Some firms measure social performance by conducting **social audits,** formal procedures that identify and evaluate all company activities that relate to social issues such as conservation, employment practices, environmental protection, and philanthropy. The social audit informs management about how well the company is performing in these areas. Based on this information, management may take steps to revise current programs or develop new ones.

Outside groups may conduct their own evaluations of businesses. Various environmental, religious, and public interest groups have created standards of corporate performance. Reports on many of these evaluations are available to the general public. The Council on Economic Priorities produces publications such as *The Better World Investment Guide,* which recommends basing investment decisions on companies' track records on various social issues, including environmental impact, nuclear weapons contracts, community outreach, and advancement of women and minorities. Other groups publicize their evaluations and include critiques of the social responsibility performance of firms. The Center for Science in the Public Interest evaluates the healthfulness of the food marketed to consumers.[21]

Many firms find that consumers evaluate their social track records through their purchase decisions in retail stores. Some consumer groups organize boycotts of companies they find to be socially irresponsible. In a **boycott,** consumers refuse to buy a company's goods or services. Mail Abuse Prevention System (MAPS) offers a new twist on the old-fashioned boycott: a service that blocks incoming e-mail from companies that it believes have sent spam. The company compiles the Real-Time Blackhole List, a list of reported spammers, and for those who subscribe, it deletes mail from those sources or returns it to the sender. Bouncing the messages back not only spares the receiver, but it can also swamp the sender's Web site so that it effectively shuts down during the onslaught. Companies that place online marketing messages treat MAPS with kid gloves. MessageMedia, for example, says it has refused to work with clients who do not adhere to MAPS guidelines because a misstep by one of its clients could land MessageMedia on the list.[22]

As Figure 2.6 shows, the social responsibilities of business can be classified according to its relationships to the general public, customers, employees, and investors and other members of the financial community. Many of these relationships extend beyond national borders.

Responsibilities to the General Public

The responsibilities of business to the general public include dealing with public health issues, protecting the environment, and developing the quality of the workforce. Many would argue that businesses also

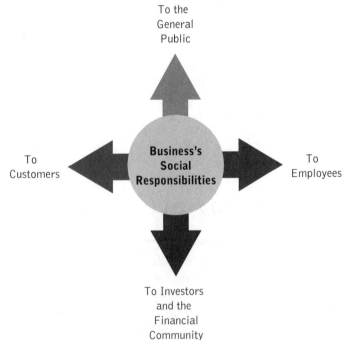

FIGURE 2.6
Responsibilities of Business

Public Health Issues

AIDS
Smoking
Alcohol Abuse
Drug Abuse

Protecting the Environment

Avoiding Pollution
Recycling
Green Marketing
Environmentally
    Friendly Technologies

Corporate Philanthropy

Monetary Donations
    to Charitable and
    Social Organizations
Support for Employee
    Volunteer Efforts
Donations of Goods to
    Charitable and
    Social Organizations

Developing the Quality of the Workforce

On-the-Job Training
Education Benefits
Operating Where
    Jobs Are Needed
Valuing Diversity

have responsibilities to support charitable and social causes and organizations that work toward the greater public good. In other words, they should give back to the communities in which they earn profits. Such efforts are called *corporate philanthropy.* Figure 2.7 summarizes these four responsibilities, which are discussed in the sections that follow.

FIGURE 2.7
Business Responsibilities to the General Public

Public Health Issues   One of the most complex issues facing business as it addresses its ethical and social responsibilities to the general public is public health. Central to the public health debate is the question of what businesses should do about dangerous products like tobacco, alcohol, and handguns. Tobacco products represent a major health risk, contributing to heart disease, stroke, and cancer among smokers. Families and coworkers of smokers share this danger as well, since their exposure to secondhand smoke increases their risks for cancer, asthma, and respiratory infections. Recently, courts have agreed with this assessment of smoking as a health risk, and tobacco companies have been assessed heavy fines to compensate for their actions. In 1998, Altria (then known as Philip Morris) and three other tobacco companies agreed to a $206 billion settlement with 46 states. Two years later, a Florida jury ordered the tobacco industry to pay $145 billion in punitive damages to Florida smokers who had developed illnesses associated with long-term smoking. Altria, whose products represent one of every two cigarettes sold in the U.S., was ordered to pay about half the entire amount. Faced with the prospect of even more legal action, the tobacco companies have spent tens of millions of dollars on socially responsible activities and causes, such as youth smoking prevention programs, food banks, and medical assistance in developing countries. But not everyone is buying the sincerity of the tobacco industry's attempts at social responsibility. In 2003, the U.S. Department of Justice filed a countersuit, demanding that the nation's biggest cigarette makers be ordered to forfeit $289 billion in "ill-gotten gains"—profits derived from a half century of "fraudulent" and dangerous marketing practices.[23]

Substance abuse, including alcohol abuse, is another serious public health problem worldwide. Motor vehicle accidents are a major killer, and drunk drivers cause many serious crashes. Alcohol abuse has also been linked to such major diseases as cirrhosis of the liver. Other risks to public health and safety come from fatty foods, television violence, and motorcycles.

Of particular concern is the impact of such products on vulnerable groups. Alcohol ads appeal to teenagers. Absolut vodka ads have even become collector's items for many teens, raising concerns that the company is encouraging underage drinking. Many consumers view alcohol advertising, whether aimed at adults or young people, as socially irresponsible. Some brewers have tried to counter these views by sponsoring advertising campaigns that promote moderation.

Businesses also face challenges when dealing with the consequences of diseases like AIDS, which is especially dangerous because, on average, five years pass between a person's first exposure to HIV and actual development of the disease. During this period, people may not show any symptoms, and they probably don't even know they have the virus, but they are still carriers who can transmit the disease to others. This large pool of unknown carriers contributes greatly to the rapid spread of the disease.

The onslaught of AIDS has forced companies to educate their workers about how to deal with employees and customers who have the deadly disease. Health care for AIDS patients can be incredibly expensive, straining the ability of small companies to pay for health-care coverage. Do companies have the right to test potential employees for the AIDS virus and avoid this expense? Some people believe that this screening would violate the rights of job applicants; others feel that a firm has a responsibility not to place AIDS patients in jobs where they could infect members of the general public.

These are difficult questions. In resolving them, a business must balance the rights of individuals against the rights of society in general.

Protecting the Environment

Businesses consume huge amounts of energy, which increases the use of fossil fuels like coal and oil for energy production. This activity introduces carbon dioxide and sulfur into the earth's atmosphere, substances that many scientists believe will result in dramatic climate changes during the 21st century. Meanwhile, the sulfur from fossil fuels combines with water vapor in the air to form sulfuric acid. The acid rain that results can kill fish and trees and pollute ground water. Wind can carry the sulfur around the entire globe. Sulfur from U.S. factories is damaging Canadian forests, and pollution from London smokestacks has been found in the forests and lakes of Scandinavia. Other production and manufacturing methods leave behind large quantities of waste materials that can further pollute the environment and fill already bulging landfills. Some products themselves, particularly electronics, are difficult to reuse or recycle. Junked parts can introduce poisons like lead, cadmium, and mercury into ground-water supplies.[24]

For many managers, finding ways to minimize the **pollution** and other environmental damage caused by their products or operating processes has become an important economic, legal, and social issue. The solutions can be difficult, and expensive. It costs computer makers about $20 to recycle each old computer, for instance.[25] Drivers may face high costs, too. Hybrid cars use a combination of gas and electricity to power their engines and promise much higher fuel efficiency than conventional autos. As gasoline prices reached the previously unheard of $2 per gallon mark, sales of U.S. hybrids reached 5,000 a month. Most of the purchasers chose the $20,000 Honda Civic hybrid, which gets about 48 miles per gallon, 30 to 50 percent better than the gas-powered version. Other hybrid auto purchasers chose the $20,000 Toyota Prius or the $21,000 Honda Insight. However, the fuel saving isn't cheap. Experts figure that adding the electric system to the car also adds about $3,500 to the sticker price.[26]

The more exotic Hy-wire, a hydrogen-powered prototype that cost General Motors $5 million to build, can reach 100 miles an hour with only water vapor as exhaust. But even though Toyota, Honda, and BMW have similar prototypes in the works, cutting costs enough to market the vehicles and earn a profit continues to be a major stumbling block.[27]

Despite the difficulty, however, companies are finding they can be environmentally friendly and profitable, too. Over the past quarter century, 3M has reduced emissions of hazardous wastes, mainly by finding alternatives to toxic solvents. The changes have saved the company hundreds of millions of dollars. And the $3.1 million that Dow Chemical has spent to reduce toxic emissions at its Midland, Michigan, plant actually resulted in savings of $5.4 million a year. These kinds of savings come

The Toyota Prius boasts both an electric motor with a battery that never needs recharging and a "super-efficient" gasoline engine. This hybrid power system is fuel efficient and less polluting to the environment. The car gets its energy economy from a system that knows which fuel source to use at which time.

Courtesy of Toyota

from sources like greater efficiency, reduced operating costs, and less money spent on complying with regulations.[28]

Another solution to the problems of pollutants is **recycling**—reprocessing used materials for reuse. Recycling can sometimes provide much of the raw material that manufacturers need, thereby conserving the world's natural resources and reducing the need for landfills. Several industries are developing ways to use recycled materials. Recycling firms in Asia, like NTT DoCoMo and J-Phone, are buying used cell phones in bulk from wireless carriers, crushing and melting them, and extracting platinum, silver, and even gold. It takes about 125,000 phones to produce a one-kilo gold bar worth $10,000. In the U.S., phones are recycled for their batteries, while larger appliances like TVs and VCRs are mined for reusable metals.[29]

recycling reprocessing of used materials for reuse.

green marketing marketing strategy that promotes environmentally safe products and production methods.

Many environmentalist groups have realized that working in partnership with companies can help them achieve their goals. One such organization, Environmental Defense, worked with McDonald's to streamline the fast-food company's waste output and has begun similar partnerships with FedEx and Starbucks, among others. Greenpeace is working with European firms to replace polluting refrigerants with a more environmentally friendly substance called Greenfreeze, and The Coca-Cola Co. and Unilever have committed to join and support the campaign.[30]

Many consumers have favorable impressions of environmentally conscious businesses. To target these customers, companies often use **green marketing,** a marketing strategy that promotes environmentally safe products and production methods. A business cannot simply claim that its goods or services are environmentally friendly, however. In 1992, the FTC issued guidelines for businesses to follow in making environmental claims. A firm must be able to prove that any environmental claim made about a product has been substantiated with reliable scientific evidence. In addition, as shown in Figure 2.8, the FTC has given specific directions about how various environmental terms may be used in advertising and marketing.

Concern had developed, though, that consumers themselves, while supportive of green products in theory, have been less willing to put their money where their sentiments are. Philips Electronics NV, for instance, increased sales by more than 10 percent for its economically friendly fluorescent light bulbs after it stopped calling them EarthLight and promoted their seven-year life span instead. Gerber Products Co. switched from glass baby-food bottles to plastic after nearly three of four baby-food shoppers said they preferred the convenience of plastic, even though plastic can't be recycled. About four in ten consumers surveyed by Roper ASW said they don't buy "green" products because they are afraid they won't perform as well. Said one, "I know the environment is going downhill, but you go in the store and buy the closest thing to your hand—something you've used before that you know works."[31]

Sometimes the new technologies themselves raise controversy. An example is **genetic engineering,** a type of biotechnology that involves altering crops or other living things by inserting genes that provide them with a desirable characteristic, such as nutritional value or resistance to pesticides. One of the most controversial of these genetically modified (GM) crops has been corn engineered to make *Bacillus thuringiensis* (Bt), a type of bacteria that acts as a natural insecticide. The potential value of such a crop is that it reduces the need for chemical pesticides. Critics warn that it could be an ecological disaster. If most corn makes Bt, caterpillars could become resistant to it, requiring more pesticide use in the long run. In addition, some research has suggested that exposure to the corn is deadly to monarch butterfly caterpillars. Critics also fear that introducing genes from one type of plant into another—for example, daffodil genes have been used to add beta carotene to rice—may create products with hidden allergens that could trigger a dangerous

If a business says a product is...	The product or package must...
Biodegradable	break down and return to nature in a reasonably short period of time.
Recyclable	be entirely reusable as new materials in the manufacture or assembly of a new product or package.
Refillable	be included in a system for the collection and return of the package for refill. If consumers have to find a way to refill it themselves, it is not *refillable*.
Ozone Safe/Ozone Friendly	not contain any ozone-depleting ingredient.

FIGURE 2.8
FTC Guidelines for Environmental Claims in Green Marketing

allergic reaction in susceptible people.

Some consumers, especially in Europe, have resisted buying GM foods, and the European Union has maintained a controversial moratorium on approving new GM crops.[32] Both U.S. and foreign farmers are uncertain whether to adopt the technology because consumer resistance could make the crops worthless in the marketplace. Already, some food processors are willing to pay premium prices for food that has not been genetically engineered. Frito-Lay asked its corn suppliers to plant only unmodified seeds, and Wild Oats Market and Whole Foods Market are eliminating GM ingredients from their store brands. An agreement negotiated under the United Nations Convention on Biodiversity allows countries to ban imports of GM seeds, animals, and crops and to require labels on living GM goods, such as animals and whole grains, saying that they may contain GM organisms. Taco Bell recently recalled its taco shells distributed through supermarkets due to concerns about adverse consumer reactions when it discovered that GM corn had been used. Still, biotech food has become part of U.S. agriculture. About one-third of the corn and almost half the soybeans currently grown in the U.S. have been genetically engineered to either include an insecticide or resist herbicides used to kill weeds around the crops. The companies that provide these technologies are hoping that sentiment will become more favorable when food producers begin offering products engineered to provide health benefits, such as eggs with reduced cholesterol.[33]

Developing the Quality of the Workforce

In the past, a nation's wealth has often been based on its money, production equipment, and natural resources. A country's true wealth, however, lies in its people. An educated, skilled workforce provides the intellectual know-how required to develop new technology, improve productivity, and compete in the global marketplace. It is becoming increasingly clear that to remain competitive, U.S. business must assume more responsibility for enhancing the quality of its workforce, including encouraging diversity of all kinds, as Eastman Kodak does.

In developed economies like that of the U.S., most new jobs require college-educated workers. Companies find it more economical to hire overseas workers for low-skilled tasks because wages are lower in developing nations. With demand greatest for workers with advanced skills, the difference between the highest-paid and lowest-paid workers has been increasing. Among full-time workers in the U.S., the top 10 percent earn an average of $1,200 per week, compared with just $275 for the average worker in the bottom 10 percent. Twenty years ago, a college graduate on average earned 38 percent more than someone with only a high school diploma, but today the typical college graduate earns 71 percent more.[34] Clearly, education is essential to the well-being of the workforce. Businesses must encourage students to stay in school, continue their education, and sharpen their skills. Companies must also encourage employees to learn new skills and remain competitive.

Organizations also face enormous responsibilities for helping women, members of various cultural groups, and those who are physically challenged to contribute fully to the economy. Failure to do so is not only a waste of more than half the nation's workforce but also devastating to a firm's public image. Some socially responsible firms also encourage diversity in their business suppliers. Retail giant JCPenney's Partnership Program is designed to foster relationships with minority- and women-owned businesses— an effort the company has worked at for more than 30 years.

Through a commitment to developing employee diversity, ChevronTexaco has successfully rebounded from a racial discrimination lawsuit. When information that the company's top managers had engaged in racist behavior became public, the company (then known simply as Texaco) was embarrassed, and its stock price tumbled. It quickly agreed to settle the lawsuit and crafted a plan to place more value on diversity among employees. Recruiting methods were revised to reach a more diverse pool of applicants, and scholarship programs were launched to develop talented minorities interested in key careers like the physical sciences and international business. The company set specific goals for hiring and promoting qualified minority employees, and to achieve those goals, it included women and minorities on human resource committees and established mentoring programs. Within three years, the company had increased its recruiting of minorities to more than four of every ten new hires, and minorities accounted for one of every five promotions.

Corporate Philanthropy   As Chapter 1 pointed out, not-for-profit organizations play an important role in society by serving the public good. They provide the human resources that enhance the quality of life in communities around the world. To fulfill this mission, many not-for-profit organizations rely on financial contributions from the business community. Firms respond by donating billions of dollars each year to not-for-profit organizations. This **corporate philanthropy** includes cash contributions, donations of equipment and products, and supporting the volunteer efforts of company employees. Recipients include cultural organizations, adopt-a-school programs, community development agencies, and housing and job training programs.

corporate philanthropy
act of an organization giving something back to the communities in which it earns profits.

Corporate philanthropy can have many positive benefits beyond the purely altruistic rewards of giving, such as higher employee morale, enhanced company image, and improved customer relationships. After the 9/11 terrorist attacks, major firms made donations that totaled over $120 million. Discover Card raised $5 million for the relief efforts by contributing portions of card member charges. DuPont donated another $5 million. The American Heroes Fund, a not-for-profit organization created by fashion clothing and jewelry marketer Polo Ralph Lauren, received $4 million from its parent organization. In an effort to maximize the benefits of corporate giving in an era of downsizing, businesses have become more selective of the causes and charities they choose to support. Many seek to align their marketing efforts with their charitable giving. For example, many

Courtesy of Concern Worldwide

Bangladesh

In rural Bangladesh there are no atm's... and no checking accounts. What there is, though, is Bank of Concern. And we're in business to help poor villagers to start their own businesses, develop their communities — and escape the poverty that's been all their families have known. When as little as a $50 loan from us can mean self-sufficiency, just think what your gift can mean.

CONCERN
WORLDWIDE
USA

PLEASE SEND YOUR GIFT TO CONCERN WORLDWIDE U.S.   www.concernusa.org
104 East 40th Street, Room 903, New York, NY 10016 212-557-8000 • 166 East Superior Street, Suite 502, Chicago, IL 60611 312-527-0679

Founded in Ireland in 1968, Concern has 3,000 personnel working in 29 countries, helping to eliminate hunger and poverty in the developing world. Concern Worldwide U.S. Inc. is a New York not-for-profit corporation exempt from Federal income taxation under section 501(c)(3). Concern Worldwide U.S. Inc. supports projects carried out in the field by Concern Worldwide, registered in Ireland.

Design donated by MCS Advertising Ltd. and placement generously donated by this publication.

Concern Worldwide is a not-for-profit corporation that employs about 3,000 people in nearly 30 developing countries, all working to eliminate hunger and poverty. The ad agency that designed this ad to raise public awareness and ask the public for financial support for Concern Worldwide donated its services, and the magazine in which the ad appeared donated the space.

companies make contributions to the Olympics and create advertising that features the company's sponsorship. This is known as *cause related marketing*.

Another form of corporate philanthropy is volunteerism. In their roles as corporate citizens, thousands of businesses encourage their employees to contribute their efforts to projects as diverse as Habitat for Humanity, the United Way, and Red Cross blood drives. In addition to making tangible contributions to the well-being of fellow citizens, such programs generate considerable public support and goodwill for the companies and their employees. In some cases, the volunteer efforts occur mostly during off-hours for employees. In other instances, the firm permits its workforce to volunteer during regular working hours. Nortel Networks offers a combination of grants, use of company facilities, and limited time off work for volunteers in the locations where it has facilities, from Atlanta to Paris to Beijing. Regional teams work with selected local community organizations to develop programs that address math, science, and technology education; health care and human services issues; and needs specific to their area. Community involvement for each city is coordinated by an employee who makes sure the efforts are in line with company guidelines.[35] Sometimes companies help by contributing resources to promote worthy causes, such as Concern Worldwide's mission to help poverty stricken people around the world.

Responsibilities to Customers

consumerism public demand that a business consider the wants and needs of its customers in making decisions.

Businesspeople share a social and ethical responsibility to treat their customers fairly and act in a manner that is not harmful to them. Consumer advocate Ralph Nader first pioneered this idea in the late 1960s. Since then, **consumerism**—the public demand that a business consider the wants and needs of its customers in making decisions—has gained widespread acceptance. Consumerism is based on the belief that consumers have certain rights. The most frequently quoted statement of consumer rights was made by President John F. Kennedy in 1962. Figure 2.9 summarizes these consumer rights. Numerous state and federal laws have been implemented since then to protect these rights.

The Right to Be Safe   Contemporary businesspeople must recognize obligations, both moral and legal, to ensure the safe operation of their products. Consumers should feel assured that the products they purchase will not cause injuries in normal use. **Product liability** refers to the responsibility of manufacturers for injuries and damages caused by their products. Items that lead to injuries, either directly or indirectly, can have disastrous consequences for their makers.

Many companies put their products through rigorous testing to avoid safety problems. Still, testing alone cannot foresee every eventuality. Companies must try to consider all possibilities and provide adequate warning of potential dangers. When a product does pose a threat to customer safety, a responsible manufacturer responds quickly to either correct the problem or recall the dangerous product. For example, the Betesh Group toy manufacturer recently recalled its Busy Bug stuffed toy after it discovered that children could chew off—and choke on—the bug's fabric antennas. A warning went out to discount department stores to pull the toys, and the company set up a toll-free hotline to answer consumer questions and concerns.[36]

The Right to Be Informed   Consumers should have access to enough education and product information to make responsible buying decisions. In their efforts to promote and sell their goods and services, companies can easily neglect consumers' right to be fully informed. False or misleading advertising is a violation of the Wheeler-Lea Act, a federal law enacted in 1938. The Federal Trade Commission (FTC) and other federal and state agencies have established rules and regulations that govern advertising truthfulness. These rules prohibit businesses from making unsubstantiated claims about the performance or superiority of their goods or services. They also require businesses to avoid misleading consumers. Businesses that fail to comply face scrutiny from the FTC

FIGURE 2.9
Consumer Rights as Proposed by President Kennedy

BUSINESS TOOL KIT

Being Considerate of One's Coworkers

Let's face it—as a new college graduate, you will not be getting the corner office with a view. More likely you will be introduced to the world of cubicles and the common work area where everyone can hear each other's phone conversations, work-related discussions, and everything else that transpires between the cubicle walls. Being a team player means being considerate of your coworkers, so here are some tips for playing it cool while at work.

1. No loud radios or CDs—keep volume low or use headphones if you have to have a radio at your desk. The same goes for conversations and phone calls; use your "inside" or library voice in order to not disturb those working. In addition, if you carry a cell phone, make sure that the volume is turned to low or on vibrate so as not to disturb others.

2. Avoid using the speaker phone unless it's for a conference call. Nothing is more irritating to your coworkers than having to listen to all of your conversations or on-hold music through a speaker phone. And although it might be tempting, try not to listen to others' personal phone calls. You don't want anyone listening to yours, do you?

3. Keep general areas tidy, put things back where they belong, and refill or replace when something runs out. This is especially true if there is a community coffeepot! And don't forget that the community kitchen is just that—a *community* kitchen that the whole office uses. Don't steal lunches or anything else that doesn't belong to you.

4. If you borrow something, return it. Good manners are part of good business communications, and they need to be practiced in the office as well as at home and in public places. You will foster good working relationships with all of your colleagues, which can only help you in your job.

5. Good manners extend to the use of the community fax or copy machine. Try to save big jobs for early or late in the day so you don't monopolize the copier and irritate anyone who only needs to make one copy.

6. Don't shout over your cubicle walls, even if it's a business-related question. Make the effort to get up, walk around, and address your colleague in a normal tone of voice so as to not disturb your other work mates. Maybe your colleague will think twice and do the same next time!

Sources: "Office and Cubicle Etiquette," http://www.business-person.com/etiquette/Officeetiquette.html, accessed January 13, 2004; Bob Rosner, "The Cubicle Lifestyle," http://more.abcnews.go.com/sections/business/dailynews/ww0227/ww0227.html, accessed February 27, 2003; Jacqueline Blais, "Mind Your Manners Even If You're at Work," *USA Today*, January 17, 2000, pp. B1, B5.

---

and consumer protection organizations. In one case, the FTC responded to complaints by filing charges against Star Publishing Group, which under the name National Consumer Services placed want ads promising as much as $800 per week for starting a home-based business. Consumers who called the toll-free number in the ad reached a recording selling a guide to start a business that the recording falsely implied would involve government work.

The Food and Drug Administration (FDA), which sets standards for advertising conducted by drug manufacturers, recently eased restrictions for prescription drug advertising on television. In print ads, drug makers are required to spell out potential side effects and the proper uses of prescription drugs. Because of the requirement to disclose this information, prescription drug television advertising was limited. Now, however, the FDA says drug ads on radio and television can directly promote a prescription drug's benefits if they provide a quick way for consumers to learn about side effects, such as displaying a toll-free number or Internet address. The FDA also monitors "dietary supplements," including vitamins and herbs. These products may make claims about their general effect on health but may not claim to cure a disease, unless the company has presented the FDA with research and received the agency's approval. For

They Said It

Suddenly our name is not so cool.

—*statement released by the band Anthrax*

FIGURE 2.10
Wacky Warning Labels
The number of product liability lawsuits has skyrocketed. To protect themselves, businesses have become more careful about including warnings on products. However, some companies may go overboard, as demonstrated by these actual product warning labels.

instance, a product may say it helps the body maintain a healthy immune system but not that it fights colds.

The responsibility of business to preserve consumers' right to be informed extends beyond avoiding misleading advertising. All communications with customers—from salespeople's comments to warranties and invoices—must be controlled to clearly and accurately inform customers. Most packaged-goods firms, personal computer makers, and other makers of products bought for personal use by consumers include toll-free customer service numbers on their product labels so that consumers can get answers when they have questions about a product.

To protect their customers and avoid claims of insufficient disclosure, businesses often include warnings on products. As Figure 2.10 shows, sometimes these warnings go far beyond what a reasonable consumer would expect.

The Right to Choose Consumers should have the right to choose which goods and services they need and want to purchase. Socially responsible firms attempt to preserve this right, even if they reduce their own sales and profits in the process. Brand-name drug makers have recently gone on the defensive in a battle being waged by state governments, insurance companies, consumer groups, major employers like General Motors and Verizon, and unions. These groups want to force down the rising price of prescription drugs by ensuring that consumers have the right and the opportunity to select cheaper generic brands. The Federal Trade Commission has even sued drug companies that it says paid generic drug competitors to keep their products off the market long after the patents on brand-name drugs have expired.[37] Other issues confront drug companies, as described in the Solving an Ethical Controversy box.

Since the long-distance telephone industry has been deregulated, some customers have also been the victims of fraud. Several unscrupulous long-distance carriers have duped customers into switching their service through an unsavory practice called *slamming*. The firms get customers to sign contest-entry forms that contain less-than-obvious wording saying they agree to be switched. In other cases, long-distance companies have switched customers without their consent after making telemarketing calls to them.

The Right to Be Heard Consumers should be able to express legitimate complaints to appropriate parties. Many companies expend considerable effort to ensure full hearings for consumer complaints. The eBay auction Web site assists buyers and sellers who believe they were victimized in transactions conducted through the site. It deploys a 200-employee team to work with users and law enforcement agencies to combat fraud. The company provides all users with insurance coverage of up to $200 per transaction, with a $25 deductible. It operates a feedback forum, where it encourages users to rate one another. The auction site operates a software program that tracks individuals' bidding performance, looking for patterns associated with fraudulent behavior. And when it receives complaints of fraud, eBay forwards them to the FTC. So, although eBay cannot prevent all instances of fraud, it does provide an environment in which buyers and sellers feel protected.[38]

Responsibilities to Employees

As Chapter 1 explained, one of the most important business resources is the organization's workforce. Companies that are able to attract skilled and knowledgeable employees are better able to meet the challenges of competing globally. In return, businesses have wide-ranging responsibilities to their employees, both here and abroad. These include workplace safety, quality of life issues, avoiding discrimination, and preventing sexual harassment and sexism. Today, they also have to accommodate office workers who fear working in tall buildings.

SOLVING AN ETHICAL CONTROVERSY

Should Drug Companies Stop Cross-Border Sales?

Because many popular brand-name drugs are cheaper to buy in Canada, U.S. consumers have begun to cross the border, often via the Internet, to fill their prescriptions for high blood pressure and cholesterol remedies. They find savings like the $150 price difference for a three-month supply of Zocor, which results from the fact that the Canadian government controls the price of brand-name drugs. Annual revenues for these cross-border sales are estimated to be about U.S. $650 million.

But one drug company has said it will cut off wholesalers who supply Canadian pharmacies selling to U.S. customers. The wholesalers feel pressured to comply with the ban on Internet sales to the U.S. or risk leaving their Canadian customers unserved. Some medicines provided by the firm, GlaxoSmithKline, have no generic alternatives. A court battle could follow on both sides of the border.

Should drug companies be allowed to ban sales of Canadian drugs to U.S. customers?

PRO

1. Real safety problems arise from variations in temperature and humidity in the shipping process, and patient monitoring suffers.
2. Many goods besides drugs are more expensive in the U.S., as are incomes and liability costs. Drug prices should not be singled out.

CON

1. The drug companies are only trying to protect the higher profits they earn in the U.S.
2. As Vermont representative Bernie Sanders says, "Americans have the right to purchase safe and affordable medicine from Canada."

SUMMARY

U.S. prices of generic drugs like amoxicillin are typically half or two-thirds their prices in Canada. So public perception that all drugs are cheaper in Canada may be wrong. Several states are poised to follow Maine in trying to use their buying power to obtain lower drug prices for the working poor, retirees, and the uninsured. Drug companies have appealed Maine's use of the federal Medicaid law; the case is before the Supreme Court. And the Food and Drug Administration has threatened legal action against businesses that "aid the practice."

Sources: "Prescription Drugs," Center for Policy Alternatives, **http://www.cfpa.org**, accessed January 6, 2004; Julie Appleby, "Stores Pop Up to Help Seniors Buy Canadian Drugs," *USA Today,* April 9, 2002, pp. B1–B2; Thomas M. Berton, "The FDA Begins Cracking Down on Cheaper Drugs from Canada," *The Wall Street Journal,* March 12, 2003, pp. A1, A2; Tom Cohen, "Canadian Wholesaler Cuts GlaxoSmithKline Supplies to Internet Pharmacies Selling to U.S. Customers," *Associated Press,* January 29, 2003; Julie Appleby, "Glaxo Wants to Keep Cheap Drugs Out of USA," *USA Today,* January 21, 2003, p. B1.

Workplace Safety   A century ago, few businesses paid much attention to the safety of their workers. In fact, most business owners viewed employees as mere cogs in the production process. Workers—many of whom were young children—toiled in frequently dangerous conditions. In 1911, 146 people, mostly young girls, died in a fire at the Triangle Shirtwaist Factory in New York City. Contributing to the massive loss of life were the sweatshop working conditions at the factory, including overcrowding, blocked exits, and a lack of fire escapes. The horrifying tragedy forced businesses to begin to recognize their responsibility for their workers' safety.

The safety and health of workers while on the job is now an important business responsibility. The Occupational Safety and Health Administration (OSHA) is the main federal regulatory force in setting workplace safety and health standards. These mandates range from broad guidelines on storing hazardous materials to specific standards for worker safety in industries like construction, manufacturing, and

They Said It

Pete, please don't do anything foolish. Please take care of yourself and don't be a hero. I don't need a Medal of Honor winner. I need a son. Love, Mom

—*letter engraved on Vietnam War Memorial in New York City*

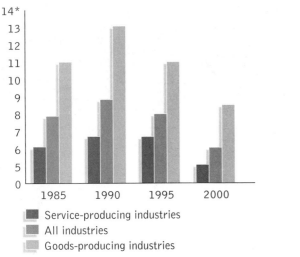

* Number of Injuries and Illnesses per 100 Full-Time Workers

FIGURE 2.11

Rates of Workplace Injuries and Illnesses

Source: U.S. Department of Labor, Bureau of Labor Statistics, "Injuries, Illnesses, and Fatalities," **http://www.bls.gov/iif/oshwc/osh/os/ osnr0013.txt**, accessed February 24, 2003.

mining. OSHA tracks and investigates workplace accidents and has the authority to fine employers who are found liable for injuries and deaths that occur on the job. As Figure 2.11 shows, workplace injuries and illnesses declined during the 1980s and 1990s. Even though rates of injury and illness are lower in service industries than in goods-producing industries, the four industries with highest injury rates are all service providers: restaurants, hospitals, nursing homes, and retail stores. Most reports to OSHA involve injuries, most of which involve disorders arising from making the same motion over and over, such as carpal tunnel syndrome.[39]

Although businesses occasionally complain about having to comply with too many OSHA regulations, ultimately management must set standards and implement programs to ensure that workers are safe in the workplace. The Jewel-Osco food-drug chain, the Midwest division of Albertson's, shows employees training videos about safe practices. The videos teach about fire safety, germs transmitted in blood, and actions to take if the store is robbed. The store makes special efforts to protect teenage employees. They are expected to read and sign a statement that they will not use any machinery, lift equipment (including the elevator), or meat slicers. Use of power equipment is limited by law to employees 18 years of age or older, and those employees must undergo training before the store permits them to use the equipment. Laws also extend extra protection to teenage workers by limiting the number of hours they work and the number of trips they may make away from their primary place of employment each day. Protection of young workers is especially significant because almost one workplace injury in three involves employees with less than a year's experience.[40]

Quality of Life Issues Balancing work and family is becoming harder for many employees. They find themselves squeezed between working long hours and handling child-care problems, caring for elderly parents, and solving other family crises. A "sandwich generation" of households, those caring for two generations—their children and their aging parents—has arisen. As the population ages, the share of American households providing some type of care to a relative or friend age 50 years or older is expected to double to more than two in five in the early years of the 21st century. At the same time, as married women spend more time working outside the home, they have fewer hours per week to spend on family. The employees juggling work with life's other demands aren't just working mothers. Childless couples, single people, and men all express frustration with the pressures of balancing work with family and personal needs.

Helping workers find solutions to these quality of life issues has become an important concern of many businesses, but finding answers isn't always easy. Some companies offer flexible work arrangements to support employees. Other firms offer benefits such as subsidized child care or on-site education and shopping to assist workers trying to balance work and family.

Another solution has been to offer **family leave** to employees who need to deal with family matters. Under the Family and Medical Leave Act of 1993, businesses with 50 or more employees must provide unpaid leave annually for any employee who wants time off for the birth or adoption of a child, to become a foster parent, or to care for a seriously ill relative or spouse. The law requires that employers grant up to 12 weeks of leave each year. This unpaid leave also applies to an employee who has a serious illness. Workers must meet certain eligibility requirements. Employers must continue to provide health benefits during the leave and guarantee that employees will return to equivalent jobs. The issue of who is entitled to health benefits can also create a dilemma as companies struggle to balance the needs of their employees against the staggering costs of health care.

The Family and Medical Leave Act gives employees the right to take time off, but because the leave is unpaid, many workers find that they cannot afford to use this right. The U.S. Department of Labor recently issued a ruling authorizing states to experiment with unemployment compensation as part of their unemployment insurance programs. States that elect to participate in this experiment can authorize partial wage replacement to parents who take approved leave. In states where it is available, the unemployment compensation would be available to employees at companies of any size, so long as they meet the state's eligibility requirements for unemployment compensation. The Department of Labor plans to evaluate whether parents who receive the benefits are more likely to remain in the workforce over the long run.[41]

Ensuring Equal Opportunity on the Job   Businesspeople face many challenges managing an increasingly diverse workforce in the 21st century. By 2050, ethnic minorities and immigrants will make up nearly half the U.S. workforce. Technological advances are expanding the ways people with physical disabilities can contribute in the workplace. Businesses also need to find ways to responsibly recruit and manage older workers and workers with varying lifestyles. In addition, beginning with Lotus Development Corp. in 1982, companies have begun to extend benefits equally to employees, regardless of sexual orientation. In particular, that means the company offers benefits like health insurance to unmarried domestic partners if it offers them to spouses of married couples. Companies that now offer these gender-neutral benefits include Boeing, Citigroup, Disney, General Mills, and Prudential. This treatment reflects the view that all employee groups deserve the right to work in an environment that is nondiscriminatory.

To a great extent, efforts at managing diversity are regulated by law. The Civil Rights Act (1964) outlawed many kinds of discriminatory practices, and Title VII of the act specifically prohibits discrimination in employment. As shown in Table 2.2, other nondiscrimination laws include the Equal Pay Act (1963), the Age Discrimination in Employment Act (1968), the Equal Employment Opportunity Act (1972), the Pregnancy Discrimination Act (1978), the Civil Rights Act of 1991, and numerous executive orders. The Americans with Disabilities Act (1990) protects the rights of physically challenged people. The Vietnam Era Veterans Readjustment Act (1974) protects the employment of veterans of the Vietnam War.

Perhaps the next round of protection will extend to the level of genetics. As scientists make progress in decoding the human genome, some people worry that employers will discriminate based on genetic characteristics, such as a gene that predisposes a person to cancer or some other costly disease. In fact, the executive branch of the federal government is now prohibited from discriminating on the basis of genetic information. When he signed the order, former President Clinton stated that he hoped it would serve as a challenge to businesses and other government agencies to adopt similar policies.[42]

The **Equal Employment Opportunity Commission (EEOC)** was created to increase job opportunities for women and minorities and to help end discrimination based on race, color, religion, disability, gender, or national origin in any personnel action. To enforce fair-employment laws, it investigates charges of discrimination and harassment and files suit against violators. The EEOC can also help employers set up programs to increase job opportunities for women, minorities, people with disabilities, and persons in other protected categories.

Fair treatment of employees is more than a matter of complying with EEOC regulations, however. Like white male employees, women and people of color want opportunities to excel and rewards for excellence. They also want to be treated with respect. A minority employee who misses out on a plum assignment may miss out on the big raise that goes with it. As the employee's salary grows more slowly, managers may eventually begin to use the size of the salary as an indicator that the employee contributes less to the organization. Chapter 9 takes a closer look at diversity and employment discrimination issues as part of a discussion of human resource management.

Age Discrimination   The Age Discrimination in Employment Act of 1968 (ADEA) protects individuals who are 40 years of age or older, prohibiting discrimination on the basis of age and denial of benefits to older employees. A recent settlement between the EEOC and the California Public Employees' Retirement System (Calpers) suggests that age bias cases are being closely watched. The settlement, the largest to date, will pay an estimated $250 million to over 1,700 retired firefighters, police, and other law officers whose disability payments were based on their age at hiring. The policy was deemed discriminatory.[43]

Table 2.2   Laws Designed to Ensure Equal Opportunity

Law	Key Provisions
Title VII of the Civil Rights Act of 1964 (as amended by the Equal Employment Opportunity Act of 1972)	Prohibits discrimination in hiring, promotion, compensation, training, or dismissal on the basis of race, color, religion, sex, or national origin.
Age Discrimination in Employment Act of 1968 (as amended)	Prohibits discrimination in employment against anyone aged 40 years or over in hiring, promotion, compensation, training, or dismissal.
Equal Pay Act of 1963	Requires equal pay for men and women working for the same firm in jobs that require equal skill, effort, and responsibility.
Vocational Rehabilitation Act of 1973	Requires government contractors and subcontractors to take affirmative action to employ and promote qualified disabled workers. Coverage now extends to all federal employees. Coverage has been broadened by the passage of similar laws in more than 20 states and, through court rulings, to include persons with communicable diseases, including AIDS.
Vietnam Era Veterans Readjustment Act of 1974	Requires government contractors and subcontractors to take affirmative action to employ and retain disabled veterans. Coverage now extends to all federal employees and has been broadened by the passage of similar laws in more than 20 states.
Pregnancy Discrimination Act of 1978	Requires employers to treat pregnant women and new mothers the same as other employees for all employment-related purposes, including receipt of benefits under company benefit programs.
Americans with Disabilities Act of 1990	Makes discrimination against the disabled illegal in public accommodations, transportation, and telecommunications; stiffens employer penalties for intentional discrimination on the basis of an employee's disability.
Civil Rights Act of 1991	Makes it easier for workers to sue their employers for alleged discrimination. Enables victims of sexual discrimination to collect punitive damages; includes employment decisions and on-the-job issues such as sexual harassment, unfair promotions, and unfair dismissal. The employer must prove that it did not engage in discrimination.
Family and Medical Leave Act of 1993	Requires all businesses with 50 or more employees to provide up to 12 weeks of unpaid leave annually to employees who have had a child or are adopting a child, or are becoming foster parents, who are caring for a seriously ill relative or spouse, or who are themselves seriously ill. Workers must meet certain eligibility requirements.

Sexual Harassment and Sexism   Every employer has a responsibility to ensure that all workers are treated fairly and are safe from sexual harassment. **Sexual harassment** refers to unwelcome and inappropriate actions of a sexual nature in the workplace. It is a form of sex discrimination that violates the Civil Rights Act of 1964, which gives both men and women the right to file lawsuits for intentional sexual harassment. More than 15,000 sexual harassment complaints are filed with the EEOC each year, of which about 12 percent are filed by men. Thousands of other cases are either handled internally by companies or never reported.

sexual harassment
inappropriate actions of a sexual nature in the workplace.

Two types of sexual harassment exist. The first type occurs when an employee is pressured to comply with unwelcome advances and requests for sexual favors in return for job security, promotions, and raises. The second type results from a hostile work environment in which an employee feels hassled or degraded because of unwelcome flirting, lewd comments, or obscene jokes. The courts have ruled that allowing sexually oriented materials like pinup calendars and pornographic magazines at the workplace can create a hostile atmosphere that interferes with an employee's ability to do the job. Employers are also legally responsible to protect employees from sexual harassment from customers and clients. The EEOC's Web site informs employers and employees of criteria for identifying sexual harassment and how it should be handled in the workplace.

Preventing sexual harassment can be difficult because it involves regulating the conduct of individual employees. Ford Motor Co. unsuccessfully tried to end sexual harassment in Chicago-area factories over the course of several years. Beginning in 1994, female workers reported to the EEOC that they had been subjected to offensive language, name-calling, and unwanted touching by coworkers and supervisors. After a two-year investigation, the EEOC agreed and reached a settlement with Ford. Then a group of women in another Ford factory complained of similar mistreatment. The company fired 10 employees and took disciplinary actions against others. Nevertheless, a group of women complained that the problems continued. After months of negotiations, Ford agreed to spend $7.5 million to compensate the victims and $10 million to train employees and managers in appropriate behavior. The company also agreed to triple the number of female supervisors in the factories and to make prevention of sexual harassment a requirement for granting raises and promotions to plant managers.[44]

To avoid sexual harassment problems, many firms have established policies and employee education programs aimed at preventing such violations. An effective harassment prevention program should include the following measures:

- Issue a specific policy statement prohibiting sexual harassment
- Develop a complaint procedure for employees to follow
- Create a work atmosphere that encourages sexually harassed staffers to come forward
- Investigate and resolve complaints quickly and take disciplinary action against harassers

Unless all these components are supported by top management, sexual harassment is difficult to eliminate.

Sexual harassment is often part of the broader problem of **sexism**—discrimination against members of either sex, but primarily affecting women. One important sexism issue is equal pay for equal work. On average, U.S. women earn 77 cents for every dollar earned by men. In the course of a working lifetime, this disparity adds up to a gap of $420,000. The percentage of women who hold managerial and professional positions has grown to 49 percent, compared with 41 percent in 1983, but that trend has not necessarily reduced the pay gap. In terms of pay, full-time female managers in some industries, like entertainment and communications, have actually lost ground since 1995 compared with men, according to the U.S. General Accounting Office. Female doctors earn just 62 cents for every dollar earned by male doctors, and female financial managers earn 61 cents for every dollar earned by male financial planners. In general, women and men start with similar salaries, and the differences develop over time, with men typically paid more than women who have comparable experience.[45]

In some extreme cases, differences in pay and advancement can become the basis for sex discrimination suits, such as those recently filed against Wal-Mart Stores. If granted class-action status, these suits, which number in the hundreds, may become the largest sex discrimination case in U.S. history. The plaintiffs in the cases say that men dominate management jobs, while women hold more than 90 percent of the low-wage cashier jobs and earn less than male Wal-Mart employees even when they hold the same jobs and other differences are accounted for. Wal-Mart could face a costly settlement; similar suits filed by thousands of female employees of Home Depot Inc. cost the firm $104 million in penalties.[46]

Responsibilities to Investors and the Financial Community

Although a fundamental goal of any business is to make a profit for its shareholders, investors and the financial community demand that businesses behave ethically as well as legally. When firms fail in this responsibility, as we saw in the story about Tyco that opened this chapter, thousands of investors and consumers can suffer.

State and federal government agencies are responsible for protecting investors from financial misdeeds. At the federal level, the Securities and Exchange Commission (SEC) investigates suspicions that publicly traded firms engaged in unethical or illegal behavior. For

Concept Check

1. What is social responsibility and why do firms exercise it?
2. How can businesses respond to consumer concerns about the environment?
3. What are quality of life issues? How can firms help employees address these needs?

example, it investigates accusations that a business is using faulty accounting practices to inaccurately portray its financial resources and profits to investors. Regulation FD ("full disclosure"), a five-year-old SEC rule, requires that publicly traded companies make announcements of major information to the general public, rather than first disclosing the information to selected major investors. The agency also operates an Office of Internet Enforcement to target fraud in online trading and online sales of stock by unlicensed sellers. Recall that the Sarbanes-Oxley Act of 2002 also protects investors from unethical accounting practices. Chapter 18 discusses securities trading practices further.

What's Ahead

The decisions and actions of businesspeople are often influenced by outside forces such as the legal environment and society's expectations about business responsibility. Firms also are affected by the economic environments in which they operate. The next chapter discusses the broad economic issues that influence businesses around the world. Our discussion will focus on how factors such as supply and demand, unemployment, inflation, and government monetary policies pose both challenges and opportunities for firms seeking to compete in the global marketplace.

Summary of Learning Goals

1 *Explain the concepts of business ethics and social responsibility.*
Business ethics refers to the standards of conduct and moral values that govern actions and decisions in the workplace. Businesspeople must take a wide range of social issues into account when making decisions. Social responsibility refers to management's acceptance of the obligation to consider profit, consumer satisfaction, and societal well-being of equal value in evaluating the firm's performance.

2 *Describe the factors that influence business ethics.*
Among the many factors shaping individual ethics are personal experience, peer pressure, and organizational culture. Individual ethics are also influenced by family, cultural, and religious standards. Additionally, the culture of the organization where a person works can be a factor.

3 *List the stages in the development of ethical standards.*
In the preconventional stage, individuals primarily consider their own needs and desires in making decisions. They obey external rules only from fear of punishment or hope of reward. In the conventional stage, individuals are aware of and respond to their duty to others. Expectations of groups, as well as self-interest, influence behavior. In the final, postconventional stage, the individual can move beyond self-interest and duty to include consideration of the needs of society. A person in this stage can apply personal ethical principles in a variety of situations.

4 **Identify common ethical dilemmas in the workplace.**

Conflicts of interest exist when a businessperson is faced with a situation where an action benefiting one person has the potential to harm another, as when the person's own interests conflict with those of a customer. One type of behavior that generates a conflict of interest is bribery. Honesty and integrity are valued qualities that engender trust, but a person's immediate self-interest may seem to require violating these principles. Loyalty to an employer sometimes conflicts with truthfulness. Whistleblowing is a possible response to misconduct in the workplace, but the personal costs of doing so are high.

5 **Discuss how organizations shape ethical behavior.**

Employees are strongly influenced by the standards of conduct established and supported within the organizations where they work. Businesses can help shape ethical behavior by developing codes of conduct that define their expectations. Organizations can also use this training to develop employees' ethics awareness and reasoning. They can foster ethical action through decision-making tools, goals consistent with ethical behavior, and advice hotlines. Executives must also demonstrate ethical behavior in their decisions and actions to provide ethical leadership.

6 **Describe how businesses' social responsibility is measured.**

Today's businesses are expected to weigh their qualitative impact on consumers and society, in addition to their quantitative economic contributions such as sales, employment levels, and profits. One measure is their compliance with labor and consumer protection laws and their charitable contributions. Another measure some businesses take is to conduct social audits. Public-interest groups also create standards and measure companies' performance relative to those standards. Consumers may boycott groups that fall short of social standards.

7 **Summarize the responsibilities of business to the general public, customers, and employees.**

The responsibilities of business to the general public include protecting the public health and the environment and developing the quality of the workforce. Additionally, many would argue that businesses have a social responsibility to support charitable and social causes in the communities in which they earn profits. Business also has a social and ethical responsibility to treat customers fairly and protect consumers upholding the rights to be safe, to be informed, to choose, and to be heard. Businesses have wide-ranging responsibilities to their workers. They should make sure that the workplace is safe, address quality of life issues, ensure equal opportunity, and prevent sexual harassment.

8 **Explain why investors and the financial community are concerned with business ethics and social responsibility.**

Investors and the financial community demand that businesses behave ethically as well as legally in handling their financial transactions. Businesses must be honest in reporting their profits and financial performance to avoid misleading investors. The Securities and Exchange Commission is the federal agency responsible for investigating suspicions that publicly traded firms have engaged in unethical or illegal financial behavior.

Business Terms You Need to Know

business ethics 40	code of conduct 48	green marketing 54	sexual harassment 62
conflict of interest 45	social responsibility 51	corporate philanthropy 56	
whistleblowing 46	recycling 54	consumerism 57	

Other Important Business Terms

Sarbanes-Oxley Act 40	pollution 53	Equal Employment Opportunity Commission (EEOC) 62
integrity 45	genetic engineering 55	
social audit 51	product liability 57	sexism 64
boycott 51	family leave 61	

Review Questions

1. What do the terms *business ethics* and *social responsibility* mean? Cite an example of each. Who are the main constituents that businesses must consider?

2. Identify and describe briefly the three stages in which individuals typically develop ethical standards. What are some of the factors that determine the stage of moral and ethical development an individual occupies at any given time?

3. What are the four most common ethical challenges that businesspeople face? Give a brief example of each.

4. What are the four levels of development of a corporate culture to support business ethics? Describe each briefly.

5. How do organizational goals affect ethical behavior? How might these goals interfere with ethical leadership? Give an example.

6. What basic consumer rights does the consumerism movement try to ensure? How has consumerism improved the contemporary business environment?

7. What are some of the major factors that contribute to the assessment of a company's social performance?

8. Identify the major benefits of corporate philanthropy.

9. What are some of the responsibilities that firms have to their employees?

10. How does a company demonstrate its responsibility to investors and the financial community?

Projects and Applications

1. Write your own personal code of ethics, detailing your feelings about ethical challenges such as lying to protect an employer or coworker, favoring one client over another, misrepresenting credentials to an employer or client, and using the Internet for personal purposes while at work. What role will your personal ethics play in deciding your choice of career and acceptance of a job?

2. "Everybody exaggerates when it comes to selling products, and customers ought to take that with a grain of salt," said one advertising executive recently in response to a complaint filed by the Better Business Bureau about misleading advertising. "Don't we all have a brain, and can't we all think a little bit, too?" Do you agree with this statement? Why or why not?

3. Imagine that you work for a company that makes outdoor clothing, such as L. L. Bean, Timberland, or Patagonia. Write a memo describing at least four specific ways in which your company could practice corporate philanthropy.

4. Imagine that you are the human resource management director for a company that is trying to establish and document its responsibilities to its employees. Choose one of the responsibilities described in the chapter—such as workplace safety—and write a memo describing specific steps your company will take to fulfill that responsibility.

5. Suppose that you own a small firm with 12 employees. One of them tells you in confidence that he has just learned he is HIV positive. You know that health-care costs for AIDS patients can be disastrously high, and this expense could drastically raise the health insurance premiums that your other employees must pay. What are your responsibilities to this employee? To the rest of your staff? Explain.

Experiential Exercise

Ethical Work Climates

Answer the following questions by circling the number that best describes an organization for which you have worked.

Questions	Disagree				Agree
1. What is the best for everyone in the company is the major consideration here.	1	2	3	4	5
2. Our major concern is always what is best for the other person.	1	2	3	4	5
3. People are expected to comply with the law and professional standards over and above other considerations.	1	2	3	4	5
4. In this company the first consideration is whether a decision violates any law.	1	2	3	4	5
5. It is very important to follow the company's rules and procedures here.	1	2	3	4	5
6. People in this company strictly obey the company policies.	1	2	3	4	5
7. In this company people are mostly out for themselves	1	2	3	4	5
8. People are expected to do anything to further the company's interests, regardless of the consequences.	1	2	3	4	5
9. In this company people are guided by their own personal ethics.	1	2	3	4	5
10. Each person in this company decides for himself or herself what is right and wrong.	1	2	3	4	5

Add up your score:_____

These questions measure the dimensions of an organization's ethical climate. Questions 1 and 2 measure caring for people; questions 3 and 4 measure lawfulness; questions 5 and 6 measure adherence to rules; questions 7 and 8 measure emphasis on financial and company performance; and questions 9 and 10 measure individual independence. *Questions 7 and 8 are reverse scored* (1 = 5, 2 = 4, 3 = 3, 4 = 2, and 5 = 1). A total score above 40 indicates a very positive ethical climate. A score between 30 and 39 indicates an above-average ethical climate. A score between 20 and 29 indicates a below-average ethical climate, and a score of less than 20 indicates a very poor ethical climate.

Go back over the questions and think about changes that you could have made to improve the ethical climate in the organization. Discuss with other students what you could do as a manager to improve ethics in future companies you work for.

Source: Richard L. Daft, *Management,* Sixth Edition. Mason, OH: South-Western Publishing, 2004, used by permission. The exercise is based on Bart Victor and John B. Cullen, "The Organizational Bases of Ethical Work Climates," *Administrative Science Quarterly,* 33 (1988), pp. 101–125.

NOTHING BUT NET

1. **Best places to work.** Every year *Fortune* magazine compiles a list of the 100 best companies to work for. Visit the magazine's Web site (http://www.fortune.com) and review the most recent year's list of the 100 best companies. Which made the top 10? What criteria does the magazine use when compiling its list?

2. **Community involvement.** Being a good corporate citizen means being involved in the community. Visit the two Web sites listed here and read about how several companies with major operations in your state are involved in community improvement. Prepare a brief oral report to your class about your findings.

   http://www.dow.com/about/corp/social/social.htm

   http://www.jnj.com/community/index.htm

3. **Protecting the environment.** Many companies are in the forefront of the environmental movement. Visit the Web site of a company you believe is committed to environmentally friendly business practices. Write a report on that firm's efforts. Examples include companies such as the following:

   http://www.ford.com/en/goodworks/environment/default.htm

   http://www.patagonia.com/enviro/main_enviro_action.shtml

   http://www.starbucks.com/aboutus/envaffairs.asp

   Note: Internet Web addresses change frequently. If you don't find the exact sites listed, you may need to access the organization's or company's home page and search from there.

Case 2.1

Strategy for Competing with Microsoft: Fight or Flight?

"Everybody should compete with Microsoft once in their lifetime," says Netscape's Marc Andreesen of his old rival, "so they have stories to tell their grandchildren. And then don't do it anymore."

The recent settlement of the U.S. Department of Justice's antitrust suit against Microsoft Corp. surprised some who had expected harsher penalties for the software giant. Found guilty of creating and maintaining a monopoly with its Windows operating system, Microsoft had fought the suit on the grounds that inextricably bundling its Internet browser with its Windows operating system was necessary for technical reasons. It now must make amends in various ways. It must reimburse the plaintiff states $25 million in legal fees; it must allow PC makers to install and promote non-Microsoft browsers, multimedia players, and other products; it cannot retaliate against those who do so; and (in settling a related suit brought by California) it must provide consumers and businesses who purchased certain Microsoft products with vouchers worth $5 to $29 toward computer products of any manufacture, up to a total of $1.1 billion. Sixteen other states and the District of Columbia have brought suits similar to California's.

But the federal settlement stopped short of forcing the company to split itself in two and softened penalties contemplated by the first judge in the case. U.S. District Judge Colleen Kollar-Kotelly's decision was based, she said, on the states' failure to show that Microsoft's devastatingly competitive business strategies hurt consumers even as they forced rival browser companies out of the market. She declined to force the firm to give up its intellectual property by licensing its Office software or providing an open-source license for its browsers. Further suits against Microsoft, AOL Time Warner, and the European Union's antitrust unit are still pending.

Microsoft founder Bill Gates called the antitrust settlement "a good compromise" and pledged to honor the agreement. "We're committed to moving forward as a responsible leader in an industry that is constantly, constantly changing," said the firm's CEO, Steve Ballmer. On the other hand, the end of the case leaves Microsoft cash-rich and free to pursue any other market it chooses, such as handheld devices, servers, applications software, video gaming, technology consulting, and Internet services. "They're absolutely more dangerous now," says Ken Wasch, president of the Software & Information Industry Association.

Meanwhile, Marc Andreesen, having lost the browser war he waged against Microsoft, has taken his new startup, Opsware Inc., into market niches that Gates's company hasn't yet touched.

QUESTIONS FOR CRITICAL THINKING

1. Was it ethical for Microsoft to force users of its Windows operating system to use its Internet browsers as well by bundling the programs together and preventing PC manufacturers from making other software available to computer buyers? Was Microsoft's behavior toward its rivals ethical? Why or why not?

2. Should Microsoft change its business practices to protect itself against future antitrust suits? How? Who would benefit from such changes?

Sources: "Billion-dollar Deal Is a Decent Outcome," *The San Jose Mercury News,* January 20, 2003, **http://www.bayarea.com/mld/ mercurynews**; Clint Swett, "Don't Expect Too Much from Microsoft Accord," *The Sacramento Bee,* January 14, 2003, **http://www.sacbee.com**; David Ho, "Judge Denies Appeal in Microsoft Ruling," *Associated Press,* January 13, 2003; Tom Bemis, "Microsoft Settles Calif. Suits for $1.1 Bil," CBS Market Watch January 10, 2003, **http://www.CBS.MarketWatch.com**; Steve Hamm, "What's a Rival to Do Now?" *BusinessWeek,* November 18, 2002, pp. 44–46.

Video Case 2.2

Timberland

This video case appears on page 603. A recently filmed video, designed to expand and highlight the written case, is available for class use by instructors.

Glossary of Important Literary Terms

action: the events that take place in a story. **Action** covers everything that happens in a story, from a character's thoughts to his or her interactions with other characters. The arrangement of the action is called **plot.**

allusion: a reference to a person, place, event, literary work, and so on. Writers generally use allusions to make their own meaning clearer or to prove a point. In "Harrison Bergeron," the Handicapper General agents are referred to as "H-G Men," an allusion to the 1930s and 1940s slang term for FBI agents: "G-Men."

ambiguity: a word, line, event, and so on that can be interpreted in more than one way. The title of Faulkner's story, "A Rose for Emily," can be interpreted in different ways and is thus ambiguous.

analogy: a comparison of one thing to another in order to clarify meaning or defend a point. In "Death and Justice," Koch makes an analogy between the death penalty and treatments for cancer. His point is that the death penalty may seem harsh as, say, chemotherapy is harsh, but both are necessary to correct problems.

climax: in a story or play, the point at which major change occurs in a character or in the action. This change affects the remainder of the story or play.

conflict: in literature, a struggle between forces: character against character; character against nature; character against society; or character against internal forces. In Brush's "Birthday Party," the conflict is between characters; in Piercy's "Barbie Doll," the main character is in conflict with the expectations of the society in which she lives.

connotation: the meaning associated with a word that goes beyond a dictionary definition. The words *woman*, *lady*, and *dame* all literally refer to a female person, but they have different connotations.

denotation: the dictionary definition of a word.

foil: a character who stands in direct contrast to another character. Through this contrast, the qualities of both characters are easier to see. In Welty's "A Worn Path," the hunter is a foil to Phoenix Jackson.

foreshadowing: a hint of something that will follow. In Jackson's "The Lottery," the boys' making piles of stones and stuffing their pockets with rocks foreshadow the violence that occurs later.

genre: kind or type; some literary genres are poetry, fiction, and essay.

hyperbole: an exaggeration used for emphasis. Hyperboles are common in everyday speech, such as "I have a million things to do."

image: a mental picture or an association created by a word or group of words.

imagery: a group of related images. Faulkner uses many images of decay to describe Miss Emily's house in "A Rose for Emily." Thus one speaks of the "decay imagery" in the story.

irony: a conflict between what seems to be and what is, or between what should be and what is. Three types of irony are **verbal, situational,** and **dramatic. Verbal irony** is created when one says the opposite of what one means. **Situational irony** is created when something happens that is the opposite of what one would expect to happen. **Dramatic irony** is created when the reader knows more than a character knows. In Piercy's "Barbie Doll," the statement is made, "To every woman a happy ending," which is an example of verbal irony. (The ending has not been happy.) Situational irony is seen in Robinson's "Richard Cory." The character Richard Cory seems to have everything, yet he kills himself.

metaphor: a literary comparison. Metaphor involves calling one thing another: "he was a lion in battle." In this example, "he" is called a "lion"; however, the comparison is between the qualities of this person and the qualities of a lion. We think of such qualities as courage, strength, and determination; thus the person was strong and brave in battle and stuck with the fight. A metaphor may be considered in terms of its two parts, the **vehicle** and **tenor.** The vehicle is the concrete image that is presented to the reader; the tenor is the idea or concept that is represented by the vehicle. In Hughes's "Mother to Son," the concrete image

363

presented is that of a stairway (the vehicle); the stairway represents life (the tenor).

motivation: why a character behaves a certain way. In some stories, character motivation is the central issue. In Brush's "Birthday Party," the central question is "Why does the husband behave the way he does?"

narrative: the name given to a piece of writing that tells a story; the word also refers to the story itself.

narrator: the person telling a story. A narrator who is involved in the action of the story should be treated as a character, and his or her attitudes and traits should be examined.

paradox: a statement that seems to contradict itself but is (or may be) true. An example of a paradox is Dickinson's statement, "Much Madness is divinest Sense."

personification: a literary device in which human characteristics are given to an animal, a thing, or a concept.

plot: the structure of the events of a story. The writer may arrange the events in the order that they occurred (as in "The Lottery"), or the writer may move back and forth in time (as in "A Rose for Emily"). The reader should distinguish between plot and theme.

point of view: the vantage point from which a story is told. A story may be told from a first-person point of view in which someone who is personally involved in the story tells it (as in Olsen's "I Stand Here Ironing"). A story may be told from third-person point of view. This point of view may be **objective,** in which case the reader is given only those events that are observable ("The Lottery"); or **limited,** in which case the reader is allowed into the mind of one central character ("Crusader Rabbit"); or **omniscient,** in which case the reader is allowed into the minds of all or several of the characters.

satire: a form of writing that ridicules or makes fun of some situation, person, or human weakness. Some satiric writing only gently ridicules its subject; other satiric writing is harsh or bitter. Satire frequently uses verbal irony. Auden's "The Unknown Citizen" is an example of satire.

setting: the time and place of the action of a story. **Time** may be as specific as a particular hour of a particular day, or it may be as vague as, say, the nineteenth century or "sometime in the fifties." **Place** may be as specific as a particular room in a house or a particular house in a town, or it may be as vague as the United States or "somewhere in the West." In some pieces, setting plays a more important role than in others. Setting in "The Lottery" and "A Rose for Emily" is very important in shaping the meaning of the story. In other pieces, such as "I Stand Here Ironing," setting is relatively unimportant in shaping the meaning of the story. The reader should consider the effects of setting on such things as character, action, and tone.

simile: a literary comparison using *like* or *as.* Thus, "He was like a lion in battle" is considered a simile, whereas "He was a lion in battle" is considered a metaphor. The function of a simile, as with a metaphor, is to explain something by comparing it to something else. The reader's job is to see what is being said about something through the use of simile. Hughes's "Harlem" is a poem developed chiefly through the use of similes.

symbol: something that represents something else. Like a metaphor, a symbol involves a comparison: what is used as a symbol has something in common with the thing it represents. Thus, a lamb may be a symbol for human qualities such as meekness, since lambs are generally meek creatures. Characters in a piece of writing may be symbols or may be considered symbolic of certain human qualities or conditions. An elderly character such as Old Man Warner in "The Lottery," for example, is a symbol for all people who resist change. (Usually, elderly people are more resistant to change.) Action also may be symbolic.

theme: the main idea or the "point" of a poem, short story, play, and so on. A piece of literature may have more than one theme, or the theme may be seen differently by different readers. With some pieces of literature, the theme can be expressed neatly in one or two statements; with other more complex pieces, theme is more effectively discussed in terms of the main issues or question raised. Theme should be distinguished from plot. In "The Lottery," for example, the plot consists of townspeople gathering together and holding a lottery. The theme, however, is not about lotteries or what happens in them. The theme is a statement about people in general or about human nature.

thesis: the main idea or the point that the writer is arguing. The thesis may be explicitly stated, or it may be implied. While the term *thesis* may be applied to any type of writing, it is always used to describe the main idea of essays.

tone: an expression of the writer's attitude. In speech, our attitudes are frequently shown by our "tone of voice"; in writing, tone is shown by such features as description of people, places, and events. Some words that describe tone in writing are "approving," "cheerful," "sarcastic," "angry," and "bitter." The tone of Owen's "*Dulce et Decorum Est*" could be described as "bitter," reflecting the poet's resentment toward those who glorify war.

Index

Authors, Titles, and First Lines

Literary Credits

Poetry

Essays

213: "Shame" by Dick Gregory, from NIGGER: AN AUTOBIOGRAPHY by Dick Gregory, copyright © 1964 by Dick Gregory Enterprises, Inc. Used by permission of Dutton, a division of Penguin Group (USA) Inc. **215:** "Daddy Tucked the Blanket" by Randall Williams from THE NEW YORK TIMES, June 10, 1975. Copyright © 1975 by The New York Times Co. Reprinted with permission. **219:** "A Hanging" from SHOOTING AN ELEPHANT AND OTHER ESSAYS by George Orwell, copyright © 1936 by George Orwell, © 1950 by the Estate of Sonia B. Orwell. Reprinted by permission of Harcourt, Inc. and Bill Hamilton as the Literary Executor of the Estate of the Late Sonia Brownell Orwell and Secker & Warburg Ltd. **222:** "Death and Justice" by Edgar Lee Koch from THE NEW REPUBLIC. Copyright © 1985 The New Republic. Reprinted by permission of The New Republic, LLC. **227:** Copyright © 1990 by Amy Tan. First appeared in THE THREEPENNY REVIEW. Reprinted by permission of the author and the Sandra Dijkstra Literary Agency. **232:** "The Myth of the Latin Woman" by Judith Ortiz Cofer from "The Latin Deli: Prose & Poetry" by Judith Ortiz Cofer. Copyright 1993 by Judith Ortiz Cofer. Reprinted by permission of the University of Georgia Press. **237:** "Making the Grade" by Kurt Weisenfeld from NEWSWEEK, June 17, 1996. Copyright © 1996 Newsweek. All rights reserved. Reprinted by permission. **240:** "What Is Child Pornography?" by George Will from the WASHINGTON POST, July 30, 2001. Copyright © 2001 The Washington Post Writers Group. Reprinted with permission. **242:** "Disgusting Doesn't Make it Speech" as seen in a Nation Review Online column by Ann Coulter. © 2001 by Ann Coulter. Reprinted with permission. Distributed by UNIVERSAL PRESS SYNDICATE. All rights reserved. **244:** "Should a Man Be Put In Jail for What He's Thinking"? by Leonard Pitts. Copyright 2001, Tribune Media

Services. Reprinted with permission. **246:** "Starved Out" by Cynthia Fox from TIME, December 1, 1997. Copyright © 1997 TIME Inc. Reprinted by permission. **252:** "Heavy Judgment" by Deborah Gregory from ESSENCE, 8/1/94. Reprinted by permission. **259:** "When Is It Rape?" by Nancy Gibbs from TIME, June 10, 1991. Copyright © 1991 TIME Inc. Reprinted by permission. **264:** "Time for a Change" by Molly Ivins from the MINNEAPOLIS STAR TRIBUNE, November 18, 1998. Copyright Molly Ivins. Reprinted by permission of Pom Inc. **267:** "Legalization of Narcatics: Myths and Reality" from USA TODAY, 3/1/97 **271:** "The Prisoner's Dilemma" by Stephen Chapman from THE NEW REPUBLIC. Reprinted by permission of The New Republic, © 1985 The NEW Republic LLC. **278:** "Violent Crimes: Myths, Facts and Solutions" by Stanley D. Eitzen from 'Vital Speeches of the Day', 61, May 25, 1995, pp. 469–72. Used by permission. **286:** "A Nasty Business" by Bruce Hoffman first published in the January 2002 (Vol. 289, Issue 1) issue of 'The Atlantic Monthly'. **294:** "Torture's Dark Allure" by Darius Rejali from Salon.com, June 18, 2004. Used by permission. **302:** "Does Torture Work?" by Darius Rejali from Salon.com, June 21, 2004. Used by permission.

Textbook

310–325: "Presidency in Crisis" by Joseph Conlin from THE AMERICAN PAST, A SURVEY OF AMERICAN HISTORY (with InfoTrac and American Journey Online) 7th edition by CONLIN. Copyright © 2004. Reprinted with permission of Wadsworth, a division of Thomson Learning: www.thomsonrights.com. Fax 800 730-2215. **326–358:** "Social Responsibility and Business Ethics" from CONTEMPORARY BUSINESS 10th Edition by BOONE. © 2002. Reprinted with permission of South-Western, a division of Thomson Learning: www.thomsonrights.com. Fax 800-730-2215.

Photo Credits

This page constitutes an extension of the copyright page. We have made every effort to trace the ownership of all copyrighted material and to secure permission from copyright holders. In the event of any question arising as to the use of any material, we will be pleased to make the necessary corrections in future printings. Thanks are due to the following authors, publishers, and agents for permission to use the material indicated.

Poetry

27: Leah McCraney

Fiction

194: © John McGinn

Essays

217: Leah McCraney

Textbook

Chapter 49. 310: Official White House Photo **312:** Official White House Photo **315:** © AP/Wide World Photos **316:** © Bettmann/CORBIS **317:** © AP/Wide World Photos **321:** Official White House Photo **322:** © AP/Wide World Photos **323:** © AP/Wide World Photos

Chapter 2. 327: © AP/Wide World Photos